Nijinsky

Nijinsky
BLUE RIBAND SIRE

Lesley I. Sampson

Colour photographs by the author

J. A. Allen
London

British Library Cataloguing in Publication Data

Sampson, Lesley
   Nijinsky.
   1. Nijinsky (Race horse)
   I. Title
   798.4'3   SF355.N5

ISBN 0-85131-411-2

© Lesley I. Sampson 1985

Published in Great Britain in 1985 by
J. A. Allen & Company Limited,
1, Lower Grosvenor Place, Buckingham Palace Road,
London, SW1W 0EL

All rights reserved. No part of this book may be reproduced, stored in a retrieval system or transmitted, in any form or by any means, electronic, mechanical, photocopying, recording or otherwise, without prior permission, in writing, from the publishers.

Book production Bill Ireson

Photoset by Rowland Phototypesetting Limited
Bury St Edmunds, Suffolk
Printed and bound by
Garden City Press
Letchworth, Hertfordshire.

Foreword

I consider it an honour to have been asked to write the Foreword for such a magnificent book, involved as I was with Nijinsky during his racing career, as racing manager to the late Charles Engelhard and later to continue my association with this great horse through perhaps his best son to be trained in England, Ile de Bourbon.

Lesley Sampson undertook, about 15 years ago, the daunting task of faithfully following Nijinsky's stud career and recording the racing deeds of his progeny having pieced together lists of the foals from mares visiting him.

Why, you may wonder, did she decide to dedicate herself to giving so much time and energy writing the history of a horse, unless it was to be a work of love? Well, that is the key, for she admits she fell in love with Nijinsky while he was racing, and determined then to chronicle everything she could, so sure was she of his ability to be a great sire. In addition to all she has written, she personally took all the colour photographs which appear in this book.

Anyone remotely interested in bloodstock breeding must find *Nijinsky – BLUE RIBAND SIRE* enthralling reading but the author, while making suggestions, still poses two tantalising questions which cannot yet be answered: will Nijinsky prove to be a really great "sire of sires"?; and which of his sons is Heir-apparent to his line? Maybe she will be able to write her verdict on all this in eight year's time . . .

Everyone could see that Nijinksy was a proud horse when he appeared in the paddock on a racecourse and 15 years have passed since he won the Triple Crown. Now rising 19, it is very fitting that Lesley Sampson should pay him this great compliment during his lifetime.

DAVID McCALL

Acknowledgements

The author wishes to thank all those who have allowed access to their Nijinsky stock both in England and Kentucky and the efforts of the staff of Pedigree Associates and Bloodstock Research in tracking them down on the Kentucky farms. Also the various associations who have so willingly provided the answers to various strange statistical queries, notably I.T.B., Fasig Tipton Co. Inc., Japan Racing Association, Japan Stallion Corporation, and the B.B.A. for the use of its library.

My especial thanks go to Stella Uttley for all her help and support – and for the photograph which adorns the back of the dust-jacket.

Contents

		Page
FOREWORD *by David McCall*		v
ACKNOWLEDGEMENTS		vii
PART ONE:	RACEHORSE AND SIRE	1
PART TWO:	BEHIND THE SUCCESS STORY	57
	1 The Leading Progeny	59
	2 An Underrated Juvenile Sire	132
	3 Durability in Nijinsky's Progeny	155
	4 Performance Ratios	173
	5 Distance and Going Aptitudes	182
	6 Quality of Mare Books	197
	7 Searching for a "Nick"	212
	8 Physiology of the Nijinsky Progeny	229
	9 A Commercial Success	243
	10 Sons as Sires	255
	11 Daughters as Broodmares	269
	12 What of the Future?	278
APPENDIX A:	Nijinsky Progeny 1972–82 and Foals of 1983	282
APPENDIX B:	Nijinsky's Stakes Horses 1974–84	293
APPENDIX C:	Pedigree and Family Details of Nijinsky	300
	INDEX OF HORSES	305

All statistics used in this book are correct to 31 December 1984. Though the events of 1985 may have reference no result from that year has been included in any statistical survey.

In general discussion the use of the term "Group" can be read as synonymous with "Grade" as employed in the North American Pattern systems.

Part One
RACEHORSE AND SIRE

Nijinsky. Panache, elegance, beauty, pride, classic conformation, the look of eagles. To many this was Nijinsky. Rarely has every arc of the perfect circle been found in one horse. Vaslov Nijinsky, the famed ballet dancer, was said to have believed his reincarnation to take the form of a horse. In many ways he could not have wished for a more faithful mirror image. Even for those who doubt the occult, the careers of racehorse and dancer reflect in an unnerving parallel. The triumph and the tragedy shadow each other in an uncanny reflection.

When you are with Nijinsky he is not with you. Though he has amiably come to inspect you readily enough and poses for the adulation like any film star, he somehow is not there. There is a faraway look in his eyes as he stares out across the other stallion paddocks to somewhere beyond, far far beyond, to where human eyes cannot follow. Nijinsky is more than a mere animal yet he is not of human quality either. It is this mystery that makes Nijinsky so magnetic. Even at 18, starting to get a little mature now, and despite the effects of his recent debilitating illness, the magic is still there. He is a champion and knows it.

Nijinsky was born to be a champion. A well-worn cliche when talk is of racehorses; but he came from the second crop of his champion sire Northern Dancer, was the second living foal from his Queen's Plate winning dam Flaming Page and he had a champion breeder in Edward Plunkett Taylor at his Windfields Farm situated in Ontario, Canada. Nijinsky came into the world of those green pastures (all too soon to become blocks of flats) on 21 February 1967, a tall strong bay colt with three white feet and the large heart-shaped star that would become so familiar to racing people all over the world. He seemed to take after his dam in size and build rather than his illustrious sire, who is of no real size himself.

Northern Dancer is too well-known to need details reiterating here and besides he is not the subject of this book. Suffice to say that Nijinsky's sire was a champion in his own right. Northern Dancer won the first two legs of the Triple Crown, the Kentucky Derby and Preakness Stakes – it appeared that he did not quite stay the twelve furlongs of the Belmont when beaten into third place – before returning for a seven length canter in Canada's premier race, the Queen's Plate. At stud he has been one of the foremost names in major classic breeding, thanks in no small part to Nijinsky's European successes in 1969 and 1970. This was to open the floodgates for Northern Dancer on that side of the Atlantic, where his reputation has really been established. Northern Dancer was by Nearco's son Nearctic and was the first foal of the high-class Native Dancer mare Natalma. She had been unlucky in chipping a bone in her knee just before the 1960 Kentucky Oaks. Though she was then retired the breeding season was practically at an end but the decision was taken to breed her to Nearctic on 28 June. The resultant foal was Northern Dancer, who, but for his dam's injury, would not have been foaled in 1961.

The world might have been fortunate to have Northern Dancer; for Edward Plunkett Taylor it might have been even more fortunate to have had Flaming Page. Taylor had sold her as a yearling but the purchaser wanted to return her as she had a swollen hind fetlock, so he took another filly in her place and Taylor kept Flaming Page. Flaming Page was one of the best fillies to race in Canada and, like Northern Dancer, won the Queen's Plate. Flaming Page had a pedigree full of black type though her dam, Flaring Top (by Menow, grandson of Nijinsky's paternal great-grandsire Phalaris), won three ordinary races but bred eleven winners. These included stakes winners Quintain and Flashing Top and also the dams of Evening Bag (Grade 3 Orchid Handicap), French Wind (Display Handicap), Fanfaron (Plate Trial), All For Victory (Canadian Derby, Grade 2) and Viendra, a stakes winner of the later 1970s; also the grandams of Group 1 winners Royal Ski and Blondy, and of the Grade 3 winner Morning Frolic. Flaring Top's dam Flaming Top, by Omaha, did not score in three outings but also more than made up for it at stud breeding eight winners including Matron and Spinster Stakes winner Doubledogdare plus Illuminable and Top Double, both good stakes winners. In addition Flaming Top was half sister to the great filly Columbiana.

Though they had both been Queen's Plate winners, Flaming Page was very different to Northern Dancer in conformation and temperament. Rangy, and with a highly nervous temperament, she was to pass these qualities on to her son. She matured late and possibly was only coming to her best when her injury occurred. This was also true of Northern Dancer in the view of his trainer Horatio Luro. This does gives food for thought as to Nijinsky's own capabilities had he remained in training as a four-year-old.

It was apparently not a hard decision to send Flaming Page to Northern Dancer for they seemed to complement each other. Unfortunately there was no fairytale ending to that union as Flaming Page produced dead twins. In 1963 Flaming Page went to Victoria Park to produce her only filly, Fleur, who won three races and gained black type with a third in the Summer Stakes. However, she was to earn her share of immortality in the years succeeding Nijinsky's career as the dam of European champion The Minstrel (by Northern Dancer) winner of seven races including the Epsom and Irish Derbies and the King George VI & Queen Elizabeth Stakes at Ascot, and also of Far North (also by Northern Dancer) a good Group 2 winner in France. In addition to these were the stakes winners Flower

Princess and The Minstrel's brother Pilgrim. For a mare who died at the age of 17 there was not much more to ask.

There were no foals for Flaming Page in 1965 and 1966 but she returned to Northern Dancer in 1966. A rather different story this time . . . Nijinsky. Flaming Page went back to Northern Dancer again the following season with Nijinsky as a foal to produce the chestnut Minsky. He was more reminiscent of The Minstrel and Be My Guest among Northern Dancer's progeny than Nijinsky. Minsky was champion two-year-old in Ireland in 1970 like his brother the previous year, and ultimately was a leading sire in Japan until his untimely early death. For Flaming Page it was the end of the road for she had had a bad birth with Minsky and never produced another foal. Had she been able to do so, with two champions and the dam of another champion from three foals, the shape of classic races might have been a shade different through the 1970s. Flaming Page and Natalma, dam of Northern Dancer, died in late 1984 and early 1985 respectively, having been pensioners together at Windfields for some years.

Nijinsky was born then on 21 February (a date he shared with another great horse, the showjumper Stroller) and was foaled on the constituent farm at Oshawa before being weaned at 17 weeks and moved on to Windfields itself. Once Nijinsky was a yearling he had a paddock of his own, quite an undertaking bearing in mind how many yearling colts Windfields produces each year. That particular paddock was eaten up by bulldozers within the time it took for Nijinsky to win the Triple Crown. Nijinsky was a well-grown yearling and at that time stood 15.3½ h.h. and clearly had a great deal of growing to do yet. Those who worked with him described him as a pleasant horse with a "nice disposition" and they remembered him particularly because of his unusually long stride and outstanding conformation.

A great many "judges" who spend their time attempting to find physical faults with the very best racehorses maybe have missed the champion feel about Nijinsky. One person who did not was Vincent O'Brien. Maybe the colt was just a little sickle-hocked but that somehow was immaterial. O'Brien had come to Windfields to inspect a Ribot yearling for Charles Engelhard (who had a particular yen for Ribots) but he was captured by the bright bay son of Northern Dancer. The Ribot yearling stayed at home as far as the Irish wizard was concerned. Windfields liked the Northern Dancer too and while every horse bred there was for sale an unusually high reserve of Can $60,000 was placed on him. Not so high as the rejected Ribot colt at Can $100,000. Nijinsky was sold to Charles Engelhard at public auction for a Canadian yearling record of Can $84,000. Ironically, while Nijinsky was sent to Ballydoyle so was the Ribot colt. Unsold, Eddie Taylor asked O'Brien to train him too. The irony does not end there for the two colts were to meet on a racecourse, Northern Monarch (as the Ribot was named) finishing fourth to Nijinsky in the Railway Stakes as a two-year-old.

Nijinsky caused concern as soon as he arrived at Ballydoyle for he steadfastly refused to eat oats having always been fed on nuts at Windfields. However the problem was resolved before the required nuts were received from North America. Nijinsky was then broken without much more note than any other yearling and, like all O'Brien juveniles, was brought along steadily and not really asked to do anything dramatic before reaching the racecourse. In that intervening time Nijinsky was ridden only by O'Brien's best and any worry that the colt was getting too much above himself was erased by their careful handling. Lester Piggott had ridden him in March, 1969, but did not do so again until the Dewhurst. At that time all eyes were on a Sea Bird II colt called Great Heron, and it was Liam Ward who rode Nijinsky for his first four outings that were to give witness of his development.

Connections were very satisfied with Nijinsky's first outing on 12 June 1969, when only four opposed him on the firm going for the Erne Maiden Stakes over six furlongs at the Curragh. Only the filly Amuigh Faoin Spier had been out before. The acceleration Nijinsky had showed on the training ground was now proved not to be merely a morning glory and though he only won by half a length from Everyday he was not pushed to do so. Runners up to great champions tend to be denigrated, but in Everyday here was a pretty able two-year-old for in his four outings he won two (including his next start by eight lengths) and was second to Nijinsky in the other pair.

Nijinsky, though starting at odds on for his debut, was now really exposed to Irish racegoers and he was the focus of attention, as he would be for the rest of his career. On 16 August Nijinsky contested his first subsequent Group race (the Pattern system was not introduced until after Nijinsky was retired) in the Railway Stakes. The Railway was run over an extended six furlongs on good going at the Curragh and Nijinsky had six opponents but started 4/9 favourite. His nearest rival in the betting was the easy Naas winner Lark Rise at 3/1, another previous winner Decies being next at 10/1. Then it was 20/1 bar. Northern Monarch was at 33/1.

It was a cruise for Nijinsky. Liam Ward let out an inch of rein and Nijinsky willingly spreadeagled the field coming home five lengths clear of Decies (who was later to win the Irish 2,000 Guineas and become a highly successful sire in the Antipodes). Nijinsky's turn of speed did not surprise Liam Ward, the other gear was there when asked for and whenever Nijinsky was wanted to go and win he could do so. The going, though declared good, was on the softish side, certainly more so than the firmness of the first outing.

Nijinsky reappeared for his third race on 30 August, contesting the Anglesey Stakes over a similar course and distance as the Railway. In many respects it was a repeat performance. Nijinsky again met Everyday. The betting had Nijinsky 4/9 favourite and Everyday at 4/1. There were four others in the field and two horses which had won their previous starts. The better of the two was the unbeaten Walky Talky, victorious in the valuable Irish Chorus Stakes and Marble Hill Stakes; the other was the subsequent Waterford Glass Nursery winner Illa Laudo who won the Vauxhall Trial as a three-year-old. Nijinsky was kept behind the leaders until asked a furlong from home and had only to increase his speed to a half gallop to go clear by three lengths from Everyday with Walky Talky five lengths behind him. This time Nijinsky had given away 7 lb to Everyday and could have won at any point. At home Nijinsky was giving older horses many lengths and cruising past them. If one did not know it before Nijinsky was now showing a little of what a champion he was – and was to become.

The Great Heron bubble had also burst. The easy winner of the Tyros Stakes at the Curragh, Great Heron met Decies, beaten so easily by Nijinsky, in the important National Stakes, about two weeks after the Anglesey. That field had included Prince Tenderfoot and Rarity; now Great Heron beat them readily enough but was in turn beaten by Decies at level weights and ultimately was second in his last start as a two-year-old to Approval in the Observer Gold Cup at Doncaster. As a three-year-old Great Heron's best performance was to win the Prix de la Porte Maillot but by only half a length from Nijinsky's 2,000 Guineas runner up Yellow God, and was beaten again by Decies in the Irish 2,000 Guineas. There was to be only one champion from that crop and that was Nijinsky.

Nijinsky's stamina was tested as a two-year-old when he contested the Beresford Stakes over eight furlongs at the Curragh on 27 September. Two races previously Everyday had won the Autumn Sprint Stakes comfortably while the stable had carried off the Irish St Leger with Reindeer, who won by six lengths from future National Hunt star sire Deep Run. Fresh from his success over Great Heron, Decies again took the field for the Beresford. In the race Nijinsky moved up steadily to be just behind Decies and Sacramento at the turn into the straight. Liam Ward found himself having to move sooner than he would have liked on Nijinsky as Decies came away from the fence and the gap was too good to miss. Nijinsky idled a little in front and with the holding ground blunting his acceleration and hampering his daisy cutting action Nijinsky recorded only a three-quarters of a length success over Decies though not having to be shown the whip and it was a very fast time. Six lengths back Greenloaning led the remainder of the seven horse field home.

Nijinsky had done everything he could to prove himself a champion in Ireland but had not faced international competition. For this he was sent to England in October to test the British on their home ground in Newmarket for the Dewhurst Stakes. Nijinsky's reputation had preceded him. He started 3/1 *on* in the six horse field, it then being 10/1 bar. His opposition was competitive if not brilliant: the future leading stayer Cumbernauld, triple winner Sayes, the pacemaker Recalled, Royal Lodge runner-up Sandal and the locally trained Thundergay.

Lester Piggott rode Nijinsky for the first time in public. He settled Nijinsky in behind Recalled and Sandal but Nijinsky was cantering all over them and it was clear that whenever Piggott chose to let him go it would be all over bar the shouting. Piggott gave him the office a furlong from home and Nijinsky strolled past without coming off the bit and the three length margin was completely effortless. Nijinsky had not beaten much in this race but could not have done so any more impressively. He had also clocked an appreciably faster time than had Ribofilio and Crepello, two previous good winners of the race. Also, most of Nijinsky's opponents were to win good races as three-year-olds.

Going on only this appearance the Jockey Club handicapper Dan Sheppard rated Nijinsky clear on the Free Handicap, though perhaps surprisingly only 2 lb ahead of the Observer winner Approval, 4 lb of Huntercombe and Great Heron and 5 lb of Prince Tenderfoot. In Ireland he was 2 lb in hand of Decies, clearly rated more on his Beresford performance than in the Railway, and 3 lb clear of Great Heron and Prince Tenderfoot. However the real debate was about what stamina Nijinsky could produce at three years. Over the winter Nijinsky was installed as favourite for the 2,000 Guineas at 3/1 and at 7/1 for the Derby. On pedigree he appeared slightly suspect over twelve furlongs and it seemed that Approval might have the greater scope. At least the English thought so . . . But in Nijinsky there were not the same limitations as for the average classic colt. Class and sheer brilliant speed counted for much more than obvious stamina.

Nijinsky was, and still is, a very active horse and did himself well over the hard winter. He enjoyed leaving his work companions standing on the gallops and therefore did not need much extra work to keep him ticking over. As a result he was always at his best when lightly trained.

Nijinsky was pointed at the Gladness Stakes on 4 April as his first outing for his classic season. The Gladness is run over seven furlongs at the Curragh and is a test for potential classic colts against older horses. Nijinsky certainly met some able horses: Coventry Stakes winner Prince Tenderfoot, the good four-year-old Deep Run and class three-year-olds Walky Talky and True Rocket. Nijinsky went off as the 4/6 favourite with Prince

Tenderfoot on 2/1 and True Rocket at ten's. The twelve horse field was the largest he had yet faced.

In the race Nijinsky settled down well galloping easily and cruised up to the leaders on the bit and won hard held, ears pricked, by four easy lengths over Deep Run and Prince Tenderfoot. On the Guineas front Gimcrack victor Yellow God had defeated leading two-year-old Huntercombe in the Trial at Kempton while the lightning fast French sprinter Amber Rama was declared to come to England accompanied by the Prix Djebel winner Roi Soleil and the horse he beat that day Without Fear. The home team for the 2,000 Guineas were ably represented by the Craven Stakes winner Tamil, Saintly Song, Free Handicap winner Shiny Tenth and Joshua, later a triple Group winner. From Ireland came Walky Talky . . . and Nijinsky. The stage was set for the 1970 2,000 Guineas, the race that would make or break Nijinsky as a truly outstanding champion.

The market for this field showed a confidence in the O'Brien colt the like of which has rarely been seen in the first classic. Nijinsky was 7/4 *on* favourite and it was 13/1 bar. Nijinsky was almost expected to win so well that the opposition would take on the appearance of selling platers.

The race was emphatic if unspectacular. There was no Lester Piggott heart stopping late charge to snatch victory as there had been with Sir Ivor. Nijinsky dominated his rivals in the paddock and dominated them in the race. Amber Rama and Yellow God shared the lead for the first six furlongs, Nijinsky close behind, and with two furlongs to go Piggott allowed him to join the leaders, glanced to the colts on either side and let him go. Yellow God kept fighting but Piggott kept Nijinsky going away for a comfortable triumph by 2½ lengths. In turn Yellow God came away from Amber Rama, who was caught near the line for third place by Roi Soleil fully 6½ lengths behind Nijinsky.

The manner of Nijinsky's victory seemed to be relatively unimportant to the media when they considered the question as to whether it proved anything about Nijinsky's staying powers. It was a question that they worried at for the next four weeks. Nijinsky had shown such speed to keep with champion sprinters such as Amber Rama and yet still had enough to power away from them. He could have beaten them at any stage and had also returned a surprisingly deceptive, and exceptionally fast, time. Was he, in a sense, too fast for Epsom?

The search was on for something to beat Nijinsky in the Derby. His winter rival, Approval – somewhat resting on his laurels having beaten a talking horse in Great Heron – had disappointed behind Cry Baby in the Royal Stakes, but came back into the picture with a four length success in the

Dante Stakes. Though the English would not admit it, any danger to Nijinsky was likely to come from over the Channel. The French were confident that in Gyr and Stintino they had something special.

The enormous gangling flashy son of Sea Bird II, Gyr was being hailed as a really great racehorse. He put the suspicions of talking horse behind him with a scintillating win in the Prix Daru when he showed incredible acceleration over the last furlong. Gyr was the horse who persuaded the retiring Etienne Pollet to stay in training another year. Just before Epsom Gyr easily added the Prix Hocquart to his tally.

Stintino carried off the Prix Lupin, his fourth victory from as many starts. In a very competitive trial Stintino had been waited with for a very long time before coming up the outside. The third horse was Sassafras. But Stintino was a son of the five furlong flyer Cynara and there were questions over whether he would last out another 1½ furlongs in top-class company. This was becoming a Derby where one wondered if there was really a genuine stayer in it.

There would be no excuses should Nijinsky be beaten if he was the champion he was supposed to be. However, with such a top-class field against him, he would certainly be the champion of his generation should he win.

Charles Engelhard usually missed seeing his horses run because they seemed to lose whenever he was there. For the 1970 Derby he defied superstition. He was not going to miss Nijinsky.

The eleven horse field included some very interesting horses and certainly the best representatives one could expect over twelve furlongs from the three leading European racing countries. Nijinsky, Gyr and Stintino were supported by sure stayer Meadowville (Lingfield Derby Trial), Great Wall (later winner of the King Edward VII Stakes at Royal Ascot), the first and second in the Royal Stakes, Cry Baby and Long Till, plus the fast Mon Plaisir and enigmatic Approval.

Had Nijinsky not been there Gyr would have won by three lengths from Stintino, been acclaimed a champion and vindicated Pollet's decision to stay to train him. But Nijinsky *was* there.

Rounding Tattenham Corner Nijinsky was in the middle of the field but only just behind the leaders, cruising and enjoying himself. On reaching the dip in the straight Piggott asked Nijinsky to go on and rather surprised to be asked to quicken from his lazy lob Nijinsky hesitated momentarily . . . and then took off. He quickly collared the leading Gyr and beat him in a couple of strides. Nijinsky cantered past the post, ears pricked, by an easy 2½ lengths in a manner not seen until Troy, Shergar and his own son Golden Fleece. It was a tremendous performance and Noel Murless is recorded as having gone up to Vincent O'Brien after the race to congratulate him and pass his verdict – "the best since Ribot". And that included Sea Bird II, one of the most spectacular of all winners.

It was the first time that Nijinsky had started at odds against though at 11/8 he was a pretty hot favourite and it had then been 100/30 Gyr, 13/2 Approval and 7/1 Stintino. The time was the fastest since electronic timing began and only 0.88 seconds outside Mahmoud's record (which still stands). Since the days of Mahmoud the course had been slowed by watering, peat dressings and, in the 1970 running, the tardy pace of the first two furlongs could not have helped. Yet Nijinsky recorded a time that appeared not feasible on a good lush grass surface.

Liam Ward had an agreement to ride O'Brien's horses in Ireland and again had the mount on Nijinsky in the Irish Derby at the end of June. In some ways it was surprising to find a larger field opposing him than there had been at Epsom but they were mainly filled by Irish nohopers attempting to grasp a share of the substantial prize money. Nijinsky's most worthy opponents seemed to be Meadowville, fifth at Epsom, Approval, whom he had defeated easily, and the French raider Master Guy, recent victor of the Prix Jean Prat. Nijinsky was kept in last place to halfway and Ward moved him up to eighth in the straight. Though quite a way off the pace Nijinsky was cruising while the majority of his rivals were already off the bit around him. Joining the leaders with two furlongs to run Nijinsky was taken to the lead a furlong out and cruised in by three lengths, the same distance separating second placed Piggott-partnered Meadowville from Master Guy. Approval was back in seventh.

Nijinsky had sweated up much more than he had in previous races as he was never one to be kept hanging around and the preliminaries are unusually long at the Curragh on Derby Day. He appeared to have already run a race before he ever got to the stalls. However, in the race, Nijinsky was never out of half speed, perfectly settled. This has also been a mark with notable members of his progeny: they become upset simply because they want to get on with the job and usually settle well in the race itself. It just depends on how much all the nervous energy has taken out of them. Not all of them can have the brilliance of a Nijinsky to surmount it.

Unlike Sir Ivor, Nijinsky showed in this race that he did get twelve furlongs. The Epsom Derby has been generally recognised as well within the limits of brilliant ten furlong horses but the Curragh is a different matter and Sir Ivor, in being defeated in 1968, definitely did not get it. It was such an easy race for Nijinsky that he lost hardly any weight and was pointed confidently for the race which has just about become the championship race over twelve furlongs for all ages, the King George VI & Queen Elizabeth

Stakes. The Arc de Triomphe comes at such a time of the year that horses are all at very different stages of their careers – Ascot in mid-July is when horses are usually trained to be at the peak of their powers and when most of the season's champions are all still in training. The Arc is almost invariably won by a fresh horse.

The field at Ascot was also the sternest test for Nijinsky in terms of class. Though there were only six runners including Nijinsky they were of the highest calibre. It was also the first time two Derby winners had met for some time; for Blakeney was in the field along with Crepellana (French Oaks), Karabas (Washington DC International), Hogarth (Italian Derby) and the Coronation Cup victor Caliban. Nijinsky had already proved that he had nothing to fear from his own generation at this stage and, to give him a further boost, Gyr had just won the Grand Prix de Saint Cloud over older horses.

The race was a formality and there cannot be many King George's where that can have been said. The winning margin of two lengths did nothing to reflect Nijinsky's superiority for he was being eased up when Blakeney came with a late run and finished far closer than had Piggott allowed Nijinsky to stride out. It was the most impressive performance seen yet. In what other race could one imagine the winner of the French Oaks starting at 20/1 (beaten six lengths), the Italian Derby winner at 33/1 (beaten twelve lengths) and an Epsom Derby winner at 100/7? Nijinsky at 40/85 favourite had proved beyond question what a champion he was.

There was very little else to prove. The St Leger was not on Nijinsky's itinerary at this stage, though it was worth bearing in mind Charlie Smirke's comment after the Derby that Nijinsky would have won even if it had been over two miles. Perhaps the tide of Press opinion swayed connections to pointing Nijinsky to the first Triple Crown victory in 35 years and as likely the last ever to be achieved.

The offers for Nijinsky were by now flooding in, anything less than £1½ million could only be seen as an insult. Engelhard's racing manager, and Lord Wigg, were keen to keep Nijinsky in England and actually gained permission from the Treasury to offer dollars for the colt for it was from the United States that the opposition came.

The National Stud in Newmarket came so close to having the super horse. All its facilities were to be made available to accommodate the Engelhard mares from the United States and their offer was £1½ million. It was followed by the late Tim Rogers organising a syndicate and offering £2 million. However it was evidently significant that Engelhard boarded all his mares at Claiborne Farm in Kentucky for, on 14 August, it was announced that Nijinsky had been syndicated to stand there for a world record

US $5,440,000 (32 shares at US $170,000) comfortably surpassing those of Vaguely Noble and Buckpasser.

Upon returning to Ireland after Ascot, O'Brien suddenly took the St Leger into his calculations. It filled a gap between the King George VI and the Arc, Nijinsky's ultimate autumn objective. Also there was the mystique of the Triple Crown, the ultimate in rarities. In Nijinsky O'Brien knew he had a horse who could achieve it. As the decision was being made the event happened that probably compromised the rest of Nijinsky's career and in all probability cost him the Arc as much as, if not more than, anything else.

Being a horse who sweated freely Nijinsky was evidently vulnerable to ringworm and like all great horses he did things properly and contracted a really bad attack. He and his two-year-old brother Minsky were the two who suffered most in the entire yard. As a result Nijinsky lost a great deal of hair under the saddle and also in front and behind the girth. He seemed to recover well however and was sent to Doncaster in the belief that the St Leger would be easy for him.

It was inevitable that the ringworm must have taken some sort of toll. There had been just three weeks in which to prepare Nijinsky and he was evidently not as fit as he might have been had he not had a lay off. The Leger is over an extended mile and three quarters and while Nijinsky won readily enough there is no telling what it might have taken out of him. He lost more weight after this race than from any other in which he ran.

Piggott rode a waiting race and kept Nijinsky right at the tail-end of the nine horse field which included some able stayers in the form of Rock Roi, Charlton and Politico. As they turned into the straight only Meadowville and the tailed off King of The Castle were behind Nijinsky. Nijinsky did not have to be ridden to weave his way through the field and win with ears pricked by a length from Meadowville. He had gone two lengths clear inside the distance and Piggott had begun to ease him up. The going was not fast yet Nijinsky covered the distance in only five seconds outside the course record.

Nijinsky was not a genuine 14 furlong horse and the St Leger certainly was not the Arc trial that it had been intended. But Nijinsky had won like a champion in defeating the odds for he had never been off the bit in this completion of the Triple Crown and rarely could it have been accomplished so easily.

If Nijinsky had been retired, like Bahram, after the St Leger he too would have done so unbeaten. With hindsight, that course would probably have been advisable – and, if it had been possible, to reserve the Arc for another year. But Bull Hancock wanted Nijinsky in the United States as soon as possible and suggested a tilt at the Man O' War and then the trip to Kentucky. But Charles Engelhard had control while the horse was racing and the connections decided the American race came too soon and it was to be the Arc.

So much has been made of the 1970 Prix de l'Arc de Triomphe that it has almost come within an ace of eclipsing Nijinsky's wins in the races which mattered just as much, if not more. In 1970 the Arc was really only just gaining momentum towards the position it holds a decade and more later. What was important was not the race but the fact that the unbeatable Nijinsky had been beaten. Looking back there were plenty of possible reasons, all now worn out because no matter the ifs and buts the result is irreversible. That Nijinsky was a superior racehorse to Sassafras is indisputable; so is the effect of the ringworm followed by the test of a distance of ground at Doncaster; so possibly the amount of ground Piggott was giving away; the bad draw; even the fact of Piggott dropping his whip while making his final run. With such short leathers Piggott found it difficult to sit down and drive the horse and, conceivably, having his weight behind the girth may have cost Nijinsky the race. But when all this is said and done the records will always show that Nijinsky lost the Arc by a head to the staying Sassafras. In Richard Baerlein's admirable book *Nijinsky: Triple Crown Winner*, he too has taken a large proportion of its pages dwelling on the Arc de Triomphe because of the sensational nature of its running. No horse could ever have had a defeat so minutely analysed and unfortunately built up out of all proportion. The picture of the flying Nijinsky in pursuit up that Longchamp straight will remain in the nightmare for ever. Had Nijinsky won that race he would have retired unbeaten and hailed as indisputably the greatest racehorse ever – had that nod on the line gone his way. Seldom has so few inches made such a difference.

In the quest for the horse to go out on a winning note Nijinsky headed for the Champion Stakes at Newmarket, his presence drawing the largest crowd in living memory to Newmarket Heath. Nijinsky was mobbed almost to the point of hysteria and it undoubtedly caused the highly strung colt a great deal of mental tension over and above that of the event itself. Nijinsky finished second to the class, but not brilliant, performer Lorenzaccio whose sole reason for his place in the annals of the Turf is really due to this single effort.

Nijinsky had been asked so much in such a short time; different countries, different tracks, different distances, different conditions. No horse had been asked to go so far to prove himself a champion. He had surmounted them all and, perhaps, if it were not for the cruel hand of Mother Nature he may well have ended up where he began his three-year-old season, as an *undefeated* champion. That it was not to be somehow recalls the career of his namesake, Vaslov Nijinsky, whose life followed the same pattern of triumph to tragedy.

Bearing in mind Nijinsky's own wish to be reborn a horse one cannot help but wonder . . .

At the end of the season Nijinsky was rated 3 lb above Sassafras and 7 lb above Gyr in the *Timeform* assessment. Even in 15 star studded years Nijinsky is still the best horse Vincent O'Brien has trained, the best horse Lester Piggott has ridden. Indeed Nijinsky was the rarest of rarities on the racetrack, an English Triple Crown winner. At stud he has become even more of a rarity. With his sire Northern Dancer, Nijinsky is the foremost stallion in the world today. Nijinsky has achieved something that many champions fail to do – follow their own blazing trail on the racecourse with the same success at stud.

E. P. Taylor took two of the shares in Nijinsky as did Jock Whitney and Captain Tim Rogers, while Engelhard retained ten himself though tragically he was to die in March of the following year leaving his Nijinsky trust in the hands of his wife, who eventually wound up the family's racing interests in 1977.

Nijinsky's new home, Claiborne Farm is situated near Paris, Kentucky, some 20 miles from Lexington, and has been in the Hancock family since 1910. The initial Hancock believed the area would become the Newmarket of the United States which in due time it did. Alongside Nijinsky now stand the likes of Sir Ivor, Secretariat, Spectacular Bid and Conquistador Cielo. Nijinsky went to the United States initially with a disadvantage as far as American breeders were concerned for, unlike Sir Ivor, he had never been seen on an American racecourse. All they really had to go on were the reports coming across the Atlantic of the "wonder horse". Such reports are often treated with scepticism as such horses are rare.

However Nijinsky certainly did not lack quality in his mares for his first season and indeed these included some very good European families too. It was overall almost a test book for Nijinsky, breeders sent mares with good pedigrees and half sisters to champions rather than the champions themselves. By any standards however they had very good credentials: champions Quill and Bowl of Flowers; Epsom Oaks victress Monade; Lady Victoria, the Canadian Oaks winning half sister to Nearctic; stakes winner Mrs Peterkin, later dam of Kentucky Oaks winner Sweet Alliance and grandam of Shareef Dancer; Round Table's own sister Monarchy plus other stakes winners in Jan Jessie, Peace, Swift Lady, Copper Canyon, Peace Movement, Rash Statement and the Uruguayan champion Lunik. In addition the dams of Bonnie And Gay, Miss Swapsco, High Echelon, Native Heritage and Moulton while the maiden mares included Green Valley (Val de Loir ex Sly Pola), Lighted Lamp (Sir Gaylord ex Chandelier) and Loyal Land, half sister to Secretariat and Sir Gaylord. The first twelve months of any stallion's career is a tense time: how many mares will prove in foal, how many foals will be healthy, will the stallion transmit any notable faults?

Nijinsky's first foal was born on 15 January 1972, a strong bay colt with a sickle shaped star on his forehead, from Prince John's half sister Scaremenot. A bonny alert individual, to be named Count Nijinsky, he was not unfortunately to be one of the several flag wavers from Nijinsky's first crop of runners, being placed as a two-year-old in England but never quite achieving winning brackets, one of the few to fail to do so.

However Count Nijinsky and the 29 foals who followed (including a Japanese representative) proved Nijinsky to be a fertile horse and one who would stamp his stock. There were no obvious defects with them other than the slight sickle hocks that some inherited from their sire. All they had to do now was learn to run.

The second season in a stallion's career is often as nerve-racking as the first, following the first covering year with as yet few foals on the ground. Memories tend to be short, especially regarding a horse standing in a foreign country from that in which he raced and who is not at all familiar to that country's people. Once the foals arrive their presence testifies to the stallion's well-being. By the next season the stallion still has no runners as his first foals are yearlings – we are now three covering seasons on, a long time in the breeding world. It is not until the mid-summer of the first yearlings' lives that the market and relative popularity of a horse can be gauged.

People were not about to forget Nijinsky. The mares sent to him in 1972 were of a higher quality than even that of his first book: Canadian Oaks winners Solometeor and the maiden mare South Ocean (later dam of Northernette, and Storm Bird); Irish 1,000 Guineas victress Lacquer; Epsom Oaks winner Monade; Princess Elizabeth Stakes winner Miba; Cheshire Oaks heroine Hardiesse; South American champions La Sevillana and Rafale; Princess Elizabeth Stakes winner Bamboozle (dam of Northern Gem); 1,000 Guineas winner Full Dress II and also the unraced maiden mare Alluvial, later the dam of Coastal and Slew O'Gold. This book produced 29 foals.

Long before any of Nijinsky's first crop of foals made their appearances centre stage at the Keeneland Sale as yearlings in 1973, Nijinsky's third book of mares had been covered. Notable names included Too Bald, Cambrienne, Gaia, Lady Victoria, Nooky, Sovereign, Tender Word, Gay Meeting, Example, So Chic, Yanina II, Monarchy and Valoris.

Nijinsky's first yearlings appeared at public auction at Keeneland in July 1973. Nine Nijinsky yearlings found new homes at the American Sales that season and were well received by any standards in a year that ushered in a phase of slump in yearling prices. The nine averaged US $114,111 which when compared to the National Average of US $12,255 immediately put Nijinsky into the top flight of sales sires. Only 3.3 per cent of all yearlings were sold for figures in excess of US $50,000. Individually, the best price for a Nijinsky was for a colt, Whiskey Road. Out of the champion mare Bowl of Flowers, Whiskey Road is now a highly successful sire in Australia. The top price for a Nijinsky filly was US $70,000 for Balletic but two other colts made over US $150,000 – Masqued Dancer (ex Bonnie Google) at US $200,000 and Lord of The Dance (ex Monarchy) at US $180,000. All of Nijinsky's yearlings were in that top 3.3 per cent.

Nijinsky had a yearling offered in England that year, a very rare event indeed. Sportsky (ex Sports Event) was led out unsold at 51,000 guineas, a considerable sum, at Tattersalls' Houghton Sales.

The 30 foals from the first crop were scattered in all directions from the Kentucky centre were they were conceived, flag bearers for their famous father and on which so much depended. Thirteen remained in North America, eleven travelled to the British Isles and Ireland, five to France and even one to Japan. They were ensconced in the leading stables: Vincent O'Brien, Peter Walwyn, Alec Head, Mack Miller, Dermot Weld, Harry Wragg, Jeremy Tree. High hopes were held as the impressive collection awaited the start of their careers. Careers that would make or break their champion racehorse sire as a champion stallion.

Nijinsky got off to a spectacular and explosive start. There cannot be many stallions, if any, whose first runners in each of the largest and most powerful racing countries of England, the United States and France, all won. The racing public in each country had not to wait long to see the first representatives of the 1970 Horse of The Year. The date when it really began was 3 May 1974 when Close Up's daughter Silky was entered for the five furlong Wilbraham Maiden Plate at Newmarket. It was as memorable a start as could be imagined. Her reputation as a flying machine preceding her, Silky started hot favourite in a 17 horse field. Backward, but impressive in scope, Silky was slowly away and was a good dozen lengths behind the leaders at halfway and seemed to be in a hopeless position. But upon really reaching into her stride Silky fairly flew. Weaving her way through the field she met the rising ground and her burst of speed was too much for her rivals.

Nijinsky's first winner in the United States was also a filly and followed only eleven days after Silky's Newmarket victory. Copernica was even more impressive in a different way for she slammed her field in a Belmont maiden over 5½ furlongs by no less than 14 lengths. Nijinsky was on his way.

The French had to wait a little longer but there again they had considerably less than half the number of representatives than did North America and England/Ireland. By the time Green Dancer made a highly impressive debut on 13 August at Deauville, Copernica had won a Belmont allowance plus finishing second in stakes races, the Fashion and the Colleen. Elsewhere Tanzor had gained black type by finishing third in the Chesham Stakes at Royal Ascot, Nijinsky's first colt to race and his first runner at that famous venue.

Having proved he could sire winners Nijinsky's next target was to sire stakes winners. He already had black type animals but the date that really set Nijinsky on the road to success in the top flight of stallions was 20 August when Tanzor fought out and won a breath-taking battle with Brilliantine for the Acomb Stakes and become Nijinsky's first stakes winner. It was a long range double for Nijinsky because his daughter Summertime Promise won her first race at Saratoga on precisely the same day.

The most significant representative of that first crop to see a racecourse was Nijinsky's first ever Group One winner and a two-year-old at that; Green Dancer carrying off the Observer Gold Cup at Doncaster at the end of the season to go into quarters as the winter favourite for the Epsom Derby.

Just as significantly, in winning that race, Green Dancer had placed his sire as the leading European First Season Sire. No one could have asked for any more than that. For the record, 16 of the 30 first crop foals ran in their juvenile season and six won accounting for nine races and Green Dancer, Tanzor, Summertime Promise, Copernica and Quiet Fling won or placed in Group and stakes races. In Green Dancer, Nijinsky had a representative in his first crop the like of which is not often seen in any crop of many stallions. Nijinsky was starting where he meant to stay – at the top.

At the American Sales that year Nijinsky's average had been almost 7½ times the National figure with Bamboozle's daughter Caught In The Act making the highest price of US $170,000. By the time the American yearling sales came round again in 1975 a great deal had taken place. Mares who visited Nijinsky that year included Areola, Black Satin, Belle de Nuit, Gleam Drumtop, Street Dancer, Croda Rossa, Prodana Neviesta, Kittiwake and Lisadell. There were foals on the ground out of such as Roseliere, Popkins, Gallant Bloom, Quill, Oraza, Alanesian, Street Dancer and Glad Rags. A veritable "who's who" of the Turf.

On the racecourse Nijinsky had secured that all-important classic win when Green Dancer had no trouble in accounting for the French 2,000 Guineas. He also added his third Group 1 race in the Prix Lupin over 10½ furlongs but failed inexplicably into sixth place in Grundy's Epsom Derby when hot favourite to give Nijinsky a Derby winner in his very first crop. Lighted Glory had also done her bit in France, finishing second to Nobiliary (second in the Derby) in the Group 3 Prix de la Grotte before a most creditable fifth place finish in the English 1,000 Guineas to Nocturnal

Spree. She then ran up to Nobiliary again in the Group 1 Prix St Alary and finished third in the Prix de Malleret (Group 2). Silky had been second to Miralla in the Irish 1,000 Guineas, turning the tables on Nocturnal Spree in the process. Elsewhere in Europe winning performances had been set up by Lord of The Dance, Caucasus, Oulanova, Krassata and Quiet Fling. Indeed, in Krassata, Nijinsky had his first two-year-old winner of his second crop before the third had even reached the sales. In the United States Nijinsky had four individual winners before mid-July, the most significant being the Woodlawn Stakes (Grade 3) victory of Dancing Champ.

Unfortunately it was depression year at the sales in 1975 before prices started to pick up again. Nijinsky's youngsters averaged US $72,778, the lowest figure ever to be recorded by his stock. Only 3.2 per cent of all yearlings made over US $50,000 and the National Average had slumped to US $10,943. Top price of the entire sale was Elegant Prince for US $715,000; Nijinsky's highest was for Masked Dancer (ex Masked Lady) at US $120,000 and the filly Nijinskaia (ex Gay Meeting) at US $115,000. He also had yearlings sold in Ireland for 35,000 and 27,000 guineas.

The Nijinsky band-waggon rolled on. Ten days after the Keeneland Sale had ended in July the two-year-old Nijana came out and won the Grade 3 Schuylerville over a classy field. Nijinsky had six individual winners in the month of August in the United States while in September he was represented by the stakes horses Silky, Masqued Dancer, Green Dancer, Krassata, Copernica and, most important, his second classic winner of the season. Not only did Nijinsky have the winner of the Irish St Leger in Caucasus but also the second in Quiet Fling. Quite a 1-2 for a first season (three-year-olds) sire. With sons winning two such diverse classics as the French 2,000 Guineas and the Irish St Leger, and a filly runner-up in the Irish 1,000 Guineas, Nijinsky was showing himself to be a most versatile sire. Nine individual winners in Europe and North America in October were headed by the top-class victories of Lighted Glory (Prix de Flore, Group 3, second Prix de l'Opera, Group 2) and that of Nijana in the Rare Treat.

European racing largely winds up in the beginning of November but Nijinsky still had two winners in the United States including Summertime Promise who triumphed in two stakes races just ten days apart. Over Served won three races in the last two months of the season and made it a Happy Christmas by winning on Boxing Day and keeping his sire well to the fore right to the end of the year. On the European Free Handicaps, Krassata was named second highweight on the Irish Two-Year-Old filly classification, while in the United States Nijana was rated joint fourth on the equivalent list just 2 lb below joint champions Dearly Precious and Optimistic Gal.

Nijinsky's first European runners in 1976 did not appear until April. By that time Summertime Promise had accounted for the Apple Blossom (Grade 3) and been placed in the Black Helen (Grade 2), Columbiana and the Grade 1 Santa Anita Invitational while Copper Kingdom became Nijinsky's first winner of the year when carrying off a Gulfstream Park allowance on 15 March.

Mares already booked to Nijinsky that year included Favoletta, Morgaise, Native Partner, Bonnie And Gay, Fleet Peach, Sign of The Times, Crimson Saint, Bold Liz, Beja, Shake A Leg, Sandy Blue, Mandera, North Broadway, Bitty Girl, Vela, Princessnesian, Lacquer, Street Dancer, Glad Rags and Shuvee. The list of stakes winners was getting forever longer.

Nijinsky did not have to wait long for his first stakes winner in Europe when four-year-old Quiet Fling scored a resounding victory in the John Porter Stakes (Group 2) at Newbury completing a double initiated by Umabatha earlier in the afternoon on the same racecourse. Seven days later Summertime Promise ran second to Deesse du Val in the record setting Gallorette. She won her second Indian Maid in May and followed that up by placing in the Hawthorne Handicap. May was a good month for Nijinsky in 1976 for Dancing Champ won the City of Baltimore, Caucasus the South Bay and finished a close second to Dahlia in the Hollywood Invitational. In Europe Krassata ran second in the Azalea on May Day and fourth in the Irish 1,000 Guineas. The best performance put up that month was African Dancer's spectacular ten length spreadeagling of the Cheshire Oaks field.

Nijinsky's first two crops of runners were going from strength to strength as three- and four-year-olds: early in June, Quiet Fling became a Group 1 winner with a game triumph over Libra's Rib in the Coronation Cup; La Jalouse became Nijinsky's tenth stakes winner by winning the Selene at Woodbine; and Dancing Champ won the Massachusetts while African Dancer kept up the classic tradition with a game third in the Epsom Oaks to the brilliant Pawneese. Krassata travelled to Bremen in West Germany to record a third against the colts in the Consul Bayeff Rennen (Group 3). Other winners included Bright Finish beginning a five-timer, Sportsky, Javamine (2), Royal Jete and Caught In The Act.

It was yearling sales time again, when the fairground merry-go-round starts revolving in its endless pursuit of equine excellence. In the run up to the yearling sales this year there were a series of near misses: a second place finish in the Monmouth Oaks (Javamine), third spots in the American Handicap (Caucasus), Sheepshead Bay (Summertime Promise), Lancashire Oaks (African Dancer) and fourth place for Krassata in the Irish Oaks and for Nijana and Javamine in the two divisions of the Sheepshead Bay. There were good wins however headed by Nijana's success in the Parlo Handicap. As July drew to a close Caucasus claimed the Grade 1 Sunset Handicap.

Nijinsky was by now an established sire. At the sales that year a share in him was sold for US $240,000. Yearlings averaged US $75,777 (National Average US $13,021), Nijinsky's most expensive yearling yet (La Nijinska, ex Street Dancer) was sold for US $232,000 while in Ireland in September Nonoalco's three parts brother went for 64,000 guineas, the second highest price at Goffs that year (named Stradavinsky he became a Group 3 winner as a three-year-old in 1978).

In August African Dancer was a desperately unlucky short head loser of the Group 1 Yorkshire Oaks being touched off by the Irish 1,000 Guineas victress Sarah Siddons. A similar story accompanied Lucky Sovereign's attempt to win Nijinsky a second Acomb Stakes when just failing to hold Lester Piggott and Padroug. However Nuclear Pulse, a son of Canadian Oaks winner Solometeor, won the Grand Prix de Clairefontaine, and Javamine won the Prayer Bell in the United States and finished second in the Grade 1 Alabama.

African Dancer caused trouble in the stalls when contesting the Group 2 Park Hill Stakes, the "Fillies St Leger", at Doncaster on 9 September, but it did not stop her from running out a convincing winner over Epsom Oaks second Roses For The Star. However, it did prevent her from contesting the St Leger proper two days later there not being time for a stalls test. In the French equivalent Nuclear Pulse had the misfortune to be brought down but an impressive debut was made in Ireland on 25 September by a two-year-old son of the Oaks winner Valoris, called Valinsky. Nijinsky was represented in England by dual winner Sportsky and in France by the Group placed two-year-old Borodine, a son of Directoire. In the United States juvenile winners included Upper Nile, while Nijana accounted for the Marconi and Caucasus the Grade 2 Manhattan. October wins were registered by Summertime Promise (Yo Tambien Handicap), Javamine (Long Island Grade 2 in a Nijinsky 1–2 over Nijana) and others including Tanzor's two-year-old sister Lady Jinsky. In England Bright Finish crowned his five race winning streak with a facile victory in the Group 3 Jockey Club Cup at Newmarket and notable juvenile winners were Galletto (out of the Irish Oaks victress Gaia) and in Japan the dual winner Maruzensky.

Far then from the season tailing off, November and December in some ways provided its highlights. Whereas racing to all intents and purposes had finished in Europe Nijinsky was represented in Japan by his champion two-year-old son Maruzensky who crowned an unbeaten first season with a huge victory in the Group 1 Asahi Hai Sansai Stakes, winning by a distance. Winners in the United States included Nijana in the Good Morning and Javamine in the Knickerbocker.

Though not an exceptional year in terms of the number of wins and stakes being accumulated by the same horses, especially in the United States with the fillies Nijana, Summertime Promise and Javamine, Nijinsky had nonetheless had a highly successful year especially in his siring of the champion Maruzensky and the versatile performances of African Dancer, Bright Finish, Quiet Fling, and some high-class two-year-old victories. Nijinsky had crept into the top twenty on the United States Sires Table and indeed was second to Sir Ivor in terms of per capita earnings. Caucasus was rated fourth (second on the *Blood Horse* list) on the handicap for turf performers while Dancing Champ was co-champion with Festive Mood for the Canadian Older Horse title. Javamine and Nijana were rated joint second on turf in the three-year-old filly division on the *Blood Horse* lists, and Summertime Promise fourth on that for older females on turf. In England and Ireland Nijinsky finished eleventh on the sires table, which was very commendable seeing that the vast majority of his 1973 crop of foals remained in North America and the representation of just six of that three-year-old crop in England/Ireland and three in France made this ranking seem almost impossible to achieve. Nijinsky's seven winners of 16 races in England and Ireland that year amassed £71,475 in win stakes, the 18 places adding further to a total of £97,261, less than £1,000 behind Exbury in tenth. Bright Finish was considered as the leading three-year-old stayer. In win money only Nijinsky was tenth on the list.

Whereas 1976 had been a year where Europe was rather unusually bereft in Nijinsky stock, the tide returned in 1977 where North America's 14 representatives were balanced by 8 in England and Ireland, 4 in France, 2 in Italy (the only foals to be born or sent there) and 2 in Japan, which usually receives one most years. These figures refer only to the juvenile crop of 1977. Nijinsky started well with Over Served winning a Santa Anita allowance as early as 19 January with the recently turned three-year-old Baldski opening his account a week later and following that up with a February success.

In Japan Meiwa Rikiya had beaten Over Served to be the first winner of the new season and won again in early February. In between Maruzensky had continued his unbeaten ways as a three-year-old. As is common with most seasons, Nijinsky took a little while to gain his first stakes success but Caucasus ably redressed the balance with a convincing win in the Arcadia Handicap at Santa Anita on 9 March. This was just five days after Nijinsky's first European runner of the season when Avodire ran second at Saint Cloud. Caucasus added to his Arcadia victory by winning the Grade 1 San Luis Rey Stakes and Summertime Promise ran third in the Columbiana and Apple Blossom on her seasonal reappearances. Six wins were totted up in March alone in the United States.

Back on the farm the stakes winners and famous names kept rolling in: Chris Evert, Drumtop, Nanticious, Bitty Girl, Chou Croute, Fish Bar, Mrs Peterkin, Miss Francesca, Street Dancer, Top Round, Java Moon, Desert Law, Singing Rain, Flying Fur, Imsodear, Syrian Sea, Full Dress II and Waterloo. Future stars conceived that year included De La Rose, Kings Lake, Leap Lively, Balletomane, Nijinsky's Secret, Sportin' Life and Shimmy. Foals on the ground included Night Alert, Nice Havrais, Muscovite, Princesse Lida, Shining Finish, Street Ballet, London Bells, Ballare and Water Dance. Not that anyone would have known that then. In the spring of 1977 these were merely four-legged pipedreams.

The more established stars kept coming up before the public eye. Summertime Promise was the centrepoint with her scintillating win in the Gallorette while Caucasus in the United States and Lucky Sovereign in England put up good performances in graded stakes. Nijinsky's new three-year-olds were beginning to prove themselves. Pas de Deux, Nijinskaia and Maruzensky scored in May but pride of place went to Lucky Sovereign's storming triumph in the Mecca Dante Stakes (Group 3), a recognised Derby trial, to become Nijinsky's 16th stakes winner. In Ireland however the odds on Valinsky had been outpointed a length in the Royal Whip (Group 3) by a 33–1 unknown called Alleged. In North America it was the older brigade which kept Nijinsky's name public, primarily with the victory of Nijana in the Shrewsbury. In a five day spell in the United States and Canada Nijinsky had six consecutive winners ranging from Nijisty's maiden at Aqueduct (completing a double with State at that racecourse on 16 May) to Krassata's Intermission. The racing world could not get away from Nijinsky if it tried.

Quiet Fling's game attempt to win his second Coronation Cup the day after The Minstrel won the Derby (defeating Valinsky and Lucky Sovereign in the process) will long be remembered. In the end he had to give best to Exceller by a neck but not first without an unflinching battle through the final furlongs. On the same day across the English Channel Pas de Deux triumphed at Chantilly. Quiet Fling then ran third to Meneval in the Hardwicke at Royal Ascot the same day as Milina won at Belmont. Lady Jinsky claimed a classic place behind Champion Northernette in the Canadian Oaks at Woodbine while Caucasus's tendency to ultra late runs cost him the Hollywood Gold Cup. On 25 May Lady Jinsky won the Arctic Dancer at Woodbine while Lucky Sovereign ran the race of his life to give The Minstrel quite a fright in the Irish Sweeps Derby. The very next day Valinsky was beaten just half a length in the valuable Group 1 Grand Prix de Paris but compensation was gained by another stakes triumph for the still unbeaten Maruzensky.

Unfortunately stakes successes were thin on the ground in the weeks preceding the opening of the sales circuit, though Pas de Deux, Baldski, Nijana and Caucasus all ran well in graded events. July was a quiet month with just three winners worldwide.

At the summer sales though no one would have noticed it. Nijinsky's yearlings averaged US $86,875 (National Average US $16,337), the top price being for Skibinoff at US $300,000 and US $210,000 for the filly Rissa, a daughter of Kittiwake. This was a year when the top priced yearling was US $725,000 for a colt and US $400,000 for a filly. Bargains were to be found however with Niniski fetching only US $90,000. It was noticeable, with hindsight, that the vast majority of the seventeen Nijinsky sales yearlings (including one in Ireland) were anything but the best of their crop.

Nijinsky had as good an August in 1977 as July had been disappointing. The European stock were fully maturing now and Nijinsky had five winners from twelve runners including Valinsky (Geoffrey Freer Stakes, Group 2), Galletto (Galtres Stakes) and also the debut of Cherry Hinton, Nijinsky's second juvenile to run, and a third in a Group 2 event to Alleged for Lucky Sovereign. In the United States Krassata ran a 1–2 with Javamine for the Quick Touch, the latter coming out again to win the Grade 2 Diana Handicap.

As September draws on racing becomes possibly even more fascinating. Now the class two-year-olds start to appear in, and often win, the type of races that makes them notable. In England, September was the month Cherry Hinton claimed her Two-Year-Old Filly Championship with a good win over experienced fillies at York and then gained a spectacular five length record breaking performance at Ascot in the Hoover Fillies Mile. Running Ballerina got the decision over the colts in her Lingfield debut while a backward brown colt bearing the name of Ile de Bourbon prefaced Cherry Hinton's Ascot win with a promising fourth on his debut. England was certainly the place to watch Nijinsky's juveniles for they were notably slow to be noticed in North America. There it was still the older generation who kept the dollars flowing to Nijinsky's total with Javamine's Arlington Matron and Nijana's Parlo (in which Krassata was third); in Europe Galletto ran two good stakes places but odds-on Valinsky could only finish fourth to Transworld in the Irish St Leger, while bidding to become Nijinsky's second winner of the race in three seasons.

European racing then began to wind down and Nijinsky's participants were few and far between. In the closing months of the season only five horses ran, the best performance being set up by Nizon at Evry but Meiwa Rikiya did win two in Japan in November.

In North America it was, of course, rather different, but even more so than usual. Nijinsky's progeny made no less than 27 starts in October, 26 in November and 17 in December. He had eight winners in that time and 26 places. Of note were Nijana's La Prevoyante in which Krassata finished third, had his twentieth stakes winner in Baldski's Gold Coast plus a notable juvenile winner in La Nijinska. The consistent fillies kept up their show in graded events. Javamine was placed second in the Queen Charlotte and Long Island Handicaps, Nijana in the Gallant Bloom and the evergreen Summertime Promise third in the Las Palmas and fourth in the Californian Jockey Club Handicap, while Krassata was knocking at the door in the Hannah Dustin, Face The Facts and La Prevoyante contests. Even now, before the advent of the Sangster/O'Brien interest in Nijinsky colts, the pattern was emerging whereby the best performances were being put up by fillies in North America.

At the end of the year Nijinsky's runners in England and Ireland had amassed eleven races and a total stakes of £97,433, comparable to the previous year. Thanks largely to Caucasus and the fillies he was ranked twelve on the United States Sires list (as compiled by the *Blood Horse* and *Thoroughbred Record* magazines), only just behind Chieftain, with 34 winners of 61 races and US $1,205,000. That was a considerably higher placing than the previous year. However he was as high as fifth on the leading sire list per capita earnings, only US $900 behind Caro in fourth, and equal fifth on the list by percentage of US $7,500 earners in the United States though quite how much that counts is open to question. Caucasus was the second highest rated turf performer, only one pound below Majestic Light. Javamine was placed second on turf for older females 1 lb below Copano. Apart from Cherry Hinton being Champion Two-Year-Old Filly in England, high ratings were given on the English and Irish Handicaps to the three-year-old Lucky Sovereign (fourth highest rated, colts eleven furlongs to two miles plus, to Alleged and The Minstrel) and also to Valinsky, and to Bright Finish and Quiet Fling on the four-year-old and up in the same distance division.

In many ways 1978 was the trendsetter, the taking-off point: the first in a succession of European Champions and the first real involvement of Sangster/O'Brien with the Nijinsky stock; their first real onslaught on the yearling market for Nijinsky colts. The worldwide distribution was a ratio becoming readily apparent. Of 35 foals of racing age, the two-year-olds of 1978 were divided so that 20 were in North America, 11 in England/Ireland and 3 in France with one representative in Japan.

Most American Nijinskys seem better with a rest during the winter months and it took until 18 February (32 starts) before Edziu opened the 1978 account scoring in an Oaklawn Park allowance. That was the last winner until Milova on 10 March though Avodire had run Copper Mel a close second in the San Luis Obispo at Santa Anita. It was merely a lull before the storm.

The stakes mares visiting Nijinsky that year were a formidable array as always: Sphere, Embroidery, Bundler, Cloonlara, Dearly Precious, Comtesse de Loir, Ivory Wand, Peace, Lassie Dear, Roseliere, Something Super and Top Round. Plus just a few others. Even more formidable were the names of those that were conceived: Golden Fleece, Hostage, Peacetime, Waving, Dearly Too, Khatango, Number and Rose Crescent.

The tempest took time to gather. Early in May, Cherry Hinton was hot favourite to claim Nijinsky's first European classic success by a filly but was a sick filly when she ran into fourth place behind Enstone Spark in the 1,000 Guineas as Newmarket. Infinitely more promising was the first outing of the season for Ile de Bourbon running the much more experienced subsequent dual Derby winner Shirley Heights to a short head the same day. Nijinsky even had his first two-year-old runner Mixed Applause, who followed up a second placed debut on 5 May with a smooth success on 20 May in the valuable George Lambton Stakes at Newmarket. The tempest gathered momentum with Pas de Deux's success in the Group 3 Prix du Palais Royal. Nijinsky had the winners of eleven races in May 1978. During that time a notable name was cropping up on the other side of the Atlantic as Terpsichorist ran up a three timer in her first three starts. That chestnut daughter of Glad Rags would keep the Nijinsky stars and stripes fluttering while triumphs were being accumulated elsewhere.

Early in June Nijinsky had three consecutive winners (that is, no other Nijinsky starter in between) on three consecutive racing days, all in allowances and all future stakes winners: Upper Nile, Summer Fling and His Honor. On the first day of the month three-year-old Baronova won on her first outing in Ireland and on 8 June Nijinskaia won at Evry while on 11 June it was Nizon's turn in the Group 3 Prix du Lys, making it five winners in seven racing days for Nijinsky. June was only half over. Upper Nile joined Terpsichorist as two of Nijinsky's most able performers in the United States capturing the Grade 3 Nassau County Handicap. In Britain, Cherry Hinton had run third to Relfo in the Group 2 Ribblesdale Stakes at Royal Ascot, her first race back from the sick list. Also at that prestigious meeting Nijinsky had had a fabulous 1–2 in the Group 2 King Edward VII Stakes, the "Ascot Derby", when Ile de Bourbon led home Stradavinsky with many established performers behind. Makarova won in France, King of Darby in England and Summer Fling in the United States to complete a highly successful midseason for Nijinsky.

But the best was yet to come. It could not have been at a better time in the two or three weeks before the sales circuit got into full swing. Upper Nile triumphed over Forego and adverse conditions when running away with the Grade 1 Suburban, Summer Fling opened her graded stakes account with a victory in the Grade 3 Open Fire while in England two-year-old Mixed Applause ran second to the flying Devon Ditty in the Group 3 Cherry Hinton Stakes. There were also five other individual winners. All before the opening of the Keeneland Sales.

All was rosy for Nijinsky that year, enjoying probably his best racing season yet. At Keeneland July the Sangster/O'Brien combine joined in the fray with a vengeance. The result was that Nijinsky's average leapt from US $86,875 in 1977 to a massive US $235,833 from which the trend was forever on the up. The National Average was only up US $3,500 to US $19,846.

Nijinsky's son Vatza (ex Shuvee) shattered the previous Saratoga record going for US $800,000 and all but two of the 18 yearlings had a six figure ring about them. It was also a season where more top-class Nijinsky racehorses were sold as yearlings than ever before. Apart from the stakes placed triple winner Vatza there were also Muscovite (US $285,000), Nijit (US $220,000), Encino (US $525,000), Street Ballet (US $200,000), Night Alert (US $190,000) and London Bells (US $185,000). More and more had a now all too familiar ring about them but then it was new. Vincent O'Brien took home Muscovite, Night Alert and London Bells, notably expensive, notably all colts.

That threatening storm finally broke on 22 July. It was not because Terpsichorist won yet again or that Mixed Applause carried off the Sweet Solera at Newmarket but because Ile de Bourbon had surged to a memorable triumph in Britain's premier all-aged race, the King George VI & Queen Elizabeth Diamond Stakes. In defeating the best Europe could throw at him, including the French Derby winner Acamas and English and Irish Derby runners up Hawaiian Sound and Exdirectory, Ile de Bourbon had proved himself the champion of his generation. It was a fabulous success for the son of Roseliere and it constituted probably the most important success for Nijinsky in Europe since the victories of Green Dancer some three years earlier.

There was room for another Nijinsky winner in July (King of Darby) and things settled down a little until mid-August. All there was to shout about were the victories for the inevitable Terpsichorist plus She Can Dance and a Graded place for Summer Fling and Upper Nile. However on 12 August Ile de Bourbon reappeared to stamp his class on the Group 2 Geoffrey Freer Stakes to make the second leg of a hat trick for Nijinsky in that particular race (Valinsky in 1977, Niniski in 1979). August was most notable then for a second place in the Grade 1 Alabama for Summer Fling.

By September one championship had been established in Europe; two with similar credentials were campaigning hard in the United States: Upper Nile's Grade 1 success having been achieved, Terpsichorist set off on the stakes trail gaining her first such victory in the Grade 3 Athenia Handicap. Stradavinsky followed up his second to Ile de Bourbon with a strong victory in the Group 3 Whitehall Stakes at Phoenix Park and later Nizon added to his Group tally with a win in the Group 3 Prix du Lutece. At the end of the month Stradavinsky came to England to run second to Homing in the Queen Elizabeth II Stakes (Group 2). Over in the United States Sis C and Excitable, both future stakes winners, opened their accounts and Terpsichorist ran third in the Gazelle and second in the Boiling Springs while Upper Nile was second in the Grade 1 United Nations and then fourth to the legendary Seattle Slew in the Marlboro Cup.

Into October and Terpsichorist was on the stakes scent with a vengeance: first the Rutgers, a slight hiccup in the Lamb Chop when third, but back for the Long Island. In a few short weeks she had established herself as the best three-year-old filly on grass in North America but unfortunately there was no divisional award of that nature open to her.

Back in Europe the most significant event in the last part of the season following the disappointment of Ile de Bourbon in the St Leger, was the victory of Nizon in the Group 1 Premio Roma. It completed a unique treble for Nijinsky: Group 1 successes in England, the United States and Italy. Not to be left out in the cold, Excitable captured two stakes in sunny Florida between 25 November and 16 December and even as late as 30 December Javamine's brother Sir Jinsky ran third in a decent stakes at the Meadowlands. In the last two months of the season Nijinsky had nine winners.

It had been a powerful year for Nijinsky with winners of 67 races worldwide. He had sired three Group 1 winners in the United States (Upper Nile), England (Ile de Bourbon) and Italy (Nizon) plus Group and stakes winners Summer Fling, Excitable, Stradavinsky, Pas de Deux and a moral champion in Terpsichorist. In Europe Ile de Bourbon was acclaimed Champion Three-Year-Old Colt, ahead of Acamas and Shirley Heights, in the United States high ratings were given to Nijana, Upper Nile, His Honor and, obviously, Terpsichorist. With Excitable's stakes successes Nijinsky now had 28 individual stakes winners to his credit in five seasons racing.

At the Keeneland November Sale a share in Nijinsky had been sold for a massive US$340,000 placing an overall value on him of US$10,880,000, exactly double that of his syndication fee eight years before.

As was only to be expected it was Nijinsky's best season yet regarding the leading sires lists: Nijinsky finished fourth on the general sires list in England/Ireland, his seven winners accumulating 13 races for a massive

£188,491, only £5,000 short of the third placed Derring Do who had 25 winners and three times as many starters. On the win money only table Nijinsky was third, ahead of Derring Do but with Mill Reef (thanks to Shirley Heights) and Petingo above. In the United States Nijinsky had risen to sixth overall, Terpsichorist being the biggest earner (US $230,095) in his US $1,529,756 total. Though these figures usually included European performances it is important to remember that European prize money is not of a comparable nature to that in the United States. That this total was achieved with more than one horse said a great deal for Nijinsky's strength in depth. Nijinsky was now really at the top and his supporters were not to be satisfied with just the successes so far achieved.

As they had hoped this tremendous success of 1978 was merely the beginning. In Ile de Bourbon Nijinsky had a worthwhile champion and certainly his best representative to date and he is all the more important for that. Even then the best was yet to come. But Nijinsky had arrived . . . and he had arrived in style.

The following year, 1979, was spectacularly successful for Nijinsky. The most important thing was that at the end of it he was able to claim another major championship with his best ever juvenile filly; and, during it, some of his best ever runners and characteristics were seen on a racecourse ranging from the speed of Czaravich to the staying power of Niniski, from the brilliance of Princesse Lida to the durable top-class jumpers Gleason and Popular Hero. At almost every facet of the sport Nijinsky had a top-class representative.

It was strange though that Nijinsky should have quite so many high-class European representatives bearing in mind that there were almost twice as many of his progeny running in North America than all the other countries of the world put together; yet it was a year when Ile de Bourbon, Niniski, Princesse Lida and Gleason dominated various different aspects. Nijinsky even had an unusually early winner in Europe when the three-year-old Stetchworth won the Ayr Spring Handicap by 20 lengths. In April Nijinsky had winning horses in England, Japan and Holland.

Of course by that time the American colts and fillies had been in action for some time; three winners in January plus stakes and graded places for the fillies Excitable, Summer Fling and Terpsichorist; five more wins in February and March including the first two outings for Czaravich, the immensely powerful chestnut son of the Irish 1,000 Guineas winner Black Satin. Terpsichorist ran second in the Orchid and fourth in the Pan American. While Excitable placed second in the Columbiana and third in the Poinciana there were also three wins in April and graded places for Excitable and Czaravich in his first stakes (and Grade 1) outing.

Mares to visit Nijinsky that year included Bitty Girl, Mira Femme, Bemis Heights, Drumtop, Divine Grace, Rose Bowl, Swingtime, Dancealot, Flying Above, Fabuleux Jane, Glad Rags, Tuerta, Java Moon, Chris Evert, Bold Liz, Like A Charm, Squander, Native Partner, Mrs Peterkin, Sweet Mist and Snow Peak. The foals of 1980 would include Beaudelaire, Bemissed, Brogan, Caerleon, Down Stage, Fabuleux Dancer, Gorytus, Rosy Spectre, Russian Roubles and Solford; the foundation for that fabulous record breaking year of 1983.

May saw the first win of Niniski and a fine Group place for Stetchworth, while amongst the four winners in North America it was stakes winner Number 29 as Czaravich claimed the Withers Stakes and was already being shouted about for the Belmont. In England, Ile de Bourbon made his reappearance a winning one with a four length romp in the Clive Graham Stakes at Goodwood. Just a few weeks later, and a week into June, Ile de Bourbon was a Group 1 winner again with probably his finest performance – a sparkling seven length demoralisation of quality horses in the Coronation Cup. It followed Troy's stunning victory in the Derby and speculation raged throughout the summer of a clash between the two. There were also winning representatives in various parts of the world. Piaffer made an impressive debut at Newbury winning by four lengths, Stetchworth made it three in England, wins for Gallantsky and Bev Bev in France, Rissa in Ireland and Ipi Tombi in Scotland. Only the highly rated flying juvenile London Bells let the side down with two relatively disappointing seconds in Ireland. June in North America saw four winners: the first two-year-old successes by a colt, Terlingua's half brother Encino (also second in the Haggin Stakes) and the daughter of Street Dancer, Street Ballet. Bev Bev had been the first in Europe.

London Bells finally came good on 4 July with a record smashing display trotting up by eight lengths at the Curragh to lower the record previously held by Nijinsky himself and his three parts brother The Minstrel. London Bells' victory was flanked by that of Yamanin Sukih in Japan and Gleason and Yeats in France and Ireland – all before July was seven days old. It was a little quieter in the United States, something which was becoming usual in the run up to the sales though Terpsichorist, Sir Jinsky and Personator recorded wins before 19 July, on which date Encino ran third in the Hollywood Juvenile Championship. This was very much a year when Nijinsky proved he could sire those class two-year-olds and that those of previous years were not atypical.

O'Brien and Sangster had already had one winner (London Bells) from their sales foray from the previous year – and they were back again. Nijinsky had eleven yearlings to sell and the average was a staggering US $390,769

(National Average US $24,768) and none sold for less than US $100,000. Nijinsky had his first representative over the million mark, the son of Secretariat's sister Syrian Sea whom the Ballydoyle team claimed for US $1,400,000 (top lot was a Hoist The Flag for US $1.6 million). This was not a one off for a Nijinsky filly smashed the Saratoga filly record when going for US $500,000. Named De La Rose she was to make this valuation look very cheap. She was however the only flat stakes winner to come from those thirteen. Altogether they combined to place Nijinsky at the top of the sires table in terms of sales prices, a great tribute to the esteem in which his stock were now held.

As if to frank that Terpsichorist lost no time in claiming the Sheepshead Bay Handicap in a dramatic finish with Late Bloomer. The second half of July was especially successful in England and Ireland with three winners and a close Group 3 place for Niniski.

August was the month to place the rest in the shade. Stakes winners Numbers 30, 31, 32, 33 and 34 all came in that month. It all started with a scintillating triumph for a dark bay filly who created an instant impression by taking the Prix Yacowlef in France. Her name was Princesse Lida and she was to keep the Autumn golden for her sire. Street Ballet earned a stakes placing as a juvenile with a second in the Blue Hen, while in an eight day spell in Europe three new stakes winners made their mark: Niniski started off this new phase to his career with a victory in the Geoffrey Freer Stakes (Group 2) to complete the hat trick in the event; then it was the four-year-old miler Piaffer's turn in the prestigious Rose of York Handicap at the big August meeting when holding off the Group winner Baptism while Yeats (ex the Coronation Stakes victress Lisadell), owned by Vincent O'Brien's wife Jacqueline, and who was enjoying an unbeaten second season, won the Herbertstown Stakes. Indeed, the same day as Niniski's Newbury success, a highly impressive winning debut was made by Muscovite another O'Brien sales purchase. Another juvenile winner was Bev Bev, her second. Back in the United States Sis C became a stakes winner by annexing the Camellia Stakes at Sacramento. The most striking success of all however was the Group 1 winning performance by a two-year-old filly when Princesse Lida defeated the colts in the Prix Morny at Deauville, following in the footsteps of some great fillies of the past.

There were some setbacks and some notable triumphs in September. It started off with defeats for Muscovite (odds on for the National Stakes behind his stable companion Monteverdi) and, even more sensationally, a short head defeat of Ile de Bourbon by Cracaval in the September Stakes but Ile de Bourbon had been off the course with a virus and was not the horse he had been in the spring. Niniski, favourite for the Doncaster St Leger, could only finish third to the French pair Son of Love and Soleil Noir, being unsuited by the slow early pace (Stetchworth ran right up behind him in fourth), while Terpsichorist was third to Pearl Necklace in the Flower Bowl. However, there were a number of consolations: Czaravich's win in the Jerome, Terpsichorist in the Violet, a winning debut for the French juvenile Nice Havrais and stakes placings for Bev Bev (Prix d'Aumale) and for Czaravich (third Woodward Stakes to Affirmed and Coastal). The greatest compensation came on 23 September when Princesse Lida made it a Group 1 double beating the colts and all comers in the Prix de la Salamandre.

There was no winding down in Europe that year though Nijinsky had few representatives to run. Just seven runners in Europe but two classic victories and a major two-year-old listed event came Nijinsky's way. It was Niniski who led the way romping to a ten length triumph in the Irish St Leger; and then travelling to France to take revenge in their St Leger for their colts having come to capture the English. In between times, the third of the O'Brien purchases at the 1978 sales had come out to win. In the Houghton Stakes, traditionally a high-class event for the following season's classic three-year-olds, Night Alert, a son of Broodmare of The Year, Moment of Truth, comfortably beat the future leading miler Posse and the 1980 Oaks winner Bireme into the minor placings. There was just one blot: the mud conditions of Longchamp prevented Princesse Lida from completing the French juvenile Triple Crown finishing third to the pacemaking Dragon and to her paternal half brother Nice Havrais in that event.

The most notable performances in the United States also came from two-year-olds, a win and a Graded place for Street Ballet and, for the future, a winning performance for the Shuvee colt Vatza, for Ballare, and for Bitty Girl's daughter Nijit. Czaravich also ran third to champion grass horse Bowl Game in the Man O'War and Terpsichorist was a game second in the Long Island. The last two months of the season went out on a high note with four individual winners and a great second spot for Street Ballet in the Tempted to Genuine Risk, the female star of 1980.

It had been a spectacular year for Nijinsky, most notable for the fact that the best performers were not concentrated in one country. In France the scintillating victories of Princesse Lida, Nice Havrais and Bev Bev placed Nijinsky clear at the top of the juvenile sires table, the only stallion whose two-year-old progeny earned over a million francs. It was also the year when the first crop of Green Dancer saw the racecourse and, with the help of Group 1 winning daughter Aryenne, Green Dancer was fourth to his own sire on the French juvenile list and was leading freshman sire in Europe following in his father's footsteps. In England and Ireland Nijinsky finished seventh on the general sires list his ten winners accounting for 19 races and the stakes won by his progeny accruing £164,548 only £900 behind the sixth placed horse Busted and £4,500 behind fifth placed Sallust. In the United States Nijinsky appeared also in seventh place with earnings of US $1,747,748 and was also the leading commercial sales sire there. On the Free Handicaps Nijinsky's progeny stole the show in France, Princesse Lida the Champion Two-Year-Old Filly (and champion juvenile with her 3 lb sex allowance) and Nice Havrais tying with Nureyev for second spot in the colts' championship – Dragon having to be placed top by virtue of his fluke win in France's premier two-year-old race. There were also very high ratings in Ireland for Muscovite and London Bells (joint fifth to Monteverdi) and also for Night Alert (3 lb below them). Of the older horses, Niniski and Stetchworth were highly rated on the three-year-old handicap (ten furlongs plus) but, of course, they had had the mighty Troy to contend with. Ile de Bourbon was the indisputable Champion Older Horse of Europe rated clear of Gay Mecene whom he had defeated by seven lengths in the Coronation Cup and who had run Troy to 1½ lengths in the King George which Ile de Bourbon had to miss due to a virus. In the United States Terpsichorist, Summer Fling and Czaravich were highly rated on the lists.

Nijinsky was certainly on the crest of a wave. Two shares in him made US $500,000, the highest figure ever attained at public auction for a share in a thoroughbred stallion giving him a total value of US $16 million. At the end of 1979, with 37 individual stakes winners to his name in his first six seasons, Nijinsky was where he would always be – at the top.

Stakes winner Number 38 was not long in coming in the new year. The recently turned three-year-old Street Ballet let the Nijinsky supporters know that 1980 was not going to pale too much into insignificance after the record breaking previous year. The new year was just three days old when Street Ballet took time by the scruff of the neck and triumphed in the La Centinela at Santa Anita. As if to prove it was no fluke Ballare opened her new season with a win at the same track two days later and, before the year was 18 days old, Nijinska Street (2) and Classical Ballet had made it five wins for Nijinsky in less than two weeks. On the 1 February there was a win for Vatza and in that month more successes for Nijinska Street, Vaslov and London Bells, repatriated from Ireland. Street Ballet suffered a slight reversal by finishing second in the Santa Ynez to her well known rival Table Hands. Wheels have a habit of coming full circle, as Table Hands was one of the mares who paid court to Nijinsky in 1981.

Before March was 21 days old London Bells, Classical Ballet and Ballare had all made it two wins each in 1980 and Nijit opened her account and won again on 2 April. Nijinsky had his first European winner on 7 April and made it stakes winner Number 39 when Nice Havrais came out to take the Group 3

Prix de Fontainebleau. Five days later it was Night Alert's turn in the Gladness Stakes in Ireland and so made it two Group winners from three winners. The next day Princesse Lida was beaten on her seasonal debut, the Group 3 Prix de la Grotte, but it was only by a neck and by Green Dancer's daughter Aryenne so it was really quite a triumph for Nijinsky. On the same day as Night Alert's win in Ireland stakes winner Number 40 arrived in the form of Ballare whose promising career was so soon to be cut short by injury. Street Ballet ran second to Ballare, as she had done in the Santa Susana to Bold 'N Determined, to give Nijinsky a 1–2 in the Senorita. Czaravich also made a winning reappearance as a four-year-old on 3 May when scoring an impressive success in the Grade 2 Carter Handicap to prove himself a force to be reckoned with for the coming season. The remainder of April in Europe had yielded a breathtaking win for Niniski in the Group 2 John Porter Stakes. Appearing well back in the ruck, with nowhere to go, he produced such scintillating speed that he got up to win by three lengths. On the same day, however, Piaffer found himself in exactly the same position as Niniski but his last gasp burst of speed left him still a short head adrift of Northleach in a race he really should have won.

Niniski repeated the performance in the Group 3 Ormonde Stakes in May when, in Chester's notoriously short straight, he just came through in time to defeat a class field. In rough races for the 2,000 Guineas and Ultramar Jubilee Handicap, Night Alert was promoted to third behind Known Fact while Piaffer decidedly got the worst of it at Kempton and his promotion to second was little moral compensation. In the French 1,000 Guineas Princesse Lida proved herself not to be quite the filly she had been at two when third to Green Dancer's daughter Aryenne once again. In Aryenne Green Dancer had a representative worthy of his first crop, as he himself had been to Nijinsky's.

Apart from Czaravich May was a quiet time for Nijinsky in North America with just three individual winners. But Czaravich was more than able to atone for it on his own. Following his Carter Handicap success, Czaravich carried off the Grade 1 prize in the Metropolitan Handicap displaying fine courage and dazzling speed.

To keep Nijinsky happy at home the mares were every bit as good as the years before. They were showing a tendency, true throughout the early years of the 1980s, towards overall younger mares than heretofore. Names to conjure with in 1980 included Fabuleux Jane, Optimistic Gal, Raise Your Skirts, Rose Bowl, Too Many Sweets, Spearfish, Miss Suzaki, Deceit, Native Partner, Something Super, Dearly Precious, Squander, Flying Above, Rosetta Stone, Smartaire, Stylish Pattern, Dancealot, Swingtime and Waya.

June opened hot and hard in England and put paid to Niniski's chances of winning the Group 1 Coronation Cup, as Ile de Bourbon had done in totally contrasting conditions in 1979. Niniski was second to Sea Chimes however and gained revenge on Soleil Noir at the same time. However, Night Alert soon made up for that disappointment travelling to Chantilly the following Sunday to take the Group 2 Prix Jean Prat.

Nijinsky had relatively few runners in Europe during June but seven winners in North America, though not of stakes calibre. Most notable amongst those American successes was the debut of the Saratoga record filly in a career that would ultimately see her a champion. In a Belmont maiden on 11 June De La Rose did not let her supporters down and nor did Czaravich whose game third to Winter's Tale in the Suburban said a great deal for his weight carrying capacities.

July in a hot Europe saw only eight Nijinskys running, pride of place going to Muscovite in becoming stakes winner Number 41 in the Ballycorus and to Piaffer who won the Crocker Bulteel Stakes at Ascot for the second year in succession and conceding no less than 32 lb to the second in the process.

It was sales time again and Nijinsky could not possibly be expected to hit the heights achieved the previous summer, though results had been good so far in 1980. He had 16 yearlings sold in North America averaging US $261,563, down on the previous year by some US$129,000. But in Golden Fleece the Sangster combine would keep going for another year or so: he sold for US $775,000, the top priced Nijinsky by US $275,000. The lowest price was US$105,000 but Golden Fleece was the only future Group winner. In England a rare offering at the Houghton Sales, a chestnut colt out of Dauntu, went for 58,000 guineas.

The older horses kept proving the Nijinsky's could run – five wins for Nijinsky in August in North America; a stakes place for London Bells and a third in the Whitney for the weighted Czaravich; and a close fourth for Street Ballet in the Delaware Oaks. But it was, again, De La Rose who stole the show, the second of her two victories being her first stakes success. De La Rose was on her way up . . . and up and all the way to the top. Five individual winners in Europe made it a comfortably successful August with juvenile Kings Lake coming out to record his first victory. A name to be heard again.

Early in September Muscovite won his Group race while Leap Lively won two races, the second of which was the Hoover Fillies Mile, establishing her as a leading juvenile staying filly much as it had done Cherry Hinton three years previously. Stakeswise the Nijinskys were running well but not quite well enough to win which was also the story in North America six winners, but the only stakes success being that of His Honor in the Governors

Handicap at Sacramento. However the two-year-old performances of Sportin' Life kept things interesting.

Princesse Lida came back to form in October to claim a listed race at Longchamp on the same day that Nijinsky's Secret and Russian Fox ran a 1–2 in a good two-year-old race there. Shining Finish had already won four races before his first Group success in the St Simon Stakes (Group 3) at Newbury later in the month while juveniles Kings Lake and Bedford (also second Houghton Stakes) kept the ball rolling in that direction. Three winners, but no stakes, was the story again in North America but the fillies De La Rose, Street Ballet and Nijit put up classy performances in being placed against top opposition.

Nijinsky had his last runner – and winner – in Europe on 18 November when Russian Fox broke his maiden at Maisons-Laffitte. By that time His Honor had run up another stakes and a notable two-year-old had arrived in Canada in Native Ballet. However, Nijinsky was going to go out on a high note with Sportin' Life who had a smashing triumph at the back end of his two-year-old career with a 7½ length stroll over classy Thirty Eight Paces in the Allegheny at Keystone on 27 December. It was stakes winner Number 46 for Nijinsky.

It was perhaps not Nijinsky's most spectacular year, but 1980 was remarkable if only for its consistency. He had had a larger number of highly rated animals in North America than probably in any other season: Czaravich, Ballare (rated fifth three-year-old filly to Genuine Risk despite her highly abbreviated career), De La Rose and the champion Canadian three-year-old filly Street Ballet, who was rated 3 lb clear of Lady Roberta and who also received a high rating in the United States. In England Leap Lively was rated joint sixth with Fairy Footsteps on the juvenile filly list behind the flying Marwell while Kings Lake, off two non-stakes victories, was given the fourth highest weight on the Irish Two-Year-Old Handicap. In France, Nijinsky's Secret gained himself a mention despite his lack of black type performance. Amongst the three-year-olds Shining Finish and Night Alert were prominent and, in the four-year-old and up, Niniski and Piaffer.

As was to be expected, Nijinsky had slipped a little in the sires' lists, his twelve winners of 21 races in England and Ireland (earning £142,909) put him 14th to Pitcairn while in the United States he sat at eleventh place with earnings of US $1,669,869, Czaravich being the major earner. However on the list, by percentage, of US $25,000 earners (minimum ten runners), Nijinsky was third behind Foolish Pleasure and the virtually unknown Pisgale who only had ten runners. Nijinsky had 43, giving him 37 per cent US $25,000.

But 1980, though quiet, was only a lull. For 1981 was to give Nijinsky a unique position – having concurrent champions on each side of the Atlantic. One was a home bred colt, the other a very expensive filly.

Neither put in an appearance for a while however. It was mid-April in Europe before any Nijinsky form was seen, Shining Finish being beaten two whiskers in the Group 2 John Porter Stakes while Nijinsky's Secret won first time out in France. Kings Lake had a first appearance which was a disastrous mystery but was soon to be put behind him. In North America the first four months had been successful with a stakes win on the very first day of the year – His Honor, in the appropriately named Happy New Year Handicap at Bay Meadows.

It was to be a happy new year for Nijinsky. Before January was out Sportin' Life, so early in his three-year-old career, had added another stakes to his tally while Vatza had come out to win twice. Conversely, there were few runners in February but Shimmy and Water Dance kept the wins clocking up while His Honor was placed in the Berkeley at Golden Gate. De La Rose made her first appearance, finishing fourth in the Forward Gal. She took a while to get going but once she did . . . Eight wins in March and April for Nijinsky's stock increased the tempo, notably His Honor annexing another stakes race.

Visiting mares to Claiborne that year included Waya, Table Hands, Mrs Warren, Spark of Life, First Feather, Ivanjica, Spearfish, Smart Angle, Dancealot, Shuvee and Street Dancer as well as the dams of Nijinsky's Secret, Sportin' Life, Solford, Western Symphony and Quiet Fling.

It all started to happen in May. On the very first day of the month De La Rose bravely ran Heavenly Cause to a short head in the Kentucky Oaks and said goodbye to the dirt track. Twenty-four hours later Shimmy gave Nijinsky another stakes winner in the Senorita at Hollywood while on the 6 May Sportin' Life gave future classic winner Summing a fright, first in the Hill Prince and then running even closer on 25 May in the Pennsylvania Derby. In between, there were four wins by Nijinsky's daughters and Nijinsky ended the month with a bang with three winners at Belmont on the 31 May from three runners, all fillies, including the first graded success for De La Rose in the Saranac, defeating the colts in the process.

Nijinsky's other champion was also on his way. In a highly controversial finish, Kings Lake prevailed over English Guineas winner To Agori Mou in the Irish equivalent only to be disqualified and then reinstated. Earlier, Leap Lively had established herself as a live contender for the Epsom Oaks with an all the way triumph in the Johnnie Walker Oaks Trial (Group 3) at Lingfield. The two Group winners were ably supported by the stakes performances of Nijinsky's Secret, Shining Finish, Susanna and Ranking Beauty.

June took off where May had ended in North America. Balletomane became stakes winner Number 49 when winning the Grade 3 Princess Stakes at Hollywood Park and, a week later, De La Rose won again, this time in the Long Island. Other performances of note were Balletomane's second to Past Forgetting, whom she had defeated soundly in the Princess, in the Hollywood Oaks. But June was altogether a quieter month in Europe with the highlights being Leap Lively's third to Blue Wind in the Epsom Oaks and the terrific battle for the St James's Palace at Royal Ascot, which Kings Lake just lost to To Agori Mou. That battle was to add fuel to the fire between those deadliest of rival camps and which had been sparked off by that controversial Irish 2,000 Guineas. It would keep the flat season in England alight the summer long.

As ever, the run up to the summer sales was relatively quiet: just five winners for the whole of July in North America but one of these was the victory for Sportin' Life in the Leonard Richards. Even De La Rose was turned over by a colt, Acaroid, in the Lexington but it was only a temporary hiccup.

Nijinsky was making headlines again at the sales. Whereas his 20 yearlings averaged US $386,900 only US $3,869 less than his record breaking year of 1979 (National Average US $35,409), he established two records – a Fasig Tipton record of US $1,300,000 for a bright bay colt out of the Cavan mare Fairness and the cheapest Nijinsky ever – US $13,000. All the others made over US $100,000 however and the O'Brien team was responsible for selecting two of them – the record breaker (the subsequent Eclipse Stakes winner Solford) and the third highest priced at US $800,000 (Caerleon, the French Derby victor). Sandwiched in between these two champions was Nijinsky's second million dollar plus colt that year, Swingtime's son Countertrade, who made US $1,107,000 and went on to win. Other stakes winners amongst these 20 turned out to be Rosy Spectre (US $250,000), Fabuleux Dancer (US $210,000) and Ultramate (US $135,000).

July in Europe saw its share of winners but nothing greatly exciting happened until 29 July which was exciting enough to last the rest of the season. The epic battle between Kings Lake and To Agori Mou continued to its climax when Kings Lake burst through in the final yards to snatch the Group 1 Sussex Stakes, his second Group 1 success: something which To Agori Mou could not achieve all year. It was a race that would burn indelibly in the memory.

Pustinya tried to set August alight with two victories starting on the very first day, but it was left to De La Rose to keep Nijinsky's flag flying high with her so easy success in the Grade 2 Diana Handicap. There were good placings too for Shimmy in the Delaware Oaks and Nijit in the Ocean City.

After that tremendous Sussex Stakes there was the almost inevitable anti-climax in Europe, though the equally tremendous race for the Yorkshire Oaks (Group 1) when Leap Lively was caught literally on the line, did try to keep things ticking over as did the juvenile success of Cloonlara's son Chivalry. The most stunning result of the month was the running of Kings Lake and To Agori Mou in the Prix Jacques le Marois, as close as it had ever been and yet both were beaten *five* lengths by the crack French miler Northjet in a performance that one still finds difficult to believe.

September in the United States was almost more notable for its near misses – that of Kyra's Slipper in the Grassland, De La Rose in the Flower Bowl and Water Dance in the Long Look. De La Rose however bounced back to form with a triumph in the Lamb Chop and a very interesting juvenile appeared called Hostage.

In Europe September saw five victories, two of a very different nature but of just as much significance. Both occurred on the same day but whereas one was a Group 1 the other was "only" a maiden. Kings Lake proved what a versatile horse he really was with an all the way victory in the *ten* furlongs Joe McGrath Memorial Stakes in which he defeated, amongst others, Erin's Isle and the dual Oaks winner Blue Wind. Previously on the card, a strapping Nijinsky two-year-old had made his debut a winning one, defeating a future dual Derby winner in the process. His name was Golden Fleece; the horse he beat Assert.

Bedford's third place in the Irish St Leger and the highly promising third place in the Houghton Stakes of the two-year-old own brother to Quiet Fling, Peacetime, were the most noteworthy performances at the end of the European season.

The season though was not finished in North America. October saw six wins, the most important being the scintillating autumn successes of De La Rose in carrying off the Athenia (Grade 3) and E. P. Taylor (Grade 3), two easy successes for her. In November came the performance that led to her officially being recognized as the Champion she was: a Grade 1 success over the colts in the Hollywood Derby. Just a day earlier Water Dance had made it half a century of stakes winners with her winning performance in the Twilight Tear and other notable successes were turned in by two-year-olds Dearly Too and Hostage, the latter also running third in the Nashua.

December eased to a close with another juvenile winner in Vestris plus those of older performers Tournament Star (ex Chris Evert), Worldwatch and Dance Call.

A remarkable 1981 then for Nijinsky with his Three-Year-Old Champion Turf filly, De La Rose, in the United States and his brave three-year-old champion miler Kings Lake in Europe. He had also clocked up 50 individual stakes winners after eight seasons of runners, a percentage which was to be improved so dramatically in the succeeding years that he would tally half as many again in just two more seasons racing, accumulating 25 additional individual stakes winners in 1982 and 1983 alone and adding ten more in 1984.

On the English/Irish Sires Table Nijinsky had risen back to seventh place, his nine winners of 15 races accumulating £212,596 (including place money) in stakes, having less runners than any of the stallions above him. In the United States he was sixth, his representatives earning US $1,967,687. He was also second on the list of American sires of average earnings per start (the leader Ole Bob Bowers had John Henry to thank for that) and also a high placing on the Average Earnings per runner. Apart from his champion filly other high ratings were given to the fillies Balletomane, Shimmy and Native Ballet while in Europe it was a second highweight in the Irish Two-Year-Old Free Handicap for the once raced Golden Fleece (top-rated was Group 1 winner Achieved). Kings Lake was jointly rated at the top of the 7 furlong –10 furlong category in Europe with To Agori Mou, Beldale Flutter and Vayrann but only he and To Agori Mou were mile performers and only Kings Lake was a Group 1 winner at both distances. Other high ratings were achieved by Shining Finish (Older Horses, ten furlongs plus), Leap Lively and Bedford.

With two champions in 1981, and 50 stakes winners under his belt, Nijinsky had quite a season to look forward to in 1982, especially in the form of the unbeaten Golden Fleece. No one even then could have predicted what heights Nijinsky was going to reach in the next 24 months.

With a share being sold at Keeneland January Sale for US $750,000 1982 got off to a pretty heady start. It was to be a rather heady season at the sales all round for Nijinsky. His fee had been revealed at US $175,000 no guarantees, which was to be rather more noticeable for the speed in which it increased rather than for the figure itself.

Nijinsky had an even greater proportion of runners than usual in North America, as opposed to Europe in 1982, yet it was horses trained in England and Ireland that were to make the greatest impact.

As ever, of course, it was the Nijinsky's in the United States that got into the swing of things first – due as much as anything else to the mere fact that the season starts earlier. The first recorded success was on 19 January when Number, a three parts sister to champion Nureyev, broke her maiden at Hialeah. Four days later the four-year-old Balletomane followed her at Santa Anita and on 2 February French import Russian Fox at Hialeah. Then the winners started to flow, though it was only De La Rose who was stakes campaigning and who was also retired after three starts. Coupled with injury, she was clearly not showing her previous zest, though she had never been an early spring type, but two defeats by Honey Fox just about sealed her fate. However, there were those to cover for her: Nijinsky sent out the winners of twelve races before the end of March.

For once, and significantly, the drought of stakes winners came to an abrupt end with the victories of two colts, one in the United States, one in Europe: significant, because they were achieved by Nijinsky's best colt in Europe that season and his best colt Stateside winning within seven days of each other.

Hostage's spreadeagling win in the Grade 1 Arkansas Derby was perhaps the more unexpected. He had earlier been a good allowance winner and his victory put him in the front rank of Kentucky Derby contenders. Unfortunately this was not to be, because he took a bad step five days before the classic and the injury was serious enough to enforce his retirement. It is more than feasible that Nijinsky would have had Derby winners on each side of the Atlantic in 1982 had Hostage been able to contest the premier Churchill Downs event.

Coincidentally, Hostage and Nijinsky's other mid-April Group winner, Golden Fleece, were bred by the same farm but the pair had gone their separate ways as yearlings – Hostage being retained to race for his breeders, Golden Fleece arriving at the Keeneland Sales to be purchased for US $775,000 and on his way to Ireland. It was in Ireland that he extended his unbeaten career with an ultra-smooth victory in the Ballymoss Stakes (Group 2) at the Curragh.

Hostage, nor Golden Fleece, had been Nijinsky's first stakes winner for the year however. That had come on 23 January in Japan when his daughter Yamanin Penny had defeated her paternal half brother Nishino Northern in the Junior Cup. On 20 February she had become a Group winner with her success in the Group 3 Yonsai Stakes.

Before eight days had elapsed, after Golden Fleece's success that pointed him to favouritism for the Epsom Derby, Peacetime proved that there was a Nijinsky representative in England worthy of Derby consideration. Peacetime triumphed in the Guardian Classic Trial in which the three previous runnings pre-Derby success had come to no less than Troy, Henbit and Shergar. Quite an act to follow.

Thahul made it a hat-trick of wins for Nijinsky by being victorious at Warwick (they win anywhere and everywhere) while back in the United States two winners at Aqueduct on the 29 April sent that month out on a high. Also, during the previous few weeks, Come Rain or Shine had run the race of his life to be second in the Grade 2 Pan American while Dearly Too, a daughter of champion Dearly Precious, had proved her stakes ability with a third in the Prioress.

As far as winners were concerned, May belonged to Europe with four winners of five races. Those five included two by now familiar names – Golden Fleece, who both lived up to his growing reputation in the race named in honour of his sire and beat Assert pointless in the process; and Peacetime, who gained a gutsy win in the classic trial, the Schroder Life Predominate Stakes at Goodwood. Nijinsky's sole winner in the United States that month was also a stakes winner: Sportin' Life in the Cochise Handicap at Delaware. Three-year-old Vestris had run a great race to be third in the Grade 1 Acorn to Cupecoy's Joy which was somewhat of a bonus. May was rather a time of what might have been and in Hostage's absence the Kentucky Derby was won by an outsider, Gato del Sol. It must surely have been the best chance Nijinsky had had of an American Triple Crown race winner.

There were no such mistakes in Europe. Peacetime went to post for the Epsom Derby but had his problems and a respiratory ailment almost certainly accounted for his relatively poor showing, being prominent at Tattenham Corner but fading in the straight. However the favourite Golden Fleece needed no such excuses. It was such a spectacular success that the race left those who know best equating Nijinsky's first European Derby winner with his own sire and also to Sir Ivor, two of the best Derby winners since the Second World War. He had made it look easy and yet the time for the race was the fastest since electronic timing was introduced. It was a scintillating victory for almost undoubtedly Nijinsky's best ever racing son.

It was a long time before the euphoria died down but the month still had days to run when the first two-year-old of the season made his appearance and with it clocked up stakes winner Number 55 for Nijinsky. His name was Caerleon, the US$800,000 purchase by Sangster and partners at the previous year's Keeneland July Sale and one of the most physically perfect of thoroughbreds one was ever likely to see. He was also one of the most courageous but that was not needed in his easy success in the Tyros Stakes at the Curragh on Irish Sweeps Derby day.

Golden Fleece was missing from that latter encounter. He had developed a lameness problem and as time wore on and the weeks available to prepare him for the big autumn races grew shorter the decision was eventually made to retire him to stud where, standing at Coolmore Stud in Ireland, he commanded a stud fee second to none in Europe. It was however sadly ill-fated for early in 1984 Golden Fleece was dead.

June in North America was somewhat quiet following the defection of Hostage to stud. There were eight wins, the most notable of which was the third of three tallied by a recent import from France, Nijinsky's Secret. With it came his first graded victory, the Grade 2 Tidal Handicap. Before that, the name of Nijinsky's Secret had not meant too much to the Americans. It would be right in front of their eyes for some time to come.

Things also wound down a little in England in July, plenty of places but no winners. Nijinsky also did his usual trick of lying dormant in the three weeks before the summer sales with just Waving and Sportin' Life winning – although the latter did account for his most valuable success, a seven length stroll in the Grade 3 William Dupont Jr Handicap. Smart performances had been put up by the sister of Nijinsky's Secret, Dancing Secret (third Martha Washington Handicap), Dearly Too (third in the Garden City) and Olamic (second Politely) and a good fourth to Christmas Past for Dearly Too in the Monmouth Oaks. But better things were just around the corner.

Despite this Nijinsky had a smashing Keeneland July and Saratoga Sales. It was not because his average for 13 yearlings was US$738,462 – his highest yet – or because all his yearlings went for prices in excess of US$120,000 or because he had two sons sold for over a million dollars. It was because he had the sales topper and, what was more, a world record priced yearling. The colt out of Spearfish, regarded as easily the outstanding offering in the blue blooded sale by the Sangster team, was bought by them for US$4.25 million. Named Empire Glory he captured the Group 3 Royal Whip in 1984 and was beaten a fast diminishing neck in the Jefferson Smurfit Memorial Irish St Leger. The second US$1 million plus (actually US$2,100,000) out of Bendara, was thus very closely related to Golden Fleece and was named Esperanto. He beat Empire Glory to the stakes draw as a three-year-old with a win in the listed Craddock Advertising Race, later to add the Shanbally House Stud Stakes. Of the 13 yearlings sold no less than ten came to Europe, a comment if ever there was one about the state of the top of the American yearling market. Others of the yearlings to have recorded stakes successes at two- and three-years-old were Greek Sky (US $200,000) in the Prix Juigne and Nagurski (US $170,000) in the Grade 3 Woodlawn Stakes in the United States. Goldye's Miss (US $210,000) also proved herself in stakes company.

On the first day of August in the United States Bemissed became the first juvenile winner for Nijinsky, breaking her maiden at the second time of asking at Belmont. The next day Number filled third spot in the Test Stakes behind the flying Gold Beauty and Nijinsky ended this summer month with three winners in three days at the big Saratoga meeting. First, Number outpointed Vestris for a valuable allowance, Topin broke her maiden the next day and then it was stakes success Number 58 when Khatango won the Graded Seneca. In Europe it was six winners for Nijinsky and, most importantly, two of them were stakes races. Caerleon followed up his Tyros

Stakes win with an equally facile victory in the Group 3 Ballsbridge/ Tattersalls Anglesey Stakes following in his sire's footsteps. On the very same day, and on the same track, Fasig Tipton record holder Solford made his debut, doing just enough to win. Three days later at the big York Ebor meeting there appeared a two-year-old about which no two-year-old had excited so much public reaction for many a year. After Glad Rags' son and Terpsichorist's brother Gorytus had smashed the two-year-old course record and, leaving his twelve rivals including Salieri seven lengths for dead, even the most cagey of race commentators were declaring that here was another Mill Reef. In Gorytus was the star to make up for the absence of Golden Fleece.

Through September it was still Gorytus who hit the headlines and his five length stroll in the Group 2 Laurent Perrier Champagne Stakes at Doncaster was only calculated to keep the euphoria and mystique surrounding this horse rising still further. Gorytus was not alone that month for Peacetime came gamely back from operations and lengthy layoffs to record a win in the valuable Valdoe Stakes at Goodwood; and over in Ireland another Sangster/O'Brien juvenile had made his first win a stakes event. This time it was a colt who was not purchased at public auction, Bitty Girl's son Beaudelaire, who gained a deserved success in the Coolmore Try My Best Stakes. Beaudelaire was stakes winner Number 59.

The North American progeny had a great deal to live up to after Nijinsky's exploits in Europe but they did their best with wins for two-year-olds White Birch (2) and, in particular, for Bemissed in the Grade 3 Natalma. Run just a day after Beaudelaire's Try My Best, Bemissed thus became the 60th stakes winner for her illustrious sire. Only six days later Dearly Too became Number 61 with a victory in the Meadowlands Starbright Stakes and, with places in Graded encounters for Number (just outpointed in the Gazelle by Broom Dance), Bemissed (third Evening Out Stakes) and Khatango (third Lawrence Realization) plus the winners of ten races, September was pretty successful in North America for Nijinsky too.

This up and up stopped abruptly in Europe. All good things are bound to end but some end rather more prematurely than others: despite the juvenile success of Drumtop's son Brogan, the defeat – or rather the virtual non-running – of Gorytus, in the William Hill Dewhurst has still to be explained. It left the racing world stunned for here was almost certainly Nijinsky's best two-year-old. No one will ever know what happened to Gorytus for certain but undoubtedly it made 1983 that much poorer. Not even Russian Roubles' game victory in the Houghton Stakes the very next day and also at Newmarket, could soften the blow.

No such misfortunes on the other side of the Atlantic; nine wins in

October alone and very successful ones too though it started with a reverse for Nijinsky's Secret in the Jockey Club Cup at Woodbine. This was quickly healed by Dearly Too annexing the Violet at the Meadowlands but then came that dreadful spill in the Jockey Club Gold Cup, which cost the life of Timely Writer, when Khatango was brought down behind the eventual winner Lemhi Gold. The very next day two-year-old Loose Cannon broke his maiden. Such are the ups and downs, sometimes quite literally, of racing. Bemissed added another stakes to her successful juvenile career on the 21 October and even improved it nine days later when she became Nijinsky's first Grade 1 winning juvenile filly in the United States by winning the Selima Stakes at Laurel, while Shimmy was a winner on the other side of the country at Santa Anita on the same day.

Nijinsky had fewer runners than usual in November and December but his important successes that year still continued unabated. Thanks to Number, Nijinsky went into 1983 with 63 stakes winners to his name as she won first the First Flight and then the Firenze. Nothing more than that game filly deserved. Number was one of four individual winners for Nijinsky in November from a few runners, and another notable performance was that of Loose Cannon in running second to I Enclose in the Nashua.

Such a successful season in England and Ireland left Nijinsky sixth on the General Sire List but, had Golden Fleece remained sound, it could have been so much higher. Still, he had sired the winners of 23 races for a total stakes of £295,602 which was less than £5,000 adrift of fifth placed Kalamoun who had Kalaglow (King George VI & Queen Elizabeth Stakes, Eclipse Stakes) to thank for his lofty placing. Thanks mainly to Assert, Golden Fleece's close relative Be My Guest was leading sire in England and Ireland. In win stakes alone Nijinsky was a clear second to Be My Guest.

In the United States Nijinsky was seventh on the Graded Sires List. His total earnings of US$2,124,624 was very creditable considering that his major successes came in Europe, where prize money is so much less, and his best horse Hostage was unable to continue past April. What was most striking and perhaps surprising was that he was fifth of the leading sires of two-year-olds with the winners of eleven races and US$503,821. On the other specific tables Nijinsky was third behind Blushing Groom and Vaguely Noble, on the list for average earnings per start and also high on the average earnings per runner.

In Europe high ratings on the European Free Handicap were recorded by, naturally, Gorytus and Caerleon. Gorytus was joint second on the English version, 2 lb below Diesis who had won that Dewhurst, while in Ireland Caerleon, like Golden Fleece, was weighted second to Danzatore while Beaudelaire was only 4 lb below him and Solford not far below that.

Needless to say, Golden Fleece was Champion Three-Year-Old, despite the fact that Assert had won both the French and Irish Derbies plus the Benson & Hedges Gold Cup in his absence, while Peacetime was high on the list of 6 furlongs–10 furlongs three-year-olds, which is a rather large division in terms of different distance performers.

So Nijinsky had had a highly successful year yet again with two of his best ever progeny in Hostage and Golden Fleece and it was sheer bad luck that neither could go on to even greater things. Yet surely no one could predict the phenomenal season to follow.

It is worth bearing in mind that at the end of 1982 Nijinsky had 63 individual stakes winners to his name, an average of almost 7 per crop. By the end of another twelve months this had shot up to 75, almost double a normal year's return and, in the process, Nijinsky smashed and set yet another record: 18 individual stakes winners in a single season. Even before this his fee had jumped to US$250,000 which was not far off double that of the previous year.

That 1983 was going to be a record breaker did not become readily apparent. There was only one winner from a limited number of runners (the million dollar colt Countertrade) and only two wins in February, both by the same filly, Dancinintherain. Another two wins in early March came and went before the first significant stakes performance: Waving's third in the Las Cienagas Handicap. Number opened her account as a four-year-old followed by wins for three-year-olds White Birch and Rosy Spectre before the stakes second of Fabuleux Dancer in the Prix Juigne in France. However the stakes tally started to mount as Nijinsky's Secret annexed the Grade 2 Bougainvillea and then became a Grade 1 winner with a memorable success in the Hialeah Turf Cup.

Number had had a reversal in being demoted from second in the Apple Blossom but ran third in the Bewitch while Bemissed ran third in the Gallorette. There were also wins for Leap of The Heart and Rosy Spectre at the end of the month. The exciting juveniles of 1982, Gorytus and Russian Roubles, were not about to excite the racing world in Europe however and it was not until 8 May that a real class performance was put up by Brogan in the Italian Derby though the exact class of that was obviously suspect. Nijinsky's first European stakes winner and Number 65 of his career came when Fabuleux Dancer, the first foal of the major stakes winner Fabuleux Jane, won the Prix de l'Avre at Longchamp. However, even better things were on the way starting with Solford's beating of stable companion Caerleon when first and second in the Craddock Advertising Race. Both would end the season as champions.

In the United States May had witnessed stakes winner Number 66, Rosy

Spectre, registering a game win in a thrilling finish to the Churchill Downs' Regret Stakes. This had followed a good third by Bemissed to Princess Rooney in the Kentucky Oaks (in which Rosy Spectre was fourth), an impressive Dixie Handicap win for Khatango and a second spot in the Shuvee for Number. May ended with a second for White Birch in the Grade 3 Hill Prince Handicap and altogether seven wins for Nijinsky.

There were some exciting foals on the ground in 1983. Colts from such as Relaxing, Late Bloomer and Riverqueen and fillies from Best In Show and Square Angel. Own brothers and sisters to Number, Hostage, Quiet Fling, Peacetime, Key Dancer, Kings Lake, Vision, Caerleon, De La Rose, Upper Nile, Western Symphony, La Jalouse and Moscow Ballet; half brothers and sisters to Nureyev, Hawaiian Sound, Northern Trick, The Very One; foals of mares who were closely related to Affirmed, Niniski, Crowned Prince, Caerleon, Vision, Mill Reef and Dahlia. Mares who visited Nijinsky in 1983 included Fairy Bridge, Glorious Song, Ivory Wings, Just A Game, Last Feather, Syria, Shanizadeh, Native Nurse, Late Bloomer, Two Rings and the dam of Seattle Slew and Lomond, My Charmer. Very familiar names in the book were Peace, Glad Rags, Secret Beauty, Spearfish, Foreseer and Like A Charm. The future for Nijinsky in the mid-1980s sire lists appears rosy indeed.

June 1982 had seen one Derby success in Europe: June 1983 saw another. Caerleon's sparkling three length triumph in the French Derby proved him unsurmountably superior to the French three-year-olds that season over twelve furlongs. It was enough to give him the French Three-Year-Old Championship though it was his solitary foray to that country. Exactly a week later Solford repeated Caerleon's journey across the Irish Sea and English Channel; this time to capture that Group 3 Prix du Lys and in the process become Nijinsky's 67th stakes winner.

France was at the mercy of the raiding Nijinskys that month; stakes winner Number 68 was totted up at Chantilly just three days after Solford's success. The English trained Brogan gaily galloped to a six length victory in the Prix Berteux. The following day Russian Roubles came back to form to run Shareef Dancer to a length in the "Ascot Derby" – the Group 2 King Edward VII Stakes – though no one at the Royal meeting could possibly have realised the significance of that form at the time. They found out just ten days later when Shareef Dancer defeated the winners of two Derbies to win the Irish Sweeps version. Caerleon, ill at ease on the rock hard ground, eventually extricated himself from the box in which he found himself to follow the Northern Dancer colt home but proved himself the superior of the two previous Derby winners by leaving Teenoso behind in third place.

With Vestris successful in a Monmouth allowance on the very first day of the month June 1983 started off well. Nijinsky had his first ever runner in an American Triple Crown race when White Birch represented him in the Belmont but he made no show behind Caveat. Number chalked up another Grade race, however, in the Grade 2 Hempstead Handicap and the number of individual stakes winners during the season was steadily totting up.

Nijinsky's Secret travelled to Canada to register an easy victory in the King Edward Gold Cup but, strangely, there was just one "ordinary" winner in North America that month (Loose Cannon at Belmont).

Early July was as quite as usual with just wins for the three-year-old fillies Start A Rumor and Down Stage though Olamic did run second in the Eatontown.

Buyers at Keeneland and Saratoga either did not notice this or chose to regard it as insignificant for the summer sales were a stunning success for Nijinsky even when compared to the previous season when he was represented by that record priced yearling. His 13 yearlings averaged US $942,593 which, compared to the National Average of US $41,255, was rather incredible. A step towards that magic one million dollar average mark. Nijinsky also had his second yearling over US $4 million in a bay colt out of Belle Of Dodge Me (subsequently named Gallant Archer). He is now resident in Michael Stoute's yard in Newmarket and won his only start in 1984. He had the misfortune however to be overshadowed by the return of US $10.2 million for Snaafi Dancer, the Northern Dancer colt also sent to England.

Nijinsky had another million plus individual in the chestnut colt, out of Our Lady Queen, Father Matthew who is with Vincent O'Brien in Ireland. He also had his first filly over that magic mark (an own sister to the previous year's sale topper) who is now in France and named Sainte Croix. As is becoming a general trend, the majority of the 13 are in Europe and no less that four with Michael Stoute. In addition to Father Matthew, Shadeed (US $800,000) and Nijinsky's Melody (US $113,708) were stakes horses of 1984 as juveniles.

July in Europe had a sensational start with a thrilling race. Solford came to England to defeat an all-quality field in the Group 1 Coral Eclipse Stakes over ten furlongs at Sandown while Russian Roubles and Brogan were first and third in the Welsh Derby at Chepstow. Nijinsky had three quick winners in France. Green Dancer's own brother Val Danseur (an American stakes winner in 1984) and juvenile Equinol, the first for the season. Two days later Beaudelaire arrived in England to smash the course record at Newcastle in the listed Beeswing Stakes, but Caerleon lost both front shoes when down the field in the premier all-aged race, the King George VI & Queen Elizabeth Diamond Stakes at Ascot, behind the filly Time Charter whom

Solford had defeated comfortably at Sandown. In the United States July had wound up with Down Stage outgunning Ile de Bourbon's sister Rose Crescent for a Saratoga allowance.

The first two and a half weeks of August proved to be a period of success to equal the victories in France of early June. Beaudelaire travelled to France to defeat Green Dancer's champion daughter Maximova for the Group 2 Prix Maurice de Gheest, while at York in the Benson & Hedges Gold Cup (Group 1) and with everything against him, Caerleon kept battling, doing it the hard way from the front, to end his career on the highest note. York, however, provided Solford's Waterloo and he too was retired to stud travelling to Kentucky while Caerleon joined Golden Fleece and Kings Lake at Coolmore.

August was full of wins for Nijinsky though none of stakes calibre though there were good runner-up performances from Number (Ballerina), Vestris (Matchmaker), Olamic (Pukka Princess) and, most importantly, the brave running of Nijinsky's Secret shrugging off a colic problem to lead his all-star field a merry dance in the Budweiser Million before just failing to hold the English raider Tolomeo and United States star John Henry.

September in North America was most notable for the return to form for the leading juvenile Bemissed and for the winning performance of the two-year-old brother to Caerleon, Vision. Most importantly for Nijinsky's mounting tally of stakes winners was that of Waving who defeated fellow Nijinsky Rose Crescent for the second division of the Lamb Chop, Olamic and Leap of The Heart being third and fourth in the first division. Bemissed followed her success in the Japan Racing Association Handicap with a game second in the Anne Arundel.

In England and Ireland there were plenty of placings but Western Symphony clocked up another juvenile winner in a highly promising juvenile crop. He finished second in early September in his first stakes appearance when hot favourite but made no mistake in his next start when humping top weight to a three length victory in the Birdcatcher Nursery and then to a Group triumph in the Group 3 Larkspur. Another two-year-old winner in Ireland had been Goldye's Miss. Western Symphony had been stakes winner Number 71 for Nijinsky as Rose Crescent had made that magic 70 figure by annexing the Grade 3 Athenia Handicap on 2 October, the same day that Nijinsky's Secret won the Jockey Club Stakes in Canada. Nijinsky had suddenly chalked up an awful lot of stakes winners that season . . .

On 19 October it was stakes winner Number 72 as Vision ran off with a division of the Grade 3 Pilgrim Stakes (the other being won by a son of Caucasus) and there were other good winners that month. But the important thing now was that time was running out and Nijinsky had 15 stakes winners, just one away from equalling the record set up by Nodouble. Also he had a real rival in his own sire Northern Dancer who was for ever only one behind him and always dangerously close.

Nijinsky had plenty of juvenile winners with Preciously Dear, an own sister to Dearly Too, and Nagurski triumphing in early November in the United States. But far more important in the stakes race was the contest of a top Italian Group 3 event for juvenile fillies. The Nijinsky representative was the English trained daughter of Waya – and the 16th stakes winner and 73rd overall could not have been achieved more emphatically. Vidalia scored by a runaway six lengths and completed a success-ridden last month of the European racing season with three winners from three runners including another two-year-old in De La Rose's full sister Rose O'Riley.

That elusive 17th stakes winner appeared so hard to come by. Nagurski was so close when second in the Hoist The Flag, Tights third in the next division of the same race, Preciously Dear running well to be fourth to Althea in the Hollywood Starlet. So close yet so far.

Then, on 30 November at Aqueduct, Down Stage came out to romp the Wistful (Vestris finishing fourth). It was stakes winner Number 74 overall and that Number 17 for the season. It was just as well, for Northern Dancer had recently had his 16th of 1983. Nijinsky could relax a little. December saw wins for Dancing Again, Ultramate, Nagurski, Dancing Lesson and Nijinsky's Secret and, just to make sure, Tights dead-heated for the Cougar II Stakes at Hollywood Park on the 17 December to make a record 18 stakes winners in a single season for Nijinsky.

It had been an unbelievable season keeping the pulses racing to the bitter end. At the Keeneland November Sales Nijinsky even outgunned his own sire in the list of covering sires, his four mares averaging US $2,612,000. At the same sale he established a new share record of US $1.4 million. For 1984 his stud fee increased to US $450,000. In Canada his son Nijinsky's Secret was named Champion Older Horse and was rated joint fourth turf horse in the United States. In Europe Caerleon was champion three-year-old in France, and Solford champion in Ireland (6–10 furlongs). Vidalia was second highweighted Italian Juvenile filly while Western Symphony was rated third to future Guineas winners El Gran Senor and Sadler's Wells in the Irish Handicap. Brogan was very highly weighted in Italy and Solford, Beaudelaire, Russian Roubles and Caerleon (second) in England.

It had been Nijinsky's best year on the sires lists too. Fifth in England/Ireland with the winners of eleven races and £298,652, just below the fourth stallion Nebbiolo, fourth on the list of win money only, just £500 short of the third horse Youth (sire of Teenoso). In the United States it had been nip and tuck with Halo all the way and, while Nijinsky's Secret was Nijinsky's leading earner with US$371,547 of his total of US$2,580,836, of Halo's total of US$2,785,836, over a million dollars had been earned by the Kentucky Derby winner Sunny's Halo. It was Sunny's Halo who just gave the Canadian stallion the edge. But there was tremendous strength in depth about Nijinsky's performance.

But at the end of Nijinsky's most successful year there was trouble back at the farm. A condition of lymphangitis was discovered in the autumn of 1983 and, by the winter months, severe laminitis set into both of Nijinsky's front feet. For a long time it appeared to be touch and go and the spring of 1984 was agonisingly long for all concerned. At US$450,000 a time the mares were brought to the aisle outside Nijinsky's box so that champions could be produced in 1985. By early May Nijinsky had improved out of all recognition and twelve months later it seems inconceivable that the stallion could ever have been in fear for his life so well has he recovered. It says much for the courage of Nijinsky that he has brought himself from the brink of disaster to return to a completely normal life. But no one connected with the horse will ever forget those nightmare months.

The fear was very very real at the time Nijinsky had his first winner of 1984. It was a tremendous start – a graded victory for the six-year-old Nijinsky's Secret in the Grade 2 W. L. McKnight Handicap at Calder. Three days later Dancing Lesson ran third in the Interborough Handicap at Aqueduct to Mickey's Echo to gain her first black type and January saw further early wins for Vestris, Dancing Lesson and recently turned three-year-olds Tights and Dancing Crown.

It was a pulsating beginning for what was to be one of Nijinsky's best seasons in the United States just as 1984 was also to see a change in the pattern hitherto established by the European raced stallion. But 1984 was too a sharp contrast to the previous season, in that Nijinsky's greatest successes were to be gained on the western side of the Atlantic at the expense of the east.

February, a dark month and one of the darkest in Nijinsky's illness, was illuminated by the successes of Nijinsky's Secret, capturing first the minor "warming up" stakes, the Miami Lakes at Calder, and then a repeat victory in the Grade 1 Hialeah Turf Cup in typically game fashion. He was supported by victories for Nagurski and Dancing Crown and a solid stakes performance by Tights.

Nijinsky's racecourse progeny were on the up and up and perhaps these first few months, when their sire's future seemed so uncertain, was when the sons and daughters did their utmost to keep the stallion's supporters spirits up. Smart Steppin, the last daughter of Smartaire, broke her maiden on 1 March and, two days later, echoed an Eastern victory when Aino Saintsky won his first start in Japan. Tights became a stakes winner of 1984 with a comfortable victory in the Santa Catalina, beating the subsequent Preakness winner Gate Dancer 3½ lengths into third place. Vision won at Gulfstream Park the same day and Ultramate at Pimlico 24 hours later. Jillinsky wound up the month winning at Santa Anita.

Nijinsky had three winners in April in the United States, the most notable being a first stakes success for the three parts brother to Terpsichorist and Gorytus, Ultramate, who, contrary perhaps to expectations, found his metier over six furlongs. April, however, also signifies the serious onset of the flat season in Europe and Nijinsky had no hesitation in showing the French that he was not to be dismissed quite yet. Greek Sky made his first start a stakes winning one, in the Prix Juigne at Longchamp, and Val Danseur was beaten only three quarters of a length into second in another listed race on the same card. Some 24 hours earlier Western Symphony had begun what was to become a disappointing three-year-old career with a third place in the Windfields' The Minstrel Stakes at Phoenix Park, but Esperanto, the US $2,100,000 close relative of Golden Fleece and Be My Guest, won his maiden impressively on the same course exactly a fortnight later.

Despite Nijinsky's debilitating illness, or perhaps indeed because of it, there were no shortage of class mares arriving at Claiborne to visit the box-confined stallion. Group 1 winners, such as dual classic queen Blue Wind, the brilliant Blush With Pride and Trillion, champion sprinter Gold Beauty, major stakes winner Afifa, the Arc heroine Ivanjica, record priced broodmare Producer, were some and there were many more.

Nijinsky's English season really opened on 5 May when Serheed began a prolifically successful season with a win at Kempton Park. On the same day at Hollywood and Pimlico respectively Nijinsky's three-year-old sons triumphed in stakes races: Nagurski in the Grade 3 Woodlawn Stakes (after a rough passage with Dr White who actually won by a head but was disqualified) and through Tights in the Spotlight Handicap.

Serheed won a further two races that month but what appeared to be the most promising European performances were in Ireland where Esperanto opened his stakes account with a success in the newly listed Craddock Advertising Stakes (this was the race in which Solford had defeated stablemate Caerleon twelve months earlier), and in the all the way win of Goldye's Miss in the Kinderhill Oaks Trial. However neither were to fulfil their apparent potential, Goldye's Miss running her best race at the end of the month being caught on the line by the subsequent Group winner Vers La Caisse in the listed Ballylinch and Norelands Stud Stakes. The inexperienced Greek Sky's limitations were apparently exposed by Truculent in the Prix La Force (Group 3) though he defeated Ti King into third place. Apart from the early victories of Nagurski and Tights the month was notable in the United States for wins for Ultramate and Lead The Dance (in the only start of his career), and the onset of the battle of three-year-old eight to nine furlong colts. This time Tights lost out to Tsunami Slew in the Will Rogers for which retribution would be swiftly claimed.

Nijinsky's best three-year-old filly in 1984, Key Dancer, opened her account at Belmont on 4 June and collected an allowance two weeks later. On 9 June, in his first start in the United States, Green Dancer's four-year-old brother Val Danseur made his first win a stakes success in the Blue Larkspur at Belmont. Ultramate captured Bowie's Terrapin Handicap and, at the end of the month, Tights extracted his revenge with a victory in the Grade 3 Silver Screen Handicap. June was a consistently successful month for Nijinsky's American stock with nine winners of ten races. Europe saw a string of near misses but five races were collected including the Group 3 success for Nijinsky's first juvenile winner; Western Symphony's own brother Moscow Ballet followed up his Phoenix Park victory on 20 June with a comprehensive success in the P. J. Prendergast Railway Stakes at the Curragh ten days later. He joined Caerleon and London Bells in winning a juvenile race his sire had won before him. Unfortunately, Moscow Ballet was to sustain a knee injury running unplaced in the Gimcrack Stakes at York in August and was not seen out again. Equinol was stakes placed in France and the first win was claimed by the world record priced yearling, Empire Glory.

The run up to the Keeneland July Sales was notably quiet in Europe with only three runners in the first three weeks of July. In the United States there were plenty of representatives on the racecourse but, apart from Nijinsky's Secret winning the Americana at Calder, there was a paucity of stakes success though there were places for Key Dancer and for Vision, first in the Grade 2 Lexington Handicap and then the Grade 1 Brooklyn Handicap behind Handicap Triple Crown seeker Fit To Fight.

The most notable aspects of the 1984 American summer sales were the new increased involvement of Arab money in Nijinsky stock and the domination of the filly representation in the final order. Previous to 1983 the bidding power of Sheikh Mohammed had only secured two Nijinsky colts at auction, both winners, Thahul and Russian Noble. In 1984 they took four, three colts and a filly to add to the colt (Gallant Archer) and filly (Abeesh) bought twelve months earlier. The filly, a chestnut daughter of Compassionately, later named Sweet Mover, was the second highest Nijinsky of the sale, at US $1.1 million. This price was a whole million short of the price paid for Nijinsky's Best, another chestnut filly. As a daughter of Best In Show and thus a three parts sister to El Gran Senor and Try My Best, it was not surprising, as she was easily the most regally bred of Nijinsky's auction yearlings. Fillies accounted for five of the top seven prices, the lone colt being the last to go over the million mark; Hopak selling at Fasig Tipton's August sale for the exact figure.

Nijinsky's average, despite the obvious scarcity of high-class colts was US $571,100 (North American sales alone) considerably down on 1983 but still over 13 times the National Average. This placed him fifth on the leading sales sire's list (including the European sold stock) and above such as Spectacular Bid, Lyphard, Alydar, Shergar, Riverman and Alleged. One of the main reasons was the lack of Sangster involvement in the Nijinsky blood and it is notable that of the two-year-old Nijinskys in Vincent O'Brien's yard in 1984 all three are "home bred" and that only one of the four three-year-olds was bought at auction (Father Matthew).

By the end of July Nijinsky was back in action. Despite the often fatal nature of such severe laminitis the danger had eased and Empire Glory seemed to underline this with a Pattern success in the Group 3 Royal Whip, a race in which Nijinsky had provided an odds-on second Valinsky (beaten by 33–1 outsider Alleged) and whose daughter Lighted Glory had produced a winner in Last Light. Equinol in France and Esperanto in Ireland were also July winners.

August saw ten races fall to Nijinsky progeny, notably the win for Tights in the La Jolla Mile beating Tsunami Slew into fourth place; and for Esperanto in the Shanbally House Stud Stakes – his second stakes success. Other commendable stakes performances were achieved by Northerly Native (France), Western Symphony and Empire Glory in Ireland, American juvenile Fortunate Dancer and also the debut of the much vaunted, O'Brien trained, Father Matthew. On the strength of whispers from Ireland Father Matthew had been backed to 10–1 clear favourite for the 1985 2,000 Guineas before he saw a racecourse but inexperience caused him to be run out of the prize of the listed Tyros Stakes by Concert Hall. Nijinsky's "horse of the month" as it were was probably Nijinsky's Secret who was defeated by only half a length in the Arlington Handicap by Who's For Dinner, giving the winner 18 lb. And, 22 days later, he led the Arlington Million field with Royal Heroine a merry dance before finally finishing fourth to the inevitable John Henry.

Nijinsky had his second (of three) Grade 1 winner in the United States early in September when Vision joined his brother Caerleon in that elite group annexing the Secretariat Stakes, thus becoming a graded stakes winner on both dirt and turf. It was the only stakes success for Nijinsky in the month but September is the time when the exciting juveniles really grace the stage. Lightning Leap, close relative of Caucasus, Maruzensky and Euryanthe, had already broken his maiden in August but, probably of much more significance, Folk Art was on her way. The own sister to Sportin' Life gained her first success on 23 September at Bay Meadows cantering home by eight lengths. In Canada, Nijinsky's Melody annexed a Woodbine maiden before finishing runner-up to Bessabarian in the Grade 3 Natalma Stakes. In Ireland Father Matthew came good, cantering in by four lengths at the Curragh to go into winter quarters as a leading candidate for 1985 classic honours.

That Nijinsky's season in Europe was not quite of the heights achieved in some years of the recent past was partially saved by the appearance in October of another so called "talking horse" – this time in England from the Michael Stoute stable. Shadeed, inexperienced and surviving a particularly unlucky passage in a Newmarket maiden to finish close behind Niniski's son Kala Dancer, followed Russian Roubles and Night Alert by carrying off the Houghton Stakes in emphatic style to become winter favourite for the Derby. In France the Niarchos owned Solstein won comfortably at Maisons-Laffitte, and at Doncaster another Stoute trained juvenile colt, the US $4 million Gallant Archer, battled his way home over a son of London Bells, Patriach, to win his only outing in 1984. Clearly, Michael Stoute has a couple of bright prospects to enliven his 1985 classic picture.

Of the older European horses Empire Glory ran the race of his life to fail by a neck in the Jefferson Smurfit Irish St Leger. Nijinsky's European season came to an end gradually with a game second in the Criterium de Maisons-Laffitte (Group 3) when the flying Solstein only just failed to catch Rapide Pied.

Back in the United States there was plenty of running to be done in the final three months of the season. The most notable performance was by Folk Art in the Oak Leaf Stakes, storming home in this Grade 1 event over some notable juvenile fillies by an impressive 4½ lengths in which, in all probability, was the best two-year-old filly race in the United States that year. In fourth place, 14½ lengths behind her, was Fran's Valentine, unbelievably to be rated on a level par with Folk Art on the Experimental Free Handicap. Never has a case of the more recent memory remaining dominant been proven more clearly.

As the early part of the year had seen Nijinsky well to the fore in the stakes front so was he represented in depth in the final quarter. Tights had not finished with Tsunami Slew and company, winning the Volante Handicap (Grade 3) while Key Dancer won the Athenia as did Rose Crescent twelve months before. In addition, October, November and December were not bleak months with game stakes placings for Vision, Lightning Leap, Key Dancer (three times including the Grade 1 Beldame and Ladies Handicaps) and Ultramate.

So, while 1984 was not quite of the heady heights of 1983, Nijinsky was responsible for 13 individual stakes winners, comfortably above his seasonal average and there was a strength in depth siring 43 winners of 78 races worldwide. And, while he may not have played his usual prominent position on the sires lists apart from Ireland, he was still in the front rank in the more specialist departments – even in England and Ireland Nijinsky is way ahead in percentages of winners to runners and also winners to runners in the juvenile department.

Nijinsky still had a highly successful 1984 season and it is reflected in his position as the leading sire in terms of weighted horses on the *Blood Horse* Handicaps. Outstanding in the United States of course was Folk Art, probably desperately unlucky not to be acclaimed as Champion Juvenile Filly instead of being placed 1 lb below Outstandingly. On the form book, Folk Art has the performances which stand up firmest under scrutiny and it was a hock injury which prevented her from contesting the Breeders Cup event, the result of which led to Outstandingly's nomination. Other notable high weightings were given to Tights and Vision in the three-year-old colt category, Key Dancer joint third in the three-year-old filly (turf) list and to the older horse Nijinsky's Secret in his last season.

In Europe recognition was given to the juvenile performances of Shadeed, Solstein, Moscow Ballet and Father Matthew while Empire Glory, Esperanto and Western Symphony were highly weighted in the three-year-old colt classification.

One of the brightest aspects of 1984 was the success of Nijinsky's sons at stud, many still with their first few crops. Of particular note was that of Niniski which made him the Champion First Season Sire like his own sire before him. He had a most impressive "strike rate" and was responsible for the leading juvenile colt Kala Dancer. Ile de Bourbon had a Derby winner in his first classic crop, Lagunas triumphing in Germany, while Green Dancer had a remarkable year in France, leading the sires table there until the Arc de Triomphe.

So, it is misleading to regard 1984 as a quiet year for Nijinsky, even though it was not quite of the magnitude of the previous season. The lack of a high placing for Nijinsky on the sires table only serves to hide the tremendous strength in depth he exhibited and that his abnormal stakes record has ably been maintained.

The previous pages have only been able to serve as a travelogue through the success story of Nijinsky from the racecourse through to his establishment as one of the world's leading sires. The remainder of this book goes behind that success, to the how and the why and to the probabilities of that success establishing new boundaries as yet almost unthinkable.

Part Two
BEHIND THE SUCCESS STORY

CHAPTER I

The Leading Progeny

Descriptions of the racing careers of twelve of Nijinsky's best progeny: Golden Fleece, Ile de Bourbon, Green Dancer, Kings Lake, Caerleon, Czaravich, De La Rose, Solford, Niniski, Caucasus, Nijinsky's Secret, Maruzensky

These arbitrarily selected "top 12" have been chosen in their position as champions and Group 1 winners who have shown consistent form in the very highest class throughout their careers. It was regretted that there was not room to include other top-class performers notably Quiet Fling and Upper Nile, while Hostage was deemed not to have revealed quite his full potential on a racecourse, his career being curtailed in the April of his three-year-old career. Nijinsky's champion and high-class juveniles Princesse Lida, Cherry Hinton, Gorytus, Folk Art and Bemissed have been accorded space in a later chapter as have those ultra-consistent fillies Nijana, Javamine and Terpsichorist who just missed Group 1 honours.

Golden Fleece

Golden Fleece was one of those rarities in the racing world: an undefeated champion. In a way horses that never see defeat are an enigma because one never really knows just how good they are. His career may have been brief and beset by problems but Golden Fleece did all that was ever asked of him and he did it in style.

Golden Fleece was foaled on 1 April 1979 but he was nobody's fool and nor were the people who bred him. Mr and Mrs Paul Hexter had two Nijinskys in their crop of foals that year and, three years later, they had favourites for the two greatest Derbies in the world. The second foal, from the Val de Loir mare Entente, was Hostage. The Hexters rarely consigned their yearlings to public auction but they decided to keep only one of the Nijinsky colts and selected Hostage, the produce of their home bred mare.

But while Golden Fleece's career was brief, in terms of years and months, that of Hostage was even briefer. Whereas we know some of the mountains Golden Fleece climbed Hostage was unfortunately a case of "what might have been". Fresh from his emphatic success in the Grade 1 Arkansas Derby, just five days short of the Kentucky Derby, Hostage sustained a base fracture of a sesamoid in his near fore and was promptly retired. Like Golden Fleece he shared the size and scope of his sire and hopefully will prove a worthy successor at stud.

Golden Fleece meanwhile, headed for the Keeneland July Sale of 1980 where he was bought for the not inconsiderable sum of US $775,000, by Robert Sangster and partners, the most expensive of the Nijinskys at public auction that year. His dam, the subsequently unraced Exotic Treat, was sold for just US $85,000 in 1972 when she was a yearling even though she was by Vaguely Noble out of the Grade 1 winner Rare Treat, a half sister to the Belmont Stakes victor Jaipur. At that time however much of the value of the pedigree that graced Golden Fleece had not come to fruition. Exotic Treat was also half sister to champion What A Treat, herself to become the dam of leading sire Be My Guest. Golden Fleece's year older half sister Office Wife had not then become a stakes winner.

Initially registered as Magnificent Dancer, Golden Fleece was very mature despite sharing his sire's size and was immediately impressive even in his early juvenile days. Like so many of the potential O'Brien stars, Golden Fleece had only one outing at two and that not until September: Nijinsky had five, starting in June. However it is unlikely that many people realised the significance of that race at the time.

Needless to say Golden Fleece's reputation had preceded him and he started evens favourite in a field of 13 over the seven furlongs of a good Leopardstown track in the first division of the Oldbawn Maiden Stakes, won before him by Valinsky who did not quite fulfil the promise he also showed in that race. With hindsight, had Pat Eddery realised what else was in that field he might have not treated the opposition with such disdain. Even three furlongs out Golden Fleece was cantering easily at the rear of the field but once the question was asked, the answer was nothing short of electrifying. Golden Fleece was in front in 100 yards and came home handily by 2½ lengths. The second horse was six lengths clear of his field. That second horse was Assert.

One of the great debates amongst Pressmen in 1982 was to ponder the relative merits of either colt. Assert took advantage of Golden Fleece's retirement to win first the French Derby and then the Irish version following up with the Benson & Hedges Gold Cup over a probably below average field before failing abysmally in the Arc on soft ground. A good many chose to overlook the fact of this first meeting – that Golden Fleece was also having his first outing – in stating that Golden Fleece had merely beaten an immature and inexperienced Assert. Perhaps the compilers of the International Classifications were executing a compromise in only weighting Golden Fleece 1 lb above Assert at the end of their three-year-old careers. As with everything it is the most recent events which have the greater impact on the memory and it is a long time between the Epsom Derby and November.

But that was all in the future. On the strength of that single outing Golden Fleece was rated second on the Irish Free Handicap just 1 lb below Achieved, winner of the Group 1 Gallaghouse Phoenix Stakes and the Group 2 Laurent Perrier Champagne Stakes at Doncaster, a race that looked better at the time than it did after the participants had closed their three-year-old careers. Even so, Golden Fleece went into winter quarters as one of the leading candidates for the 1982 middle distance classics. But even then he was beset by a problem. Not one of illness or unsoundness but one probably due to his size: he hated starting stalls.

The problem did not seem to pose many difficulties for the colt at three years; the behind-the-scenes men had evidently worked tremendously hard over the winter. After impressive work-outs in which he was comfortably leading Flying Childers (Group 2) victor Peterhof five or six lengths, the race lined up for him as his debut in 1982 was in actual fact not one in which the O'Brien stable had been particularly successful in recent years. However this did not dissuade the punters for on 17 April Golden Fleece was 4/5 favourite for the Sean Graham Ballymoss Stakes (Group 2) over ten furlongs of the Curragh on what the Irish quaintly call "good to yielding" going. Unlike his sire, Golden Fleece could not be accused of frightening the opposition away; indeed he never faced a field of single figures. However lacking in quality, the Ballymoss field were certainly not lacking in quantity. Golden Fleece had 14 opponents. On the same day that Achieved won the Group 3 Tetrarch Stakes and Raconteur beat Lords for the Ballysax Race, Golden Fleece cruised home pulling up by three lengths from 33/1 shot Future Spa and 12/1 third favourite Salutely. On the face of it this was not an exceptional performance, albeit a classy one, and the sceptical media were quick to label it as not measuring up to Epsom Derby class. However, behind Salutely were the leading stayers Ore, Karol, The Neurologist and Noelino and back in thirteenth place was a four-year-old mare Stanerra, future winner of the Japan Cup (Group 1). Golden Fleece had beaten his elders and beaten them pointless. What more could a three-year-old, having his first race of the season and only the second of his career, do?

The response of the bookmakers was clear: Golden Fleece was

immediately installed as joint favourite with Craven Stakes winner Silver Hawk at 10/1 for the Derby.

Racegoers did not have to wait long for confirmation of the form. Golden Fleece's pre-Derby test was on 8 May, three weeks after the Ballymoss. Fittingly it was the race named after his sire run over ten furlongs at Leopardstown. Vincent O'Brien made a special journey to inspect the track at Leopardstown before allowing Golden Fleece to take his chance in the Group 2 event though the going was eventually officially described as "firm"!

Again, with the aid of hindsight, the field Golden Fleece faced that day was quite possibly the stiffest he met in his career, and overall a higher class field than that paraded in the Epsom Derby, if only for the nature of one of the horses he beat that day. It read like a "Who's Who" of Irish racing at that time: Stanera, Lords, Senior Citizen . . . and Assert.

It was clear which horse was rated the superior by the racing public for Golden Fleece was installed 3/1 *on* favourite with Assert as second choice at no less that 6/1. They again had the finish to themselves. This time Golden Fleece lay up in third place behind Senior Citizen and Grundy's half brother Chronicle until he was sent to the front approaching the home turn and quickened clear two furlongs out and galloped relentlessly further and further away. The recorded 2½ length margin was entirely due to Eddery taking a long look round and easing Golden Fleece down well before the post. Twice Golden Fleece had met Assert and twice he had given him a sound and unequivocal beating. Surely there could be no argument now? In fairness the argument did not start until Fleece had been banished to stud and Assert was winging his merry way through all the major prizes that Golden Fleece had necessarily forsaken (apart from the King George VI & Queen Elizabeth Diamond Stakes in which Assert was narrowly beaten by Kalaglow). At this point Assert had done nothing out of the ordinary. For the record Lords finished 1½ lengths behind Assert in the Nijinsky with no less than eight lengths separating him from Stanera, the future "wonder mare".

Golden Fleece's size made many question his aptness for Epsom but he had already proved he could handle the turns of Leopardstown and that he had all the speed in the world. Like all horses that run in the Derby the big question was one of temperament when subjected to the bustle of Derby Day and its parade. But Nijinsky, more highly strung than his son, handled it and so did his three parts brother The Minstrel (though with the help of cotton wool in his ears), who also had that question mark put over him. Snow Knight was more upset than most and it certainly did not seem to affect him because he led from start to finish and won at 50/1. But the drama, even before Golden Fleece was flown to England, was still to come.

On 18 May, fifteen days before the premier classic, the headlines rocked to the news that Golden Fleece was lame. He had unshipped "T. P." Burns on the gallops but had instinctively returned to his own yard and the injury was not reported as serious. The media reaction was caused by his withdrawal from the Gallinule Stakes which it had been decided was to be Golden Fleece's last Derby trial. Vincent O'Brien stated calmly that the affliction was only slight but the immediate reaction was to take Golden Fleece completely out of the Derby betting. The following day Peacetime, another son of Nijinsky, impressively won the Schroder Life Predominate Stakes at Goodwood and threw the whole book into confusion.

On 21 May Golden Fleece was declared sound and was cantering both morning and afternoon but the ever cautious bookmakers, still with the spectre of Storm Bird hovering over them from the previous year, still offered a "with a run" clause on the Ballydoyle colt and Simply Great and Peacetime became their leading lights. The lack of a statement stating categorically whether Golden Fleece would definitely run did much to undermine the good relations Robert Sangster had worked so hard to build up. Rumours were rife, as with all Derby favourites: temperament, unsoundness and an apparent aversion to travelling each took its turn. However, Golden Fleece's training as a juvenile when he was travelled around in a horsebox so as to become accustomed evidently put paid to that. There was even a tale that he had tried to break out of O'Brien's air transporter.

But on the morning of 1 June, 36 hours before the world's greatest classic, Golden Fleece was out in the mists of early summer on Epsom Downs, sporting an unfamiliar white sheepskin noseband, perfectly sound for all to see. He had come over on the Saturday just in case he became upset by flying and a switch could still be made to a boat if it were necessary. It was not. By the end of 2 June Vincent O'Brien was talking about Golden Fleece in the same breath as his sire Nijinsky.

Golden Fleece did get a little warm in the pre-race parade and was always on his toes. However it was a most stifling day with scattered fierce thunderstorms which caused the opening two-year-old race to be run in a deluge and which a drenched author has especial cause to remember. Many of Golden Fleece's opponents, notably Peacetime, were awash with sweat. In the stalls there was no sign of the claustrophobia so enlarged upon by the Press.

Long before Florida Son led them into Tattenham Corner, Pat Eddery had settled Golden Fleece back in the last half dozen while Yves Saint-Martin, perhaps his main rival, had dropped Persepolis out last of all. Norwick and Touching Wood were in particularly good positions down the hill while Jalmood was just behind but it was Peacetime who was probably in the best "winner's position" of them all, bidding to give Joe Mercer his first ever Derby.

Surely no Derby winner was in quite such a position rounding Tattenham Corner since Psidium came from last to first in the 1961 running. Golden Fleece had only three behind him, including Persepolis. Norwick and Peacetime went on but the latter, possibly still showing immaturity or that the muggy nature of the day was not to the liking of a hobdayed horse, once asked to go and win his race found nothing. Meanwhile Touching Wood was threading his way between Peacetime and Norwick to take up the running. Behind them, still in the tail of the field, Pat Eddery asked his colt to quicken and, the fifth gear being engaged, Golden Fleece had dramatically reached the front in less than 100 yards. For those watching, one minute Golden Fleece was completely out of the picture, the next second he was powering majestically into the lead and, despite leaning in, by the line there was effectively nothing else in sight. The official distance of three lengths could have been so much more.

Joe Mercer was heard afterwards to say of the winner "He went past me as if I was standing still. He must be brilliant." This sentiment was echoed by TV commentator Lester Piggott, for perhaps the first time in his riding life a spectator of the world's greatest race following the injury to intended mount Simply Great. Pat Eddery had no hesitation in stating that Golden Fleece was undoubtedly the best horse he had sat on, which necessarily included Grundy, and stated that at no stage had Golden Fleece been extended. Touching Wood, subsequently to win the St Leger, ran on gamely to take second spot with Silver Hawk and the fast finishing Persepolis behind him. Persepolis, ridden differently, might well have claimed the runner up position. So fast did Golden Fleece finish that the time was the fastest since the race was electronically recorded.

In all the euphoria that followed Robert Sangster even talked about Golden Fleece possibly being trained as a four-year-old but Golden Fleece was to see a racecourse no more. On 20 June it was announced that Golden Fleece was suffering from a nasal discharge and would be unable to work for several weeks. Once back in work Golden Fleece sustained a recurrance of the lameness that had affected him before Epsom. It was then decided that there was not enough time to prepare him for the major events remaining and, on 20 August, Golden Fleece was officially retired.

Golden Fleece was installed at Coolmore Stud for the 1983 season at a fee of 100,000 Irish guineas making him the most expensive stallion in Ireland or yet in Britain. His first book of mares was made up of champions and dams of champions. They included Group 1 winners Detroit, Ukraine Girl, Sarah Siddons, Dunette, Enstone Spark, Typecast, Arctique Royale, Sweet

Mimosa, plus Lisadell, Arkadina, Amaranda and the dams of Harbour, Dunette, Phydilla, General Assembly, River Lady, Erin's Isle, Star Pastures, Ardross, Greenland Park, Monteverdi, Thatching and Shirley Heights.

It all looked good for the best racing son of Nijinsky. Taking a great deal in physical appearance after his sire and matching him exactly in height, Golden Fleece had all the hallmarks to become a sire of the same calibre. Sadly it was not to be.

In February 1984 Golden Fleece was reported to have cancer; despite one apparently successful operation after which he resumed covering, he then contracted colic attacks and was operated again for a strangulated intestine but was again stricken with colic resulting this time in a perforated bowel. That was 18 March and later that Sunday he died.

His death followed all too hard on the heels of that of Troy and the disappearance of Shergar and his loss stands on a par with either of these tragedies. European breeders have now lost the services of three of the last four Derby winners to stand at stud here, which must be rated a severe blow to the breeding industry. As with Golden Fleece, an undefeated champion, there will not be many to replace him.

Ile de Bourbon

Like Nijinsky, Ile de Bourbon was bred to be a champion and like Nijinsky he was a champion at three years. Unlike his sire he was not a leading juvenile but was Champion Older Horse in Europe as a four-year-old, which Nijinsky never had the chance to be. Much of the reason for the late development of Ile de Bourbon lies in his very late foaling date of 23 May. Ile de Bourbon was never going to be a two-year-old though he did show some promise and it was only at four years that the two halves of his physical make-up finally knitted together.

Ile de Bourbon is an all-brown horse who, for a good deal of his racing career, certainly appeared as two horses joined together in the middle. With maturity all this changed but that was not until well into his third racing season and by then he had already won the King George VI & Queen Elizabeth Diamond Stakes. This fact more than anything illustrates just what a brilliant racehorse Ile de Bourbon became.

Like his sire he was by a champion out of a champion and had the additional distinction of being half brother to a champion (Minsky came a little later for Nijinsky). His dam Roseliere was the leading three-year-old filly of 1968 in France where she won the French Oaks (from Pola Bella), Prix Vermeille (by four lengths from Pola Bella and La Lagune), Prix de Pomone (Group 3) and Prix Penelope (Group 3, by six lengths) and beat all but Vaguely Noble, Sir Ivor and Carmarthen in the Prix de l'Arc de Triomphe. Her first foal Rose Bed (by Habitat) won the Group 3 Prix Chloe. Her second, a full sister to Rose Bed called Rose Bowl, established herself as one of the leading mile fillies of the decade, winning the Queen Elizabeth Stakes (Group 2) twice and culminating with a victory in the Group 1 Champion Stakes in which she defeated the great Allez France. At stud she has produced the listed race winner Golden Bowl (by Vaguely Noble) and two daughters of Nijinsky, the unraced Browser, and Crystal Cup, who had only two outings.

Then came Ile de Bourbon. Perhaps more than anything else he was important at this time as the last surviving thread of the involvement of Nijinsky's owners, the Engelhards, with the succeeding generations. Mrs Jane Engelhard was even then winding down her operation and, at the time of Ile de Bourbon's arrival at the Blewbury Stables of Fulke Johnson-Houghton (trainer of Rose Bowl), there were only ten horses in training left in the United States and two in England.

Ile de Bourbon ran in the Engelhard name for his juvenile career which spanned just two races. He was still very light and ran very greenly on his debut at the back end of September in a good £6,000 race at Ascot. Ridden tenderly by Tony Murray he was in the rear for much of the seven furlongs but ran on really strongly to be fourth to the accomplished juvenile Home Run. Separating them that day were Dactylographer, also having his first run, and previous winner M-Lolshan, of whom Ile de Bourbon was to see much more. For such an immature colt it was a promising run, so promising in fact that Ile de Bourbon was next pointed for the Group 1 William Hill Futurity over eight furlongs at Doncaster, four weeks later.

It was almost certainly asking too much of such an immature specimen but Ile de Bourbon was well supported behind favourite Home Run. Ile de Bourbon, ridden for the first time by John Reid, his future regular partner, was last out of the stalls and never got into the race and he eventually finished ninth to Dactylographer, Julio Mariner and Home Run. Also down the field that day were Hawaiian Sound and Whitstead. However it was not a result to cause connections any discouragement as Ile de Bourbon had not been given a hard race and obviously needed more time to strengthen.

Such was the esteem in which Ile de Bourbon was held at Blewbury that when Mrs Engelhard decided to sell him, by then her last remaining thoroughbred, her racing manager David McCall, who had first option, was hell-bent on buying him. To raise the capital that was needed he enlisted the help of Fulke Johnson-Houghton, the latter's mother Helen and Sir Philip Oppenheimer. Having 30 per cent of the holding in Ile de Bourbon, McCall's colours were sported on the colt for his second season.

Jane Engelhard had sold all of her bloodstock in the United States to Paul Mellon, owner of Mill Reef, who suddenly found himself the owner of Roseliere, carrying the future Group winning own sister to Ile de Bourbon, Rose Crescent, Rose Bowl, about to foal to Nijinsky, and the yearling Golden Bowl, her stakes winning daughter by Vaguely Noble.

Ile de Bourbon had not matured greatly over the winter and still appeared unfurnished. His first outing of his second season was at Newmarket at the beginning of May in the Heathorn Stakes, just half an hour after Enstone Spark had upset Nijinsky's champion daughter Cherry Hinton in the 1,000 Guineas. Lester Piggott was on board Ile de Bourbon for the first time and with Ile de Bourbon set to carry 8 st 5 lb had to do 1 lb overweight on the day. The pound proved crucial. Ile de Bourbon failed to wear down the more experienced Shirley Heights by a short head. Few watching could ever have dreamt that they had seen the winners of two Derbies and a King George doing battle on the racecourse that day.

Three weeks later Ile de Bourbon appeared at Goodwood in the Predominate Stakes but was evidently still feeling the effects of a Piggott driving finish from Newmarket. He was stepping up to twelve furlongs for the first time and Piggott allowed English Harbour to make all the running and just possibly steal the race and there was still 1½ lengths between them in the end. It appeared a relatively disappointing performance from a colt expected to be something special but behind him that day were the likes of Nicholas Bill and Home Run.

Johnson-Houghton had promised Reid that he would only be taken off one of the stable's horses for Piggott or Carson. They were both claimed by other stables for Ile de Bourbon's next objective, the King Edward VII Stakes (Group 2) at Royal Ascot. Ironically Piggott was aboard the only other maiden in the field, a second Nijinsky colt, Nonoalco's close relation Stradavinsky, but who was in a very different mould to Ile de Bourbon. His tenth place finish in his only previous start, the Irish 2,000 Guineas, did not stop this huge colt from starting favourite. Five of the field had run in the Derby and included Dactylographer, Julio Mariner and English Harbour.

Ile de Bourbon was run off his legs in the early stages but Reid did not ask him to close until the final turn. English Harbour had again set a strong pace but this time dropped out about three furlongs from home allowing Dactylographer to go on. Ile de Bourbon went past him a furlong and a half out with Stradavinsky challenging several positions wide of him. If lack of experience was still Ile de Bourbon's problem then it was doubly true of Stradavinsky, having only the second outing of his life. But the two Nijinsky colts had the race to themselves with Ile de Bourbon coming clear for a 2½ length victory with the remainder four lengths and more behind.

It is not often that a three-year-old colt breaks his maiden in a Group 2 race at Royal Ascot and Ile de Bourbon's connections were leaning towards a crack at the Irish Derby. In the event Ile de Bourbon and Stradavinsky both by-passed the classic for Group 1 races in England: Stradavinsky finished fourth in the Coral Eclipse Stakes at Sandown to Gunner B while Ile de Bourbon went straight to the premier all-aged contest in Britain, the King George VI & Queen Elizabeth Diamond Stakes, sponsored by Sir Philip Oppenheimer's firm De Beers. Ile de Bourbon's connections knew that the race was probably too soon for their horse and that he would make a better four-year-old but they were confident that Reid would give him an understanding ride and were hopeful for a place.

Between the King Edward VII and his next trip to Ascot, Ile de Bourbon was worked basically over a mile but did have two gallops over twelve furlongs. He was not a horse that needed a great deal of work and was doing very well at the time anyway. On the day before Ascot Ile de Bourbon had a 5½ furlong pipe-opener and there was nothing else to be done.

The field assembled for the 1978 King George, just eight years on from Nijinsky's finest performance, was truly international and worthy of any of the previous runnings. Shirley Heights, unable to run after the Irish Derby, was not there but the Epsom form was represented by Hawaiian Sound, ridden by American jockey Bill Shoemaker, whom Shirley Heights had beaten only inches at both Epsom and the Curragh and by the unlucky Curragh runner-up Exdirectory. The French Derby victor, Acamas, the last classic winner in the famous Boussac colours, had arrived, accompanied by Trillion, Guadinini and Montcontour. The champion from the Antipodes, Balmerino, was also there, later to run Alleged all the way to the line in the Arc, as was New Zealand star Silver Lad. English classic form of the previous year was represented by the dual classic winning Royal filly Dunfermline. That's A Nice, probably the first American trained horse to come across the Atlantic specifically for the King George, Irishman Orchestra, and Dunfermline's pacemaker, Sea Boat, made up the field.

Ile de Bourbon was improving hand over fist throughout his three-year-old days. This time he could lay up as Sea Boat set a blistering early pace. Indeed, going into the turn Ile de Bourbon was just about the only one in the star-studded field who could. Reid had him cruising smoothly alongside Hawaiian Sound at halfway and a good ten lengths and more adrift of Sea Boat and Dunfermline but when Ile de Bourbon moved up in Swinley Bottom it was not Dunfermline who drew away from her pacemaker. Neither could Acamas, the favourite, stay with Ile de Bourbon's relentless surge. Ile de Bourbon was still on the bridle and after rounding the final turn into the home straight, had swept past the toiling Dunfermline into the lead, Reid making the best of his way home and defying the others to try and catch him. It must have seemed a very long straight to Reid as it certainly did to those cheering him on. But Ile de Bourbon was never going to be caught.

There were 1½ lengths between Ile de Bourbon and Acamas at the line and over 20 to Trillion who had only two behind her, the pacemaking Sea Boat and the American hope That's A Nice. Hawaiian Sound, in finishing almost two lengths third, paid a great compliment to Ile de Bourbon for he had defeated the Epsom Derby runner-up by a far greater distance than Shirley Heights had ever achieved. Ile de Bourbon was now certainly a far different proposition from the immature colt who had given the future Derby winner such a fright back in early May.

The wheel had turned full circle. The Engelhard success story of Nijinsky had ended with the Engelhard bred Ile de Bourbon taking England's richest race. But while the last page of one book was closing another was opening in Ile de Bourbon's career.

Ile de Bourbon recovered so well from his exertions at Ascot that his return to the racecourse was only three weeks later, on a longer course and over a more testing surface. Only six opposed him in the extended 13 furlong Group 2 Geoffrey Freer Stakes at Newbury but they included M-Lolshan, Royal Hive and Dunfermline. Unlike Ascot these were not weight-for-age conditions.

Valuation was employed as Dunfermline's new pacemaker but he missed the break altogether and it took him two furlongs to gain the lead and within another half a mile he had exhausted himself completely. The ex-French four-year-old Paico was left in front and, after a brief struggle, he relinquished that to Ile de Bourbon who was hand ridden to quicken clear in the final furlong, without being asked more than necessary, to win by 1½ lengths with the future Irish St Leger winner M-Lolshan running on to be a three length third. Dunfermline followed at a respectful four lengths distance and was forthwith retired to an unfortunately all too unsuccessful visit across the Atlantic to Nijinsky.

By this time Ile de Bourbon's connections had made a firm decision to keep the colt in training as a four-year-old and with this in view it was decided to give the Arc a miss and to concentrate on the St Leger. In doing so Ile de Bourbon became the first King George winner to compete in the final classic since his sire back in 1970.

Quite what happened at Doncaster nobody knows. Ile de Bourbon was never going well over the 14 furlong trip and although put under pressure with two furlongs to go did not make up enough ground to trouble the leaders and eventually finished sixth to horses he had beaten comfortably on previous occasions which included the winner Julio Mariner, third placed

M-Lolshan and Obratzsovy, fourth here as he had been in the King Edward VII. The race was delayed twenty minutes with the runners at the start due to the tragedy that befell Easter King in the stalls when he reared up and fractured his skull, but it seemed to have no more effect on Ile de Bourbon than on any of the others. John Reid reported that his colt would not have won no matter what the distance of the race. It was, and still is, a complete mystery. The only logical explanation was that the colt had gone over the top and he certainly did not impress in the paddock beforehand. Maybe he was particularly a summer horse and let us not forget that Ile de Bourbon was still not a fully mature horse.

The international handicappers did not allow this performance, or lack of performance, to cloud their judgement however. Ile de Bourbon was rated Champion Three-Year-Old of Europe, clear of Acamas and Shirley Heights, both placed 3 lb below him. For the record Tromos headed the juvenile classification ahead of Irish River and Sigy, and Alleged was declared Champion Older Horse.

Ile de Bourbon's connections mapped out a tough programme for their champion in 1979, beginning with the Clive Graham at Goodwood, followed by the Coronation Cup, Eclipse Stakes, the King George and, finally, a tilt at the Arc. However Fate can never be disregarded and had more than a little to say before the campaign was half completed. During the winter Ile de Bourbon improved dramatically to such an extent that here at last appeared the complete racehorse and optimism could only run high. In his four-year-old career Ile de Bourbon was to carry the colours of Sir Philip Oppenheimer, now the largest shareholder, which had been borne so successfully back in 1976 by his previous best horse, Nijinsky's daughter African Dancer.

Ile de Bourbon appeared on schedule on 22 May at Goodwood to contest the Clive Graham Stakes over ten furlongs. The going was yielding which Ile de Bourbon was known not to like but his five opponents were not considered to be in the same class, the best of them being Crimson Beau, Town and Country and Jellaby. The race worked out that way and Ile de Bourbon had only to be ridden with hands and heels to coast home by four lengths from Crimson Beau, who was to run Troy so close later in the year.

Everything was going very much to plan and Ile de Bourbon was on course for the Coronation Cup a day after Troy had spreadeagled the Derby field. However the elements then decided to play a part and torrential rain turned the course into a quagmire necessitating the delaying of the race for 24 hours. The field was small but very select and stood their ground: Ile de Bourbon, M-Lolshan, and two top-class raiders from France, Frere Basile and Gay Mecene, subsequently runner-up to Troy in the King George.

Ile de Bourbon had been kept at Epsom overnight but in the race proved emphatically that neither the delay nor the change in the going would inconvenience him. None of the other jockeys would make the pace so John Reid had no choice but to go on himself and in doing so Ile de Bourbon probably gave his best and certainly his most spectacular display. Ile de Bourbon was never off the bit and never out of a hand gallop. The way that he cruised home by seven effortless lengths from Frere Basile was nothing short of stunning. Gay Mecene finished ten lengths behind him here – at Ascot in July he was to run Troy to 1½ lengths.

It was all looking good. And then Fate intervened. Everything was prepared for the clash between Troy and Ile de Bourbon, the leaders of their generations, at Ascot, when the virus descended on Blewbury. With coughing sweeping the yard, and much of Berkshire, Ile de Bourbon missed the Eclipse. He was not at this stage affected himself but his connections did not wish to take any chances.

Then Ile de Bourbon was taken ill and the Troy confrontation was off. Ile de Bourbon was off the course for more than three months during which time Troy carried off the Irish Derby, The King George VI & Queen Elizabeth Diamond Stakes and the Benson & Hedges Gold Cup, and when Ile de Bourbon returned he was but a shadow of his former self. The form book supported McCall's assertion that Ile de Bourbon would have won by 2½ lengths at Ascot had he run and the conviction that Ile de Bourbon would have shown too much speed for the three-year-old Troy to have stayed with him. But it was all sadly nothing but conjecture.

The September Stakes, instituted in 1979 as a stepping stone to the major autumn prizes, was Ile de Bourbon's first racecourse venture since early June. Obviously he could not have been back to his best for although he gave Cracaval 10 lb he was expected to win by five lengths and was beaten a short head. The remainder of the field were seven lengths away and Cracaval was a pretty able colt but not that good as his subsequent performance in the St Leger showed. Although Ile de Bourbon quickened again at the line the protracted battle for the length of the straight found out the reserves in a rusty Nijinsky colt.

Such a hard race was not likely to do his Arc prospects any good, especially if Ile de Bourbon had not shaken off the effects of the virus. However he was allowed to take his chance in the Arc but was evidently not the horse he had been in the summer. Added to this the colt had had a severe fright on the flight over when a light aircraft flew across the path of the aeroplane carrying Ile de Bourbon and Double Form just as it was landing. It had to take off sharply again having delivered a fairly hefty bump to the occupants.

In the race Ile de Bourbon was never going well after being hampered early on and eventually finished in mid-division behind the filly Three Troikas. Evidently, on the performances of his two champion seasons, Ile de Bourbon was clearly best in the spring and summer and did not hold his form through to the autumn though the months off the course as a four-year-old must have had a bearing on the latter part of this career.

The international handicapper saw it that way as well for Ile de Bourbon was rated above Gay Mecene and Thatching in the classifications for the older horse. In the English equivalent he was placed comfortably clear of Gay Mecene and the leading stayers Le Moss and Buckskin.

In the summer Ile de Bourbon had been syndicated by the British Bloodstock Agency to stand at Banstead Manor Stud, at Cheveley just outside Newmarket, for a value estimated, and not denied, at around £4 million pounds, then the highest figure for which any stallion had been syndicated in England. Having got 35 of his 38 first season mares in foal Ile de Bourbon has been rewarded by a champion juvenile in his first crop to race. Lagunas, who was the highest rated two-year-old in Germany in 1983 and the subsequent German Derby winner in 1984, was his sire's first Group 1 winner. He was ably supported by the stunning Glowing With Pride, owned by Sir Philip Oppenheimer, the highly promising juvenile filly of 1984 Kashi Lagoon and the other stakes horses Bonne Ile, Rye Tops and Bourbonel. Clearly Nijinsky's best racing son trained in England and his most accomplished son standing here, Ile de Bourbon clearly has the brightest of futures at stud and with his yearlings of 1983 averaging 57,000 guineas clearly the breeders think so too.

Green Dancer

Green Dancer was the horse who made Nijinsky the leading first season sire in Europe in 1974; he was also the horse who set breeding pundits forecasting, correctly as time unfolded, that Nijinsky was to blaze a trail as bright through his stud career as he had on the racecourse.

Bred by his owners, the Wertheimers, Green Dancer was the first foal from an unraced daughter of Val de Loir, Green Valley. Although with no racing or winner producing credentials on her side Green Valley was nonetheless worthy of her place in the first band of mares to visit Nijinsky. She was a daughter of Sly Pola, winner of the Group 1 Prix Robert Papin, the Prix de l'Abbaye de Longchamp (Group 1), the top sprint race, and the French Guineas Trial, the Prix de la Grotte (Group 3). One of her daughters, El Palomar, later produced the Gran Criterium (Group 1) winner Pareo who also won the Gran Premio d'Italia (Group 1). Sly Pola was herself a half sister to the top-class sprinter Takawalk II and to Polamia, herself dam of champion Grey Dawn, the only horse to beat Sea Bird II and subsequently a leading sire in the United States, and Right Away who won the French 1,000 Guineas. Green Valley was acquired by Green Dancer's trainer Alec Head for 410,000 F as a yearling at the Widener dispersal sale and was responsible for using up sufficient of Head's funds that he could not win the battle for the yearling colt that later became Amber Rama. When Green Valley had an accident in training that necessitated her retirement to the paddocks it must have seemed that Head had allowed the big fish to get away. But all clouds of this nature have a silver lining, and this one was very silver indeed.

Ensconced in Head's Chantilly yard Green Dancer was to be associated with Head's stable jockey and son Freddie for much of his career. Although a big strong colt Green Dancer was able to see a racecourse in August, at Deauville, in a six furlong race often known for the classic potential of its entrants. On this occasion the Prix de Tancarville attracted twelve runners and by the finish Green Dancer, whose reputation had preceded him, had them nicely strung out without being asked any questions at all.

However this was only a maiden race and Green Dancer found out what it was like to really have to run on his second outing. In the Group 3 Prix des Chenes at Longchamp on 22 September Green Dancer was asked to go eight furlongs against a colt destined to be the two-year-old champion of France, Mariacci. In the event Green Dancer was an unlucky neck second, Freddie Head appearing to be surprised by the late challenge of Mariacci, not pressing Green Dancer once he had headed Primo Rico at the distance. The two principals had drawn so far clear that the third horse Mister Jacket was eight lengths away. With hindsight, it was a very good performance for a slightly leggy, rather green youngster against a horse who was to put Green Dancer's stable companion Val de l'Orne and other pretenders in their places in the Grand Criterium (Group 1).

Just whether Green Dancer's single foray to England in preference to the larger French prizes (Alec Head evidently felt that Val de l'Orne could scoop them on his own) cost Green Dancer the French championship is never to be known. However Green Dancer was certainly a stronger individual by the end of October and could well have put Mariacci in his place on good going at Longchamp. England's championship was firmly in the grasp of Grundy, who had climaxed an unbeaten first season with a stroll in the Dewhurst Stakes (Group 1), England's most prestigious juvenile contest. Whatever Green Dancer did in the Group 1 Observer Gold Cup at Doncaster was not going to usurp the English bred and raced Grundy from his crown.

All Green Dancer could do was win and win well. Against him was the yielding going at Doncaster which over eight furlongs for a two-year-old can prove quite a test. No Alimony, stablemate of Grundy, was sent off as favourite but with Green Dancer only a few fractions of a point longer and being afforded the respect that most French raiders deserve when they choose to challenge for England's top prizes.

In the race Freddie Head had to keep a very tight hold of the free running Green Dancer's head but by the time they reached the turn into the straight Green Dancer was already running all over his rivals. Green Dancer was in fifth place on the rails when No Alimony made his move but was quickly extricated, had mastered No Alimony at the distance and steadily forged clear. At the line there was 1½ lengths between Green Dancer and the Irish raider Sea Break who had followed him through. No Alimony was three quarters of a length back in third followed by Whip It Quick, runner up to Grundy in the Champagne Stakes, leading home Anne's Pretender and the rest at a respectful six length distance. In this authoritative performance Green Dancer showed that he had the stamina as well as his undoubted speed.

Immediate bookmaker reaction was to make Green Dancer winter favourite for the Derby and to bemoan that once again the English prospects for its premier classic were looking grim. However the English handicapper took an altogether more restrained view and placed Grundy top of the Free Handicap by 1 lb from Green Dancer, preferring to rely on the solid consistency of a horse that never left Britain to one whom he had seen only once. In France Mariacci had annexed the Grand Criterium beating Green Dancer's stable companion as Green Dancer had defeated Grundy's, and was weighted 2 lb clear of Green Dancer which, considering that there was only an unlucky neck between them when they had met, appeared very generous to Mariacci.

Green Dancer, while alert and on his toes at Doncaster, was never overwrought and on the matter of temperament did not seem badly suited for Epsom on Derby Day. He was evidently well balanced and appeared to have the blend of stamina and speed necessary to win European classic races. As with his sire, and most Derby favourites, the doubts voiced were as to his ability to stay twelve furlongs at Epsom. Being by a Triple Crown winner, out of a mare by a French Derby victor, Green Dancer seemed to have no problems on that score but the female line of his family did display a preponderance of speed.

Green Dancer had no introductory race in any Guineas trial at the beginning of his three-year-old season but made his first appearance in the Poule des Poulains (French 2,000 Guineas) itself on 27 April. With the going on the firm side of good, Green Dancer started odds-on in a field of twelve which included Condorcet, Free Round, Dandy Lute, Monsanto and the lone English challenger Record Token, probably sent to act as a thermometer in the waters of Green Dancer's potential by Grundy's trainer Peter Walwyn. Green Dancer had had little work leading up to the race due to fears of the cough, whereas all his rivals had had a previous outing. Alec Head ran Methane as a pacemaker for Green Dancer and the job he did was so effective that the race was run in a time far faster than average.

Condorcet struck the front a furlong out but Green Dancer, who had been kept going easily on the heels of the leaders, needed only to be shaken up two furlongs out and ran on steadily and, without having to show any real burst of speed, defeated Condorcet a comfortable length. Record Token was back in sixth. Green Dancer had given Nijinsky a classic winner in his first crop (Caucasus was to make it two later in the year) and on the same card Val de l'Orne made it a double for Alec Head in the Group 2 Prix Noailles.

The selected race for Green Dancer's final outing before the Epsom Derby was the ten furlong Prix Lupin (Group 1) and despite the presence of the still unbeaten Mariacci, who had begun his second season by winning the Group 2 Prix Greffulhe, Green Dancer started an odds-on favourite. Head again ran a pacemaker, this time in the shape of Brenn, but also in the field were Trepan, Val de Loir's half brother Val de Fier, Matahawk and Condorcet. The epic battle that resulted on Longchamp's soft going could have done neither Green Dancer or Mariacci's Derby chances any good. The two were locked together for the duration of the final furlongs after Mariacci had taken it up coming into the straight, and while Green Dancer was being vigorously ridden, Freddie Head did not have to recourse to the whip. Green Dancer was the victor by half a length though it did seem as if it could have been extended had there been farther to go. The time was good and the performance very good but no one realised just how much it had taken out of both horses at the time on Longchamp's yielding going. For the record Matahawk led Condorcet, Trepan and Val de Fier home some six lengths behind Mariacci.

In the race preceding the Lupin, Dandy Lute, third in the French 2,000 Guineas, had franked the form by taking the Prix de la Jonchere (Group 3). Despite Grundy's success in the Irish 2,000 Guineas following a second place to Bolkonski in the English version, Green Dancer was hardening all the time as Derby favourite. Grundy had only beaten Monsanto 1½ lengths in the Irish classic whereas the colt finished fourth to Green Dancer in the French equivalent.

The ground was riding a good deal firmer at Epsom on 4 June and Green Dancer was by now almost as short a favourite as Nijinsky had been. Second favourite Grundy was at 5/1 to Green Dancer's 6/4 and it was then 11/1 Sea Break with everything else at 16/1 or longer. Green Dancer had run in the

Lupin as if he needed further than the 10½ furlongs and had shown no signs that the Derby Day furore would possibly upset him. However, perhaps the warning signs were out even in the paddock for the magnificent specimen seen on Lupin day appeared perhaps a little hard trained at Epsom.

It is history now that Green Dancer did not win the 1975 Derby, that Grundy defeated the filly Nobiliary by three lengths and went on to become one of the great English champions with further victories in the Irish Derby and King George VI & Queen Elizabeth Stakes. So what went wrong? The instant reaction of his jockey was that the horse had "run out of gas" after going easily to the top of Tattenham Corner and that Green Dancer had no apparent answer when the pace quickened. It was clearly not the colt's true form and Alec Head was quick to have him tested. Other theories concluded that it was the firm going and the connotations of the Epsom track or even the distance of the race. It is true that Green Dancer was never to win over a longer distance than 10½ furlongs but his performance in the Lupin had suggested that any extra ground would not be too much of a test for him. He did run well over eleven furlongs subsequently though the pace on that occasion was admittedly slow. Alec Head is now of the opinion that the Prix Lupin was to blame for the defeat of France's best Derby prospect since Sea Bird II and Head blamed himself for giving Green Dancer one race too many: Mariacci, who denied him the title of France's champion juvenile, was to prove Green Dancer's evil talisman even in defeat.

Green Dancer was given a lay off after his English exertions. He did not reappear again until 7 September in the eleven furlong Group 3 Prix Niel at Longchamp. Only four turned out to oppose him and he started hot favourite. It had been the intention to run him in the Prix Jacques le Marois (Group 1) at Deauville in August but he had coughed shortly before the race. The French contenders consisted of Green Dancer's pacemaker Leros and the short of top-class Lioubov. The foreign representatives were Vincent O'Brien's Guillaume Tell who had won the Group 3 Gordon Stakes and was being aimed at the Arc, and Anne's Pretender who had finished fourth to Green Dancer's sixth in the Derby and, despite the three lengths between them then, he was not expected to confirm the placings.

Leros did not do the effective kind of job that Methane and Brenn had done in Green Dancer's spring triumphs and the race was run at a moderate pace: the race turned into a sprint and the 6 lb weight concession allowed Anne's Pretender to catch Green Dancer, who had been sent on at the two furlong marker, and beat him by a neck. Neither horse had had a particularly hard race and, all things considered, it was a good enough performance by Green Dancer, conceding weight after a lay off, even if not up to those Group 1 triumphs. Guillaume Tell broke down in the race and he was retired forthwith to earn his own piece of immortality as the sire of the great racemare Stanerra.

Green Dancer's performance was thought of sufficient merit to earn him a place in the field for the Prix de l'Arc de Triomphe. Grundy's exploits against Bustino at Ascot had finished him and he was already retired and so did not appear at Longchamp. However it was quite a field that was assembled including some of the best fillies ever to meet on a racecourse: Allez France, Dahlia, Ivanjica, Comtesse de Loir and Nobiliary; the French colts were represented by Green Dancer, Kamaraan, Duke of Marmalade, Citoyen, Henri le Balafre and Kasteel; England by St Leger winner Bruni; the United States by Intrepid Hero; and Germany by Eclipse victor Star Appeal.

Even in this company Green Dancer was strongly fancied but had no luck in running, being one of those who had a particularly rough passage down the hill. In the end he finished eighth over all but third of the ten three-year-olds and he beat Dahlia, Ivanjica and Intrepid Hero. The winner was the 119/1 shot Star Appeal from the virtually unconsidered On My Way with Comtesse de Loir the first filly home. She was followed by Un Kopeck, Allez France, Nobiliary, Bruni and then Green Dancer. At the distance all these were in the firing line, Green Dancer racing one away from Allez France on the outside, Star Appeal bursting through at the last moment on the inner. Green Dancer finished only about four lengths off the third horse Comtesse de Loir, less than 1½ lengths off Allez France. All this considered Green Dancer ran an honourable race in his final appearance.

In the French Three-Year-Old Handicap Green Dancer was fourth, 3 lb behind his French Derby winning companion Val de l'Orne. Patch, who had so courageously run Val de L'Orne to a head in that race was on 9 st 12 lb (1 lb below the champion) and the three-year-old filly champion Ivanjica on 9 st 11 lb. Mariacci was weighted 2 lb below Green Dancer and equal with Washington International victress Nobiliary, on 9 st 8 lb.

Green Dancer appeared to have a bright future as a four-year-old but it was not to be. In November the announcement was made that Green Dancer had been retired to Alec Head's Haras du Quesnay, offering to French breeders the type of horse the French breeding industry seemed to be unable to produce for themselves; the classic racehorse with speed and middle distance ability blessed also with a top-rank pedigree.

In many ways the outset of Green Dancer's stud career mirrored that of his sire. He was represented by a Group 1 winner in his first crop which also went on to win a Guineas classic, like Green Dancer had represented Nijinsky's. Green Dancer was also champion first season sire. However it was more of an indication that could be realised at the time in the fact that

Green Dancer's representative was a filly, Aryenne. Taking Green Dancer's stud career as a whole to date it appears that he does sire a greater percentage of top-class fillies than colts.

Green Dancer had made such an impact on French racing and breeding in his early years that, considering the trend French breeding seems to be taking, it was really no surprise when the United States came in for him with an irresistable bid at the end of the 1981 breeding season. By 1982 the leading French stallion was safely ensconced at Gainesway Farm in Kentucky.

Green Dancer, on his best performances, has every right to be rated among Nijinsky's very best progeny in terms of racecourse ability and he is certainly the best of the French based racing sons. Green Dancer represented far more for Nijinsky than just a multiple Group 1 winning classic winner though that would be enough for most stallions. Green Dancer was the one horse who really set the standard of Nijinsky's success as a stallion and it brought him instant success and recognition. In these early days, Green Dancer has already established himself as currently Nijinsky's best son at stud though there are those even younger that promise to challenge in the future. It is to be hoped that Green Dancer finds both the opportunities in quality of mares and the best conditions for his racing produce in his new base in the United States as he would have had in France had he remained there.

Kings Lake

Kings Lake was undoubtedly one of the leading milers of the early 1980s. Yet he leaves behind a doubt about a potential unfulfilled for on breeding alone he would have been expected to excel at distances in excess of a mile. In his career Kings Lake ran only three times at ten furlongs or more. His sole attempt at twelve furlongs proved that distance was indeed too far but in winning a Group 1 event over ten furlongs beating a star studded field of middle distance performers makes one wonder what heights could have been achieved with a four-year-old campaign over this kind of trip. Therefore, though Kings Lake's most memorable performances were over eight furlongs it might well be unfair to regard him merely as a specialist miler and capable of no other versatility.

Bearing in mind Kings Lake was a half brother to the brilliant speed queen Cloonlara, it is perhaps not unreasonable to expect twelve furlongs to be too far for Kings Lake and that his best distances would be short of that trip. However, his dam Fish Bar won over 12½ furlongs in France when capturing the listed Prix de l'Elevage at three years and his third dam

Herringbone, won both the eight furlong 1,000 Guineas and the 14 furlong St Leger and was dam of Entente Cordiale (Doncaster Cup), Dogger Bank (Princess of Wales's Stakes) and ancestress of Castle Keep and Gold Cup winner Ragstone, both top-class stayers. Herringbone's dam Schiaparelli bred the twelve furlong specialist Swallow Tail and was ancestress of Shantung, Roi Dagobert, Sassafras, Irish Ball, Bikala and Assert, all top-class middle distance performers. So there is plenty of support for the theory that a ten furlong campaign would have suited Kings Lake admirably.

His juvenile career perhaps reflected this intention. His first outing in the colours of Monsieur Jean Pierre Binet was in August over six furlongs at Phoenix Park. Ridden by Tommy Murphy, stable jockey for Vincent O'Brien when Pat Eddery was needed or riding elsewhere, along with Christy Roche, Kings Lake started like most of O'Brien's debutants, at odds on. The result must have been a surprise when Master Thatch outgunned the immature Kings Lake by half a length. After all, Kings Lake had not been foaled until 14 May and he had quite a bit of growing to do and quite a few weeks to give to his older colleagues. However his performance was heartening for, having missed the break, Kings Lake mounted a strong challenge from fourth place half a furlong out and was running on well at the finish.

His second start was much more up to expectations. Some three weeks later at the Curragh Kings Lake went to post for the Rathangan Maiden Stakes, also over six furlongs but on the more taxing "good to yielding" going, whatever that exactly entails. He was again opposed by Noble Mark who had finished third, beaten 2½ lengths by the Nijinsky colt, at Phoenix Park. This time there were four lengths between them and with Tommy Murphy up, Kings Lake had a comfortable race once he had taken up the running two furlongs from home. The opposition was not strong but, as with so many of the potential O'Brien stable stars of the future, Kings Lake was to have a relatively quiet first season. His first winning performance had been overshadowed on the day by the equally impressive performance of Storm Bird in the National Stakes later on the card. Storm Bird might have been the horse of the moment at this time and reported to be comfortably beating Kings Lake and the rest of his contemporaries at home but it was a very different story less then twelve months hence. But that was for the future.

Kings Lake's final outing for his first season was some six weeks later at Naas over seven furlongs on yielding going. Not the sort of race for any potential sprinting type. Kings Lake was long odds on and was only hand ridden to beat Tellurano, no mean horse himself, by half a length with the remainder well outpaced. There was no point in asking too much of a horse whose three-year-old career was evidently in mind. The performance however caused *Timeform* to state unequivocally that Kings Lake would stay "at least" ten furlongs at three years.

Kings Lake was rated fourth on the Irish Two-Year-Old Free Handicap on 8 st 8 lb. Storm Bird was pounds clear on 9 st 7 lb with the wayward Critique, then trained by O'Brien, on 9 st 1 lb and Prince Echo on 8 st 11 lb. It was a comfortable first season for the future European champion without being asked too much.

Kings Lake's first outing of 1981 was over ten furlongs. With the aid of hindsight this distance was, perhaps, a little over-optimistic at that time and Kings Lake was obviously being regarded as a potential middle distance classic horse. The performance quickly altered that opinion, at least at that stage of the colt's development. The Ballymoss Stakes had seen the initial steps towards a champion's career for more than one of O'Brien's classic heroes, though not for Nijinsky himself. On this occasion Kings Lake was 9/1 to beat his Eddery-partnered stable companion, Critique. O'Brien had three runners in the event and the Irish public evidently decided to follow the jockey's choices. However Kings Lake ran much better than Critique, even though the latter was to prove himself endowed with more stamina than Kings Lake. Ridden by Christy Roche, Kings Lake was running on at the end, 2½ lengths behind Erin's Isle and three quarters of a length behind another stable companion, Magesterial. Critique was 1½ lengths behind in fourth. In yielding or soft going this was evidently as far as Kings Lake wanted to go.

However, it was perhaps still something of a surprise when it was Kings Lake who was selected to represent the stable in the Airlie/Coolmore Irish 2,000 Guineas in place of Storm Bird. Apparently it was now Kings Lake who was beating Storm Bird dramatically at home. Unfortunately the drama surrounding this race was to colour the rest of Kings Lake's career to the point of extinguishing the real merits of the horse. There were 13 runners at the Curragh and the going was officially described as good. The English 2,000 Guineas winner To Agori Mou was odds on favourite with Kings Lake second in the market at 5/1. The field also included Mattaboy, a close second at Newmarket, Dance Bid, Ore and Prince Echo. Eddery had the mount on Kings Lake for the first time and the result could hardly have been more controversial. He slipped Kings Lake into the lead two furlongs from home and To Agori Mou ranged up outside of him to challenge a furlong out. In the final furlong the colts certainly bumped and with Greville Starkey standing up in his stirrups on To Agori Mou the Stewards took note. Kings Lake held his lead to the line to win by a neck, the first time he had really been in a race. Kings Lake was the better horse on the day but it was found that he was the transgressor and was promptly disqualified.

To the media it was sensational for the Irish stewards to demote one of their own runners in favour of an English raider; what was more sensational was Kings Lake's reinstatement after O'Brien's appeal. The controversy it generated set alight the fuel to a fire which would burn throughout the 1981 season and keep its audience on the edge of their seats for many months to come. The saga did not end with the declaration of Kings Lake as the classic winner, it merely sparked the conflagration. The shame of it all was that in these clashes, involving human personalities, the horses themselves got somewhat neglected and it was a tragedy that throughout Kings Lake was seen as the villain of the piece instead of being recognised as a top-rate racehorse. The whys and wherefores of the legal wrangles involved in the Irish 2,000 Guineas are not for our concern but what the race did prove and which was confirmed throughout the coming season was that there was not only one champion miler in England and Ireland that year but two. But what made Kings Lake different was that he had the class and stamina to win a Group 1 race over ten furlongs. But that was not until September.

If the furore involved in the Irish 2,000 Guineas was in any way diminished with time, and other races and other horses superseded it in human memory, it certainly flared again at Royal Ascot in June. Kings Lake made his first visit to England to contest the eight furlong St James's Palace Stakes (Group 2) in whose field reappeared To Agori Mou and Prince Echo and which also included Bel Bolide and Robellino plus Great Substence from France.

This time it was Kings Lake who started a narrow favourite over To Agori Mou and the race also ended in a neck victory but this time for the Englishman. Greville Starkey could not disguise his satisfaction as he passed the post when looking across at Eddery. Starkey had gained first run by pushing To Agori Mou through a gap entering the last two furlongs through which Kings Lake had to follow. The pair quickly went six lengths clear of Bel Bolide and though Kings Lake was coming back at To Agori Mou at the finish the English Guineas winner had enough to keep him at bay on the line.

Kings Lake had lost nothing in defeat and had done nothing to dissuade his connections from taking on To Agori Mou for a third time. The 1981 Sussex Stakes at Goodwood proved as temperature-raising as any of the previous encounters and a more dramatically exciting race would be hard to find anywhere. Apart from Kings Lake and To Agori Mou seven others turned out for the eight furlong feature on Royal Wedding Day and included Belmont Bay, Mattaboy, Noalto, Dalsaan, and the French 2,000 Guineas winner In Fijar. It must be some time since the victors of the three top European mile classics met in one contest later in the season. Lester Piggott took the field along at a tremendous pace on the four-year-old Belmont Bay.

Greville Starkey decided to employ the same tactics as had been successful at Ascot and to gain first run on the Irish colt. Kings Lake was looking for, and not finding, a gap between Last Fandango on To Agori Mou's inside, and Belmont Bay. Then suddenly with time running out the space briefly appeared and the Nijinsky colt burst through on the inside of To Agori Mou who had gained the advantage. With less than 100 yards to go Kings Lake was level and at the line had gained victory by a head and, the surprise of the race, Noalto was flying at the finish to be only a neck behind To Agori Mou. Kings Lake was unusually in quite a lather in the preliminaries but it did not stop him running with as much courage and determination to go through with his challenge through the narrowest of gaps as could be asked of any horse. It was the first time that the colt who had got first run had not won.

At this stage Vincent O'Brien was not even considering any ten furlong races for Kings Lake but maybe what happened in the Prix Jacques le Marois, the fourth meeting between Kings Lake and To Agori Mou, changed his mind. Kings Lake did not travel until the day previous to the eight furlong event at Deauville, just over two weeks after the Goodwood battle. The going at Deauville was firm, far firmer than Kings Lake liked and he looked ominously ill at ease in running. However it says much for his courage and class that he ran To Agori Mou to a nose when Eddery asked him for his effort two furlongs out. However neither To Agori Mou nor Kings Lake connections had reckoned on Northjet. Quite how Northjet managed to slaughter the British champions by five lengths is something of a mystery. Northjet was doubtless a cracking miler but had hardly shown quite the form of this calibre beforehand. He had been beaten before by one or two members of the field which included Group 1 winners The Wonder and Ukraine Girl plus Cresta Rider.

Suddenly the ten furlong Champion Stakes was being mooted as the next objective for both Kings Lake and To Agori Mou. The Nijinsky colt's next race was preparatory to that, the Irish equivalent, the Joe McGrath Memorial Stakes at Leopardstown. An hour after a highly successful debut by a certain colt called Golden Fleece, Kings Lake faced a field made up of class ten and twelve furlong horses including dual Oaks winner Blue Wind, Arctique Royale, who had been the first leg of a Guineas double for Jean Pierre Binet, the good English middle distance performer Kind of Hush and the future American champion Erin's Isle, who had defeated Kings Lake in the Ballymoss.

Blue Wind started favourite but once Kings Lake turned on the style she could not live with him. Kings Lake produced a burst of brilliant speed at the end of the ten furlongs to defeat Erin's Isle a very comfortable length indeed to give the Nijinsky colt his easiest win since his juvenile days. Kind of Hush was three lengths in third and Blue Wind finished 6½ lengths behind Kings Lake in fourth. Kings Lake could not have been more impressive in his first attempt over ten furlongs since the Ballymoss.

If the matured Kings Lake had had more opportunities to show what he could do over distances around ten furlongs, who knows, maybe we would have seen a rarity indeed – a proven champion at eight and ten furlongs. Perhaps had he remained in training as a four-year-old the likes of Kalaglow and Assert would have had something to fear in their challenges for the Eclipse and Benson & Hedges Gold Cup respectively. But that is all conjecture.

Kings Lake did not start in the Champion Stakes in which To Agori Mou was a dismal flop but ran instead in the twelve furlong Prix de l'Arc de Triomphe, for which he started second favourite. The soft going in a field of the stiffest class imaginable over this kind of distance proved that Kings Lake's forte was over rather shorter distances than this. However he was not disgraced in finishing eleventh, in a field which included such middle distance stars as Gold River, Bikala, April Run, Perrault, Ardross and Argument and he did finish comfortably ahead of Lancastrian, Cut Above, Blue Wind, Condessa, Detroit and Beldale Flutter.

Kings Lake was retired to Coolmore Stud. In the European Three-Year-Old Handicaps of 1981, cunningly divided into a category encompassing 6½ to 10½ furlongs, Kings Lake was rated equal with To Agori Mou, Vayrann and Beldale Flutter, the latter pair best at ten furlongs. Indisputably, Kings Lake and To Agori Mou were the champion milers of their generation. Kings Lake was the only Group 1 winner of the four to win Group 1 races over eight *and* ten furlongs at three years and also won three Group 1 events to To Agori Mou's single success.

Kings Lake's first book of mares was as impressive as the horse himself and included the Arc heroines Detroit and Ivanjica; classic winners Arctique Royale and Lagunette, plus Catherine Wheel, Typecast, Piney Ridge, Sassabunda, Val's Girl and the dams of Shirley Heights, Jacinth, Monteverdi, Treizieme and Thatching. The resultant foals were rated outstanding and were well in demand at the foal sales in 1983; the four offered in Ireland averaging 203,750 Irish guineas and the sole representative at England's December Sales bringing a bid of 160,000 guineas, the highest prices being for colts out of Hard To Tell (275,000 Irish guineas) and Yankee Lady (255,000 Irish guineas) making him the leading foal sire (with two or more sold). His first yearling representatives in 1984 resulted in an average of 241,297 for 12 yearlings sold in Europe second only to Shergar in the first season yearling sales sires list.

Rarely can a horse have given so much to English racing. Brilliance, courage, controversy, thrilling excitement. Kings Lake was an outstanding individual and racehorse and hopefully will pass all these qualities to his progeny which are due to race in 1985. The world awaits them with anticipation.

Caerleon

For anyone who loves to see a gutsy, honest, game performance from a racehorse then Caerleon's performance in the 1983 Benson & Hedges Gold Cup will remain in the memory for ever. A more genuine battling effort will be hard to witness and, when people remember Caerleon, will probably eclipse the brilliance of his three length win in the French Derby.

Perhaps it is all the more remarkable because of the way one has become accustomed to seeing flashy, spectacular performances that could mean anything from the O'Brien horses and perhaps indeed from Nijinsky's stock. Caerleon and Kings Lake before him proved there was another dimension. With Caerleon the race was never lost or won until the winning post.

Caerleon was not cheap. At US $800,000 he was the third most expensive Nijinsky colt sold at auction as a yearling in 1981, costing less than only Solford and Countertrade (ex Swingtime) both of whom fetched over a million dollars. As yet Countertrade is the only one not to score in a Group 1 race. Yet Caerleon's price so upset Seth Hancock of the vendors, Claiborne Farm, that he vowed never to submit yearlings for public auction again. The immediate result of this was that Swale won two legs of the Triple Crown in 1984 for the home stable.

A late March foal, Caerleon is a medium-sized dark bay with only a faint star to testify to any white about him. He is a son of the Round Table mare Foreseer who won three races and was stakes placed herself and who had already produced the American Stakes winner Palmistry (by Forli) as well as Good Thyne (by Herbager) who was a good Group performer in Ireland and the stakes placed Reviewer colt Old Testament. Palmistry is the dam of Nadeed, a Nijinsky juvenile of 1985 and resident in Michael Stoute's Newmarket stable. The cross was a proven one, for Nijinsky on Round Table had already been responsible for De La Rose, Upper Nile, Ballare, Sportin' Life and Waving and, still to come Brogan, Tights, Folk Art and Caerleon's own brother Vision, who at the time of Caerleon's sale was just a foal. Foreseer was a daughter of Regal Gleam (by Hail To Reason) the champion juvenile filly of 1966 whose victories included the Grade 1 Frizette and Selima Stakes and was responsible for Royal Glint, successful 21 times including the Grade 1 races, the Santa Anita Handicap, Amory L.

Haskell Handicap and United Nations Handicap. The family traced back to the great matriarch La Troienne, possibly the most influential modern tap root in the United States today.

Caerleon had it all: pedigree, looks and ability. Trained by Vincent O'Brien for Robert Sangster Caerleon arrived at Ballydoyle with Solford to join the year older Golden Fleece, Nijinsky's other Group 1 winning sons in the yard that year. Solford may have been more striking to look at with his bold white blaze but it was the bright-eyed Caerleon who was the flag bearer in the two-year-old Group contests though given an easy first season like most of O'Brien's classic candidates.

O'Brien had the most incredible strike rate that season (1982). Of the stable's 18 individual runners, 17 won a race. Caerleon was one of the first juveniles to see a racecourse. Along with Treasure Trove he made his debut on Irish Derby Day in the six furlong Tyros Stakes (listed race) at the Curragh. Caerleon was hot favourite while Treasure Trove, unbelievably for a Ballydoyle runner, started at odds of 40/1! The field of 13 was full of previous winners but the two Ballydoyle representatives effectively had the race to themselves. Caerleon joined the leaders quickly, took the advantage just after half way and held the run of Treasure Trove by two comfortable lengths. Three of the field had fallen just after halfway in an almost unprecedented situation but this did not in any way detract from the satisfactory performance of the favourite. It is doubtful that those who suffered would have been any real threat to the winner.

While this was easy black type gained by Caerleon, his second outing was gauged to be much more of a test. A runny nose had kept Caerleon out of the Group 1 "Heinz 57" Phoenix Stakes but the setback did not keep him off the course for long. Though only four opposed him in the Ballsbridge/ Tattersalls Anglesey Stakes (Group 3) at the Curragh on 14 August, the quality was certainly not lacking. Caerleon was accompanied by Storm Bird's US$3½ million brother Ballydoyle, making his first appearance, and they were opposed by Virginia Deer, previously successful in the Group 3 Curragh Stakes; Burslem, the six length winner of the valuable Ardenode Stakes, and Rock 'n' Roller, a well regarded previous winner, who was to chase Horage home in the Group 2 Gimcrack Stakes five days later. On paper they were certainly sure to give Caerleon a race he would remember.

Caerleon, odds on, had a very tardy start and trailed by four lengths after a furlong and a half. However Eddery elected to stay behind as Rock 'n' Roller and Virginia Deer disputed the lead and did not ask him to make up the ground until well past halfway in the extended six furlong contest. Caerleon cruised up in style, went to the front smoothly inside the distance and ran on well to beat Rock 'n' Roller and Burslem 2½ lengths. Ballydoyle was five lengths back in fourth. In the previous race on the card stablemate Solford had successfully made a pleasing debut.

There was talk of the Prix de la Salamandre (Group 1) but Caerleon met with a slight setback and was retired for the year. Though not as spectacular as stablemate Danzatore, Caerleon had done enough to suggest that he would continue to improve to be a force to be reckoned with in 1983, and very much to be regarded as a live Derby hope. In the Irish Free Handicap he was given second spot, as had Golden Fleece before him, his stable companion Danzatore being placed 5 lb ahead.

Caerleon was geared towards a Derby programme in his early races as a three-year-old. His first appearance was in the ten furlong Rogers Gold Cup Ballymoss Stakes (Group 2) at the Curragh in late April, following in the footsteps of Kings Lake. But while King Lake's performance in finishing third was maybe disappointing, Caerleon's was downright baffling. Starting odds on in a field of ten Caerleon was in the rear throughout, dropped out next but one to last rounding the turn and managed to beat only two home. Though Caerleon did appear backward in the paddock beforehand he had done nothing to suggest his running would be anything but that of an odds-on favourite. It was reported however that somehow Caerleon's nostrils had become clogged with mud. Effectively a tilt at the Epsom Derby was ruled out.

Caerleon was next seen in public on 28 May at Phoenix Park when, along with Solford, he was sent to post for the ten furlong Craddock Advertising Race. He was asked to give 8 lb to Solford which, in the face of Solford's subsequent performance in the Coral Eclipse Stakes, was asking a great deal. Also in the field were highly regarded stablemates Delgado, Heron Bay and South Atlantic, all of whom were making their three-year-old debuts. None of these were in the shake-up however. Eddery had chosen to partner Solford so Caerleon was ridden for the first time on a racecourse by George McGrath. In running Solford to three quarters of a length Caerleon put up a much better performance than people could have realised at the time. The pace was very slow on that occasion and Solford was too far ahead by the time Caerleon mounted his challenge.

Along with Lomond, Salmon Leap, Shearwalk, Solford and The Noble Player, Caerleon was a Sangster representative in the 32 four-day acceptors for the Epsom Derby but both Caerleon and Solford were kept back for races in France. While Solford won the Group 3 Prix du Lys a week later, Caerleon's selected race was the Group 1 French Derby in which he naturally faced his stiffest test yet. Eleven opposed him, the favourite being the French 2,000 Guineas victor L'Emigrant, who ran in the colours of Stavros Niarchos, who also had a share in Caerleon. L'Emigrant, a son of

The Minstrel, had also won the Derby trial, the Prix Lupin (Group 1). Margouzed, third in the Guineas, and Lovely Dancer (by Green Dancer), runner-up in the Lupin, were also in the field accompanied by the Prix Hocquart first and second, Jeu de Paille and Esprit du Nord; Dom Pasquini, successful in the Prix Greffulhe (Group 2); Nijinsky's lightly raced stakes winning son Fabuleux Dancer (ex Fabuleux Jane) plus English challengers Cock Robin and Jasper. The field was in all probability a great deal stronger than that which opposed Teenoso in the English equivalent.

In the muggy atmosphere which preceded the race and in which it was run, many of the colts became extremely warm in the paddock. Caerleon, however, remained calm and perfectly behaved throughout. Caerleon was settled by Pat Eddery in third or fourth place on the rails behind Pietru and alongside Dom Pasquini, but Caerleon was going so well that upon entering the straight Eddery moved him into the lead past the struggling pacemaker over two furlongs out. Fabuleux Dancer went with him but inexperience found him out and he could not match the power showed by his paternal half brother. L'Emigrant was moving up behind them from about eight lengths off the lead apparently eating up the ground in the middle of the course but his stamina ran out to leave Caerleon accelerating strongly to an easy three length success. L'Emigrant just managed to hold second place from the Piggott-partnered Esprit du Nord who was to run champion filly Sun Princess close in the St Leger later in the year.

Due to the late cancellation of the Irish air traffic controllers industrial action, O'Brien was unable to make the journey to France but watched the race on television. He later declared that it was only now that Caerleon had had the good going he needed and that he was regarding the Coral Eclipse as Caerleon's next target leaving Solford the Irish Derby. One can only conjecture upon the possible results of those races had this plan been adhered to.

Pat Eddery was elated by Caerleon's performance saying that Caerleon was always going so well that no matter how fast they went he would have been happy. Caerleon had accelerated well to erase any worries L'Emigrant's run might have caused. His biggest problem was avoiding the rapidly tiring pacemaker. It was a great race too for Northern Dancer for the first three home were by his sons Nijinsky, The Minstrel and Lyphard. In a way it was a galling result for L'Emigrant's trainer Francois Boutin. He had advised Niarchos, a quarter share owner in Caerleon, to buy the colt outright for himself at the Keeneland Yearling Sale.

Though the going at Chantilly was good and suited Caerleon admirably it was a little too much of a good thing at the Curragh where Caerleon made his next start in the Irish Derby. The going was nearer rock hard and proved the undoing for more than one of the field. However it did suit Shareef Dancer, the US $3.3 million son of Northern Dancer and the Kentucky Oaks victress Sweet Alliance, whose best performances had not been put up in muddy conditions. The field for the race was, on paper, the strongest of the classics of 1983 for it not only contained the winners of the French and English Derbies but also the runner up in the latter, Carlingford Castle, plus the Irish 2,000 Guineas winner Wassl.

A rash had appeared on Caerleon's back in the morning and in an unprecedented move he was allowed to be led down to the start.

Unfortunately for Caerleon this race uncharacteristically did not see the best of Pat Eddery. Caerleon was in close touch from the start but found himself trapped on the rails. Halfway up the straight and Swinburn was making his way for home as fast as Shareef Dancer could hear his hooves rattle and storming away from the toiling Teenoso who was hanging right on the ungiving ground. As Carlingford Castle dropped back Eddery and Caerleon found themselves trapped in all directions except that behind. With Wassl and Teenoso outside him Eddery could only take that course and pulled Caerleon back around three horses to make his challenge up the outside. Becoming, not surprisingly, unbalanced Caerleon took a second to get into his stride and though he ran on well and cut the deficit considerably Shareef Dancer was long gone and had three lengths at the line in what was later judged to be the best performance over twelve furlongs by a racehorse for the season. Caerleon won the battle of the Derby winners, Teenoso being a footsore two lengths back in third, never the same horse as he had been at Epsom until his four-year-old days. O'Brien declined to offer Caerleon's skin problems as an alibi but simply said that they were beaten by a better horse on the day. Caerleon had, however, put in a highly creditable performance and would at least have been considerably closer with a clear run.

Caerleon had an even less happy run in the King George VI & Queen Elizabeth Diamond Stakes at Ascot. He started joint favourite with runaway Oaks victress Sun Princess but, having moved readily up in Swinley Bottom, he lost his action on the final bend and it later transpired that he had lost both front shoes coming around the home turn and was virtually pulled up. The race was left open for Time Charter to storm home. Two shoes were found later near the crossing half a mile from home.

These two visits to the racecourse inevitably placed question marks over Caerleon even though he had more than adequate excuses. Though the Benson & Hedges Gold Cup (ten furlongs) comes at a difficult point in a middle distance classic colt's career Caerleon was sent to York as Assert had been twelve months earlier. It was his fourth Group 1 race in ten weeks. As the rain poured down Shareef Dancer was withdrawn at the last minute defying the old adage that a good horse should be able to win on any going. Caerleon could not have liked it either but O'Brien was not to follow the same cautious course as that of his main rival. Caerleon was there and was there to run. He was not going to be taken back to Ballydoyle because the going was turning soft, though the going had changed from the firm side of good in a matter of hours, one of the fastest changes of going ever recorded.

It was not Pat Eddery's plan to make the running but the slow gallop set for the first half furlong meant that he took the initiative and sent Caerleon to the front with ten furlongs of the 10½ furlongs still to travel. By doing so he challenged the rest of the field to come and catch him. The eight who opposed him included the Nijinsky "wonder horse" Gorytus, still out to redeem a slightly tarnished reputation, the Mecca Dante winner Hot Touch, Henry Cecil's representative John French and Shareef Dancer's substitute Electric.

Caerleon ran with his tongue strapped down for the first time. Hot Touch, who went well in the ground, got very close two furlongs out and seemed poised for victory with Gorytus and John French also challenging outside of him. Caerleon stuck grimly to the rails as Hot Touch drew almost level but Caerleon kept finding a bit more and still more. Caerleon was not going to be beaten. A more courageous performance would be hard to imagine: the middle distance classic colt, having to make his own running in ground he did not like over a short ten furlongs. Hot Touch had no more to give and was a neck adrift at the line with the easy Gordon Stakes victor John French depriving Gorytus of third spot by a head some 1½ lengths behind the two principals.

Eddery declared that Caerleon would have won on the bit had the ground been on the firmer side and O'Brien, though considering the Arc, was very hesitant to commit himself to pointing his colt towards that goal fearing a repetition of the soft going that usually so characterises Longchamp in October. However none of the European Derby winners saw Longchamp in October: Shareef Dancer, following his withdrawal at York, was promptly retired to Dalham Hall Stud at Newmarket; Teenoso injured himself in finishing third in the Great Voltigeur two days later and was out for the season though he ran with great success as a four-year-old; and the Benson & Hedges also saw Caerleon's last appearance in public.

He was due to run against Sun Princess in the Doncaster St Leger but it was decided not to travel him after Town Moor was soaked for the week, though unfortunately it was made too soon as the ground dried out considerably the next day, the Friday. By that time of course it was too late to fly Caerleon from Ireland. However rain fell again and Sun Princess slogged on well to win on the Saturday.

It was then decided to retire Caerleon to the Coolmore Stud in Ireland where he stood his first season in 1984 at a fee of 80,000 Irish guineas. He was rated the champion middle distance performer in France over eleven furlongs plus, above Sun Princess and second in England and Ireland only to Shareef Dancer, who was rated on that one championship performance in the Irish Derby.

Caerleon proved himself a true champion in the Benson & Hedges Gold Cup confirming the performance he had given at Chantilly. He had defeated championship fields in all types of conditions proving himself able to adapt to all circumstances – the good going at Chantilly when majestically accelerating away from the best opposition France could muster, and outgunning and outbattling the best ten furlong horses in Britain in the bog-like ground at York when having to make his own running and holding off all challenges as they came. If Caerleon can pass on this blend of speed, stamina and courage to his progeny with his own spotless pedigree they will be something to adorn our racecourses in the years to come. Along with Ile de Bourbon and Kings Lake it is largely on his shoulders that the reputation of Nijinsky as a sire of sires will rest in Europe.

Czaravich

Czaravich is the epitome of the difference in American and European racing trends. Although he is regarded as an eight furlong specialist, had he raced on British tracks he would probably have stayed a great deal further. Unbeaten at distances short of 8½ furlongs Czaravich nevertheless showed top-class form over longer distances when asked. In the middle of his three-year-old season Czaravich was still thought of as a twelve furlong horse, and it must be erroneous to consider him necessarily being considerably better over shorter distances.

Czaravich was foaled in Kentucky on 29 March 1976, bred by his owner William L. Reynolds. A massive chestnut with two large stockings behind and a wandering white blaze, he was the product of two European classic winners: the bay Nijinsky and his contemporary, the dark brown Irish 1,000 Guineas victress, Black Satin, who in turn was by the almost black Linacre. Black Satin had bred nothing of note beforehand and has bred nothing of importance since. However, her dam, the bay Panaview (by Panaslipper) had also bred another Irish 1,000 Guineas winner in Front Row and the classic placed Ragapan and Kingsview, plus the Australian champion Panamint.

The third dam April View (by Panorama) was dam of April Slipper, the grandam of April Run and Northern View.

Trained by Billy Turner, Czaravich was too big and backward to be trained as a two-year-old. Instead American racing had to wait until March of his three-year-old year to witness the debut of this striking colt. In view of his later performances, 9½ furlongs on his debut on fast going might have seemed quite a test for Czaravich. However the six who turned out against him at Aqueduct proved no match at all. Starting evens favourite and ridden by Jean Cruguet, Czaravich won comfortably by two lengths from Mystic Era.

Czaravich was brought back to Aqueduct for an allowance contest eleven days later. Over a furlong shorter to travel but this time Czaravich did not start favourite; that honour fell to Pillar Farms' Pianist, having his first start since the previous December. The two finished almost eight lengths clear of the third horse in the five horse field but it was second favourite Czaravich who came away to win by 1¼ lengths.

That was enough to convince the Aqueduct crowd. Czaravich was way odds-on for his third start, this time returning to a mile in mid-April. The four who opposed him may not have been top-notch but Czaravich could not have been more impressive in his nine lengths stroll over Crown Thy Good and Beautiful Contest.

Now was the time for Czaravich to embark on a stakes career. He had had three very easy races and no one was quite sure just how good he really was. While they suspected they could only speculate.

Czaravich's first stakes start was in a Grade 1 race, which illustrates the heights Billy Turner thought his horse could achieve. The Wood Memorial, run over nine furlongs at Aqueduct, was New York's gateway to the Kentucky Derby. In three of the previous four years the colt who won this race went on to win the Derby. It was quite an assignment. Secretariat's Gotham Stakes winning son General Assembly was the public's choice as the winner and indeed that colt was to enhance his reputation – but at a later date. Also in the field were Smarten, Screen King and Instrument Landing, yet Czaravich was the strong second choice despite having only competed in allowances. Czaravich's connections felt that they had only General Assembly to beat. Screen King had won three in a row but had been beaten a head in the Bay Shore and then disappointed to finish fifth in the Gotham. The Grey Dawn colt Instrument Landing had won the Remsen and Nashua Stakes at the back end of his juvenile career but had not had a glorious winter campaign at Santa Anita. The Woody Stephens trained Smarten had been beaten only a neck by Golden Act in the Arkansas Derby but had not been nominated to the Kentucky Derby because of a quarter crack which ultimately had not proved as serious as was first thought. The only other serious contender in the field of ten was Picturesque who had already won four of his six starts that season including three stakes. But of all of them none was such an unknown quantity as Czaravich.

Instrument Landing was left to make the running and set a very moderate pace considering the strength of the field. The pacemaker for Screen King, Four Kids Only, beaten pointless by Czaravich in his second start, was never in the hunt and may have been responsible for the slow pace which suited Instrument Landing maybe best of all. Cruguet had wanted to stay away from the lead for as long as possible yet, after six furlongs, Czaravich was only half a length behind Instrument Landing. Czaravich had before distinctly shown signs of idling in front. General Assembly made ground to be only just behind with Smarten and Screen King breathing down their necks. Upon turning into the stretch General Assembly took second place from Czaravich but Instrument Landing opened up an immediate lead of 1½ lengths at the furlong pole and General Assembly began to weaken. Screen King, on the outside, began to rally and also Smarten along the rail. Czaravich meanwhile was launching his bid between Screen King and Smarten. Instrument Landing, hugging the rail, hung on grimly to the line, only holding a nose advantage over Screen King with Czaravich only half a length behind, inching out Smarten for third money.

Turner was the first to admit after the race that though Czaravich had turned in a highly satisfactory performance he had asked a great deal of a colt to run four times, culminating in a Grade 1 effort, in four weeks having never seen a racecourse previously. Many New York horsemen viewed Czaravich as a "Belmont horse" and Cruguet was quoted as predicting flatly that his horse would win it. Turner, aiming his colt for that classic, did not want to ask Czaravich for too much too soon and decided to head next for the Withers, leaving the Kentucky Derby at the mercy of Spectacular Bid.

In the Withers at Aqueduct on 12 May Czaravich met Instrument Landing again but this time he was an odds-on favourite to reverse the placings of the Wood Memorial. None of the other Memorial competitors decided to take them on and none of the other seven runners were expected to be in the shake up at all. Czaravich's way of running suggested twelve furlongs would not be beyond him and he gave the strong impression that the further to go the better he would like it. The furlong shorter distance of the Withers following the Wood Memorial seemed likely to suit Instrument Landing the better. Either way it was expected to be a two-horse race and so it proved. On a wet drizzly day and on a greasy track Czaravich was settled in seventh place as Prodigo and Bishops Choice showed in front early on. Going into the turn following the backstretch Cruguet tapped Czaravich with the whip and the chestnut simply took off. In a few strides he was level with Instrument Landing who by now had the lead. However Instrument Landing was not about to let the rangy chestnut go by him and fought back to maintain his narrow lead into the straight. Czaravich, hanging left, as had been his habit, regained the lead and was going away at the line, scoring a three quarters of a length victory.

Turner, now his colt had achieved the first objective and claimed a major stakes race, was not going to be tempted to veer from his course for a crack at the Preakness just a week away. Though Reynolds was especially keen to run, Turner managed to convince him that the colt still did not have enough experience. Turner still felt that only 80 per cent of the real Czaravich had been seen in the Withers. Instead he stuck to his original plan and pointed Czaravich next for the Peter Pan.

They say that all the best laid plans will go wrong and Turner's certainly did with Czaravich. Cruguet's confident prediction that the ever improving Czaravich would win the Belmont no question, was never able to be proved. Just before the clash between Czaravich and Coastal, the subsequent Belmont winner and conqueror of Spectacular Bid in the Peter Pan, Czaravich succumbed to a respiratory ailment which was sweeping Belmont. Just as he seemed to be recovering from that Czaravich then threw a splint. Turner had known that there had to be a reason for the way Czaravich leant in during his stretch runs. Off the course for almost four months it was a frustrating summer for all concerned. So it was not until August that Czaravich returned to serious training and not until 3 September that he returned to the track.

Turner felt that the Jerome at Belmont had still come a little early for the Nijinsky colt and that the field, even without intended starter General Assembly, was an especially tough one. He had had to push Czaravich for the race and feared that he could still be a little short of his best. The public had not forgotten Czaravich however and he started favourite over a field which included Valdez, Clever Trick and the old rival Instrument Landing.

To compound matters Czaravich was almost left at the post. Though Cruguet had wanted to wait with Czaravich he probably had not quite reckoned on that. After two furlongs Czaravich was stone last and trailing by ten lengths. After four furlongs, the half way point, he had passed just one horse and was still eight lengths adrift. But in two furlongs Czaravich was in the lead, striding past the opposition majestically in a show of sheer power. It was all over as soon as he hit the front. At the line he had two easy lengths over Swaps victor and fellow top weight Valdez.

Turner, still considering twelve furlongs to be perfect for his colt, was thinking in terms of the Jockey Club Gold Cup as Czaravich's autumn objective. Czaravich had never run over a distance short of a mile and he was not to for the rest of his three-year-old career. Three weeks later Czaravich was lining up for the ten furlong Woodward Stakes in a field which included the four-year-old Triple Crown winner Affirmed and the Belmont victor Coastal. The Italian champion, Sirlad, acclaimed the best since Ribot, came out to oppose them in a field of five.

The Argentine bred Mr Brea cut out the early pace but allowed Czaravich and Coastal to go on. By the time they reached the final turn Sirlad was tailed off and Affirmed was only now getting into gear. He slipped through between Mr Brea on the rails and Czaravich and there was no catching him. Czaravich, perhaps caught a little by surprise, battled on but could make no impression. It was the late finishing Coastal who got within 2½ lengths of Affirmed with Czaravich back in third.

Czaravich had already had enough after his long lay off racing in the very highest company. The final start of his much abbreviated three-year-old career was in October over eleven furlongs, his only attempt on a turf course, in the Man O'War. He finished third, beating Fluorescent Light but on this occasion was no match for champion grass horse Bowl Game.

Czaravich was weighted joint fifth in the three-year-old handicap, 7 lb below Spectacular Bid. However Czaravich's greatest days were still to come.

The four-year-old season of the much stronger Czaravich began in mid-April when only three opponents turned out in a six furlong allowance race at Aqueduct. Czaravich had never been asked to race against this type of speed horse before but it proved little more than a training spin for him. He was odds on favourite and had his rivals well strung out at the end.

Czaravich really came back to the big time in the seven furlong Carter Stakes (Grade 2) at Aqueduct in early May. Many of the six horse field he had encountered before and as a result he was sent away long odds on. However he was also giving away lumps of weight. It seemed a great deal, considering the New York Handicap Triple Crown was still ahead. Turner did not like the thought of what Czaravich would be asked to shoulder should he win well here.

The 1980 Carter was one of the fastest seven furlongs ever run in New York. The only faster Carter was run by Kings Bishop at Belmont Park, where at that time it was still a track record. Czaravich also put in his straightest stretch run which was just as well. A tribute to the handicappers weightings, the first four home were separated by a neck, a head, and a neck. Czaravich was furthest away from the rail and was running outside his opponents all the way. Although it looked anyone's race Larry Adam, who had first been aboard Czaravich in the six furlong allowance, had only to keep

Czaravich concentrating and did not have to recourse to the whip. Tanthem, who had been runner up to Czaravich in that Aqueduct allowance, was second again. Czaravich maturing, and Adam concentrating on holding his horse together rather than trying to bully the colt into refraining from his leaning habits, were the instrumental pointers in making Czaravich an even more potent force to be reckoned with. Czaravich was back.

The scene was set for the New York Handicap Triple Crown, along with the classic races the most prestigious series in American racing. The first leg was the Grade 1 Metropolitan Handicap run over nine furlongs at Belmont in late May. The opposition included State Dinner, who was the only horse rated capable of beating Czaravich. Giving 6 lb and more to his rivals, Czaravich gave 9 lb to State Dinner. The race was one of the most pulsating seen on American racecourses in 1980.

Laffit Pincay, jr, had the ride on the Turner colt for the first time and Turner felt he moved a little too soon off the false pace on a fast track but acknowledged that he had had no choice. Czaravich liked to run in company with pressure on all the time. He had all that here. Czaravich had been in close attendance all the way through the race and opened up a clear lead of a length turning into the stretch but State Dinner was flying behind and cutting down Czaravich's lead with every stride. At the line no one knew who had it. A second print convinced the judge that the race was Czaravich's. It was quite a horse race. Of those behind, the fourth placed Ring of Light collapsed on the track from sheer exhaustion and the contest left racegoers and connections alike breathless.

It was Czaravich's finest hour and probably his gutsiest performance, shouldering 126 lb as he was. He next headed for the second leg of the series, the ten furlong Suburban, just under six weeks later. State Dinner, Czaravich and Ring of Light renewed rivalry but the field was also spiced with the addition of Winter's Tale and the ex-English Lyphard's Wish.

The race was just as thrilling as the first encounter. Czaravich had gone up 1 lb in the weights, State Dinner remained as he was with Winter's Tale receiving 3 lb from State Dinner. In all it was quite a task for Czaravich now giving 10 lb and more to his field. State Dinner was sent off the marginal favourite over Czaravich.

Around the final turn Winter's Tale and Ring of Light seemed to be having their own private battle in the lead with the favoured pair not very far back. Suddenly both moved together, sweeping past the leaders but Czaravich going the widest. Ring of Light faltered and Winter's Tale was left alone with the two principals bearing down on each side of him. Pincay thought that he had Czaravich's nose just in front at the furlong pole but the weight anchored him and at the line he was two heads adrift of Winter's Tale and

State Dinner. In winning the Suburban, following up on a Nassau County success, Winter's Tale was following in the footsteps of the Nijinsky colt Upper Nile two years before.

Winter's Tale went on to win the Brooklyn, the third leg of the Handicap Triple Crown. Czaravich had no chance now of completing the triple and he was bound to be shouldered with as much weight as he could possibly carry. Czaravich was given a rest.

All the principals from the previous two races met again in the nine furlong Whitney Stakes four weeks after the Suburban. Czaravich was this time receiving 3 lb from Winter's Tale and in the event beat him 13 lengths. Czaravich was assigned second top weight with Ring of Light on 123 lb, State Dinner receiving 3 lb from them. Czaravich was still odds on to defeat his old rivals. Outsiders made the early running but with three furlongs to go the race began in earnest. Dr Patches shot to the front with Czaravich and State Dinner beginning their runs behind him. Winter's Tale was never in contention and wound up last but one in a field of eight. Czaravich made his effort on the inside of Dr Patches with State Dinner on the outside. Czaravich took a narrow lead but it was only momentary as Dr Patches fought back to be half a length clear of the Nijinsky colt but could not hold off State Dinner who cut down the margin steadily to score by half a length.

It was the end of the racing road for Czaravich. He wrenched a suspensory ligament in the running of the Whitney and had to be blistered. Definitely sidelined for the rest of the year it was decided to retire him to Gainesway Farm where his first foals were juveniles of 1984. Czaravich possibly had everything: pedigree, size, power, class and speed. Added to all this is the consideration of the weights he was assigned. He should do well for American racing, for a gamer and more consistent horse would be hard to find.

De La Rose

De La Rose was not Nijinsky's first champion filly, the two-year-olds Cherry Hinton and Princesse Lida had beaten her to that; nor might she have been in the United States had the category which she won, and Eclipse award been available, when Terpsichorist was eligible. What made De La Rose special was that she was capable of beating the colts at any time and at any place.

De La Rose was outstanding even as a yearling, breaking the Saratoga Sales filly record when purchased for half a million dollars by Henryk de Kwiakowski, a Polish fighter ace of the Second World War and later the owner of Conquistador Cielo. The previous record had stood at US

$275,000 so De La Rose must even then have been something special. On paper her credentials were first-class: an own sister to the Grade 1 Suburban Handicap winner Upper Nile from a half sister to Rosalba (Coronation Stakes, Group 2, Queen Elizabeth II Stakes, Group 2) and to the dam of Champion Grass Horse Bowl Game, and England's evergreen Sea Pigeon. Her dam Rosetta Stone was by Round Table, a cross that had so far produced excellent results.

Trained by "Woody" Stephens, De La Rose was an able juvenile, in the top-notch of her filly contemporaries if not the leader of her division. Her first start was in mid-July, cantering home by 3½ lengths in a Belmont maiden on a fast dirt track. Despite being left at the start she was very impressive. Despite Stephens' declaration that he expected De La Rose to be even better over longer distances he next headed her for the Grade 3 Schuylerville Stakes, again over six furlongs, at Saratoga along with stablemate Heavenly Cause. Heavenly Cause finished third, De La Rose seventh in the field of eleven behind the narrow winner Sweet Revenge.

De La Rose then turned her attention to the turf courses, a surface on which later in her career she was to prove almost invincible. Two furlongs further to travel this time and De La Rose gave Eddie Maple an armchair ride finishing five lengths ahead of her nearest rival Picture Pretty. Heavenly Cause was back in seventh place.

At this stage Stephens was working particularly on De La Rose's tardiness from the stalls. It was a problem that one day could make the difference between winning and losing a major prize. But once De La Rose had grasped the idea there was no stopping her improvement. Her first stakes victory was on grass, in the Evening Out Stakes over seven furlongs at Belmont, for which she was co-topweight with Rubescent Rumor. De La Rose was well back but rallied with determination to defeat Bravo Native by a head. The first two were ten lengths ahead of Prime Prospect and Heavenly Cause. Future Eclipse filly Wayward Lass finished last in the seven horse field. It was all in all a highly promising performance but, as Stephens feared, most of the two-year-old filly championships are on dirt and De La Rose did not seem terribly enamoured with that particular surface.

The Matron Stakes at Belmont in September is one of the legs of the juvenile filly Triple Crown. And the 1980 running did nothing to detract from standards set in previous years. Heavenly Cause was back on her best surface, De La Rose was not. In a thrilling race Prayers 'n Promises, a half sister to Little Current and the Nijinsky stakes winner Water Dance, outgunned De La Rose's stablemate by a head. Sweet Revenge separated Heavenly Cause from De La Rose. It was a Grade 1 field for a Grade 1 event; De La Rose was not disgraced.

It was a similar story in the Frizette, held also at Belmont on the main track but over a furlong more. The same fillies were out to do battle but this time it was Heavenly Cause who came out best by 1½ lengths from Sweet Revenge and Prayers 'n Promises. De La Rose was fifth.

De la Rose at last returned to her favourite surface at Aqueduct at the end of October. Over nine furlongs, a long race for two-year-old fillies in any country, De la Rose was second favourite to Smilin' Sera in the Miss Grillo in a field of eight. Both fillies were undefeated on grass. De La Rose had to give 3 lb to Smilin' Sera and it made all the difference as Smilin' Sera eroded De la Rose's advantage to score by a length.

De la Rose was returned to the dirt track for her last start as a juvenile. This time it was decided to employ tactics launching a bid off the pace and challenge up the final stretch thereby reverting to her previous successful style of running. The Demoiselle was run over nine furlongs and De La Rose comfortably defeated Prayers 'n Promises but came up against another real star in Rainbow Connection who had enough class to repel De La Rose's challenge along the rail by a head. Tina Tina Too and company were six lengths in arrears. Rainbow Connection was already the leading filly in Canada having accounted for the Grade 1 Princess Elizabeth Stakes and the Grade 3 Natalma and the Halo filly was certainly not one to be dismissed lightly. De La Rose had proved herself to be no pushover on the main track and on the Free Handicap that year she was rated 7 lb below her stable companion, Heavenly Cause, whom she had defeated every time they had met on grass.

The dirt track has such a hold on American racing that Stephens found it hard to map out a top-class grass campaign for De La Rose, so her first four starts as a three-year-old were on the "main" track. Fourth, rallying on the outside and catching her rivals hand over fist, in the Forward Gal (to stablemates Dame Mysterieuse and Heavenly Cause), fourth again to Dame Mysterieuse in the Bonnie Miss at Gulfstream Park and yet again to Dame Mysterieuse in an allowance at Keeneland were De La Rose's rewards. However her next outing on dirt, and her last for some while, showed De La Rose as a top-class filly on any surface.

By the line in the Grade 1 Kentucky Oaks Woody Stephens knew he had won – but with which filly? De La Rose had worked so well on the Sunday before the race that Stephens decided she was worth an entry. Unhurried early, De La Rose was allowed to launch her bid on the outside in the stretch and closed relentlessly on leader Heavenly Cause. Heavenly Cause would not let the Nijinsky filly go past however and at the line had just enough left to repel the flying De La Rose. Wayward Lass was five lengths back in third. It was quite a performance from a filly who had shown quite clearly that she was not as at home on the dirt surface as her stable companion.

Stephens had long promised De La Rose a return to the grass. The races were now available for her, his filly was now much more mature and ready to assert her superiority on her favoured surface ... and to do what only the very best fillies could do. Defeat the colts on their own ground.

De La Rose was re-introduced to her preferred surface in an allowance at Belmont three weeks after the Oaks. It was as nice an introduction as one could wish for. De La Rose won comfortably by almost four lengths from Explosive Bid. As the only filly in the field she had claimed her first scalps.

The last day in May was an auspicious one for Nijinsky. Not only was Kings Lake reinstated to his position as the winner of the Irish 2,000 Guineas but he had a treble of winning fillies at Belmont. Dancing Secret, older sister of Nijinsky's Secret, and Prayers 'n Promises' half sister Water Dance, won allowance races while De La Rose was about to score her first victory in graded company over the colts. The eight furlong Saranac Stakes was worth US $35,400 to the winner and De La Rose could hardly have had to have done so little to earn her extra ration of oats. Admittedly she was receiving weight from her male contemporaries but not enough to have affected the 6½ length margin of her victory. A distant last in the early stages De La Rose, the only filly in the field, moved boldly up the outside after rounding the turn and left the colts, headed by the useful Stage Door Key, trailing in her wake. De La Rose was on her way.

De La Rose now travelled to Monmouth Park for her next contest against the colts. Stephens was eyeing the Belmont classic, the CCA (Coaching Club American) Oaks, and needed a race for De La Rose before it. The long Branch seemed an easy US $34,400 and a Grade 3 cap into the bargain. The race would set her up nicely for the Oaks. As was her custom De La Rose was unhurried in the first part of the race, moved up with a rush on the outside leaving the backstretch and gained command on the turn. Increasing her advantage into the straight De La Rose ran away from Century Banker to win by 8½ lengths. The power of the filly was unbelievable; Maple allowed her to take off when she felt like it and De La Rose knew just when it was time to go. Even challenging six horses wide into the turn made no difference to De La Rose who drew out exactly as she chose to dictate to her jockey to score her most emphatic victory yet.

Maybe Stephens allowed all the euphoria surrounding De La Rose's grass victories to cloud his judgement a little for De La Rose was brought back to the dirt track to contest the CCA Oaks, admittedly America's premier event for three-year-old fillies. In finishing sixth to Wayward Lass, De La Rose ran her last race on the main track. For the future she was to be kept where she evidently liked it best and clearly where she wanted to be – on grass.

However connections must have been surprised at the very least when De La Rose was upended by a colt in the Grade 2 Lexington Handicap a month after the Oaks. This was De La Rose's one and only attempt at twelve furlongs on turf and she was up against an unbeaten (on grass) runner in Acaroid, to whom she was conceding 4 lb. Acaroid made the most of his light weight and had opened up a substantial advantage in the straight, setting sail for home. De La Rose rallied with her customary long stretch run from the back of the field but her weight disadvantage anchored her and she failed to peg back the colt by 1¼ lengths. The ex-English Wicked Will led the remainder four lengths adrift.

There was no change in riding tactics for De La Rose's trip to Saratoga in mid-August for the Grade 2 Diana Handicap. Again "out with the washing" early on De La Rose was on the heels of the leaders approaching the end of the backstretch and went after leader Rokeby Rose. The yielding going for the nine furlong feature did not blunt her speed for, accelerating rapidly, she caught Rokeby Rose midway up the stretch and eased off for a 1¾ length victory.

De La Rose and her supporters suffered a reversal in the ten furlong Flower Bowl in early September when Rokeby Rose claimed her revenge by 1¾ lengths. Memory Best led by seven lengths down the backstretch with Rokeby Rose inching forever closer to her and then, catching Maple napping, she drew away with sudden acceleration on the turn and leading by two lengths at the furlong pole there was no chance for the fast finishing De La Rose to catch her.

Not to be disheartened in his quest for an Eclipse award for De La Rose, Stephens next pointed his turf star to the 8½ furlong Lamb Chop Handicap and a field which included two granddaughters of Nijinsky in Wings of Grace (out of Nijinsky's first crop daughter Far Beyond) and Dancing Champ's daughter If Winter Comes. As usual, De La Rose lagged behind under her considerable top weight and then rallied strongly to defeat Andover Way by 1¾ lengths with Wings of Grace a neck behind. De La Rose was back on course.

She was brought out again for the ten furlong Athenia Handicap at Belmont in mid-October. This time she was assigned an impost for the Grade 3 event of 125 lb with a massive 9 lb and more to give away to her main rivals. It did not prevent her from running and nor did it prevent her from winning in the style of the champion she was. Racing last around the clubhouse turn and down the backstretch, Maple sat quietly oozing confidence and at the far turn, allowing Noble Damsel to go to the front, he set De La Rose to deliver that deadly burst of acceleration. As the field negotiated the far turn De La Rose went from last to first and led by 1½ lengths at the two furlong marker and was three lengths ahead at the furlong pole. From then on the contest was merely a procession, Noble Damsel staying on to be second ahead of Andover Way.

Stephens, despite his sights being on an Eclipse award, chose the first running of the E. P. Taylor Stakes at Woodbine for De La Rose. It was only five days after the Athenia and was her first visit out of the United States but the winners purse was Can $69,000. That was more for this Grade 3 race than De La Rose would earn in any of the options left to her; more in fact than the Grade 1 Hollywood Derby.

The field comprised the most international assemblage De La Rose had faced and included Sangue and Sajama from France, Condessa and Viendra from England and Ireland and the ex-Irish Fair Davina from the United States. For once De La Rose was coping with weight-for-age conditions and was not asked to concede weight to her contemporaries. The E. P. Taylor, formerly the Nettie Stakes, was run over ten furlongs on a firm course. De La Rose settled in at the back of the field for the early stages of the race and the jockeys on board the horses in front of her must have been very aware of her presence there and wondering when she would pounce. De La Rose moved up slightly in the backstretch but found her opening closing in front of her. Coolly Maple dropped his filly back next-to-last before coming around the entire field in barely a furlong. De La Rose stayed outside around the far turn and swept into the lead, galloping away to win with ease, Maple looking behind him at the opposition of which Sangue proved best. Her turn was still to come.

At this point de Kwiakowski and Stephens were planning a West Coast campaign for De La Rose to sign off her second season. The intentions were for De La Rose to race at four with Europe's Prix de l'Arc de Triomphe as her main target. Accordingly De La Rose was shipped to Hollywood Park for a crack at her first Grade 1 race on turf, the Hollywood Derby. Established now as one of the great international races of the autumn the Hollywood Derby, as often as not, has had to be divided and 1981 was no exception. De La Rose found herself the only filly in the field of eight.

De La Rose was off slowly and was ten lengths back but moved up after five furlongs, and as was her wont circled the field to vie for the lead with Partez entering the stretch. Gaining eight lengths before the field had reached the turn De La Rose was executing the kind of rally to which Easterners had long become accustomed. Before coming out of the turn De La Rose had the lead and refused to let High Counsel rally back at her. Hand ridden by Maple De La Rose held the colt safely by a long neck. The rest of the field were five lengths back and the time was considerably faster than that clocked by Silveyville in the second division.

De La Rose had done everything: carried all the imposts of weight she could have been assigned, defeated her filly contemporaries and the older mares and had firmly proved that she was more than a match for any colt. She duly won her Eclipse award as the Champion Grass Filly having held her form right through the season, showing admirable consistency. The female turf division was exceptionally strong that year and De La Rose defeated Turf Classic victress and Washington DC International runner-up April Run for the award. Other contenders had been the Japan Cup and Matchmaker Stakes winner Mairzy Doates, Santa Barbara Handicap victress The Very One, plus Yellow Ribbon winner Queen To Conquer, the multiple Group scorers Kilijaro and Just A Game. But De La Rose had earned her recognition.

Unfortunately the plans for 1982 did not come to fruition. De La Rose was not an early season filly; both her previous seasons had proved that and her third campaign did nothing to alter that fact. Her first start was in mid-February after a three month break from her very full three-year-old season. In the Columbiana Handicap at Hialeah, De La Rose finished second under 124 lb beaten 3¾ lengths by a new rising star Honey Fox. De La Rose was again slowest to begin, raced on the outside and caught third placed horse Shark Song in the closing strides but could not close on the winner. Over a longer distance, Stephens thought, the result would have been different. Honey Fox had won her previous outing and it was not a bad showing by De La Rose.

De La Rose next met Honey Fox in the Grade 2 Black Helen Handicap, over half a furlong further. Again De La Rose was slowest away but rallied around the final turn and was gaining at the finish up the outside. But Honey Fox was long gone and De La Rose could only manage fourth. De La Rose had been made the odds-on favourite despite her earlier defeat at the hands of Honey Fox.

The lack of instantaneous speed in response from De La Rose baffled Maple. After a sixth placed finish in the Suwannee River Handicap behind Teacher's Pet, Maple was sure he was not on the same filly who had won the Eclipse award: "Not within ten or twelve lengths of herself." Woody Stephens agreed and decided the filly did not like Florida, pointing out that a filly did not win eight races and then suddenly throw it all in. De La Rose was taken off the track for a while. Hindered by an ankle injury it was a little longer than anticipated and necessitated her missing all the major summer contests.

Even in mid-June her connections were still hoping for a crack at the Prix

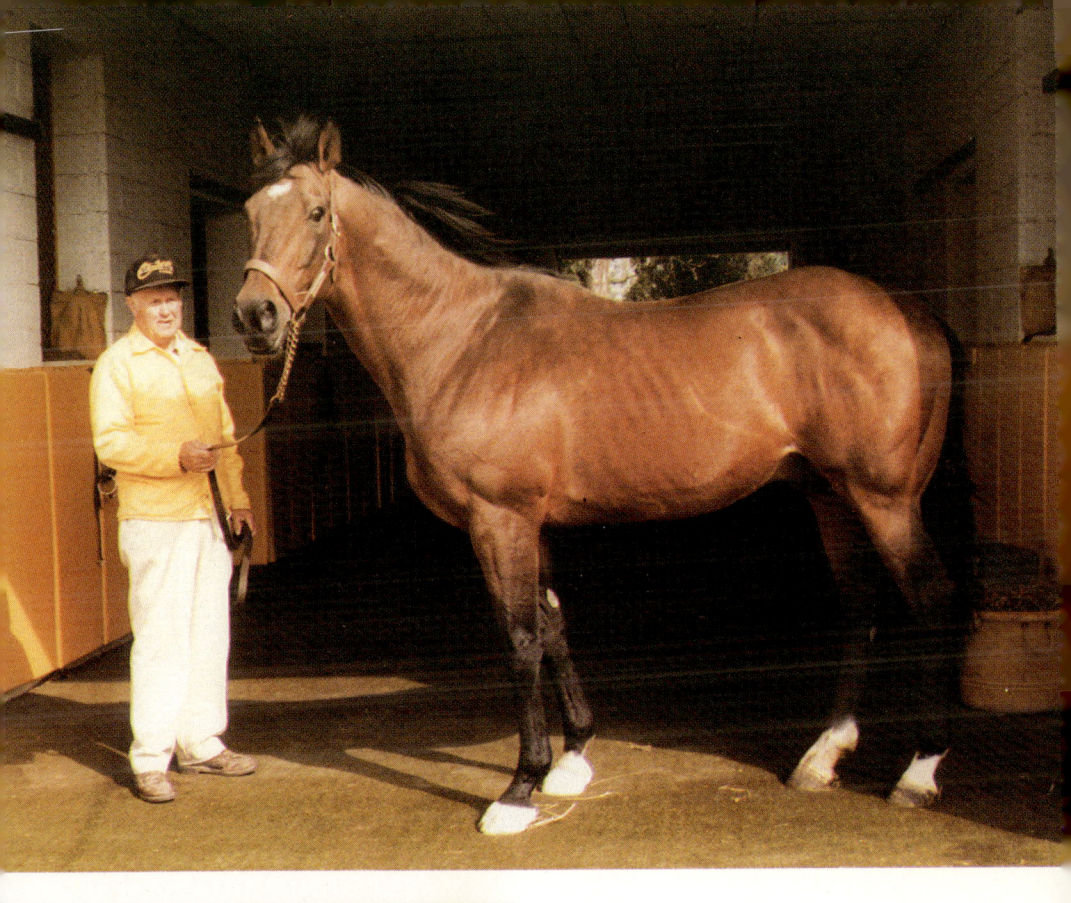

ABOVE
Nijinsky. At 17 years of age the magic is still there

LEFT
Nijinsky's best son to be trained in England, Ile de Bourbon is one of only two standing there at present

ABOVE
Perhaps the most courageous of Nijinsky's sons, Caerleon goes to post with Pat Eddery up

RIGHT
One of the most accomplished of Nijinsky's American sons, Czaravich was probably also the one most endowed with speed

ABOVE
The ill-fated Golden Fleece wins the 1982 Derby to climax an unbeaten career

LEFT
Green Dancer, the first classic winner and Nijinsky's most successful sire son to date. Green Dancer is now at stud in the United States

RIGHT
Nijinsky's only American champion, the filly De La Rose, about to foal to Conquistador Cielo

BELOW
Solford wins the Coral Eclipse Stakes from the accomplished performers Muscatite, Tolomeo, Stanerra and Time Charter

de l'Arc de Triomphe after De La Rose had been fired in mid-May. However De La Rose was never again given the chance to return to the races in the attempt to recover the form that took her through such a triumphant summer and autumn campaign of the year before. Maybe she would have come good as she had the previous seasons after a tardy start. Who knows?

De La Rose was officially retired in September and, in 1983, was sent to the court of her owners more recent champion Conquistador Cielo. The outcome of this union between Nijinsky's only Eclipse award winner and the champion colt of 1983 was a colt. His appearance will be something to wait for. If he takes after his brilliant parents then he will be a holy terror on the track. De La Rose will not be forgotten.

Solford

Everything in life is relative and so it is with champions and championships in racing. A champion in one country may not be regarded as so in another. Solford's form is very difficult to evaluate because he only ever did enough to win and, but for one inexplicable flop when he did not put in a run at all, Solford would have been an *undefeated* champion, a rare specimen whose limits are very difficult and well-nigh impossible to assess accurately. But in defeating Caerleon in his first outing as a three-year-old and then coming to England and claiming victory over the likes of Tolomeo, Time Charter and Stanerra, Solford has very strong claims to justify his elevated position.

Foaled on the last day of January 1980 Solford was a far more mature individual as a yearling than many of Nijinsky's progeny at the same stage. A striking bright bay with a long narrow white blaze kinking to the right a little, rather like that of his grandsire Northern Dancer, and sporting white socks on both hind feet, Solford was not going to be overlooked in the paddocks at yearling inspection time. He was bred by Helen Alexander at King Ranch from the unraced Fairness, a daughter of Cavan.

Fairness was 17 when Solford was foaled (and there were only two to follow) and she had already bred the major winner No Bias (by Jacinto) and the CCA Oaks placed fillies Equal Change and No Duplicate, both daughters of Arts and Letters. The dam of Fairness, Equal Venture (by the St Germans stallion Bold Venture) also never saw a racecourse but had bred the graded winners Prove Out, Heartland (dam of Distant Land) and Saidan and was herself own sister to Horse of the Year Assault, winner of the Triple Crown.

Despite his tremendous pedigree and physical credentials Solford was entered for the Fasig Tipton Kentucky Sale towards the end of July 1981. Already exhibiting that "look of eagles", so characteristic of his sire, Solford had been well spotted by Vincent O'Brien representing Robert Sangster and partners and maybe this colt was worth stopping by for at the Fasig Tipton Kentucky Sale after all.

After the sale, Helen Alexander was quoted as saying she had expected the Nijinsky colt to go for around US$300,000. Events, and the determination of men with money to obtain the colt, dictated otherwise. The early bidding started at US$100,000 but the packed sale ring had agreed with the Sangster camp's appraisal that this was going to be something special. It was a two pronged battle which took on the bidding – Dick Warden representing Sheikh Mohammed, and Tom Cooper of the British Bloodstock Agency (Ireland) representing Sangster. The million dollar mark came and was left behind. The top price at the previous year's sale had been US$325,000. At US$1.2 million Warden decided to call a halt but was persuaded to try an additional US$50,000 more. It was not enough and the record breaker was heading for Ireland with a price tag of US$1,300,000 hanging around his princely neck.

Solford's naming commemorated the horse with which Vincent O'Brien's father, Dan, had won the 1938 Irish Cambridgeshire and who went on to win the Champion Hurdle for Dorothy Paget.

Like Kings Lake and Golden Fleece before him, Solford was not hurried in his two-year-old season. He made his debut on 14 August 1982 at the Curragh on going on the firmish side of good. The six furlong Dunmurray Maiden, run on the same day as fellow Nijinsky colt Caerleon carried off the Ballsbridge/Tattersalls Anglesey Stakes (Group 3), attracted 16 runners. Solford started at 5/2 on to beat the more experienced Winning Feature and Bushti Music which he did cleverly by three-quarters of a length. Four lengths back, in fourth place, was the future Stewards Cup (Goodwood) winner Autumn Sunset. It was a good day for Eddery for apart from comfortable wins on Solford and Caerleon he also scored neck victories on Lords in the Group 2 Blandford Stakes for the Ballydoyle stable, and on African Pearl for John Oxx.

Solford's second and last outing of his first introductory season was at Leopardstown on the first Saturday in September, A furlong further to travel and nine opponents but Solford came with a wet sail to overhaul the grey Moral Leader on the line in the Wexford Race, thus completing a stable double initiated by future champion Danzatore having his first outing in the first division. Solford and Moral Leader were four lengths clear of the accomplished Iron Leader. It was again Eddery's day with no less than five winners from his five rides – apart from Solford and Danzatore he also scored on debutant Beaudelaire (Nijinsky-Bitty Girl), Punctilio in the Pacemaker International Whitehall Stakes (Group 3) and, again, on African

Pearl. It was quite an occasion for Irish racing too, witnessing the winning debuts for three future champions and near champions. Also in the beaten two-year-old fields were Give Thanks, Cremation and Autumn Sunset, all of whom were to become familiar names in the following year.

That was it for the season for Solford. He had not been excessively impressive as one had come to expect from O'Brien's representatives but he had done all that was asked of him and had not over-exerted himself. In the Irish Free Handicap he was assigned 15 lb less than stable companion Danzatore and 10 lb below second rated future French Derby winner and fellow Nijinsky colt Caerleon.

Solford was scheduled to make his reappearance in April in the Ballysax Race. But he looked dreadful in the paddock and was withdrawn when the vet diagnosed a raised temperature and reported that the colt was erupting with a skin condition. In Solford's absence the race was won by subsequent Derby runner up Carlingford Castle.

It was virtually under the conditions of the Irish Handicap that O'Brien elected to allow Solford and Caerleon to meet in the Craddock Advertising Race on 28 May at Phoenix Park over ten furlongs. Solford was set to receive 8 lb from his stable companion. Caerleon had had the dubious benefit of a previous run but that had been the highly unsatisfactory Rogers Gold Cup Ballymoss Stakes when, reportedly, mud clogged his nostrils which accounted for his poor showing on that occasion. Despite the presence of the much vaunted Heron Bay and South Atlantic, yet more stablemates, the race was seen to be between the two sons of Nijinsky. Eddery elected to partner Solford, which automatically meant that he started evens favourite with Caerleon at 5/1, shorter odds than any of the remainder of the field except Alleged's unraced brother Delgado. The pace was very slow for a classic trial with Solford making or sharing the pace and he held on well to keep the improving Caerleon at bay by three-quarters of a length.

Eddery reported that Solford had appeared to lose interest a little for a spell in the straight at Phoenix Park, though he ran on again when challenged. Perhaps this led to Solford sporting blinkers for the first, and only, time for his trip to France in mid-June. Seven days before Caerleon had captured the French Derby by an easy three lengths. That form made Solford a certainty for the Group 3 Prix du Lys over twelve furlongs at Chantilly. The race before had seen an Oaks victory for Escaline; there was nothing of her class in the Lys. The European record priced yearling South Atlantic had travelled with Solford but he might as well have stayed at home. He finished last of the six runners, some 10¾ lengths behind his stablemate. Solford won easily, disposing of able animals in future 1984 Group 1 winner Romildo and Jabal Tarik, but again was not extravagant in his length success.

While the opposition may not have been of the highest calibre in France, Solford certainly took some on in the third start of his second season. Vincent O'Brien's representative for the Group 1 Coral Eclipse Stakes at Sandown Park, Solford was seeking to establish himself well and truly in the top flight by a victory in England's premier summer ten furlong race. On paper he had no easy task: representing the English three-year-old classic colts were Tolomeo, Muscatite and Guns of Navarone, the older horses (who incidentally filled the last three places) by Lafontaine, Prima Voce and Lobkowiez and the best of the females in training from the previous year, Oaks victress Time Charter and the "mare of the moment" Stanerra, who had achieved a rare Group double at the 1983 Royal Ascot meeting. Subsequently these horses were to account for races as prestigious and diverse as the King George VI & Queen Elizabeth Diamond Stakes at Ascot, the Budweiser Million at Arlington Park and the Japan Cup. Against horses of this calibre Solford was almost an unknown quantity. However he still started second favourite behind Stanerra.

Possibly no one was any wiser as to just how good Solford was after the event than before it. Eddery rode a perfect race following pre-race planning exactly. The pace that had been set by Lafontaine and Lobkowiez was barely faster than a snail and caused all sorts of problems for all the runners in the straight. Eddery was quick to see the situation and kept Solford out of the melee and held him back until a furlong and a half from home when he allowed his colt to hit the front. Tolomeo went with him but the remainder of the field were still attempting to tie themselves in an intricate series of knots. Stanerra, Muscatite and Guns of Navarone all attempted to make their runs at the same time but Time Charter seemed to have no challenge to give at all. Muscatite was the only one moving fast enough under Lester Piggott's driving to get up to pass Tolomeo but he was not going to peg back Solford who was still being ridden with hands and heels by the ice-cool Pat Eddery.

The confidence Eddery showed in his riding of the Irish colt had to be seen to be believed for the challenges were coming thick and fast from all sides at once: Solford had only Tolomeo inside him but looming up on his outside were Muscatite and Stanerra while Guns of Navarone was vainly looking for an opening between Muscatite and the winner. However, all this did not worry Eddery, nor Solford either. Eddery at no stage had to resort to the whip while all his rivals were hard at work and it was a great credit to Solford that he could adapt to the conditions of the race when it became clear that it would develop into what was basically a four-furlong sprint.

It was as thrilling a spectacle as one could hope to see in a horse race. The first five home were separated by a head, a neck, a head and another neck with Time Charter 1½ lengths back in sixth. Solford maintained the male domination of this race – no filly had won it in the 97 years of its history. (Pebbles became the first in 1985).

Solford had now grown into the massive frame he inherited from his sire, much like Golden Fleece had, and as O'Brien knew he would given the time. Luckily, Nijinsky had also passed on the sheer power and speed that went with it.

On their reappearance Time Charter carried off England's richest race, the King George VI & Queen Elizabeth Diamond Stakes, while Tolomeo travelled to the United States and picked up the Budweiser Million from John Henry and Nijinsky's Secret. Later in the year, Stanerra claimed the Japan Cup and the Joe McGrath Memorial. It was quite another story for Solford.

Finding it rather difficult to set out a programme for Solford, O'Brien decided to send him over with Caerleon for the big York meeting in August. While Caerleon ran his heart out to win the Benson & Hedges Gold Cup (Group 1) on the rain soaked ground, Solford was scheduled to meet the Derby winner Teenoso in a battle of the giants the following day.

But whereas Solford had looked the perfect specimen he was, and the epitome of hard fitness, on Eclipse Day this was quite a different horse who paraded at York. He was again showing traces of a skin rash, was decidedly disappointing in his coat and, surprisingly for an Eclipse winner, he was being niggled at in the race before they had gone three furlongs. The race itself proved an anti-climax for neither Group 1 winner was in the hunt at all: Teenoso broke down and could only finish three lengths third to runaway winner Seymour Hicks while Solford was virtually pulled up. He was beginning to labour turning for home and was hanging to the right all the way up the straight. The reason for this lack lustre display, the only blemish on an otherwise spotless record, has never been revealed.

Whatever it was, it necessitated Solford's retirement and he travelled back across the Atlantic to stand at Winfield Farm in Kentucky where he should let down into a truly magnificent stallion. The international handicappers did not forget Solford. He was acclaimed champion in Ireland in the 6½–10½ furlong division, clear of the Guineas victors Lomond and Wassl and was certainly worthy of the recognition. Solford was not even a black type performer in Ireland but he had certainly flown the flag with style when sent to Chantilly and Sandown. In the International Classifications he was rated on 84 kg, below only L'Emigrant, Luth Enchantee, Tolomeo and Sackford, three of which were best at a mile. In England he was third behind the last two named. Rating Tolomeo above Solford is probably paying a little too large a compliment to the Arlington Million winner who was certainly beaten on merit at Sandown. *Timeform* rated them equals, yet rated Caerleon (in a different division) on 132 to Solford's 127, O'Brien having said, following Solford's Eclipse, that they were virtually the same horse.

Whichever was truly the better horse we shall never really know. One can only reflect on what a shame it was that we did not see more of this striking colt whose ability to stay and yet display such brilliant speed should be an asset to the bloodlines in the United States. The physical appearance of the first Solford progeny in 1985 bodes well for their sire's future.

Niniski

In appearance Niniski can be described as the image of his sire but a whole hand smaller. Perhaps not quite a whole hand. But Niniski has the bright bay colour, the intelligent Nijinsky expression, the bold white star and three white feet though there is a little of Tom Rolfe in his compactness too. Being by Nijinsky, out of a granddaughter of Ribot, one might suppose that Niniski has some of the nervous temperament exhibited by those two brilliant stallions. However he has not and is a real delight to behold. But whereas Niniski is quite typical of his sire in appearance he was quite a different racehorse.

The first foal from his winning dam from the family of Riboccarre, Cyane and Yelapa, Niniski cost US $90,000 at the Saratoga Yearling sale of 1977 on behalf of Lady Beaverbrook. Famous for her lucky seven figure names Lady Beaverbrook called the colt Niniski which proved to be quite a tongue twister, many preferring to refer to him as Nininsky or Nininiski.

Niniski was not hurried as a two-year-old by trainer Major Dick Hern who, after all, had other juveniles far more forward in his mind – Troy, in particular. Niniski had also had a traumatic journey to Britain after his purchase in which his flight was transferred to Germany due to industrial action and the Niniski that walked off the aeroplane for the first time in England was a complete wreck. The son of Nijinsky therefore made only one appearance, not being seriously questioned in a six furlong maiden race at Newbury at the back end of October.

Niniski was forward enough by May of his three-year-old season however and, at the Newmarket Guineas meeting, he met the subsequent good handicapper Steeple Bell and beat him a neck over a mile. Niniski started at 10/1, Steeple Bell at 25's: someone, if not Major Hern, was surprised. The next outing was only thirteen days on, over 2½ furlongs further at York. Having been ridden by Willie Carson in his previous races, Lester Piggott was now in the saddle and after a desperate battle Niniski went down by a neck to the Peter Walwyn trained New Berry. Ivatan and Masked Marvel were 2½ lengths behind in a field of twelve.

Even after this not guaranteed-to-make-the-headlines performance, Niniski was thought worthy of a place in the Derby field. Given a quiet ride by John Reid, partner of Ile de Bourbon, Niniski finished a respectable ninth behind his spectacular stable companion Troy. Niniski was four lengths behind the third horse, Northern Baby, and had finished in front of the much vaunted, Piggott-partnered stablemate Milford and also the Guineas and St Leger victors Tap on Wood and Son of Love. Not too bad for an 80/1 shot having only his fourth start.

Niniski was given a rest after the Derby and his next outing was again over the classic distance and gave notice of the promise later to be fulfilled. In the Group 3 Gordon Stakes ridden by Eddery, Niniski ran his more experienced stablemate More Light to three-quarters of a length with Haul Knight 2½ lengths in third. More Light had led all the way but he had just enough left to hold Niniski's late challenge.

Niniski was improving hand over fist and his performance in the Group 2 Geoffrey Freer Stakes at Newbury in August not only proved him a genuine stayer and battler but made him the leading British representative for the St Leger. Starting second favourite in the 13 furlong feature, Niniski wore down first Vital Season and then Pollerton in the last three furlongs, having been last but one and ten lengths off the pace at halfway, to win comfortably going away by three lengths from the Irish St Leger winner of the previous season M-Lolshan. In winning this race Niniski had enabled Dick Hern to pass Vincent O'Brien's record for the total winning stakes in a single English season. In the paddock Niniski had appeared to have put on a great deal of muscle and he was now fit for a tilt at the leading autumn staying events.

Carson chose Niniski in preference to Milford for the Doncaster classic. Niniski started joint favourite with Cracaval whose short head defeat of Ile de Bourbon in the September Stakes at Kempton had put him bang in the picture. Also in the field, apart from Milford, were Imperial Fling, Noelino, Reprocolor, fellow Nijinsky colt Stetchworth, and the French raiders Scorpio, Son of Love and Soleil Noir, who between them represented the best French staying form with not a great deal to choose between them. In the event Soleil Noir and Son of Love reproduced their running in the Grand Prix de Paris almost to the pound with Son of Love this time reversing the places by a short head. A thrilling finish to the Group 1 event but for Niniski, who along with Stetchworth led the rest of the field home, the abysmally slow early pace killed any chances he had of victory. He went on himself early in the straight and fought off the persistent efforts of Scorpio but could not hold the challenges of the first two inside the final furlong.

Contrary to general belief Niniski was not finished for the season: anything but. Indeed the best was still to come. Four weeks later Niniski started hot favourite for the Irish St Leger at the Curragh on the famous Irish good to yielding going. He was accompanied from England by Torus and the opposition included Bohemian Grove, Hypermetric and Bustino's brother Parva Stella. There was just no contest. This time there was a realistic gallop set by Parva Stella, which was taken up by Torus half a mile out when the Irish horse ran out of steam. Carson switched Niniski to the outside at the two furlong marker and the colt quickened stylishly with nonchalant ease in the manner of a top-class horse to cruise home by ten lengths yet not really being asked for an effort.

There was no stopping Niniski in his quest for the staying classics which now seemed at his mercy. His next and last outing for his three-year-old career was the French St Leger over $15\frac{1}{2}$ furlongs at Longchamp, controversially open for the first time to older horses. There were actually only two older horses in the race though neither made any show. Niniski, for the first time, had to cope with really heavy going. His most dangerous opponents seemed to be the fillies Singapore Girl, who had defeated Son of Love in the Prix Maurice de Gheest (Group 2) and Anifa, though the colts Shafaraz, Stout Fellow and Prove It Baby had proved themselves no slouches.

Niniski took command early in the straight and Anifa was the only one with any chance of getting anywhere near him. She was unable to do so and failed honourably by $1\frac{1}{2}$ lengths with Prix de Pomone (Group 3) victress Bolsa leading the rest of the field home at a respectable distance of five lengths.

Over the winter Major Hern was faced with a choice over his dual Leger winner: whether to keep Niniski in staying races and go for the Gold Cup or to allow him to compete against the best over twelve furlongs. Just as the season was beginning to get under way Hern decided to find out and Niniski's answer was electric.

The Group 2 John Porter Stakes, run in mid-April at Newbury, had always proved to be a leading guide to the well-being of the forthcoming season's top older horses. Run over a mile and a half, the going for the 1980 version was reported as firm and had attracted a strong, if not top-quality, field of 16. This large field was almost Niniski's undoing.

Dropped right out as Beau Reef cut out the early pace Carson allowed Niniski to make progress with four furlongs to run. However another furlong and the picture had changed dramatically. Carson found his path blocked and he decided to go around the outside. Having to pull back Niniski was left with ten lengths to make up in a furlong and a half. To all watching the race, very few could have believed that this was anything but a hopeless position. But the burst of speed that Niniski produced had to be seen to be believed:

Niniski had caught the leader Morse Code in 100 yards and had turned his ten length deficit into a three length victory at the line. Niniski had answered his trainer's questions: the four-year-old Niniski was a new Niniski, equipped now with an undeniable extra gear.

It was no fluke. The next foray might have been over an extended 13 furlongs but it was also around the tight track at Chester. Niniski was set to concede 8 lb to his principal opponents in the ten horse field and it was hardly an ideal track for him. However despite all this Niniski was odds-on.

Taking third place turning into Chester's short straight, Carson was again forced to switch to the outside. Chester's straight is barely two furlongs and a horse like Niniski needed to get balanced. Ground was running out. Two of Diamonds, who had once given Troy a hard race, had taken the lead and was setting sail for home. However Niniski was not to be denied. Battling his way past the leaders he was in front 50 yards from home and, in the end, won a great deal more comfortably than the neck verdict suggested.

Though the going at both Newbury and Chester was officially firm it was almost rock hard at Epsom on Coronation Cup day. Though more suited by the course, Niniski was also facing Soleil Noir for the first time since they had met at Doncaster the previous September. It was a hard battle on the concrete ground and Niniski got the better of the French colt by a neck. However by that time Sea Chimes had gone beyond recall.

The defeat did not stop Niniski heading for the King George VI & Queen Elizabeth Diamond Stakes, which says a great deal for the esteem in which Niniski was held by his trainer. However a bruised foot, a relic from the hard going at Epsom, ensured that Niniski was not in the line-up at Ascot. In his absence his stable companion Ela Mana Mou proved an able representative.

So, Niniski came to the Prix de l'Arc de Triomphe without a preliminary race but was not without his supporters. However Niniski would undoubtedly need some give in the ground and for one of the rare occasions at Longchamp in October he did not get it. The result was a thirteenth place finish behind Detroit, Argument, Ela Mana Mou and Three Troikas, but it was not a field to be disgraced in.

Niniski's final outing was back at Longchamp for a second crack at the Prix Royal Oak, the French St Leger. The going had by now turned to the other extreme. But evidently soured by earlier races on firm going Niniski disappointed to finish six of thirteen. But maybe with hindsight it was not such a bad performance after all; the winner by an easy three lengths was the future Arc heroine Gold River and back in third place was the champion stayer of the early 1980s, Ardross.

Niniski was syndicated by the British Bloodstock Agency for £800,000 and retired to Lanwades Stud near Newmarket, which is in the charge of the extremely knowledgeable and able Swedish manager Kirsten Rausing. In some ways being a dual Leger winner Niniski has had an uphill battle to establish himself as a commercial sire with the current prejudice against stayers. Being only the second son of Nijinsky at stud in England perhaps breeders should avail themselves more of a horse who possessed obvious top-class speed at the classic distance over twelve furlongs, as well as being one of the few reasonably priced representatives of the most sought after sire line in the world today.

Where else can breeders go to use a dual Group 1 winning son of Nijinsky at only £6,000? The fact that the only other Group 1 winning sons of Nijinsky at stud in England and Ireland are Kings Lake, Caerleon and Ile de Bourbon plus the new arrival from the United States, Vision, is worth bearing in mind. And, if breeders are determined to label Niniski as a stayer pure and simple, they would do well to keep in mind one other previously written off stayer . . . High Line.

Buyers have not forgotten Niniski however. His first yearlings were well received in 1983, the nine on offer grossing 150,810 guineas (which does not include a US $95,000 representative sold in the United States). These were headed by an outstanding individual, out of the Petingo mare Sushila, who made 90,000 guineas at the Highflyer Sale. Maybe the buyers remembered the victory over a mile early in Niniski's three-year-old career and his highly compromised juvenile days.

Niniski had his first runners in 1984 and it was only they who could provide the answers. The reply was emphatic. First there was Petoski, the 90,000 guineas yearling. Carrying off the listed Champagne Stakes at Salisbury, displaying an unanswerable burst of speed, Petoski then went on to halt Provideo's run in the Lanson Champagne Stakes at Goodwood. Only a particularly unlucky passage deprived him of a "Champagne Triple" in the Group 2 event at Doncaster. But, apart from Petoski and a staggering percentage of able juveniles to runners, the moment that established Niniski as a sire to be respected and confounded the critics was Kala Dancer's momentous battling triumph over Law Society and Local Suitor in the William Hill Dewhurst Stakes to give Niniski the first season sire's championship like his sire before him. It was a moment for his supporters to savour and on no occasion was unshakable faith so richly rewarded.

Caucasus

Caucasus, along with the fillies Summertime Promise, Javamine and Nijana, probably was the first horse to open the eyes of the Americans to the durable qualities of Nijinsky's stock. But for Green Dancer he would have been

Nijinsky's first classic winner in Europe but he was certain Nijinsky's first really top-class son to race in the United States.

Caucasus was a member of Nijinsky's first crop foaled in 1972. He was in good company: Quiet Fling, Dancing Champ, Green Dancer, Lighted Glory, Summertime Promise. Nijinsky's first book of mares had included such racing stars as Mrs Peterkin, Rash Statement, Monarchy, Monade, Lunik, Swift Lady, Lady Victoria and Bowl of Flowers and the dams of Sweet Alliance, La Dorga, Blade, High Echelon, Native Heritage, Title, Fabled Monarch, Bonnie And Gay, Northern Taste, Titled Hero and Royal Bowl. Caucasus's dam Quill was one of the very best. She was the Champion Two-Year-Old Filly of 1958 and her 14 wins included the Acorn Stakes and Mother Goose Stakes. She was already dam of One For All (Laurel Turf Cup, Sunset Handicap) and First Feather (dam of Run The Gantlet). Her daughter Shill was to produce Nijinsky's champion son Maruzensky two years later.

Caucasus was bred by Mrs Jane Engelhard, wife of the owner of Nijinsky. Quill had been bought by Charles Engelhard in foal to Native Dancer (which resulted in Bandarilla) for US$365,000 then a record for a broodmare. Caucasus was sent to the stables of Vincent O'Brien in Ireland where Nijinsky had been trained. He was brought along slowly and did not see a racecourse at two years. Also at Ballydoyle among his contemporaries were Gay Fandango, Caucasus's future deadly rival and American stablemate King Pellinore, and the fillies Karelina, Gallina, Swingtime and Tuscarora. He was also in company with other Nijinsky colts Lord of The Dance and Whiskey Road.

Had Caucasus been kept in Ireland for the entirety of his three-year-old career he would probably have been unbeaten. He made his debut at Phoenix Park on 3 May in a maiden race for three-year-old colts and geldings. He did not even start favourite: that dubious honour fell to Robbie Burns, a Sea Hawk II colt from Paddy Prendergast's stable who was having his first outing of the season. Running very green Caucasus won the ten furlong contest by a short head from Megalomania who had benefitted from a previous outing. Robbie Burns was three lengths back in third.

Tommy Murphy had been in the saddle at Phoenix Park: Lester Piggott had the ride in Caucasus's next race which was on Irish Sweeps Derby day. In the Derby itself Masqued Dancer (Nijinsky ex Bonnie Google) ran down the field behind Grundy and King Pellinore. It was a much sterner task for Caucasus in the twelve furlong Enniskellen Memorial Handicap in which he was opposed by Lucky For Me who was later so impressive in winning at York's big August meeting. Lucky For Me, later the dam of Grand Prix de Paris victor Yawa, was receiving 16 lb from the colt who was carrying top weight in the seven horse field. It was not really a race for Caucasus as he strolled home for a recorded six length victory over the filly. He evidently preferred the firm ground at the Curragh to the soft encountered at Phoenix Park.

Caucasus next went in search of a stakes victory, travelling to Down Royal two and a half weeks later. The distance of the Ulster Harp Derby was only 11½ furlongs, perhaps a little short considering Caucasus would be running next over a mile and three-quarters. He started 5/1 *on* and only four turned out to oppose him. Dowdall was 5/1 second favourite and that was how the race went. Caucasus, partnered by Tommy Murphy, won easily by three lengths, ten lengths and twenty lengths.

Caucasus carried his unbeaten record to England. He contested the St Leger trial, the March Stakes, at Goodwood on 23 August. Caucasus started odds on in a field of five which contained a few very experienced horses, especially Whip It Quick, who had finished ahead of Green Dancer when fifth in the Derby, and Caucasus found himself engaged in a battle up the final two furlongs with the English colt which, receiving 5 lb, won by half a length.

It was decided to send King Pellinore to Doncaster (in which he was upset by Bruni) and Caucasus was the stable's representative in the Irish equivalent. He was opposed by another Nijinsky colt in Quiet Fling, who was to win the Coronation Cup the following year, as well as future Cesarewitch winner Shantallah and the horse who at one stage was all the rage for the English Derby, Nuthatch.

Caucasus wore blinkers for the first time. Contrary to his usual style of running Caucasus went into the lead before two furlongs had been covered and, by the time they turned into the straight, all but Shantallah and Quiet Fling were toiling in his wake. No one is quite so adept as Lester Piggott in employing waiting in front tactics. Shantallah proved no match but at the 1½ furlong point Quiet Fling loomed up on Caucasus's outside and appeared to be going the better. Caucasus responded to Piggott's coaxing and fought back to regain the lead 150 yards out and drew clear to win by two lengths. While the two Nijinsky colts had given their sire a sparkling end to his first classic crop, Caucasus had given O'Brien his first Irish classic success since Nijinsky had won the Irish Derby over five years before.

Caucasus was sent to the United States to continue his racing career along with King Pellinore. Both were for sale by their respective owners and both found their way to the same stable. Dempsey and Sahadi, who purchased Caucasus for their Cardiff Farm, bought Caucasus for long distances (the American term) and on grass, having in mind the San Juan Capistrano and Hollywood Invitational. Caucasus went into the care of Charlie Whittingham who had charge of many European raced horses including Dahlia and Youth. Caucasus's new owners had had to decide between him and King Pellinore and, after much consideration, they found Caucasus the better proposition. Whether they were right or not both horses had their share of success and there was not that much between them. They got King Pellinore in the end but at a much inflated price. Once both horses were in the same ownership they could keep them apart and stop them from cutting each other's throats any longer.

Caucasus made his first American start at Hollywood Park in an allowance over eight furlongs on turf. The distance was clearly too short for him and with the unfamiliar surroundings there were enough reasons for Caucasus's satisfactory fourth placed finish, beaten three lengths by the favourite Pisistrato.

Twelve days later Caucasus turned out again for an allowance at the same track but over a furlong further. Some allowance. Carrying only 7 st 13 lb and receiving 5 lb from Caucasus was a certain chestnut daughter of Vaguely Noble called Dahlia. She won by only half a length from Caucasus who had run just the right sort of preparatory race for his first graded start in the United States. The South Bay Handicap (Grade 2) was run eleven days later over eleven furlongs at Hollywood. Caucasus was an odds on favourite and had no easy run. He was caught short for early speed but had to be checked after running into numerous pockets on the rail and did not get a clear run until well onto the home straight. Once he saw daylight he made steady headway to catch Copper Mel who had taken up the running two furlongs out. It was an impressive performance by Caucasus for he had been giving 7 lb and more to his rivals and 11 lb to Copper Mel, no mean stakes performer himself.

Eleven days later Caucasus again met up with Dahlia, this time receiving only 2 lb from the colt. King Pellinore led the rest of the star studded field for the eighth running of the Hollywood Invitational over twelve furlongs which also included Avatar, Top Command, Landscaper and Pass The Glass. The race drew the largest crowd for five years to the track. As before Caucasus needed time to find his rhythm but moved closer at the far turn. Dahlia took the lead at the mile pole and was winging her way home. Caucasus rallied steadily and strongly but could not quite reach the mare, missing by half a length but without being punished. The remainder, led by Pass The Glass and King Pellinore (giving Caucasus 2 lb) were four lengths and more behind.

Caucasus was given a five week rest after this game performance against one of the world's greatest ever mares. His next start was the nine furlong American Handicap in which he was set to receive a pound from King

Pellinore. Also in the line-up were Riot In Paris and Ancient Title, two established turf stars. Caucasus was dropped right out as Zanthe made the early pace. By the time Caucasus was allowed to get into his stride, and boldly charge up the straight catching the leaders hand over fist, King Pellinore was virtually home and dry beating Riot In Paris three-quarters of a length. The fast finishing Caucasus was just three-quarters of a length behind.

Twenty-two days later Caucasus met King Pellinore again. Though trained by the same man they were running for different interests. It was also Caucasus's third meeting with Dahlia and old friend Riot In Paris, while Avatar and One On The Aisle were also in the field for the Grade 1 Sunset Handicap. Caucasus broke alertly but was held up as a traffic jam occurred. Toro kept Caucasus on the inside after his path had been blocked. Dahlia, as was her wont, was merrily doing her Pied Piper act having taken it up from King Pellinore after half a mile. However this time Dahlia could not maintain her lead and faltered to finish seventh. Two and a half furlongs out Caucasus had got some space having been manoeuvred neatly to the outside and engaged King Pellinore in a battle royal all the way up the straight. The two quickly went 2½ lengths clear of Riot In Paris. During the last furlong the two horses touched more than once and which led Laffit Pincay, jr, to lodge a claim of foul against the other Whittingham trained colt. The stewards quickly determined that it was half a dozen of one and six of the other and Caucasus was declared the winner by a nose. It was Caucasus's first Grade 1 win on American soil but it was not to be his last.

Eight weeks later Caucasus took on a 13 horse field for the Grade 2 Manhattan Handicap at Belmont Park over eleven furlongs without King Pellinore. They were not all unfamiliar faces however. Also in the field was the year older Hail The Pirates, a colleague of Caucasus at Ballydoyle. He led a number of European exiles including Kamaraan and Recupere. Despite the lay off Caucasus was patiently waited with early on as Kamaraan made the pace. Upon entering the backstretch Caucasus made ground between horses but was left looking for room approaching the straight. However once he had got out Caucasus fairly flew. He wore down Trumpeter Swan who had taken over from Kamaraan on the far turn, and got the better of that colt by half a length, the latter receiving 7 lb from Caucasus, who was carrying the second highest weight in the 13 horse field. Hail The Pirates finished last.

Caucasus's last race of his first campaign on American turf was his most disappointing. Starting hot favourite for the Man O'War at Belmont two weeks later in weight-for-age conditions he finished tenth, two places behind Dahlia, and behind Erwin Boy, Kamaraan and Trumpeter Swan, all of whom he had beaten easily in the Manhattan. The race was won by

Effervescing. After the race it was discovered Caucasus had bruised a foot and was off the course for four months afterwards.

On the turf handicap that year Caucasus was placed fourth behind King Pellinore, Youth and Intrepid Hero, not all of them having run in handicap company and it is difficult to see how Caucasus could have been separated from King Pellinore by anything but an extremely narrow margin.

Caucasus's first start in 1977 was merely a training exercise. Carrying top weight over all but Bruni, Caucasus ran in a nine furlong handicap at Santa Anita at the end of February. He finished fifth of the six runners and Bruni finished last.

However Caucasus was on the ball for the Grade 3 Arcadia Handicap ten days later. Again, only Bruni was carrying more weight (125 lb to Caucasus's 124 lb). As was his habit Caucasus was kept far back along the inside. He found himself pocketed at the quarter pole and had to swing wide to come around horses in looking for room into the straight. Then he closed fast to win, going away by 2½ lengths. Among the beaten horses were Bruni (seven length conqueror of King Pellinore in the Doncaster St Leger), Riot In Paris back in mid-division.

Caucasus met up again with King Pellinore, now carrying the same Cardiff Farm colours, in the twelve furlong San Luis Rey Stakes (Grade 1). This was the first time they had met at level weights, as indeed were all the field. A true championship race. The two Whittingham stars headed a field of seven which included Bruni. Top Crowd took an early lead with King Pellinore closest of the pursuing bunch. Caucasus, after being taken in hand and allowed to settle on the rail, closed a little at the far turn only to get trapped momentarily. Gold Standard dropped back just at the right moment and, coming into the final two furlongs, Caucasus was upsides Top Crowd and King Pellinore. For a moment they were almost in a perfect line; King Pellinore for a second appeared in front and then Caucasus was gone. King Pellinore fought back but Caucasus was getting stronger the further he went and he was past the post for a two length victory which was only two and three fifths seconds outside the course record. The result led Whittingham to decide that King Pellinore was possibly the better horse up to ten furlongs but Caucasus the stronger over distances in excess of that. Caucasus was a good deal smaller than King Pellinore but proved himself equal to carrying a similar amount of weight.

Caucasus was the stable representative for the San Juan Capistrano at Santa Anita on 10 April. The Grade 1 race over one and three quarter miles is one of the longer races in the American calendar and seems a perfect target for many ex-European horses as their American counterparts are often not trained to race over this kind of distance. King Pellinore was kept in the barn, leaving Caucasus to carry top weight of 128 lb, giving 6 lb to recent import Anne's Pretender, 8 lb to Properantes, 10 lb to Top Crowd and more to the remainder of the eight horse field. Caucasus went off 4/5 favourite and broke faster than usual to be close up on the rail, Properantes close behind him. When horses began falling over each other Darrel McHargue switched Properantes to the outside in a lightning move that possibly won him the race. Top Crowd had opened up a lead at the top of the straight as Caucasus came off the rail looking for room, could not find it and had to go back to the rail. When the gap opened for Caucasus it was too late. Properantes closed on the outside and Top Crowd was caught inside the final furlong, the pair finished clear of a weight anchored Caucasus who only then saw daylight. It was the first notable occasion that these tactics had probably cost him a major race.

Three weeks later Caucasus turned out for the Grade 1 Century Handicap over eleven furlongs at Hollywood Park against many of the horses he had met countless times before: Effervescing, Top Crowd, Anne's Pretender and Properantes. He was again top weight, giving 4 lb to Properantes and 6 lb to Anne's Pretender and Effervescing. Caucasus broke very slowly and, again, got caught up in traffic but this time there was no way through at all. He finished fifth behind Anne's Pretender and Properantes.

It was another Grade 1 outing for Caucasus at Hollywood Park at the end of May. This time the twelve furlong Hollywood Invitational in which he had been beaten the year before by Dahlia. No Dahlia but instead 126 lb and a grey ghost called Vigors to whom Caucasus was giving 9 lb. Yet again Caucasus found his late rally checked by heavy traffic at the far turn. By then Vigors had launched himself clear on the outside and fast as Caucasus stormed through on the inside in the final furlong it was too late and Vigors was home by three-quarters of a length. Anne's Pretender was third, Properantes fifth, Effervescing sixth, the Antipodean superstar Balmerino seventh and Top Crowd last of the twelve runners.

Caucasus seemed cursed with ill luck as long as he was kept far back and racing on the inside. Unfortunately the tactics remained the same for the ten furlong Hollywood Gold Cup (Grade 1) on 18 June. For the first time in several months Caucasus was not carrying top weight – that fell to Crystal Water. The race was a particularly rough one even though it ended up as a contest for just three of the field of twelve. Caucasus did not begin to close from his distant position and when he did he ran into a solid wall of horseflesh. Agonisingly he had to wait for room, wait and wait. Suddenly the opening came between horses nearing the quarter pole and Caucasus got his clear run up the middle. Ahead Crystal Water and Cascapedia were engaged in a battle royal which the former just won by a neck. Caucasus however was bearing down on them eating up the ground like a hungry tiger. At the wire he was a nose short of Cascapedia and in another two strides he would have won.

All these hard races were bound to have a mark on any horse and especially one who had tried so hard, only to be thwarted and frustrated at every turn. Caucasus made just two more starts at Hollywood in July. The American Handicap (Grade 2) which he had won the previous year found him trailing around the far turn and coming with a rush as usual. And, as usual, Hunza Dancer, Anne's Pretender and Legendaire had gone beyond recall. Perhaps the nine furlongs did not leave enough scope for Caucasus to truly get into top gear.

His final appearance was in the Grade 1 Sunset Handicap which he had also won the previous year. After being frustrated in heavy traffic yet again, this time Caucasus decided enough was enough. The race was won by Today 'n Tomorrow who had been left for dead by Caucasus on previous encounters.

Caucasus was retired to E. P. Taylor's Windfields Farm in Canada with earnings from nine victories of US $411,555 and £14,728. This time he was weighted on the turf handicap second only to Majestic Light (126 lb to Caucasus's 125 lb), equal with Exceller and ahead of King Pellinore and Washington DC International winner Johnny D.

Caucasus presently stands at the Hurstland Farm in Kentucky, alongside, ironically, King Pellinore. Caucasus is outgunning King Pellinore in the stud stakes too though he himself has been a little disappointing. His first crop reached the races in 1981 and so far he has been represented by the stakes winners Casus Belli, Royal Anthem, Trust Us and Dundrum Dancer plus his best progeny to date Pied à Terre who won the Grade 3 Pilgrim Stakes as a juvenile by seven lengths at the back end of 1983 having finished third in the Grade 1 Laurel Futurity. Like his races on the track maybe after this slightly tardy start Caucasus will come with a rush and leave them all standing.

Nijinsky's Secret

Nijinsky's Secret differs from the rest of Nijinsky's progeny selected here in that he was not a major Group winner at either two or three years of age. Indeed, he did not mature sufficiently to prove himself amongst the best of his contemporaries until he returned to his native North America to race at four, five and six. As Nijinsky's leading money earner Nijinsky's Secret has nevertheless done enough to be ranked worthy as one of the best representatives of his sire to date.

Nijinsky's Secret was not at all a late foal. Born on 11 February 1978 he is a dark chestnut with a small round star and an independent narrow vertical stripe down the nose and two white socks. His dam Secret Beauty was a contemporary of Nijinsky's. Although she had only been placed herself she was a daughter of Raise A Native from the Vagrancy Handicap winner Dandy Blitzen (by Bull Dandy), dam in turn of Great Career. Dandy Blitzen was half sister to Venomous who won 15 races including the Colonial Handicap and who bred the successful sire Explodent plus the graded stakes winner Treacherous. The cross of Nijinsky on Raise A Native mares had been responsible for producing Night Alert, Muscovite and London Bells and Formidable's half sister Bev Bev. However, Nijinsky's Secret is the only Grade 1 winner as yet to come from that combination.

Secret Beauty had already produced winners from a variety of stallions including Bold Hour, Call Me Prince and West Coast Scout. Her foal preceding Nijinsky's Secret was, however, her first stakes performer, the bay own sister to Nijinsky's Secret called Dancing Secret. She won six races at four and five years showing the same lack of precocity as her brother. She never quite claimed a stakes race for herself but was third in the Martha Washington Handicap. Secret Beauty also has a chestnut full sister to the pair called Dancing Brownie, an unraced three-year-old of 1985.

Nijinsky's Secret did not go through the sale ring but was sent to France under the care of J. Cunnington, jr. He was bred and raced by the Oxford stable of Ralph C. Wilson, who sent one or two horses outside the United States each year and who were to be responsible for shipping Nijinsky's Secret back to the United States at the end of his three-year-old career and ultimately to sell him after his first graded success and therefore miss the development of Nijinsky's Secret into a Group 1 performer.

Although Nijinsky's Secret was such a big colt and obviously would need time to grow into himself he did start twice at two years. His first race was in late September at Longchamp in an eight furlong affair for previously unraced colts. The Prix de Villebon had a good reputation for throwing up a good horse or two and Nijinsky's Secret had a nice introduction finishing fourth to Great Substance who went on to win the Group 3 Prix Gontaut Biron and Prix Quincey later in his career.

Nijinsky's Secret was next seen out three weeks later in the Prix de Louvre, again over eight furlongs at Longchamp. He won comfortably by 1½ lengths and five lengths over a field which included Yumi, who had finished second to his fourth in the Villebon. The second horse was Russian Fox (Nijinsky-Flying Fur) who was having his first outing. He was to follow Nijinsky's Secret back to the United States but not to such outstanding success.

Nijinsky's Secret was put away for the winter and allowed to mature. He was always a character and maybe his three-year-old season also saw the onset of the muscular problems that were to compromise his career so much in the United States. If so the answer was not found in France . . .

Nijinsky's Secret made his three-year-old debut on 14 April at Saint Cloud in the Prix Jean le Gonidec over the full classic distance of twelve furlongs. His main rival in the seven horse field was undoubtedly Marasali who would later win the Prix de Barbeville (Group 3) and the Group 2 Prix de Conseil de Paris, and who had the advantage of a previous outing. Ridden, as he was throughout the majority of his French racing career, by Maurice Philipperon, Nijinsky's Secret was engaged in a rousing battle up the straight with the Saint-Martin partnered Marasali. The two had the race to themselves, Nijinsky's Secret eventually triumphing by a neck with the Group 3 Premio Lazio victor Shamstar four lengths back in third.

Nijinsky's Secret made his stakes debut on 10 May in the Prix Hocquart (Group 2) at Longchamp. The going was very heavy which did not suit the Nijinsky colt and, possibly, also not the favourites Mariacho and Vanann. Gap of Dunloe set a very fast pace with Vanann and Nijinsky's Secret some way adrift and clearly not going very freely. Mbaiki went on as Gap of Dunloe dropped out but Mariacho was looking all over the winner. However Rahotep found an opening between them inside the final furlong and ran out a comfortable winner. Nijinsky's Secret led the remainder home in fourth place clearly bogged down in the Longchamp straight.

Nijinsky's Secret went straight to the French Derby on 7 June at Chantilly despite not having had much of a race in the Hocquart. The twelve horse field for the classic was full of quality and controversy. The favourite was No Lute, sensationally disqualified along with Explorer King from their spring Group successes due to the apparent presence of steroids. Recitation, winner of the Grand Criterium and French 2,000 Guineas was sent from the English stable of Guy Harwood; The Wonder and Bikala, beaten by No Lute in the Lupin and who were promoted to first and third in that race, and the first four in the Hocquart plus Gap of Dunloe made up the rest of the principals. Plus Akarad. Unbeaten, he had never run in Group company but he wound up the season as Arc favourite and started second favourite here.

Fast going and a muggy atmosphere led to a fast early pace set by Magnum, running for No Lute, followed by Bikala, Mariacho and Gap of Dunloe. Nijinsky's Secret was at the absolute rear of the field after five furlongs. Coming into the straight Bikala had stormed clear but two furlongs out Nijinsky's Secret was bang there in line with Gap of Dunloe, Rahotep and Akarad about three lengths behind the leader. Instead of Bikala coming back to his field however he kept piling on the pressure. Apart from these five colts there was nothing else in sight. While Bikala was making for the post,

Akarad swept through to take second ahead of Gap of Dunloe, Rahotep and Nijinsky's Secret. Maybe Nijinsky's Secret had been given a lot to do, and had made up his ground from the rear rather rapidly, to be in the firing line so soon in the straight. However, he finished a good deal closer to Rahotep than he had in the Hocquart and was obviously a better horse on faster going. He also never gave up the fight and was only a short head behind Rahotep at the finish and less than a length out of third place. Toiling 2½ lengths behind him was Mbaiki, second in the Hocquart and further behind were Recitation, The Wonder, No Lute and Mariacho, third in the Hocquart. The first two of those last named were either multiple Group 1 scorers before the Derby or after it.

As Kent Stirling was to find later in the United Stakes, Nijinsky's Secret needed time between races. His next outing was four weeks later in the Grand Prix de Paris (Group 1) run over 15 furlongs back at Longchamp. Still a Group 1 race, but not carrying the prestige it once had (formerly a superior prize to both the French Derby and the Arc), it nevertheless carried a hefty prize (450,000 F to the winner) and attracted a top quality field in 1981. Only Mbaiki and Nijinsky's Secret made it from the French Derby, but the Epsom second, Glint of Gold, was there plus future Champion Stakes winner Vayrann and the first three in the Group 3 Prix Berteux, headed by Le Mamamouchi. Tow led by a wide margin in the early stages but Glint of Gold was keeping a close eye on him from mid-division and when the time was right pounced for a convincing victory. Nijinsky's Secret stayed on to be fifth but possibly did not want too much further to go.

After the Grand Prix de Paris Nijinsky's Secret was off the track for six weeks. Then he was entered in an eleven horse field for the Group 2 Grand Prix de Deauville over 13½ furlongs. He and Top Dancer (by Green Dancer) were the only three-year-olds in the race, which was headed by the English raiders Castle Keep and Nicholas Bill with the future American champion Perrault representing France. Nijinsky's Secret was clearly not right and made no show at all behind Perrault. Nijinsky's Secret was having problems, but for which the French found neither the cause nor an answer. It was left to Kent Stirling to come up with that.

Nijinsky's Secret had just one more race either as a three-year-old or in France. He fared no better in the 15 furlong Prix du Lutece (Group 3) on 20 September, a distance over which he was clearly not at his best and was virtually pulled up behind Tipperary Fixer who had been runner-up to Glint of Gold in the Grand Prix de Paris. Marasali and Mbaiki, whom he had beaten convincingly before, were the placed horses on this occasion. Nijinsky's Secret had been ridden in his last two starts by Jackie Taillard.

Ralph Wilson knew that his colt was better than he had shown in public.

Clearly there was a problem and clearly it was not to be solved in France. Accordingly it was decided to send Nijinsky's Secret back to the United States which offered a greater range of competition for him as a four-year-old. The European system of top-class racing is not geared to lucrative rewards for its older horses over the whole season. In the United States the scope is enormous.

Nijinsky's Secret was kept at Aiken all winter and got a good deal of serious and valuable training on the sandy surface of the tracks there. His new trainer Bill Hirsch, who also had charge of Dancing Secret, took Nijinsky's Secret north in the spring of 1982 to begin his four-year-old career. As soon as the grass season opened Nijinsky's Secret was entered for a mile race. He was fractious at the start, bolted when he got out of the stalls and clearly was unhappy with the tight turns at Aqueduct. He ended up fourth, beaten almost six lengths by Folge in a field of nine.

It was quite a different story once Nijinsky's Secret had adapted to his new conditions. His second start was at Belmont in an 8½ furlong grass allowance race where he ran out an impressive 5½ length winner over Foolish Tanner despite being very slowly away. He had taken his own time in catching the leaders and the whole operation could not have been smoother.

A repeat performance eleven days later in another Belmont allowance, this time over eleven furlongs on the turf. There he beat another European exile, End Of War, half brother to Quiet Fling and Peacetime, which set him up nicely for his first graded stakes attempt in the United States.

Nijinsky's Secret was a narrow favourite for the Grade 2 Tidal Handicap at Belmont over the eleven furlong turf course. He was ridden for the first time by Jeff Fell, his previous jockeys being Eddie Maple and Angel Cordero. It must have been a bitter sweet experience for his trainer. Nijinsky's Secret had been sold to influential Canadian owner Mrs John A. McDougald who had been looking for a horse of this kind. All her horses were trained in Canada by Kent Stirling and Hirsch knew that Canada was where Nijinsky's Secret would be heading no matter what the result.

Nijinsky's Secret was kept back behind the leaders Folge and Bottled Water but started his run in the backstretch, earlier than Hirsch would have liked. Nijinsky's Secret was in front fully four furlongs out but quickly drew away and had plenty left in a 3½ length victory. His time equalled the stakes record set by Noble Dancer five years before.

Nijinsky's Secret had provided a quick return for his new investors who had beaten Californian rivals to him by half an hour, but his first venture in Canada was a big disappointment. He was widest around the far turn in the eight furlong contest at Woodbine, and level with the winner Lord Elgin a furlong out, but faded to finish sixth, about 4½ lengths behind.

He was next sent to Saratoga for a raid on the big August prizes. He started in the Grade 3 Bernard Baruch Handicap over nine furlongs, again racing wide into the stretch and rallied well but failed by less than a length and a half to catch Pair of Deuces and finished fourth.

Fifteen days later he turned out for the Grade 3 Seneca Handicap over 13 furlongs, ridden by Jeff Fell who accompanied him in both his Saratoga forays. Moving up on the outside he finished fifth to Khatango, Nijinsky's son from the Damascus mare Penny Flight.

Perhaps a little bewildered about the obvious potential of the spring being unfulfilled in the summer, Stirling took Nijinsky's Secret back to Canada and began to try and analyse the problem and to sort it out. A month after the Seneca Nijinsky's Secret ran in a nine furlong allowance at Woodbine on a sloppy dirt track. He obviously did not like it one bit and he finished a distant last of four.

Stirling was, however, getting to know his horse a little better. The problem the horse was having to contend with was a back muscle ailment, a cure for which has still not really been found to this day. Stirling realised that Nijinsky's Secret was a horse who needed a little time between races and that he needed an extraordinary amount of warming up – some three-quarters of an hour trotting around – before he went to post for each race.

The new programmes were evidently having some effect by the beginning of October when Nijinsky's Secret reappeared in the twelve furlong Jockey Club Stakes, a Grade 2 race on turf. Although the going was yielding, Nijinsky's Secret, unhurried early on, came readily on the outside around the final bend and finished with great determination to beat all but the champion Frost King.

The Rothmans International was not quite such an occasion. The yielding 13 furlong course, against some of the best horses two continents could provide, was not to Nijinsky's Secret's liking at this stage. He finished seventh to Majesty's Prince and Thunder Puddles.

Nijinsky's Secret made two starts at Calder in December but it had been a long season. He managed a fourth place finish in an 8½ furlong allowance and was running on steadily at the end. It had been a satisfactory start, seeing as he had been off the course for a month and was in unfamiliar surroundings. However, twelfth place in Nijinsky's Secret's second start baffled and concerned Stirling. The horse now came down with severe muscle spasms after the race which no one could explain. He had also thrown a splint after the Rothmans. Nijinsky's Secret was given four months off the track and, during the winter, his training routines were taken back to scratch and turned upside down. At his West Palm Beach farm Stirling was able to formulate a way of training his horse that was so different from any other that, had he not been on private grounds, it would surely have upset those also wishing to use the same stretch of track. Stirling had discovered that it took Nijinsky's Secret's muscles some time to relax. While his father worked with the colt an hour and a half every day walking, trotting and galloping, Stirling devised an interval training scheme for Nijinsky's Secret to prepare him for his races during 1983. When worked, Nijinsky's Secret would go two furlongs the right way round the track then slow down to a walk for a few minutes. Then he would be turned around and breezed another quarter of a mile the wrong way and then work the final quarter. On courses where there were no training track facilities Nijinsky's Secret would have to improvise but he had proved himself an adaptable horse.

Whatever caused the back problems of Nijinsky's Secret, which are with him still today, Stirling's interval training certainly had an effect. At the end of 1982 Nijinsky's Secret had been rated 12 lb behind Perrault and 10 lb behind John Henry, the leading grass specialists of that year. But 1983 would see Nijinsky's Secret rather closer than that.

Nijinsky's Secret started over 36/1 for the Grade 2 Bougainvillea Handicap at Hialeah over 9½ furlongs on 9 April; he would never start at those odds again. Stirling had intended it as a preparatory race for a shot at the Grade 1 Hialeah Turf Cup but Nijinsky's Secret turned it into an impressive and substantial victory. Stirling instructed Jose Velez, jr, now Nijinsky's Secret's regular partner, not to press the horse too early but to let him make his run in the straight.

The field was a tough one, including Thunder Puddles who had finished second in the Rothmans, when Nijinsky's Secret was seventh, and also the experienced stakes horses Super Sunrise, Field Cat, Data Swap and the recent Irish import Day Is Done. Nijinsky's Secret was well placed behind Fabiano and Day Is Done who battled for the lead. He saved ground and despite one anxious moment when it looked like he would be trapped on the rail, Nijinsky's Secret slipped through on the inside about a furlong out and drew away to win by 1¼ lengths from Data Swap, Super Sunrise and Field Cat. Thunder Puddles finished tenth. The time was only three fifths of a second outside the course record.

Nijinsky's Secret had given Stirling a pleasant surprise and also his first victory of 1983. But the trainer's patience had been rewarded and he had the satisfaction of knowing that what he was doing was right. Nijinsky's Secret had been walked and trotted up and down for 50 minutes before he went to the paddock; was then given a sponge down and kept moving. His rider Jose Velez then warmed him up for a mile. Such had been the impression given in the works Nijinsky's Secret put in before the race that clocker Ted Tamer had been forced to admit to the Press that Nijinsky's Secret had worked "tremendous" on the turf. Few, if any, took notice of the prophecy.

Nijinsky's Secret was bang on course for the Turf Cup over twelve furlongs twelve days later. Ten opposed him in the Grade 1 event, including his fellow top weights, the European Group 1 winner Pelerin and Field Cat, out for revenge. Contrary to his previous style of running Nijinsky's Secret took the lead before the first of the three turns. He had broken fastest and Velez took the lead when no one wanted to take it from him. Despite being under pressure all the way and surrendering the lead briefly to Fray Star, Nijinsky's Secret resumed command, repelled the challenge of Discovered inside the final furlong to win by half a length. The time was, again, three fifths of a second slower than the course record, held by The Bart. This time Nijinsky's Secret had only had thirty minutes warming up prior to the race. He had had only one piece of work beforehand – three furlongs the wrong way and half a mile the right. The rest of the time Kent Stirling's father got on Nijinsky's Secret for 20 minutes and warmed him up to a long slow gallop, asking him nothing.

Nijinsky's Secret was sent back to Canada, though only temporarily, following his Grade 1 success. He was given almost two months off before starting favourite, despite carrying top weight of 126 lb (giving 7 lb and more away) in the Grade 3 King Edward Gold Cup over nine furlongs at Woodbine. On the firm track Nijinsky's Secret equalled the course record set by L'Enjoleur. He had 90 minutes warming up this time: walking for 20 minutes, trotting for 20 minutes, then bathed and blanketed before going through to the paddock. While the other runners were parading to the post Nijinsky's Secret was warmed up by Velez by trotting and cantering a mile. In the race he was away smartly and took a brief early lead but dropped back a little behind the leaders in the backstretch before beginning his run around the far turn. He opened up a furlong out and had 2½ lengths over Determinant at the line.

As a preparatory race for the Budweiser Arlington Million Nijinsky's Secret was next posted for the Grade 2 Bernard Baruch Handicap at Saratoga. He was top weight by 7 lb but had a rough passage just before the straight which knocked the stuffing out of him. Eventually he finished fifth to Fray Star, whom he had defeated easily in the Turf Cup.

On 28 August Nijinsky's Secret took on a crack field in the Budweiser Million over ten furlongs at Arlington Park . . . John Henry, Hush Dear, Thunder Puddles, Majesty's Prince, European representatives Tolomeo, Muscatite, Bold Run, Be My Native and The Noble Player, plus the European exiles Erin's Isle, Trevita and The Wonder. Quite a task. Nijinsky's Secret ran a brilliant race in his own right. He had given Stirling a few anxious moments during the week, with a high white blood cell count and attacks of colic, but had impressed in his work outs before the race. He was now solidly regarded as the pacesetter but this was in fact a role only lately taken on by the big chestnut.

Nijinsky's Secret took the lead, holding the rail, from the start. Tolomeo was settled by Pat Eddery just behind him with John Henry going very easily farther back. The pace dropped dramatically after the first two furlongs and John Henry ranged up to dispute the lead with Nijinsky's Secret. The big battalions were gathering and in the sudden upsurge in the pace they left the rest of the high-class field for dead. Between the three, Nijinsky's Secret, John Henry and Tolomeo they executed one of the most breathtaking final quarter miles ever witnessed. Straightening up around the final turn Nijinsky's Secret still held the lead on the rails with John Henry outside him. Tolomeo was biding his time to pounce and suddenly Nijinsky's Secret came away from the rail and the English horse was through. John Henry battled on all the way up the straight to defeat Nijinsky's Secret but saw Tolomeo too late and the Newmarket horse had won by a neck, Nijinsky's Secret half a length back in third and the rest of the fourteen horse field out with the washing.

After this race Nijinsky's Secret was given a well deserved five week lay off. He returned to Woodbine for the Jockey Club Stakes over ten furlongs in which he had been second the previous year. He stayed off the lead and came around the outside into the straight, challenged a furlong out and drew clear to win by 1¼ lengths hand ridden. He stayed at Woodbine for the Rothmans International. He ran second for the early part of the race behind Half Iced with Thunder Puddles just behind. For eleven of the 13 furlongs it stayed that way but behind, steadily making headway through the yielding ground, was the French filly All Along, fresh from her Arc de Triomphe success and heading for the Horse of The Year honours. She won easily. Nijinsky's Secret finished a creditable fourth, beaten only three lengths.

The race had taken a great deal out of Nijinsky's Secret, along with the recurring colic attacks which kept him out of several of his intended races during the year, and he had a nine week break before the winter campaign in Florida. On 23 December he beat Open Call over 8½ furlongs at Calder conceding 5 lb in a preparatory race for the W. L. McKnight Handicap. Nijinsky's Secret had had a different build up that day. On the main track he had been walked for five minutes, trotted for ten minutes and then galloped for three-quarters of a mile. He was taken back to the stable, bathed and then given a light warm up in the post parade and ran a brilliant race.

The American public did not have to wait long into the New Year to see Nijinsky's Secret again. He lined up with ten others as the odds on favourite for Calder's Grade 2 W. L. McKnight Handicap over twelve furlongs. He was top weight by 7 lb over the next in the betting, the ex-English Pelerin.

After Nijinsky's Secret had held the lead to the first turn, it was possibly a surprise to Jose Velez, jr, to find Four Bases, receiving 12 lb, heading him. Intent upon not allowing his horse to be caught up in a speed duel Velez settled Nijinsky's Secret behind the new leader content to sit there until the mile mark had been passed. When Velez let Nijinsky's Secret go the result was decisive. Nijinsky's Secret had no difficulty in thrusting Four Bases aside in the straight and had gone well clear before Don Menzotti (receiving 10 lb) could conjure up any sort of run. As ever with Nijinsky's Secret there was a story behind the success. In a not dissimilar repetition of the attack immediately before the Arlington Million, Nijinsky's Secret had been struck down by colic the night before.

Nijinsky's Secret was off the course for six weeks before he reappeared in the Miami Lakes at Hialeah over 1½ miles. This was a preparatory race for a tilt at a second Hialeah Turf Cup. Top weight by 8 lb Nijinsky's Secret was sent away as the long odds on favourite over a field of ten and won comfortably by two lengths, repelling the occasional challenge and barely turning a hair in the process.

The Hialeah Turf Cup followed ten days later. For the third time in 1984 Nijinsky's Secret faced ten opponents; for the third time he claimed the prize. This time, however, it was not without a fight. For the entire twelve furlongs Nijinsky's Secret was involved in a battle with Four Bases and, as in the McKnight, Nijinsky's Secret had to allow the other colt to go to the front and raced within half a length of him. For a brief spell first one had his head in front and then the other but it was going into the final furlong that Nijinsky's Secret, giving the other horse 13 lb, really threw down the gauntlet. There was nothing in it until, just before the wire, Nijinsky's Secret changed his lead to his left and snatched the US $136,650 prize by a nose. It was four lengths back to the third horse Tonzarun and the time was exceptional, considering that it had rained enough for the other turf event to be switched to the dirt track. As ever, Nijinsky's Secret had experienced the preparation unique to himself before the Turf Cup: three-quarters of an hour before he was due to leave for the paddock Nijinsky's Secret was walked for 25 minutes, ridden and trotted for 15 minutes, walked for a further five, given a second bath and was on his way.

Now the weight was beginning to compromise Nijinsky's Secret's tilt at the very top turf races. He was assigned 126 lb for the Americana Handicap on 4 July at Calder; 10 lb more than the second weighted horse Discovered. He had been off the track for almost four and a half months with leg trouble, which besets so many with Raise A Native blood.

Nijinsky's Secret set off in front but, as with Four Bases, he allowed Bold Frond to take it up at the first turn but confidently regained the lead by a head in the straight and ran out a 3½ length winner over Ronbra (received 10 lb) in a time only one and three fifths seconds slower than the course record.

What had threatened in the spring races occurred in the ten furlong Grade 1 Arlington Handicap, Nijinsky's Secret's "prep" race for the Million. Nijinsky's Secret was caught in a dangerous speed duel. Top weight by 8 lb he found himself in a field with other horses of early speed and one of them, Explosive Bid, led the field passing the stands for the first time with Nijinsky's Secret settled in third place. Halfway up the backstretch Nijinsky's Secret engaged Explosive Bid and it was a battle all the way to the furlong pole. Having dispatched that horse there was no time left for Nijinsky's Secret to renew his effort to repel the late challenge of Who's For Dinner who bested Nijinsky's Secret by only half a length receiving no less than 18 lb.

Nijinsky's Secret was not to win again but he was not to be disgraced. As ever he made the early pace in the Arlington Million, the race in which he had been third the previous year, but was soon content to allow the English classic filly Royal Heroine, now trained in California, to prompt the pace. This time when Nijinsky's Secret drifted out in the final furlongs it was John Henry who took the advantage and it was he who ran out the winner from Royal Heroine while Nijinsky's Secret was just run out of third money by a nose by Kentucky Derby winner Gato del Sol.

Four weeks later Nijinsky's Secret was back in Canada to contest a nine furlong allowance race in preparation for the Rothmans International. Again carrying top weight and starting way odds on, Nijinsky's Secret allowed Gun Carriage to make the early pace and came on the outside to challenge in the straight. He failed by a head.

After leading for eleven of the 13 furlongs in the Rothmans International on 21 October, Nijinsky's Secret tamely resigned his place to Majesty's Prince, fading to finish fifth. Nijinsky's Secret had had enough for the season. He was named Champion Canadian Turf Horse, as he had been in 1983, although he had not actually won in that country and was rated fourth amongst the turf males in the United States to John Henry.

At the beginning of 1985 it was announced that Nijinsky's Secret had been retired and would stand at Beaconsfield Farm just inside the New Circle Road in Lexington, alongside his paternal half brother Alezan Dancer. At a fee of US$15,000 live foal, this classy and ultra-consistent horse must represent a bargain.

Maruzensky

Not many English Derby winners domiciled in the United States can claim to have sired a Japanese Champion. Conceivably Maruzensky ranks with the very best of Nijinsky's sons and, had he been standing at stud in the West, could possibly have been the son to succeed the father. The first of Nijinsky's progeny to race in Japan, Maruzensky had to be rated amongst the most brilliant of champions in the last decade.

In 1973 the unraced Buckpasser mare Shill, a daughter of champion Quill, was bought at Keeneland November Sales for US $300,000 by Heron Bloodstock on behalf of Mr Z. Hashimoto, carrying a three parts brother to the then yearling, later classic winning, Caucasus. The resultant produce, the brown colt Maruzensky, can be regarded as the Japanese equivalent of Golden Fleece: an undefeated champion. Unlike Golden Fleece, Maruzensky was a champion Group 1 winning juvenile but never had the chance to win a Derby at three. But both had careers curtailed by injury, though Maruzensky has not suffered Golden Fleece's fate at stud.

Maruzensky also had twice as many races as Golden Fleece. He started his career on 9 October 1976 when he won a newcomers race by a distance over six furlongs on turf at Nakayama. He was ridden by S. Nakano Watari, who was to ride the colt in all his races. Twenty-one days later he duplicated his success with another score over six furlongs (on turf) at Nakayama, this time by nine lengths from Shiyada Etsuse.

By 21 November he had travelled to Tokyo to claim the eight furlong (turf) Fuchu Sansai Stakes, though this time by only a nose. However, Hongou, his trainer, evidently knew the capabilities of his colt and had not instructed Watari to be too insistent. On 12 December Maruzensky returned to Nakayama for what was, with hindsight, the highlight of his career, the Group 1 Asahi Hai Sansai Stakes. The going was good and the presence of Maruzensky had caused only five horses to challenge him. The result could not have been more emphatic. Another distance win, this time over Hinshi Suphido, the horse which he had only defeated by a nose in the Fuchu Sansai. In the process Maruzensky smashed the course record time of one minute 34.4 for 1,600 m. He was instantly acclaimed Japanese Champion Two-Year-Old colt.

To a certain extent Maruzensky's career as a three-year-old was inevitably to be an anti-climax. The Japanese classics were barred to foreign bred horses. Unfortunately for Maruzensky those horses conceived abroad were also embraced in this exclusion. Though a move was at foot to redress this situation it would come too late for Maruzensky and others like him. So, the only race for which Maruzensky could aim was the Arima Kinen. Japan's major race for three- and four-year-olds, it is the equivalent of a King George & Queen Elizabeth Stakes or an Arc de Triomphe.

However, Maruzensky suffered recurring lameness. Despite this and despite one of the worst winters on record when the Japanese stud farms were buried in anything up to six feet in snow, Maruzensky appeared on 22 January at Chukyo to win a three-year-old race by 2½ lengths from Jiyou Kuitsukirih. But, he did not reappear again until 7 May when he won another three-year-old race at Tokyo, this time by seven lengths.

Maruzensky began his build up seriously for the Arima on 26 June at Nakayama when he won the stakes race, the Nihontapa Shou, by seven lengths in heavy going. The nine furlongs was the furthest he had been asked to travel. For the third successive time Maruzensky carried top weight against his three-year-old contemporaries.

A month later he was put on dirt for the first time, over six furlongs at Sapporo in the Tankyori Stakes. It was also the first time he had met older horses but that evidently did not trouble the Nijinsky colt. He won by ten lengths in record time from Hinshi Suphido who must have been glad to see the metaphorical back of Maruzensky as much as he must have hated the literal view.

But that was the last trip to the races for the hot ante-post favourite for the Arima, subsequently won by the leading older horse Tenpointo. Maruzensky was syndicated for stud at a record equivalent of £500,000 in 1978.

Quite how Maruzensky would have fared if Shill had not gone to a Japanese destination at that sale is, of course, conjecture but there is nothing to say that he would not have done equally well anywhere else. He was certainly a distance in front of anything Japan could pitch against him. There was no lull in the meteoric transition between racecourse and stud. Maruzensky's first foals arrived in 1979 and included the Japanese St Leger (Group 1) winner Horisky. The second crop included Group 1 winning juvenile Nishinosky who was weighted second on the Japanese Two-Year-Old Handicap. In 1982, Maruzensky was the leading juvenile sire (money won) echoing Green Dancer in Europe and following closely in his own sire's hoofprints. But this was not to be unexpected. Maruzensky was a true champion by any standards.

CHAPTER 2

An Underrated Juvenile Sire

Charting the reasons behind Nijinsky's underplayed success as a sire of two year olds

Nijinsky was a champion two-year-old. In light of his later and greater triumphs and in assessing him as a sire many critics seem to lose sight of this fact. Nijinsky was not only a champion two-year-old but an unbeaten one and one who never looked like being beaten. There was, and still is, no reason why Nijinsky should not be capable of siring good juvenile winners – as indeed he has done, but this somehow tends to be overshadowed by those two-year-olds' later performances. The best of champion racehorses are good two-year-olds, a high-class or unbeaten juvenile season is part and parcel of the make up of a true champion of champions.

The facts speak for themselves. From 243 winners Nijinsky had 86 individual two-year-old winners; and no less than 20 which won at two years did not win in later life, including the class Cherry Hinton, Gorytus, Mixed Applause, Silky, Western Symphony and Vidalia. In the 1970s, and into the 1980s, the breeding world had an increasing tendency to regard Nijinsky wholly as an influence for stamina, and not one to be expected to sire precocious horses and those with exceptional (black type) ability. In the past few years it has been the fashion to keep promising Nijinsky juveniles for their three-year-old season, probably giving them only one or perhaps two outings as two-year-olds. However, the two-year-olds that have been trained have often proved themselves capable of holding their own at the highest level.

Nijinsky of course, himself made five appearances as a two-year-old and triumphed in all of them. We recall that he made his first appearance in July 1969 and won a six furlong maiden race easily. He followed this up with an impressive display in the Group 3 Railway Stakes cantering home by five lengths from the subsequent Irish 2,000 Guineas winner Decies. Next it was a three length romp in the Anglesey Stakes and he repeated his success over Decies in the eight furlong Beresford Stakes.

It was then time to come to England. After his comfortable and deeply impressive three length win over Recalled, Nijinsky was immediately installed as the clear winter favourite for the 2,000 Guineas and Derby. The rest is history. In his unbeaten, barely extended, first reason Nijinsky was the only winner of any of the Triple Crown races to win as many as five for years before and none since.

Nijinsky was the product of two champion middle distance (by American standards) performers who could obviously produce champion two-year-olds (Minsky was to follow Nijinsky's example in Ireland). Nijinsky was not long in proving he could do the same. From his very first crop came a Group 1 winner and, in 1979, he culminated his performance as a juvenile sire by being the leading two-year-old sire in France. The one he had to thank for that was the scintillating Princesse Lida. She was only one of 22 juvenile stakes and Group winners Nijinsky has sired to the end of 1984 and she has quite a supporting cast. In looking closer at her exploits and that of her fellow champions and highly rated two-year-olds it will be seen that she was no "flash in the pan".

Princesse Lida

Princesse Lida crowned a memorable season in France in 1979 for Nijinsky by attaining the Champion Juvenile Filly title. Indeed, if her 3 lb sex allowance is taken into consideration, Princesse Lida would also be the champion two-year-old ahead of Dragon, Nureyev and her paternal half brother Nice Havrais. Her exploits that year, added to those of Nice Havrais and the Group 3 placed Bev Bev, combined to place Nijinsky top of the Juvenile Sires List in France in 1979.

Foaled on 4 February 1977, Princesse Lida was the first foal of her dam, the Habitat mare Princess Lee who had been a high-class two-year-old winner herself, being also placed in the Group 1 Prix Robert Papin and Prix Morny at that age. A bright bay, with her sire's head and star and one near hind sock, Princesse Lida was trained for Jacques Wertheimer (like Green Dancer) by Alec Head.

She made her first appearance in the listed Prix Yacowlef at Deauville on 5 August. This race is very similar to the Acomb Stakes at York at around the same time, in that it encourages the very best bred and promising of many hitherto unraced juveniles to make their first appearance. They knew Princesse Lida was coming for only five opposed her, all fillies and all were left trailing four lengths in her wake strung out like a line of washing hung out to dry. There were nine lengths between first and fourth. Quite clearly this was a flying machine, clocking just over 59 seconds for the five furlongs on very soft going yet not even having to be asked a question.

The performance had been impressive but it was still a giant step to the Group 1 Prix Morny run over six furlongs at Deauville 14 days later. Princesse Lida started only fourth favourite in the field of ten, behind the Coventry Stakes victor Varingo (who had defeated the Nijinsky Irish two-year-old flyer London Bells in the process), the Prix Robert Papin victor Choucri plus Comtesse de Loir's half sister by Nonoalco, Firyal, who had made a deep impression in her newcomers race a little more recently than Princesse Lida.

Varingo broke very smartly and took the lead from Prince Dias before the first three furlongs were completed. With two furlongs to run two English colts, Varingo and Durandal, were ahead of affairs. However as soon as Firyal made her challenge on the outside Durandal's faded away. Meanwhile inside the final furlong Freddie Head asked Princesse Lida to go through a gap between Durandal and Choucri who had been close behind the leading pair all the way. However Durandal hung to his left and Princesse Lida thought twice about trusting the narrow gap to stay open. By the time she had made up her mind it had closed. However with just 300 yards to run and when it looked like Varingo was home and dry Princesse Lida went smoothly through her second chance at an opening and went after the leader up the rails. Varingo had no more to give and the filly shot past in the final yards to score by 1½ lengths with Firyal a similar distance in third, Durandal leading home the others at a respectful distance.

Princesse Lida had not had a hard race and had succeeded where her mother had failed in her quest for juvenile Group 1 honours. She had run very green in not going for the first gap that had opened for her.

It had been rumoured that she would be put away until the top fillies race, the Criterium des Pouliches on Arc day, but the Heads knew that they had an exceptional two-year-old filly. Princesse Lida was therefore sent out to tackle the colts again in the Prix de la Salamandre (Group 1) run at Longchamp over seven furlongs on 23 September.

She was opposed again by Firyal and Choucri, and also by the English raider Teacher's Pet, plus Try to Smile, a distinctly unlucky loser of the Robert Papin.

Princesse Lida was settled into fourth place at the beginning of the straight but settled the race much earlier than she had the Morny. She burst through a gap between Green Dancer's daughter Bold Green and Teacher's Pet two furlongs out and the race was over. Teacher's Pet kept on but Choucri stole past her 50 yards from home to snatch second place by half a length, some

1½ lengths behind the cruising Princesse Lida. Teacher's Pet had some trouble with a slipping saddle which caused her to interfere with Firyal's pacemaker Koboko, the placing on these two ultimately being reserved.

Instead of heading for the Criterium des Pouliches Princesse Lida was pointed at the eight furlong Grand Criterium, which had not been won by a filly since the Criterium des Pouliches had been instituted. That race was won in Princesse Lida's absence by Green Dancer's daughter Aryenne, of whom Princesse Lida was to see a great deal more in 1980.

In attempting a hat-trick of Group 1 wins over the colts, Princesse Lida was going for a feat only achieved by four fillies (Hula Dancer, Appollonia, Bella Paola and Silver Cloud) since the war. Her career so far had been ominously similar to the French 1,000 Guineas and Oaks winner Appollonia and also to the 1,000 Guineas victress Hula Dancer. Both had also been unbeaten at this point and had been successful in the Prix Yacowlef, while Princesse Lida had now won the Prix Morny, like Appollonia, and Prix de la Salamandre like Hula Dancer.

Princesse Lida started odds on in a field of eight to achieve that feat. With hindsight it was a formidable field which she was so confidently expected to beat. She was the only female representative against the likes of Choucri, In Fijar, the subsequent French 2,000 Guineas winner, and Nijinsky's son Nice Havrais. More importantly, the going that October day at Longchamp was heavy in the extreme and it was notable that other American breds completely failed to act on it. In Fijar's pacemaker, Dragon, a son of Vitiges's sire Phaeton, ridden by a work rider having his first ride of the season at Longchamp, set a strong gallop with the rest of the field following at a discreet distance. All the spectators confidently expected to see either the pacemaker come back to his field or the field increase their speed and get closer to him. He did not . . . and neither did they until it was all over. In Fijar and Star Way kept Dragon in their sights until the distance and then both dropped out quickly. Princesse Lida meanwhile was obviously anything but happy on the ground and could not find that blistering turn of foot she had shown on the better going of previous victories. At the line she was 3¾ lengths adrift of the pacemaker having been caught in the final strides for second place by Nice Havrais – whose jockey, Phillippe Pacquet, had been guilty of watching Princesse Lida too closely and confidently expecting Dragon to come back to his field.

Not only could Princesse Lida not cope with the ground but possibly eight furlongs was as far as she wanted to go in it at that stage. Dragon never again did anything to suggest that his run was a gauge to his true merit and it was perhaps as big a surprise as the race itself when he was placed top of the French Free Handicap on 9 st 10 lb, 1 lb clear of Nice Havrais but also of the unbeaten Nureyev with Princesse Lida rated 1 lb below them. Ominously breathing down the back of her neck was the unbeaten Aryenne, a first crop daughter of Nijinsky's son Green Dancer. However it was quite a triumph for Nijinsky with a son, a daughter and a granddaughter rated in the top five. On good going Princesse Lida would doubtless have claimed the Handicap Optional for herself without having to recourse to the filly allowance.

On the face of it Princesse Lida looked as if the future would lie at distances around a mile. Nijinsky's best distance was around 10–12 furlongs and Princesse Lida came from an able sprinter and a fast female line. She was confidently expected to make a first rate miler at the very least and, but for that infamous Longchamp going in October, she would have been hailed as another Hula Dancer or Bella Paola. In the event Princesse Lida was never tested over distances in excess of a mile in her second season.

On the face of it Princesse Lida's three-year-old season was a disappointment. After the scintillating triumphs of her two-year-old year anything less could not be regarded as much else. If it were not for a certain Green Dancer filly by the name of Aryenne all would have been well at the onset of her three-year-old career. Princesse Lida followed in the footsteps of another leading Head filly, Riverqueen, by heading for the French 1,000 Guineas via the eight furlong Prix de la Grotte (Group 3) at Longchamp in April. Odds on, Princesse Lida took the lead over the eight filly field with 1½ furlongs to go and looked all over the winner but Aryenne challenged and, though hanging, the Green Dancer filly just got up to score by a neck. Pompoes was 2½ lengths in third. Aryenne certainly had the scope for longer distances and though it had been a good performance by Princesse Lida first time out the writing was on the wall about her stamina.

She and Aryenne started in the French 1,000 Guineas accompanied by only four other fillies including the lightly raced Safita and Teacher's Pet. This was the last attempt at eight furlongs for Princesse Lida and just as it appeared obvious that she did not stay Aryenne clearly was looking for a longer trip. Aryenne came through at the distance and ran on to defeat Safita by a short neck, Princesse Lida holding her place 1½ lengths behind. In the French Oaks Aryenne had to give best to Mrs Penny by only a short head. Princesse Lida had been abreast of the first two in the Guineas with 150 yards to run but her stamina just ran out in the end.

That race was on 4 May. Princesse Lida was not seen out again until 29 June when, on very soft going, she was clearly unhappy behind Luck Of The Draw, Hilal, Suvero and Kilijaro in the Group 3 Prix de la Porte Maillot. Ya Zaman won the race but was disqualified.

On 3 August Princesse Lida was ignominiously blinkered for her fourth outing of the season. The combination of that and the holding going at

Deauville put paid to any chance she had in the 6½ furlongs Prix Maurice de Gheest (Group 2) though she started second favourite that day. Boitron won by a short neck from champions Moorestyle and Kilijaro.

Princesse Lida's dam Princess Lee had trained off very early in her three-year-old career and had a much less successful second season than her daughter. Alec Head persisted with Princesse Lida and she rewarded him with a victory in the listed seven furlong contest, the Prix du Pin at Longchamp, over Safita and Teacher's Pet. Lightly raced, Princesse Lida made just one more appearance, finishing sixth to Moorestyle in heavy going at Longchamp on 26 October in the Group 1 Prix de la Foret.

Though Princesse Lida had appeared to have had a disappointing second season she did win a listed contest and place in a classic and was raced against the best sprinters Europe could offer throughout. She was often compromised by heavy going with which she had no means to cope. After her dazzling juvenile performances, however, her three-year-old career did not live up to the brilliance of her two-year-old season. If she had she would truly have been a filly in a million.

Cherry Hinton

Nijinsky's other European champion filly was in a rather different mould altogether. Built anything but like a greyhound, Cherry Hinton was as unlikely a champion two-year-old filly as one could expect. She was built and bred for the Oaks trip and gave the impression that she would do much better in her second season. The fact that she was good enough to be acclaimed champion juvenile filly and that she was so compromised by the virus that her three-year-old season was virtually non existent, makes one wonder just what might have been.

Cherry Hinton was foaled on 7 April 1975 so it is not as if the maturity of an early foaling date gave her an advantage over her contemporaries of that spring. Her dam, the Romulus mare Popkins, had won six races including the Princess Elizabeth Stakes (Group 2), Sun Chariot Stakes (Group 2), Prix des Lilas (listed), Prix de la Nonette (Group 3) and Prix de Psyche (Group 3) and also finished third in the French 1,000 Guineas, none of which were two-year-old contests. She had bred nothing of note beforehand and has not since. Cherry Hinton was her fourth foal. The rest of the family showed a preponderance of staying blood.

Owned and bred by the Moller family, who were such sturdy supporters of Nijinsky at that time (before the current policy of restricting their mares to generally home based stallions), Cherry Hinton was put into training in the care of Harry Wragg.

Cherry Hinton was a striking two-year-old, big and strong and very attractive and very easy to recognise. Immediately impressive to anyone who saw her, Cherry Hinton was given a gentle introduction to the racecourse on 6 August in a six furlong contest at Haydock. Tenderly ridden by Tony Murray she coasted into third place to Bolak in a field of twelve.

Her next start was a maiden race. It was probably the best maiden race of the season. Cherry Hinton found herself racing on her own on the far side of the course, the width of the track away from her nearest rival. She had started favourite and was well clear of her field but was unaware of John de Coombe on completely the opposite side of the racecourse. John de Coombe got up to win. At the time the result seemed disappointing but Cherry Hinton had won the race as far as she was concerned and it had been a good performance for such a big filly having only her second outing. It looked rather better when the winner went on to defeat the likes of Super Concorde and Kenmare in the Group 1 Prix de la Salamandre and when the third horse, Formidable, carried off the Group 1 Middle Park and Group 2 Mill Reef Stakes. Some maiden race!

Cherry Hinton made her third start a winning one. She was pointed for the six furlong Tadcaster Stakes at York on the 1 September in a select field of six. She was vying for favouritism with the Lowther Stakes third (to Enstone Spark) Be Sweet. Be Sweet made the running and Piggott seemed so at ease on Cherry Hinton that it looked for a dangerous moment that he was letting the narrow favourite get away. Still he waited but for any anxious supporters the writing was on the wall for Be Sweet. Fully two furlongs out she was being vigorously ridden along while Cherry Hinton was merely cantering behind and the sight of that famous Piggott rear rising loftily in the air must have calmed many a fluttering heart. Just as many scribes thought that it was all too late Piggott let out an inch of rein and Cherry Hinton cruised past to win by a hard held neck without knowing she had been in a race. The winning margin gave no indication at all of Cherry Hinton's superiority.

Punters had taken note however. Cherry Hinton's next, and last, outing of her first season was the Group 3 Argos Star Fillies Mile (now the Hoover Fillies Mile) at Ascot on 23 September, the unofficial championship for staying fillies. Cherry Hinton was odds on in a field of eight, her greatest danger appearing to be the Acomb and May Hill Stakes victress Tartan Pimpernel, carrying the Royal colours borne with such distinction by her half sister Dunfermline. The other fillies comprised the second and third in the May Hill and all those who had finished so close to the other leading two-year old filly of 1977, Cistus, in the Waterford Candelabra.

Lady Abernant led for four furlongs but after that gave way to Pearl

Strand. Two furlongs out Fiordiligi was in front but Piggott was sitting ominously easily about two or three lengths behind. There was no noticeable command as Cherry Hinton lengthened her stride and smoothly went past the struggling leaders. She took the lead a furlong and a half out and drew right away in a common canter to register a long looking five length success over Tartan Pimpernel who had found it difficult to go the early pace and who stayed on to take second a length in front of Watch Out. The rest were well strung out. Despite the ease of her success Cherry Hinton had lowered the juvenile course record time for the round mile, held by the colt Adios and which had stood for five years.

The performance earned superlatives from all directions. Even the sometimes reserved *Timeform* ranked her victory with that of Noblesse in the *Timeform* Gold Cup, Soft Angels in the Royal Lodge and Cantelo in an earlier victory in the same race. On a line through the fourth filly Caraquenga, Cherry Hinton appeared some 10 lb better than anything the French could put up as opposition.

The two-year-old Cherry Hinton was very reminiscent of her sire at the same stage. She was so well developed that she could easily have been mistaken for a three-year-old, much like the impression her sire made when he came to England to claim the Dewhurst some eight years before. Additionally, the further Cherry Hinton went at two the better she ran and high hopes were held for the Oaks. She was very much bred to be a twelve furlong filly, but on her performance at Ascot the sky was the only limit and Cherry Hinton was pointed at the eight furlong 1,000 Guineas early in 1978.

On the Free Handicap Cherry Hinton was weighted 5 lb ahead of any other filly, that being the Irish Sookera. Even more importantly, perhaps, she was only 4 lb adrift of the champion colt Try My Best which at that time was being talked about as somewhere in the region of a Nijinsky. With the 3 lb filly allowance Cherry Hinton was in truth rated only 1 lb below him.

Bad luck as much as anything else contributed to the disappointing second season. There were plenty of excuses for her second place finish behind Shapina in the Fred Darling Stakes, Group 3, at Newbury over an extended seven furlongs in mid-April. Cherry Hinton badly needed the race and reportedly blew up. It did not dismay Lester Piggott who was unusually optimistic about her chances at Newmarket. The seven furlong Newbury track was decidedly too sharp and Cherry Hinton looked almost too big and well beforehand. She simply dwarfed her four rivals which were made up of an old adversary in Lady Abernant, the future Oaks winner Fair Salinia and top sprinter Smarten Up plus Shapina. Slow to come to hand Cherry Hinton was still evidently a little backward.

By the time Newmarket came around Cherry Hinton was already carrying a virus though that was not apparent until after the race, as is common with many viruses. In it she finished fourth to Enstone Spark, Fair Salinia, whom she had defeated so easily at Newbury, and Seraphima. The illness also caused her to miss the Oaks. She made her reappearance at Royal Ascot and clearly needed the race when finishing close up third in the twelve furlong Group 2 Ribblesdale Stakes to Relfo and Be Sweet, who had been defeated so easily by Cherry Hinton the season before.

Then followed an abortive trip to Ireland for the Irish Guinness Oaks when a terrible journey over necessitated her withdrawal. It later transpired that she had injured her back at some point and this, combined with her appearance of having already run up very light, ensured a poor display in the Group 1 Yorkshire Oaks behind Fair Salinia who had got the Irish Oaks on a disqualification. Cherry Hinton was retired to stud.

Yet again, one can only wonder about what might have been had everything gone smoothly for Cherry Hinton in her second season. The illness which caused her to miss her prime objective, the Epsom Oaks, compromised the whole of the rest of her career. But, as her performance at Ascot as a juvenile showed, she was a worthy champion by any standards.

Bemissed

Nijinsky's second Group 1 winning filly, Bemissed, was probably the best two-year-old female representative of her sire to race in the United States until Folk Art. Though she made nine starts as a two-year-old and "only" won four of them, Bemissed ran consistently against the best, claimed her Grade 1 with a most tenacious performance and never finished worse than fourth.

Bemissed was the first foal of her stakes winning dam Bemis Heights, who was by Herbager. She was thus bred for distance and turf. Bemis Heights and her daughter were the best performers produced by the female line for some generations. A chestnut with a large star and thin stripe on her head Bemissed was foaled on 15 February 1980, just eight days after another notable Nijinsky two-year-old, Gorytus.

Homebred, Bemissed raced for James Ryan's Ryehill Stables and was trained by Woody Stephens. He had also conditioned Nijinsky's champion daughter De La Rose and planned a campaign for Bemissed similar to that filly.

Bemissed made her first start at Belmont in a six furlong dirt maiden event on 23 July when she ran second, showing early speed to the odds on favourite Cryptic who was no slouch herself. A fellow Nijinsky filly Dancing Lesson was a length behind her in third. Bemissed was learning fast and at Belmont on 1 August on a turf track, which she evidently preferred, she had a saunter around the seven furlongs to defeat seven rivals by no less than twelve lengths. She closed in on leader Whites Creek all of a sudden and was gone with the power of a jet engine. Bemissed had arrived.

However on 19 August Bemissed came up against Cryptic again. On a dirt track Cryptic was not about to allow the Nijinsky filly any room. Bemissed, this time starting favourite, was well to the fore throughout but weakened a little to finish third to Cryptic in the six furlong allowance event, beaten 1¼ lengths by the winner.

Bemissed then returned to her favourite grass surface for the Evening Out Stakes over eight furlongs at Belmont, the race in which De La Rose scored her first stakes win. Bemissed did not much like the yielding going and faded to finish third to Cryptic and stablemate National Banner.

Only 16 days later however, Bemissed chalked up her black type. She travelled to Woodbine to capture the Grade 3 Natalma Stakes over an eight furlong turf course – again on yielding going. She was away quickly, tracked the leader to the far turn, challenged around the final bend and drew away in the final furlong to score by 1¾ lengths from Hold Me Closer and collect Can $35,640 in the process. She then headed for Bowie and the Kindergarten Stakes on a fast dirt track over seven furlongs. It was anybodys race for second behind easy victress Singing Susan and Bemissed lost out by two noses making a bold late bid from the rear.

Returning to the grass for the nine furlong Grade 3 Miss Grillo Stakes at Aqueduct on 21 October, just five days after the Bowie event, Bemissed rallied down the backstretch and loomed up boldly to join the leaders in the straight and outlasted Cryptic in a battle royal. National Banner finished fourth.

Bemissed was on a high now. She travelled to Laurel for the Grade 1 Selima Stakes over 8½ furlongs. The only snags were that the race was run on dirt and that Singing Susan was in the field. In the event neither was a problem. For a purse of over US $240,000 it had been worth a try under any circumstances and Stephens had triumphed before with Dancealot, Smart Angle and Heavenly Cause, the last two claiming the prize en route to an Eclipse award. Singing Susan, a doubtful stayer, was reserved in the race, as was Bemissed. The difference was that Frank Lovato was sitting very comfortably on his Nijinsky filly while Rivera was nursing Singing Susan in front for she led into the stretch and weakened dramatically to finish next to last. Bemissed, on the other hand, came from behind at the entrance to the straight and once she was in front there was nothing that was going to get past. Her winning margin was an easy 3¼ lengths in front of 41/1 outsider

Icy Time. Apart from Singing Susan another notable runner back in the dust was National Banner.

It is just possible that had Bemissed been retired for the season on the strength of that Grade 1 win she might well have been in the firing line for an Eclipse award. But she was given one more outing that season, in the nine furlong Grade 1 Demoiselle on dirt, and had clearly had enough for the time being. She tired very early in the straight eventually finishing fourth to Only Queens, Gold Source and National Banner.

Despite this Bemissed was rated fourth top filly in the Experimental Free Handicap, 4 lb behind joint champions Landaluce and Princess Rooney, both outstanding fillies in any year. Bemissed had proved herself a tenacious and consistent individual. Never out of the first four and with enough speed to claim a Grade 1 two-year-old race on a surface far from her best.

Bemissed was not given an easy second season in the top flight in which she ran. In no less than 16 appearances she scored one success, in the Japan Racing Association Handicap over 8½ furlongs on turf at Laurel in September. She had, however, had a remarkably consistent season and finished third in the Kentucky Oaks to Princess Rooney and Bright Crocus on that dirt surface. She was also placed in the Grade 3 Gallorette and Anne Arundel Handicap and ran fourth in the Grade 1 Fantasy Stakes.

Though Bemissed's form did not quite match up to her juvenile performances she was undoubtedly a top-class two-year-old and well able to hold her own in top-class company. Throughout her career she was forever raced against the best and perhaps suffered as all horses do when there is severe competition inside one stable, because there are stablemates with just as strong claims to be in the best races.

Folk Art

It would not be a point of controversy to suggest that, in all probability, Folk Art was Nijinsky's best juvenile filly. It is a cause for surprise and, on the formbook, for disbelief, that she was not officially accorded the filly championship and an Eclipse award in 1984. Never has a case of a relatively minor injury cost so large a crown. For here it was not a matter of a horse not proving itself; Folk Art assuredly had and her form was undoubtedly the most consistent and spectacular compared with that of her rivals.

Folk Art was foaled on 29 March 1982, an own sister to Sportin' Life, another deeply impressive juvenile who did go on to gather other similar victories in later years. Sportin' Life was a seven and a half length winner of the Allegheny Stakes in 1980 and clocked up eight wins in all including five stakes contests. Their dam, the Round Table mare Homespun, was a stakes placed winner and was drawn to public attention in 1984 through another outstanding juvenile, Local Suitor. As a son of Homespun's daughter by Vaguely Noble, Home Love, Local Suitor was one of the best colts seen in England and was well to the fore in the epic battle for the William Hill Dewhurst Stakes, the race which decided the destination of the Free Handicap leadership.

Like Sportin' Life, Folk Art does not lack for size which, as with Cherry Hinton, made her two-year-old performances all the more meritorious. She has also proved her worth on a dirt surface and, should she follow De La Rose in preferring the more natural tracks, then Royal Heroine et al had better beware.

Inexperience was Folk Art's watchword in her first outing at Hollywood on 17 June over a fast five furlongs, surely on the short side even for a filly with such blazing speed. Indeed, carrying 1 lb overweight, Folk Art was taken off her feet early on but found her stride coming into the final straight. She finished with a very strong run which carried her to within two lengths of the winner, the favourite Winter's Love and only half a length behind Princess Cabrini who had the benefit of a previous outing.

Neil Drysdale then pointed his filly for a confidence booster, at Bay Meadows on 23 September. She had had a long rest after her trip to Hollywood and came to the races a fresh filly. It was, again, a fast dirt surface but this time over an extra furlong. Folk Art did not even have to grow warm. Cantering just behind the early leader Capture The Heart, the odds on favourite moved up to join that filly at the turn and smoothly opened up a considerable advantage in the straight. The official margin was eight lengths. Folk Art first, the rest nowhere.

Folk Art took the step into allowance company two weeks later at Santa Anita. Again, sent off at odds on, she was making her first attempt at a mile. Laffit Pincay had been reunited with her, having missed her easy victory, but it probably made no difference for there was no stopping Folk Art. Content to sit behind Sweet Caprice and Paisana, Pincay waited until they were turning for home before launching his filly. Striding out, Folk Art cruised past Pet Bird inside the furlong marker. Within the final eighth of a mile Folk Art's lead had extended to five lengths. Pet Bird had a further eleven lengths over Sweet Caprice. Folk Art's performance paled the following Anoakia Stakes into insignificance. That race was won by Wayward Pirate and both fillies were to meet in the very near future.

Folk Art was scheduled to meet Wayward Pirate in the Grade 1 Oak Leaf Stakes on 20 October, also at Santa Anita. The allowance winner was sent off odds on, the stakes winner at 4/1, second in the betting. It was a small but select field and included stakes victresses Fran's Valentine and Lady's

Secret, apart from Wayward Pirate. There was an extra half furlong to travel but it could have been four and a half for all the difference it made to Folk Art.

As others battled for the lead Folk Art sat back and laughed at them all the way to the post. She could win whenever she wanted, at whatever point she chose. For half a mile she waited and at the midway point of the race Folk Art became bored with playing with her rivals. With one swoop she had collared the leader Lady's Secret, disdainfully swept aside the game response of Pirate's Glow and the race was over barely as the striaght was sighted. Folk Art passed the post 4½ lengths in front of Pirate's Glow looking as if she could go round again. The six runners were strung out in respectful procession – 6½ lengths from Pirate's Glow to the third filly Wayward Pirate. In terms of the Eclipse award and the subsequent battles between Fran's Valentine and Outstandingly it is important to remember that Folk Art left Fran's Valentine standing by *over 14* lengths.

The first Breeders Cup series was to be held in 1984 and as a result it seemed doubly important for trainers to do well. Accordingly, Folk Art was pointed at the juvenile fillies event for Drysdale knew it was there for the taking. Then tragedy struck. The curb which developed on Folk Art's hock not only kept her away from Breeders Cup Day but also out of the fillies championship. In her absence a most unsatisfactory race ensued with the ultimate winner Fran's Valentine being disqualified in favour of Outstandingly. Fran's Valentine had beaten Outstandingly on merit for it was not that filly who had suffered as a result of Fran's Valentine's wayward course. Outstandingly later went on to win the Hollywood Startlet by 2¾ lengths over Fran's Valentine which still put Folk Art over ten lengths in front of the champion on the book. But, because Outstandingly was the only filly to claim two Grade 1 juvenile filly events, she got the all-important vote and gained the Eclipse Award. In the Experimental Handicaps she was rated a single pound above Folk Art and Fran's Valentine who, unbelievably, were assigned the same weighting, though in many polls Folk Art was the undisputed champion but not, unfortunately, on the one that mattered.

So, 1985 will be a fascinating year. It will, hopefully, prove that Folk Art's promise was for greater things to come though whether her future lies over grass or dirt only time and opportunity will show. One can only hope that she will have a second chance to be acclaimed the champion she obviously is. By the time this book has been published we shall know.

Gorytus

Of all Nijinsky's progeny and of racehorses in general, undoubtedly the one around which the most mystique has been woven is Gorytus. Quite what happened on that never to be forgotten day in October 1982 will probably never come to light. It was only some 18 months after the event that foul play has seriously been hinted at by someone close to the horse. But one thing is clear: that the Gorytus which ran in the William Hill Dewhurst on 15 October 1982 was not the Gorytus described by his trainer as "the best two-year-old I have ever seen". Major Dick Hern should be in a position to judge and is not one to eulogise unnecessarily.

Gorytus was the product of the third union between his parents. His dam, Glad Rags, had carried off the 1966 1,000 Guineas having had a successful two-year-old career in which she won the Railway Stakes (as did Nijinsky four years later) and placed second in the Royal Lodge Stakes. To previous unions with Nijinsky she had produced the multiple Group winner Terpsichorist, one of the best fillies on grass of her generation. Two years Terpsichorist's junior came Vaslava who never saw a racecourse and then Gorytus. Previously Glad Rags had produced the useful Mirthful Flirt and the dam of a Nijinsky stakes winner (Ultramate) in Gala Party. Gorytus took more after his sire than Terpsichorist and other of Glad Rags foals who mostly resembled herself.

Gorytus was a strapping and handsome bay colt (though erroneously described in the American Stud Book as a chestnut) whose coat gave off a gleam rarely achieved on many hides. Like most of Glad Rags's progeny he was home bred by Mr and Mrs Mills at their Hickory Tree Farm but, unlike them, he was trained in England.

The question was, could Gorytus run as well as he looked? By 5 pm on 17 August 1982 everyone knew that he could. Gorytus had gone to post with Willie Carson in the saddle for the listed Acomb Stakes, a recognised birthplace of potential champions, at York as 5/1 second favourite. Favoured in the betting was the experienced dual winning Salieri trained by Henry Cecil, who was later to win the Group 2 Mill Reef Stakes to complete a highly successful season in which, but for Gorytus, he would have been unbeaten. Salieri had won his previous outings by five and twelve lengths and he developed into probably the best seven furlong performer in England in 1983.

After this particular seven furlongs had been completed however, Salieri was looking very ordinary indeed. Gorytus was one of only four debutants in the field, which also included another son of Nijinsky in Brogan (ex Drumtop). But for Gorytus, Salieri would have won by three lengths and been acclaimed as a certain champion. Gorytus, however, left the racetrack earning the kind of accolades that only surefire wonder horses get and already being quoted as Guineas and Derby favourite and at seemingly ridiculously low odds. In storming home unchallenged by seven lengths Gorytus smashed the two-year-old course record by over a second.

Henry Cecil was known to consider Salieri as much the best of his 90-plus two-year-olds in the yard at the time. The last juvenile to have lowered a course record on his debut in this kind of class was Shergar and before him Mill Reef. Gorytus was clearly something special. On that one outing the hallowed *Timeform* bestowed a rating of 120 on the colt, which was clearly in advance of the likes of Mill Reef at the same stage.

The racing world buzzed with talk about Gorytus. His next appearance was awaited eagerly. It was a long time since a once-raced juvenile colt had captured the imagination so entirely. The public were treated to the next act in the racing play of the season when the star performer reappeared on 10 September at Doncaster.

It was a select field which opposed Gorytus in the Group 2 Laurent Perrier Stakes that day: All Systems Go, a course record holder himself and who had won his previous four races off the reel including the Group 3 Seaton Delaval Stakes and the Lanson Champagne Stakes at Goodwood over a class field; the crack sprinter, On Stage, confidently expected to make the West Ilsley flyer "go a bit"; Proclaim, who had won his previous two starts; and Top O' The North, who had been an impressive winner of the Champion Two-Year-Old Trophy.

Despite the assembled talent Gorytus was odds on to repeat his York success. Gorytus's performance made even those odds seem mighty generous. As he quickened, fully 2½ furlongs from home, Gorytus cruising had all his rivals off the bit and had them all beaten as soon as Willie Carson let out an inch of rein. It was an electrifying performance, as outstanding as one would ever see. The further they went the further Gorytus sprinted away and, despite the sheer effortlessness of this win, his time was only just outside the record and well above average. Had Carson pushed him out or the runners not been faced with a head on breeze that record too would surely have fallen.

Bookmakers thought so too and Gorytus was 5/1 for Epsom. No one could remember a colt being called as low as that since the days of Colombo and Bahram, some fifty years before. The colt had so mesmerised everyone who watched him that it is true to say that the Press, public and even his usually cautious connections, did get a little carried away. But in his two races Gorytus had created that kind of magical impression.

All the furore had made no adverse impression on Gorytus and he never turned a hair throughout the proceedings before or after the Doncaster race. This is a fact to note – as is also that that the horses he left struggling in his wake in both races came out again to capture important events.

But for some mysterious being of one form or another, Gorytus could well have been claimed the greatest two-year-old ever seen on a racecourse by the time he went into winter quarters. He might also have had a subsequent career as stunning and worthy of superlatives to equal with those early performances. Instead Gorytus, mainly from people speaking through their pockets, was a figure of derision and ridicule and labelled as ungenuine. Whatever happened to Gorytus in the Dewhurst, and undoubtedly something did happen, ruined as bright a career for good as any colt could possibly have had.

It is history that Gorytus did not win the William Hill Dewhurst and that Diesis became the first colt since Bayardo to complete the Middle Park/Dewhurst double. The odds on Gorytus trailed in some thirty lengths behind his opposition to all intents and purpose being pulled up in the process. He had looked magnificent beforehand, Diesis not being able to hold a candle to him, but before the runners had traversed a furlong on that nightmare day at Newmarket something was palpably amiss. By the time the runners were in the winning enclosure Gorytus was in a distressed and terrible state. Enquiries were held for weeks afterwards and nothing proven to be awry was published. However, Gorytus himself was clearly not to blame even if his superstar reputation had lost a little of its gleam.

What is certain is that whatever ailed Gorytus that day compromised the entirety of the remainder of his career. He made just three starts in England as a three-year-old, finishing a close fifth in the 2,000 Guineas and Waterford Crystal Mile and fourth in the Benson & Hedges Gold Cup behind Caerleon. Though creditable enough performances they were not of the standard expected of that two-year-old wonder. Shipped to the United States, Gorytus had just two runs there at the beginning of 1984 finishing a close second in the Royal Palm Handicap, obviously needing the race, and then fourth in the Grade 2 Bougainvillea Handicap. Gorytus was then purchased to stand alongside such celebrities as Kings Lake, Caerleon and Golden Fleece at Coolmore Stud in Ireland where his flawless looks and pedigree have ensured that he has been very well received.

Gorytus was in all probability not only Nijinsky's best two-year-old but also one of the best two-year-olds seen on British racecourses for many years. It was a tragedy of the utmost proportions that he should not be allowed to prove that potential. We can only think ourselves very lucky that the sons and daughters will be given a chance to prove what their sire might have been.

Green Dancer

Nijinsky's other Group 1 winning two-year-olds have already had their racing careers described in detail and at length but emphasis must be made here of their outstanding quality as juveniles even though Green Dancer, in particular, went on to even greater successes at three.

To recall, Green Dancer made his first appearance as a juvenile in August 1974, in a six furlong maiden race at Deauville in which he faced a strong field of eleven potential classic horses and defeated them comfortably. His second outing was a much stiffer affair in which Green Dancer had to battle with the future champion juvenile, Mariacci, but one in which Green Dancer was not hard ridden. Green Dancer was still undoubtedly backward and this was also his first attempt in Group company.

His third and last race as a two-year-old was an even bigger step and involved his first trip to another country. He came to England to challenge for the Group 1 Observer Gold Cup, a race which attracted several class colts and which was deemed to be England's top race for staying two-year-olds. Green Dancer won with authority, pulling away from rivals who represented some of the best stables in England and Ireland. Possibly because Green Dancer was a foreigner, and had made just one foray to England, he was placed second on the Free Handicap to Grundy and, because he had missed the Group 1 events in France in order to challenge in England, he was also placed second to Mariacci though there was only a matter of 2 lb in it.

That Green Dancer went on to triumph in the French 2,000 Guineas and Prix Lupin as a three-year-old is now history, but that fact should not be allowed to overshadow the outstanding performances of a classic colt at two years. Some of its significance lies in the fact that he was the first Group 1 winner for his sire and ultimately the first classic winner. But Green Dancer had proved as a sire that he too is capable of siring two-year-olds of his own class, notably the fillies Maximova and Aryenne.

Maruzensky

Maruzensky was the other Group 1 winning juvenile and a true champion at that. His reputation as a racehorse largely rests on that fact. He was a champion two-year-old in Japan in 1976 but was ineligible to run in the Japanese classics and thereby gain future and more prestigious successes. Maruzensky was unbeaten in eight starts, though hardly extended, and was clearly head and shoulders above his contemporaries.

He had four races as a juvenile and won all of them with consummate ease.

He made his debut in October and won a six furlong turf event by a distance and which in actual fact was a good deal further than the 240 yards accredited. His second outing was again over a six furlong turf course and also at Nakayama. This time he won by nine lengths.

He had to be shaken up a little to score in the eight furlong Fuchu Sansai Stakes on 21 November but Maruzensky stamped his class for all to see in winning the Group 1 Asahi Hai Sansai Stakes on 12 December. Very few horses can claim to have won a Group 1 race by a distance, even in Japan. In smashing the two-year-old course record in the process Maruzensky revealed himself an outstanding champion. He could do no more than win the four races he was asked to contest as a three-year-old before injury curtailed his career.

That precocity he is now passing on to his stock along with a great deal of his parental stoutness. In his first two crops he is already sire of a Group 1 winning juvenile in Nishinosky (second top rated Japanese two-year-old), and a St Leger winner in Horisky. Bred to race in the West one can only conjecture on Maruzensky's possible achievements had he not raced in Japan. Perhaps the West missed another champion and perhaps J. O. Tobin and Seattle Slew just might have had something to worry about.

As will be shown in later chapters, Nijinsky has an extremely high proportion of two-year-old winners and a large number of juvenile stakes winners. Apart from the seven detailed above a further 15, whom we look at below, won stakes races in their first season showing an amount of precocity that is sometimes overlooked when evaluations are made on Nijinsky as a sire. Some, of course, went on to greater achievements at three but others, like Cherry Hinton, Princesse Lida, Bemissed and Gorytus achieved their best performances at two years.

The Houghton Stakes at Newmarket is often a stepping stone to the higher echelons for potential classic candidates. The race is run on Champion Stakes day and is often used to unravel the better candidates for the following season's Derby amongst those horses who have not before been exposed to the public eye. Often the first three home, and many unplaced, prove themselves exceptional performers in their second season. Nijinsky has done particularly well in this event having several placings and three who won. The ill-fated **Night Alert**, a contemporary of Princesse Lida's, won a particularly hotly contested running in 1979 pushing in the process the leading miler Posse and the future Oaks winner, Bireme, into the minor placings. Night Alert won from these accomplished horses by an easy 2½ and three lengths, it being only his second appearance on a racecourse having commenced life with a third place in the Group 3 Larkspur Stakes, later won by Nijinsky's son Western Symphony. Night Alert went on to win the Gladness Stakes (Group 3) and Group 2 Prix Jean Prat at three years, as well as being placed in the 2,000 Guineas, Waterford Crystal Mile and Joe McGrath Memorial Stakes, never being out of the first three in Europe. After just two outings in the United States Night Alert developed colitis and died early in his four-year-old season.

The second winner of the race, **Russian Roubles**, came from the same crop as Gorytus and Bemissed. He won the Houghton Stakes in 1982, but he did not accomplish it so easily as Night Alert and nor did he have anything like the calibre of Posse or Bireme to beat. However, he ran on very tenaciously from being quite a way off the pace to score from Vaisseau, ridden by Lester Piggott, in a thrilling finish. The following season Russian Roubles won the Welsh Derby very easily. But he only gained places in the King Edward VII Stakes (Group 2), though only beaten a length by champion three-year-old Shareef Dancer, and the Group 3 Gordon Stakes which, after the promise of his first season, was a trifle below that expected of him.

Nijinsky's third success in the Houghton Stakes came in 1984. The infinitely promising **Shadeed** came to the races two weeks earlier at Newmarket, just across town from his stable, with a reputation as high as a kite. A very immature sort of two-year-old he became involved in a rough passage, being dreadfully squeezed for room and eventually was beaten 1½ lengths by a 33/1 winner named Kala Dancer. Two weeks later everyone knew the exact value of that form. Kala Dancer won the Dewhurst to become champion and the next day Shadeed roundly turned the tables on Al Riyadh who had just pipped him for second in that previous race. Shadeed won the Houghton unchallenged by 2½ lengths with Al Riyadh almost three lengths behind him in third. In the close season it is, of course, very difficult to evaluate form but the manner of Shadeed's victory sent him into winter quarters as Epsom Derby favourite. In early 1985 he saw classic success.

The Larkspur Stakes, mentioned above, was won in 1983 by **Western Symphony**. A son of Mill Reef's half sister, Millicent, and himself being a three parts brother to the flying Peterhof, Western Symphony had a successful first season, winning two races and being placed in two others. He had first won the listed Birdcatcher Nursery by an easy three lengths under top weight and was beaten a length in the listed Tap On Wood Stakes. His victory in the Group 3 event was his last start and he achieved it comfortably from the useful Without Reserve. Unfortunately, Western Symphony did not quite live up to the promise of his first season, achieving second, third and fourth places in listed and Group events at three years, his only starts before travelling to Australia to stud.

Western Symphony's year younger brother **Moscow Ballet** became Nijinsky's first juvenile stakes winner in 1984 when he captured the P. J. Prendergast Railway Stakes (Group 3) on 30 June by a very comfortable 2½ lengths from Stanhoe. He had earlier broken his maiden at Phoenix Park by a length and five but is impossible to evaluate with any degree of confidence. Moscow Ballet only made one further trip to the races at a two-year-old running too badly to be true in the Group 2 Gimcrack Stakes at York. It was subsequently discovered that he had injured a knee and was not seen out again. It must be hoped that his three-year-old career does not prove to be as anti-climatical as that of his brother.

The listed Acomb Stakes is a race similar in nature to the Houghton Stakes but, as we have seen, it comes a good deal earlier in the season, at York in August. Nijinsky has done especially well in the Acomb, as he has in the Houghton, and apart from placed performers he has had two winners in Gorytus and **Tanzor**. Tanzor's chief role in Nijinsky's stud career was that he gave him his first stakes success when getting the better of Brilliantine in a driving finish. He had previously been third on his debut at Royal Ascot in a similar contest, the listed Chesham Stakes. Disappointing at three his best performance in three starts was probably a third in the Hethersett Stakes, for which he started odds on, though he did injure himself when unplaced in Grundy's Derby for which Green Dancer was hot favourite.

Leap Lively was a similar performer to Cherry Hinton in that she won the Hoover Fillies Mile (Group 3) as a two-year-old but was not quite so impressive in doing it. She too was a big rangy staying filly but differed from Cherry Hinton in her coat colour (Leap Lively is chestnut) and that she went on to Group success as a three-year-old and, also, ran third in the Oaks to Cherry Hinton's fourth in the 1,000 Guineas. Leap Lively did not start favourite for the Fillies Mile, even though she had won her previous start, but defeated the favoured Exclusively Raised comfortably by 1½ lengths, breaking Cherry Hinton's course record set up in the same race. She had earlier triumphed in the eight furlong Goldener Oktober Stakes at Goodwood when trouncing a class field by three, five, six and twelve lengths. She had taken some time to find her feet having had two fifth place finishes in good events such as the Waterford Candelabra (to Fairy Footsteps) previous to that.

As a three-year-old Leap Lively won the Johnnie Walker Oaks Trial (Group 3) by an easy three lengths from Allegretta and Condessa, then attempted to lead all the way in the Oaks only to be caught by Blue Wind and French Oaks victress Madam Gay. She eventually fell to the late charge of Condessa in the Group 1 Yorkshire Oaks after she bravely repelled all challenges only to be caught on the line by her nippier rival who won by a neck. It was a performance very reminiscent of African Dancer in the same race five years before, beaten a short head by the late challenge of Sarah Siddons.

Nijinsky's other Group 3 winning juvenile filly was **Vidalia**, a two-year-old of 1983. An aristocratic but rather temperamental tall leggy bay filly she wound up the season being rated second to Sly Moon in the Italian Handicap for two-year old fillies after her smashing six length success in the Criterium Femminile from two leading Italian fillies in Clair Matin and Philyra. It was her only success as a juvenile from four starts, in two of which she had been placed. As a three-year-old it seemed that temperament finally got the better of her for, in five outings, her best performance was a fourth placed finish (beaten a short head for third) in the Group 3 Cheshire Oaks to Malaak over an extended eight furlongs, but she is stakes placed in the United States in 1985.

Caerleon does not need any introduction as a great deal has been said already. Suffice to say that he was unbeaten as a juvenile in two starts. He won both comfortably, starting with the listed Tyros Stakes at the Curragh in June and then annexing the Group 3 Ballsbridge/Tattersalls Anglesey Stakes beating a class field by a comfortable 2½ lengths. He was rated second in the Irish Free Handicap behind Danzatore but proved much the better three-year-old with successes in the French Derby and Benson & Hedges Gold Cup.

His contemporary and stablemate **Beaudelaire** was to make his name over shorter distances but also had an unbeaten and quiet first season. Out of the brilliant speed queen Bitty Girl, Beaudelaire made a smashing debut at Leopardstown in September over five furlongs winning a well contested maiden by five lengths over the future Stewards Cup winner Autumn Sunset with the rest four lengths and more behind. He next came out in the listed Coolmore Try My Best Stakes over seven furlongs (the furthest distance over which he was ever to win) at Leopardstown later in the month and won very easily again from Gormanstown Prince. Beaudelaire went into winter quarters rated 6 lb below Caerleon. As a three-year-old he had just five starts, won two and placed second twice. He was successful in the Group 2 Prix Maurice de Gheest over 6½ furlongs, in which he triumphed over Green Dancer's daughter Maximova, and the Beeswing at Newcastle when slaughtering the course record. He was beaten narrowly on his first two outings, both in listed races in Ireland, but was undoubtedly one of Nijinsky's fastest sons.

Nijinsky's other juvenile stakes winners are all in North America. **De La Rose** is also a well known figure having been Nijinsky's first Eclipse winner. She may not have been the leader of her generation at two but she was certainly amongst the best. She won three of her eight races at two, including the Evening Out Stakes at Belmont over seven furlongs and she was placed second in the Grade 2 Demoiselle and Miss Grillo Stakes and fourth in the Grade 1 Matron. At three, De La Rose was the leader amongst the turf fillies winning eight races including the Grade 1 Hollywood Derby.

One of the best Nijinsky fillies to race in the United States, **Nijana** kept her form remarkably through several seasons and 28 races. She won three of her seven races at two when rated fourth leading two-year-old filly, 2 lb from the top. These wins included the Grade 3 Schuylerville Stakes over six furlongs by two lengths from Future Tense and Crown Treasure, who was later to make quite a name for herself in another sphere. Nijana also won two good class allowances, the Singing Rain and the Rare Treat. She was never worse than fourth in her other four appearances, the fourth place being in the Grade 1 Frizette Stakes. Nijana went on to win seven further races including the Shrewsbury Handicap, Parlo Handicap (twice) and the La Prevoyante Stakes at three and four years.

The four years older own brother to Folk Art, **Sportin' Life** had only three outings at two years culminating in the stunning 7½ length victory in the Allegheny Stakes at Keystone over seven furlongs from Thirty Eight Paces. He had already won his maiden and been placed in his other appearance. Sportin' Life won a further six races in the next two seasons, including the Philmont Stakes (by 3¼ lengths), Leonard Richards Stakes (by nine lengths) and the Cochise Handicap (by 1½ lengths) and the Grade 3 William Dupont Jr by seven lengths. A spectacular performer Sportin' Life also ran the Belmont victor Summing to 1½ lengths in the Grade 3 Pennsylvania Derby.

Nijinsky's last two stakes winning juveniles, Tights and Vision, were both two-year-olds of 1983, both colts and both winners in the United States. **Tights**, a full brother to stakes placed Dancing Again and a son of Selima Stakes victress Dancealot, accounted for the Cougar II Stakes at Hollywood Park though he had to dead heat with French Legionnaire to gain the distinction. He had been a winner earlier and been placed in the Hoist The Flag Stakes and placed fourth to Caucasus's son Pied à Terre in the Grade 3 Pilgrim Stakes. He was a most consistent performer at eight and nine furlongs in 1984 winning six races including three Graded events and twice in listed contests.

Vision, an own brother to Caerleon, won the second division of that Grade 3 Pilgrim Stakes by 5¼ lengths spread-eagling the field in his wake. It was also his second win of his two-year-old season but this first attempt at a stake or graded race. As a three-year-old Vision followed in his brother's footsteps by becoming a Grade 1 winner capturing the Secretariat Stakes on turf.

On the surface all this seems highly impressive indeed – below the surface it is even more so. Of Nijinsky's 402 foals of racing age to date (of which a proportion did not run at all during their lives and which necessarily included a large number of unraced juveniles of 1984 which will make their debuts at three years) 187 did run at two years and some of them up to 14 times. No less than 86 were juvenile winners of which 22 were stakes winners and a further 25 were stakes placed. Added to this are a number (43) who showed some ability to be placed. It is all the more remarkable when it is realised that 47 only ran once and 48 twice.

Of Nijinsky's 85 stakes winners to date a quarter won stakes races at two years. When one considers that Nijinsky is the youngest stallion to have reached that mark then it is clear how important those juvenile successes are.

The Nijinsky influence is now being felt in the next generation. Of course, it is too early to make many conclusions as the first full crops of his own progeny did not appear on a racecourse until 1979 but there is enough to be more than encouraging. Most of his sons at stud have already sired two-year-old stakes horses while Nijinsky's daughters are responsible for nearly 20 stakes winners. Of these Kirtling (Grundy-Silky), Delices (Artaius-Rasimova), Air Distingue (Sir Ivor-Euryanthe), Eastern Dawn (Damascus-Euryanthe), Defecting Dancer (Habitat-Running Ballerina) and La Lorgnette (Val de l'Orne-The Temptress) were stakes winners at two.

The future appears rosy indeed.

CHAPTER 3

Durability in Nijinsky's Progeny

The ability of Nijinsky's stock to withstand training, contrary to one school of thought.

We have seen how Nijinsky has been represented by a good proportion of precocious and classy juveniles. The other side of the coin is his fair share of the most durable of representatives who carry their ability through several seasons, often in the very top-class of competition.

Not surprisingly, most of these have been racing in North America where the emphasis is on racing older horses and, equally unsurprising, is the fact that the majority of the better ones are fillies. The Americans are much keener in racing their fillies than are Europeans and there are a great many opportunities for them to do so. Nijinsky had a great start in this sphere: Summertime Promise, Nijana, Javamine and Krassata all came from his first two crops. They were more than ably supported in latter years by the likes of Terpsichorist, De La Rose, Kyra's Slipper and Excitable. As we shall see, in a later chapter, Nijinsky has a far higher proportion of top-class fillies in North America than in Europe, standing as testament to their durable qualities.

Summertime Promise

Probably the most resilient and toughest, and certainly one of the most talented, of Nijinsky's top-class American winners, Summertime Promise in five seasons of racing went to post no less than 47 times. She won 10, placed second 9 times, third 10 times and fourth in a further three, accruing US $396,077 in the process. She contested at the highest level from her juvenile season in 1974 right through to six years of age.

Summertime Promise was almost certainly the best filly from Nijinsky's first crop which also included Copernica, Lighted Glory and Silky. Her dam, Pride's Promise, a year Nijinsky's senior, had produced nothing with her first foal by Jaipur and has produced nothing of similar class since her second, which was Summertime Promise. Pride's Promise was only placed at three years herself, her only season to race. However she was a half sister to major winner Pride's Profile who was to breed the able performers Winds of Thought and Elegant Tern, in turn the dam of good European performers Elegant Air and Fairy Tern.

Summertime Promise raced for the Rokeby Stable of her breeder Paul Mellon, and made her debut over six furlongs at Saratoga in mid-August of her juvenile season. On that occasion she was beaten a neck but made absolutely sure of winning brackets ten days later when, on the same track but over a furlong further, she won her maiden easily by nearly four lengths over Slip Screen. This was followed by another success, her first in allowance company and this time at Belmont back at six furlongs. Another easy success, so Summertime Promise was pointed at one of the very top races for two-year-old fillies, the Grade 1 Frizette at Belmont. Needless to say it was a hot field, which also included a fellow member of Nijinsky's first crop, Copernica. On the day it was Copernica, whose best performances were at two years, who ran the better finishing second to the easy winner Molly Ballantine. Summertime Promise was beaten some way but was only a neck out of fourth place.

In her next outing, also in a Grade 1, Summertime Promise ran a much better race this time at Laurel over 8½ furlongs in the Selima, half a furlong further than the Frizette. She was just over three lengths off the winner Aunt Jin and a head out of second place.

For a filly who was to capture graded events for some time to come Summertime Promise was not too far off the best of her age and sex in 1974. In her sixth and last outing as a juvenile she was beaten two necks into third in the Remove at Aqueduct over a fast six furlongs by Funalon and Quick Tempo, for which she started favourite. In the Experimental Free Handicap that year she was rated some 14 lb below the magnificent and ill-fated Ruffian.

Summertime Promise took a little time to find her form as a three-year-old making her debut as early as March when third in an allowance at Aqueduct. After her second start, fourth in the Khalita, she was off the course until August. She made just two starts and was off again until October. A second in a Belmont six furlong allowance and Summertime Promise was on her way. She gained her first stakes success in the Indian Maid at Hawthorne on a soft seven furlong course with a tenacious nose victory over Cute Kiss.

Tenacious was the word to describe Summertime Promise for her style of running, leading from an early part of the race, invited her opponents to come and catch her. In the highest class she was not to find it quite so easy as her first victory in the Yo Tambien Handicap ten days after the Indian Maid. Here there were no challenges, Summertime Promise responding readily as Victorian Queen and Sixty Sails came at her and she drew away again for a 3¼ length success. Summertime Promise had been sold not long before from the Rokeby Stable to Ken Opstein for a cheap looking US $145,000 from a reduction consignment, and it now appeared that Opstein had gained a very valuable proposition.

Summertime Promise disliked the muddy conditions of the Next Move Handicap held in December, her last run as a three-year-old. Her four-year-old season was not even three weeks old before she made her debut, a neck second to Katonka in the Old Hat Purse. The remainder of the nine horse field were five and six lengths behind.

In the prestigious Columbiana at Hialeah at the beginning of February, Summertime Promise was caught in the very last stride by Redundancy but had Yes Dear Maggy (later dam of Stalwart) a comfortable 2½ lengths in arrears. But Yes Dear Maggy got her revenge in the Black Helen ten days later, St Valentine's Day. They were level at the half furlong marker but Yes Dear Maggy just outlasted her by half a length. Summertime Promise turned the tables on Katonka, however, beating her into third place. Summertime Promise was setting up a sequence of near misses. The most important was on 29 February when she travelled to Santa Anita only to be beaten a nose by Fascinating Girl in the Grade 1 Santa Margarita Invitational.

Summertime Promise gained her just deserts a month later when holding off Baygo and Costly Dream by a neck and a length. She was all out but giving the second and third 5 lb and 6 lb respectively.

It was back to being caught close home again in the Gallorette at Pimlico over 8½ furlongs on turf. This was as far a distance as Summertime Promise was to win over. In winning the prestigious event Deesse du Val equalled the course record, prevailing by a neck. On 8 May Summertime Promise repeated her success of the previous year by winning the Indian Maid by an easy three lengths. It must have been a nice contest for her to win as she pleased.

Carrying top weight and starting favourite, Summertime Promise weakened to finish third in the Hawthorne Handicap but carried off an allowance nicely from Kissapotamus. That was a prelude to a rough race for the Sheepshead Bay in which Summertime Promise was disqualified after finishing a neck second to Fleet Victress and placed third. Following that she was pitched in against the best in the Grade 1 Matchmaker, having the honour and anchor of carrying top weight. Summertime Promise ran fast for seven furlongs but possibly found the 9½ furlongs too far in this type of company and wound up fifth to Dancer's Countess. Then it was a crack against the colts and a sixth place finish in the 9½ furlong United Nations Handicap (Grade 1) to Intrepid Hero.

Brought back to eight furlongs for her last visit to the racecourse of the year, Summertime Promise annexed the Yo Tambien for the second season in succession. She started odds on and conceded 10 lb to 13 lb to her six rivals. As was her wont Summertime Promise sprinted clear from the start and held off Rocky Trip by half a length. In the American Handicap Summertime Promise received 119 lb, 6 lb below top rated Bastonera.

The plan of action for Summertime Promise's five-year-old season was a carbon copy of the previous year. This time she failed to win the Apple Blossom and Indian Maid but triumphed in the Gallorette. She had been beaten two lengths in the Columbiana by Regal Gal, conceding the winner 6 lb but found the 8½ furlongs a shade too far under that kind of weight. It was also her first start since September. In the Apple Blossom she wound up third to Hail Hilarious having led for six furlongs. However she scored a scintillating triumph, and possibly her best, in the Grade 3 Gallorette. Sent away odds on, and top weight by 5 lb, she lasted the 8½ furlongs this time and galloped her rivals into the ground. She took the lead after two furlongs and had nine lengths in hand at the line in a time one and two fifths seconds slower than the course record.

Twelve days later she was asked to give 6 lb to her field and 10 lb to the filly who beat her. She just failed by a neck to last home from General Partner.

For her next three starts Summertime Promise was giving away lumps of weight in top-class company. It resulted in three sixth place finishes including the Ak-Sar-Ben Queens Handicap and the Sheepshead Bay in which she was used up through making the pace. However she showed signs of returning to her best, though tiring in the last furlong of the nine furlong Las Palmas Handicap at Santa Anita coming third to two ex-European fillies in Swingtime and Theia. Summertime Promise finished up the year carrying top weight in the Yellow Ribbon and finishing down the field behind Star Ball, Swingtime and Theia and then being fourth in the California Jockey Club Handicap to Hail Hilarious.

Summertime Promise was not quite the same filly at six though she won a Santa Anita allowance by two lengths and was defeated narrowly in the Ak-Sar-Ben Queens Handicap (by Gladiolus and Proper Princess) and in a handicap at the same course by Lady Randolph. However Summertime Promise carried enormous weights and ran creditably in several top-class events.

Ultra consistent over several seasons at the top Summertime Promise was retired to the paddocks midway through the season but too late to be bred.

The foals she has to run for her in 1985 include a three-year-old filly by Blushing Groom and a juvenile daughter of Alydar, both as yet unraced.

Javamine

Javamine was a member of perhaps Nijinsky's best crop for outstanding fillies, those foaled in 1973 when his first representatives, including Summertime Promise, were yearlings. Alongside Javamine there were also Nijana and La Jalouse in North America and African Dancer and Krassata in Europe. Krassata re-crossed the Atlantic to make quite a mark there too.

Javamine was the first foal of her dam Dusky Evening who won three races at three years and later bred a stakes placed own brother to Javamine in Sir Jinsky. Javamine raced for the Cragwood stable of Mrs Jane Engelhard, widow of Nijinsky's owner. Unraced at two years, Javamine "only" ran at three and four years of age but clocked up 22 appearances for 7 wins, 8 seconds, one third and a fourth for US $243,235. She competed in the very top-class of runner and did so with notable success. She was a quadruple Graded winner and placed second in four others.

Javamine did not see a racecourse until April of her three-year-old season, when she had a gentle introduction in an Aqueduct maiden. She knew a great deal more by mid-May when she was a close second to Miss Prism in a six furlong Belmont maiden and even closer to Queens Gambit two weeks later. Javamine broke her maiden on 7 June and did so in style romping to a 6½ length success over 8½ furlongs at Belmont, her first trip over grass. The second filly A Happy Butterfly was not looking quite so happy at the winning post.

Javamine followed up with an equally impressive performance in a Belmont allowance, cruising home by a spectacular six lengths. She was all set then for her debut into Graded company and a revered collection they were. The odds on favourite was the CCA Oaks winner Revidere who was confidently expected to thrash her field. She was given quite a fright then, when Javamine had the temerity to head her in the straight but Revidere recovered her equilibrium to come back to win by a head. Javamine's jockey Jorge Velasquez objected for interference but it was overruled. Still, Javamine had proved herself capable of taking on the very best. Twelve days later she finished well to take fourth in the rough contest for the Sheepshead Bay behind Fleet Victress, Redundancy and the disqualified Summertime Promise.

Then followed a stunning success in the Prayer Bell at Saratoga over nine furlongs, starting at odds on and storming home by a smashing eleven lengths. Starting second favourite she was promoted to second in the Grade

1 Alabama behind easy winner Optimistic Gal after Dona Maya had been disqualified.

After this Javamine was a creditable fifth in the Diana and second to No Duplicate in a Belmont allowance but, eleven days later, Javamine was sent out to claim her first graded success. It was a magnificent success for Nijinsky and the stable of Mackenzie Miller who saddled the first three and the sixth from four runners in the Long Island. Javamine and paternal half sister Nijana came to the front together at the furlong pole but Javamine's white starred head held off her blinkered stable companion by 1¼ lengths in a time one and three fifths seconds off the course record. Javamine had been bumped by her stablemate coming around the final turn.

Javamine followed up this triumph with another to round off her three-year-old season. This time it was a victory over the colts in the Grade 3 Knickerbocker Handicap. Javamine was sent off favourite and comfortably caught the experienced Recupere in the straight to win by 2½ lengths on a soft turf course in a comfortably faster time than in which the second division of the race was run.

Javamine started 1977 beaten two lengths into third by Lady Singer in the Office Queen over a short seven furlongs. An uncharacteristic eighth place followed in the New York Handicap to Fleet Victress. In the Quick Touch at Saratoga she gave 1 lb to another Nijinsky filly, the recent Irish import Krassata, and was beaten a head with the rest of the field strung out behind.

Javamine then returned to her favourite surface and probably to her most significant success and in twelve days she was to mark herself as one of the very best turf fillies of that year.

The nine furlong Grade 2 Diana Handicap at Saratoga is regarded as one of the top races for older fillies and mares in the United States and the field for the 1977 renewal did not let the reputation down – Glowing Tribute, Krassata and, most importantly, Pearl Necklace. The three-year-old Pearl Necklace was receiving 5 lb from her year older rival and second favourite Javamine. Javamine lay fifth after the first four furlongs and then drew away to an easy five length triumph over Pearl Necklace. It was quite a performance, more important in hindsight than it was at the time.

Twelve days later Javamine was sent to Arlington for the 44th running of the Grade 2 Arlington Matron. Even money favourite Javamine was allotted joint top weight with Star Ball and Merry Lady III, the other six fillies receiving between 1 lb and 9 lb from the trio. Javamine was trailing for more than six of the nine furlongs of a soft turf course but her jockey Velasquez, who was quite familiar with the filly, was sitting comfortably and was happy to wait until the absolute last moment. At her best he rated Javamine the best grass filly in training and he rode her like one.

On that day she proved it. One moment Star Ball was comfortably clear and the favourite nowhere in sight, and the next Javamine was looming down her neck. By the line Star Ball was an easy second but Javamine had long gone beyond recall.

Javamine was not given much of a rest after her two most notable triumphs. She might well have needed one however for she was fifth to What A Summer on the dirt of Belmont in the Grade 1 Maskette and sixth to the colts over a most unsuitable twelve furlong dirt track in the Grade 2 Manhattan for which she was second favourite.

However Javamine closed her career with two most creditable seconds: top weight by 4 lb when finishing fast but too late in the Queen Charlotte and again finishing strongly to just fail to catch Pearl Necklace in the Long Island.

That Javamine was an exceptional filly was indisputable and on grass she was one of the very best around that year. The handicapper agreed for in the division for fillies and mares on grass Javamine was weighted equal with the brilliant Swingtime and just one single pound below Dancing Femme. It was reported that she had died in 1984 and if that is the case it will be a great shame for Javamine was just proving herself as a broodmare. Javamine's second foal, the Blushing Groom colt Spicy Story, showed plenty of stamina as a three-year-old in 1984 in Europe winning two races over good company as well as finishing a desperately close third in the Group 1 Grand Prix de Paris and then being runner up in the Italian St Leger. He remains in training in 1985 where he will be joined by a two-year-old filly by Damascus.

Nijana

Nijana was Javamine's contemporary and stable companion and there was certainly not much between them. Unlike Javamine, Nijana ran at two years and was a Graded winner at that age. Nijana represents one of the rarest of all species of the thoroughbred: the speed and precocity to be in the top-class at two and the stamina and endurance to be still in the higher echelons at three and four. In three seasons Nijana ran 28 times, winning 10, being placed second 6 times, third 3 and fourth a further 6 totalling US $242,180. Her successes were not quite so notable as Javamine, with just the one Graded stakes, but she was certainly even more consistent, not that Javamine could be regarded as much else.

Nijana was a chestnut daughter of Prodana Neviesta, herself a winner of the Diana Handicap and who had bred a couple of useful performers in Prod and Zingari before Nijana but who has not produced much since, apart from

Nijana's winning own brother Quick Dance who unfortunately had a tragic accident early in his stud career necessitating his destruction.

Nijana began her racecourse career on 30 June at Belmont and finished second over 5½ furlongs. She repeated the performance three weeks later but opened her account with a bang when she contested the six furlong Schuylerville Stakes (Grade 3) on 28 July over a star studded field. Coming from far back Nijana stormed past Future Tense and Crown Treasure (the latter became a familiar name in English breeding circles through her sons Glint of Gold and Diamond Shoal) to draw away for an impressive two length success. Somebody was obviously impressed for Nijana was given top weight for the Rose O'Neill but could only finish third to Artfully. Such are the ways of horses when they are expected to win. This was followed by a fourth place in the Grade 1 Frizette to Optimistic Gal and Artfully before Nijana turned her attention to the turf, to become by far her most familiar surface. Starting odds on Nijana stormed to a 6½ length triumph in the Singing Rain at Belmont over eight furlongs. Dotties Doll was disqualified from second and that place awarded to Wajima's half sister Veroushka and thus Nijinsky had first and second in that respected allowance contest. Nijana repeated her victory over Dotties Doll seven days later in the Rare Treat, this time at way odds on and by 3½ and eight lengths from that filly and Prowess.

That was it for her juvenile season, which gave every promise for the future but also pointed Nijana's way led towards a turf surface. Nijana had been weighted just 2 lb below the champions Dearly Precious and Optimistic Gal in the Two-Year-Old Filly Handicap. Yet it was on dirt that Nijana made her reappearance in May 1976 when beaten three lengths by Funny Peculiar in the Imperial Hill when evens favourite.

Returning to turf the New York Handicap winner Sugar Plum Time outlasted her for the La Corredora but it was soon back to winning ways for Nijana. Sent off favourite for the sixth Parlo Handicap Nijana was the sole three-year-old in the field of eleven. She was forced to race very wide for most of the 8½ furlong trip but she rallied well to outduel Flama Ardiente by three-quarters of a length. Djaura was four lengths back in third. Nijana had followed in the footsteps of two other Nijinsky offspring, Caucasus and La Jalouse, in becoming the third 1976 stakes winner to be bred by the Cragwood stable of Mrs Engelhard.

This all meant that Nijana started favourite for the Sheepshead Bay (Grade 2), not the luckiest of races Nijinsky's daughters but later to be won by Terpsichorist. This time Nijana was fourth to Glowing Tribute, a performance that was to be repeated when third to the same filly in the Diana.

Nijana then carried off the Marconi Purse giving 5 lb to the second and winning easily from Hinterland and Pass A Glance and also Sun And Snow, who had defeated her in the Polonaise between the Sheepshead Bay and the Diana. Nijana then was fourth on a muddy dirt track in the Margate on which she was hardly expected to excel but returned to a much better performance in the Long Island when giving the winner Javamine 2 lb and being interfered with by other runners when trying to make her challenge. Nijana followed this 1–2 for her sire with a win in the Good Morning over Thirty Years.

Nijana's four-year-old career dawned with a hard won victory in the Red Carmelia over Pacific Princess on 3 May on a fast six furlong dirt track at Aqueduct. As a result of this effort she started favourite and top weight by 4 lb for the Intermission at Aqueduct but disappointed behind fellow Nijinsky filly Krassata.

However Nijana bounced back to form on 30 May in the Shrewsbury Handicap over 12 furlongs, the furthest by a good two furlongs she was ever asked to travel. Sharing top weight with Krassata, giving the rest of the field at least 3 lb, and 14 to Sans Arc, Nijana raced well behind as Krassata went on. Sans Arc took the lead after four furlongs but as Krassata stopped abruptly Nijana went on to catch Sans Arc on the line in a course record time, fully a second up on the old mark.

The race under top weight and over a distance must have taken something out of Nijana for it took her some little time to regain that form. A relatively disappointing performance in the New York Handicap behind Fleet Victress, and fourth places to Glowing Tribute and Fleet Victress in the Sheepshead Bay and to Fleet Victress again in an allowance, led to a second place in the Green Glade where she was clear top weight and failed by a head to overhaul Small Raja.

However Nijana was leading towards a grand finale when she went to post bidding for a repeat success in the Parlo Handicap. Even money favourite and clear top weight, Nijana raced last in the eight horse field after two furlongs. At the top of the straight she came between rivals and drew clear for a comfortable success from Time For Pleasure and Krassata.

In the Gallant Bloom Nijana was asked to give weight to Pearl Necklace and the combination of that and the muddy dirt track combined to place her second to that filly. Probably the best daughter of Hoist The Flag, Sensational, was third. Nijana came fifth to Pearl Necklace again, in the Long Island when Javamine was second, but she had saved her best for her last visit to the racecourse with a storming ten length triumph in the La Prevoyante at Aqueduct on a sloppy dirt track over Sweet Bernice and Krassata.

Clearly a top-class filly, especially on grass, Nijana was probably not quite the equal of Javamine in her later seasons but she could hardly have been more consistent over an arduous career. Already at stud she has been represented by a Graded placed winner in Secret Sharer, sired by Secretariat. She has an unraced four-year-old in 1985 by Sir Ivor and a three-year-old filly, Secret Script, by Secretariat so the reputation of Nijana should live on for a while yet.

Krassata

Krassata was a filly not quite of the status of a Nijana or Javamine, her contemporaries, but she had to travel far further to earn her reputation. In three seasons Krassata ran initially 10 times in Europe recording a win, a second, 3 thirds and 2 fourths (in Ireland and Germany) and then made 22 further starts in the United States registering 5 wins, 3 thirds and 4 fourths in good-class company. Much of her race record has necessarily been recited above for she raced in the best company and particularly that of Javamine and Nijana.

Krassata had been produced by Bonnie Google, the winning dam of the Matron winner Bonnie And Gay, as had Krassata's year old brother, Masqued Dancer, who had been successful in Ireland and stakes placed at Royal Ascot.

A leading juvenile, Krassata scored a scintillating six length success in a Curragh maiden on her first appearance. On the strength of that she started hot favourite for the prestigious Moyglare Stud Stakes but finished down the field behind Petipa. Despite this Krassata was favourite again for the Silken Glider (Group 3) but was well behind winner Glenoe in third place. However, Krassata must have made quite an impression because she was the second highest weighted filly in Ireland that year just 3 lb below champion Welsh Garden.

With this rating in mind Krassata was sent off favourite to make a winning start to her three-year-old career in the listed Azalea Stakes at Phoenix Park over ten furlongs but she was beaten a head by Gorse Bush. The useful Countess Eileen was a length away in third.

Undaunted by this reverse Krassata was in the line up for the Group 1 Irish 1,000 Guineas and ran very well to be fourth to Sarah Siddons, Clover Princess and Lady Singer, who was to accompany Krassata across the Atlantic. Krassata herself then travelled to seek Group 3 honours in Germany contesting the Consul Bayeff Rennen and she ran well to be third, less than two lengths off the exceptional colt Lepanto. Returning to Ireland, Krassata ran next in the Group 1 Irish Guinness Oaks and, leading into the final furlong, it looked for a moment that Nijinsky was going to have his first

European filly classic winner. In the end the French filly Lagunette won the race comfortably but Krassata was only beaten a short head and a head by Sarah Siddons into fourth place, instead of the 3½ lengths as in the 1,000 Guineas.

Krassata was then pointed for the Brownstown Stakes at the Curragh and started favourite but was outlasted by a neck and a head by Slap Up who started at 14/1. Krassata wound up her European career out of the first four in the Irish St Leger (to Meneval) and Youghal Stakes (to Serencia).

Krassata ran twice in the United States in December 1976 but hardly had time to acclimatise. It was not until March 1977 that she found her form, winning three 8½ furlong and nine furlong (twice) Santa Anita allowances off the reel, the first on dirt and the other two on turf. Krassata was then thought worthy of contesting the Grade 1 Top Flight but made no show. After finishing third in the Queen of The Stage under top weight (conceding 5 lb to the field) Krassata carried off the Intermission with Nijana well in arrears. Nijana gained her revenge in the Shrewsbury however and after one brief return to the dirt Krassata was quickly sent back to the grass surface.

After being beaten a length into fourth in the Captain's Gig under top weight (conceding 4 lb to the winner Notably) Krassata beat Javamine a head in the Quick Touch. She then saw quite a lot of her fellow Nijinsky fillies when sixth to Javamine in the Diana and third to Nijana in the Parlo Handicap. Krassata ran reasonably well in the Black Curl behind Pearl Necklace and again in the Hannah Dustin carrying top weight, to Lady Subpet. After a fourth in the Face The Facts, beaten a nose and two heads by Carolina Moon and Glowing Tribute and being top weight with the latter, Krassata wound up her career by a third place finish to Nijana in the La Prevoyante.

An able performer, Krassata was perhaps unlucky not to win a stakes event but ran consistently on two continents for three seasons. In 1983 her daughter Safe Process, by Bold Forbes, repeated her mother's performance by being a good winner in Ireland and finishing fourth in the Irish Oaks.

Terpsichorist

Just as Javamine missed the leading filly or mare on grass title by the narrowest of margins Terpsichorist was in a way even more unlucky. It has been said by many good judges that had there been a divisional award when Terpsichorist was eligible, then De La Rose would have been Nijinsky's second Eclipse winner and not the first. Terpsichorist only ran at three and four years but totalled 28 starts for 11 wins, 2 seconds, 4 thirds and 2 fourths for US $426,986.

Terpsichorist, a large chestnut filly encompassing all her sire's size and power, was foaled 10 March 1975, a crop which included the stakes fillies Summer Fling, Excitable, She Can Dance, Cherry Hinton and La Nijinska and also one of Nijinsky's very best colts, Ile de Bourbon. She was also the daughter of the 1,000 Guineas winner Glad Rags, being the first of Glad Rags's three Nijinsky foals of racing age (Glad Rags also has a 1984 filly) of which one never ran and the other was Gorytus. Unlike Gorytus, Terpsichorist was kept in the United States by her owner breeders Mr and Mrs James Mills and sent into training with Woody Stephens. Way over 16 hands at two years and bred to be a stayer (by American standards) Terpsichorist was given plenty of time, unraced at two years, and made her debut at Gulfstream Park in late March of her three-year-old career finishing fifth to Evening Boo Boo, evidently concentrating more on learning about the game.

Terpsichorist had learnt enough by 20 April when she contested an eight furlong maiden at Aqueduct over a sloppy dirt track, not the type of surface for many Nijinskys to show their best. Terpsichorist won handily by 1½ lengths from Key To The Saga, herself an accomplished filly. Terpsichorist took it in her stride and was also to win her next two starts by a resounding seven lengths (coming from 16 lengths off the pace) in an Aqueduct 8½ furlong (turf) allowance and again by four lengths on dirt, two weeks later at Belmont. Terpsichorist was then thrown in at the deep end but found the Grade 1 field for the Mother Goose just a little beyond her at that stage competing against the very best of dirt fillies in Caesar's Wish, Lakeville Miss, Tempest Queen and White Star Line.

Terpsichorist came back to a fourth in a Belmont allowance and a second to fellow Nijinsky filly Milina ten days later. She then carried off an allowance by six lengths over a turf mile at Belmont and again on 4 August on a seven furlong muddy dirt track at Saratoga, though conditions were sufficiently against her to reduce her winning margin to a head.

Terpsichorist now took on the two crack fillies Waya and Pearl Necklace in the Diana, finishing a creditable fifth. She followed this up with a third in the Grade 2 Gazelle to Tempest Queen on the muddy Belmont surface. However, eleven days later Terpsichorist scored an easy success for her first graded stakes, the Grade 3 Athenia Handicap (to be won in 1983 by Rose Crescent and in 1984 by Key Dancer) when accounting for eleven opponents on a yielding surface at Belmont over ten furlongs, much more her distance. Terpsichorist had worked her way through the field before drawing away to a comfortable three length success.

The ultra-consistent Key To The Saga, beaten 3½ lengths in the Athenia gained her revenge in the Boiling Springs at Meadowlands 15 days later over a very firm 8½ furlongs. It was Key To The Saga's fifth win in seven grass starts. It was certainly too short a distance for Terpsichorist but she was a very comfortable second.

Terpsichorist took on the colts in her next start and was the only filly in the nine horse field for the Rutgers Handicap (Grade 3) over eleven furlongs at the Meadowlands. Second favourite to Roberto's best son to date in the United States, Darby Creek Road, Terpsichorist was a long way back for much of the race but came through strongly. She made up eight lengths in 36 seconds to catch the pacemaker, and later the Laurel Turf Cup victor, Native Courier just yards from the line. Not only had Terpsichorist lowered the course record but had blown it to smithereens by seven and two fifths seconds. Darby Creek Road finished three lengths back in third.

It was a pretty impressive performance by Terpsichorist and, as a result, she was given a high weight in the Lamb Chop on 25 October at Aqueduct over 8½ furlongs. She was last for a good part of the way, came flying but could not get up to catch Misgivings and Invision.

This race, however, really sharpened her up for the Grade 3 Long Island at Aqueduct four days later, where the twelve furlongs was much more to her liking though she was giving lumps of weight away to older fillies and mares. Mike Venezia, who had partnered Terpsichorist for her previous ten races, had a prior commitment to Magnificent and Terpsichorist was ridden by Angel Cordero. This time Terpsichorist lay a close fourth pulling all over her rivals as Fabulous Fraud led from the Prix Vermeille winner Kamicia and Magnificent. Kamicia took over the slow pace until Magnificent assumed a length lead at the two furlong pole. Terpsichorist was taken to the outside to challenge at the final turn. The battle was brief. Terpsichorist had a narrow advantage at the furlong marker and 2¾ lengths at the line.

Terpsichorist was thus unbeaten at distances in excess of nine furlongs. In beating colts readily in the Rutgers, and in that performance in the Long Island, Terpsichorist stamped herself as almost certainly the best three-year-old filly on grass that year.

Her four year old career started with two second spots. Attempting to give classy Calderina 5 lb she was beaten three-quarters of a length, with the Nijinsky filly She Can Dance 3¾ lengths in third, in the Suwannee River on 31 January at Gulfstream Park. Then it was the Orchid where Terpsichorist was engaged in a rough race before winding up 1¾ lengths adrift of Sans Arc when third but comfortably ahead of Calderina. Terpsichorist was moved up to second as Time For Pleasure was disqualified for interfering with the unlucky Nijinsky filly. Terpsichorist ran a good race against the colts in the Pan American to finish fourth to Noble Dancer; and followed that up with two not so good performances when fifth in the Grade 2 Bougainvillea and behind Calderina in the Gallorette, which had been switched from turf to dirt due to heavy rain.

Any doubts Terpsichorist connections might have had about keeping her in training as a four-year-old were erased with a solid win in a Belmont allowance over Sans Critique over 8½ furlongs. Then came her major triumph in the Grade 2 Sheepshead Bay when Terpsichorist took on the best on a rather firm surface over Belmont's ten furlongs. Terpsichorist had Waya and Late Bloomer to beat and, bearing in mind Waya had defeated the Nijinsky filly 7½ lengths in the previous year's Diana, Terpsichorist had quite a sizeable task. Also, Waya had not been beaten by a female since the Sheepshead Bay twelve months earlier; and that was Late Bloomer by a neck. Late Bloomer went on to be named Champion Older Filly or Mare.

Eddie Maple was on Terpsichorist as he had been in that allowance three weeks before. That had been the first time he had ridden her since her first three victories early in her three-year-old career. He saved ground on Terpsichorist well behind the leaders, came out from the rail as the field came into the straight and, going wide, found a sudden gap between the outside horses. Late Bloomer came upsides and it was a battle all the way to the line. Terpsichorist had the lead by a nostril with 100 yards to go and gamely held that advantage to win by a nose. It was not Waya back in third but her half sister Warfever.

After this battle of a race Terpsichorist was third on a yielding surface for the nine furlong Diana to Pearl Necklace and was then beaten half a length and the same by Pearl Necklace and The Very One (giving 6 lb to the second) in the Flower Bowl. However it was soon back to winning ways in the 8½ furlong Violet Handicap under the lights at the Meadowlands. Upon Terpsichorist's announcement to run six of the 17 horse field defected leaving Terpsichorist top weight over the likes of Navajo Princess, The Very One, Spark of Life and Sans Arc. The eleven left were made up of eight stakes winners and three stakes placed horses. Terpsichorist came from even further back than usual having broken last and was ninth after four furlongs. Terpsichorist was really upset that night before they even left the paddock, perhaps by the glaring artificial light, but it did not stop her running, despite having to go around five horses to find space. However, Terpsichorist was in sixth position after six furlongs, less than five lengths off the lead. A furlong out and leader Spark of Life had four lengths over her but Terpsichorist was closing with every stride and got up by half a length and travelling away the further she went.

Calculations were upset when the Queen Charlotte at Meadowlands was moved to the dirt track and Terpsichorist could only finish fifth to Water Malone, giving 6 lb to the winner. Terpsichorist's last race of her 28 race career was to seek a repeat victory in the Long Island but giving 15 lb to Flitalong was just beyond her on the yielding surface coming from so far off the pace.

In Terpsichorist, Nijinsky had possibly his most durable and ability-endowed American filly representative and she was very unlucky to race at a time when turf courses were not considered of equal standing by those who ascertained divisional awards. Terpsichorist was certainly one of the very best.

There are several reasons why horses remain in training past their three-year-old season. In the case of colts the large majority tend to be moderate racers for there is not much of a future for them after their racing careers are terminated. Fillies tend to be the best around for there is more opportunity for them to do so in the United States than Europe and, of course, there is a future for them in the paddocks no matter at what stage they retire.

Javamine, Nijana, Terpsichorist and Krassata were four of Nijinsky's best fillies and who proved it past their three-year-old careers. The most obvious is **De La Rose** whose career has already been described in detail and suffice to say she was champion turf filly in 1981. In three seasons she made 26 visits to the racecourse for 11 wins, 6 seconds and 5 fourths for a total career earnings of US $544,647. Her victories included the Grade 1 Hollywood Derby, Grade 2 Diana Handicap, Long Branch Stakes and Saranac Stakes and the Grade 3 Anthenia Handicap, E. P. Taylor Stakes. De La Rose defeated the colts on more than one occasion. On her less favoured dirt surface she was a narrow loser of the Kentucky Oaks.

But De La Rose was not the only one.

In three seasons, **Excitable** ran 32 times, winning three races and being in the first four on no less than 20 occasions. Among her victories were two stakes performances, the Miss Florida and Miss Tropical Handicaps, and being in the money in stakes on eight other occasions. Not in the class of her contemporary Terpsichorist, she was nevertheless a tough and durable racehorse and, as the Americans say, "ran big races" against Calderina in the Columbiana, Late Bloomer in the Black Helen, Unreality in the La Prevoyante and Navajo Princess in the Suwannee River. A half sister to the speedy English juvenile, Bel Bolide who did so well in the United States in 1984, Excitable should also probably have won the Vizcaya on her first ever appearance but ran into a fence.

Other classy Nijinsky fillies to have clocked up over 20 appearances are Canadian Oaks placed **Lady Jinsky**, Canadian stakes winner **La Jalouse**, Bitty Girl's daughter **Nijit** (43 appearances for 5 wins, 13 places, second and third), Nureyev's three parts sister **Number**, other stakes winners **Down Stage**, **Rose Crescent** and **Rosy Spectre**, plus **Olamic**, **State**, **Water**

Dance and **Vestris**. Grade 1 winning juvenile **Bemissed** made 25 appearances in just two seasons winning 5 and being second and third in 8 others.

Of the colts a number were good performers, notably **Nijinsky's Secret**. As already described Nijinsky's Secret made eight outings in France and 28 in North America. His twelve victories included the Hialeah Turf Cup (Grade 1) twice, Tidal Handicap (Grade 2), Bougainvillea Handicap (Grade 2), Jockey Club Stakes (Grade 3), W. L. McKnight Handicap (Grade 2) and King Edward Gold Cup (Grade 3) plus good performances in the Budweiser Million.

He is ably supported by the stakes winning half brother to Exceller, **Baldski**, who ran 27 times for 7 wins and 6 places and who is now making his name as a leading young sire. **Caucasus**, whose 22 races in Europe and the United States included Group 1 success in the Irish St Leger, Sunset Handicap and San Luis Rey Handicap, raced until five years.

His Honor, whose 35 races over five seasons, yielded four stakes success among his nine victories and four stakes and Graded places among his eight seconds and thirds. Others include: **Come Rain or Shine** (23 starts, 4 wins, 11 places); **Avodire** (35 starts in North America and France, one win, and 16 places including Graded stakes); Graded winner **Khatango** (24 starts, 6 wins, 6 places); stakes winner **Nuclear Pulse** (31 starts in Europe and the United States for 3 wins and 13 places); Javamine's brother **Sir Jinsky** (32 starts, 3 wins, 8 places); and **Ultramate** (24 starts, 7 wins including two stakes, 9 places). In 1984 the two three-year-olds, **Tights** and **Dancing Crown**, made 43 appearances between them incorporating 10½ victories.

There is little or no place for useless colts at stud so these sons of Nijinsky represent the cream of the crop, all having been able to accumulate black type. Obviously, the majority raced or are racing, at least eventually, in the United States as racing there is geared to horses making more appearances in any one season than they would in Europe. There are also more incentives to keep horses in training for one or two seasons beyond that of their three-year-old career. Lesser colts do race on but still prove their toughness and durability. For example, in 1983, Amen Wadeen, Nijinsky's son out of the Epsom Oaks winner Monade, won his first flat races in the United States at the age of ten after a successful jumping career.

The European Element

As with a large number of European champions whose stud careers take place in the United States, many of Nijinsky's progeny returned to race in Europe. Because of the relative shortness of the racing season in Europe and the relative scarcity of a top-class handicap Pattern for older horses (witness the importance in the United States of the Handicap Triple Crown) European horses very rarely make anywhere near the appearances of their American counterparts.

It is unusual, in particular, for the best and classic racehorses to make as many outings as their less endowed companions: trainers in Europe like to "lay out" their champions for particular races. Take, for example, Nijinsky's three-year-old career of the classic trial (Gladness Stakes) followed by the 2,000 Guineas, Derby, Irish Derby, King George VI & Queen Elizabeth Stakes, St Leger, Arc and Champion Stakes. Very few champions since have contested all the last three, at most it has been two or often one or maybe even none at all. For example, no Epsom Derby winner since Nijinsky has even contested all three of the classics that constitute the Triple Crown and no less than ten ran in the Derby alone. It is probable that had Nijinsky won the Arc he would not have re-visited Newmarket. But the point here is that Nijinsky had eight races as a three-year-old and most have barely had six. In latter years few leading contenders have that, note Shareef Dancer, three outings at three years yet acclaimed a champion. And he only won two of them. Rather different to the way of racing in the United States.

However, Nijinsky's stock have shown their durability in other ways than sheer number of runs. Firstly, stamina. Horses such as Bright Finish, Thahul, Niniski and Quiet Fling, regularly race over distances in excess of 13 furlongs and are able to hold their own in the very best, and very British, of racing traditions against the more traditionally stoutly bred indigenous stock. Secondly, the courage and determination shown by many in hot competition, notably, as we have seen, the brave competitiveness of Kings Lake and Caerleon; and the memorable performances given by Peacetime, returning from hobdaying and a soft palate operation to defeat a class field in the Valdoe Stakes (listed) at Goodwood; and the two-year-old inexperienced Russian Roubles's last gasp victory in the Houghton Stakes. Less brave animals would have surrendered a long way from the finishing post.

Nijinsky cannot help it if his produce win flamboyantly on the first start of their lives (58 of his 243 winners worldwide won first time out) and do not quite develop into the champions they are then acclaimed as. It should be noted that many of these races take place in Ireland, where the competition is less harsh. As many of these horses originate from the most powerful stable of Vincent O'Brien most whose juveniles and first time outers are expected to win this way, it is often regarded as a catastrophe if they do not. Also, in Ireland, there are more Nijinskys per head of thoroughbred population than there are in other parts of Europe. It would be interesting to see just how many other stallions' stock have this high flying reputation before or after their first appearance on a racecourse.

There will always be those who will attempt to crab and criticise a leading stallion no matter how successful he is. Often it is relatively unimportant to his success. Nijinsky has been accused of producing notably unsound stock. Nijinsky's stock are not soft. Nijinskys also often exhibit great determination and "guts". None of Nijinsky's best raced stock or such as Kings Lake, Caerleon and Peacetime in Europe and the above mentioned progeny in the United States can be said to be prone to shirking the issue though occasionally, as with all sires' stock, some do appear. In Europe "hard" racing of the very top classic bracket has become a thing of the past and it is to be noted that the apparent Sangster/O'Brien policy of the potential stallion consideration is a general one and not just with Nijinsky's in particular. Nijinsky cannot be judged on European stock alone no matter what mitigating circumstances prevail in the United States. Having witnessed dirt racing there it is not hard to see how any stallion could be regarded as a progenitor for unsoundness.

Yet it is noticeable regarding Nijinsky animals who have raced in Europe, or returned for the Stateside campaign, that many of them have held their form and maybe even lost it while few or virtually none have gone from a second rate performer to a potential champion. If they appear to have done so there are usually other reasons for it, particularly simple maturity. This state of affairs is quite notable as latterly European "handicappers" have done very well in the United States stakes races.

As will be shown, in later chapters, there may be other reasons for any unsoundness: the influence of the female line and, in particular, the male line of the dams of the stallion's foal; the effects of the virus stricken 1970s in Europe; or, a mere unlucky bad step such as that which ended the careers of Ballare and Hostage and the simple fact that bigger horses carrying so much more weight in themselves and pressure in their sheer size are more likely to come up "unsound" than the smaller variety. The main characteristic of most, and all of the best, is the size and power Nijinsky imparts. One would, therefore, expect more of his stock to have soundness problems than, say, the more characteristic of Northern Dancer's progeny.

Overall one would have to say that Nijinsky's progeny show a remarkable resilience to training, taking all other factors into consideration. For a horse that stands in Kentucky and has the majority of his runners there it is unfair to take European racing alone to judge his capabilities as a stallion. The detrimental statements about the early brilliance of progeny unfulfilled only serve, in a roundabout way, to pay a great compliment to Nijinsky, by expecting each easy juvenile winner to automatically develop into a champion. How many stallions can have had that said about them?

CHAPTER 4

Performance Ratios

The real basis of Nijinsky's success: ratios of winners to runners, stakes winners to winners, etc; Average Earnings and Comparable Indices; world distribution of progeny; relative merits of colts and fillies

Like all the leading sires Nijinsky is best known and most highly regarded for producing stakes winners. It is obviously the best horses which keep their sire's names in the headlines. But to make a stallion a great sire there must also be great strength in depth and great reliability placed on the "backroom" support. Nijinsky is not only one of the leading sires in numbers of stakes winners (he sired 18 alone in 1983) but also as possibly the leading stallion in the world in terms of his ratios of winners to runners and associated criteria.

To assess any stallion there must be a usable number of progeny by which to gauge an accurate assessment of the ability of that sire. Nijinsky has had 402 foals of racing age worldwide (that is, up to and including two-year-olds of 1984) and it is these that we are concerned with here. Emphasis is now placed heavily on percentages of all spheres of racing whether it be stakes horses or number of foals who actually started.

So, what degree of success would a buyer of a Nijinsky foal or yearling reasonably expect? Well, to start with he would have a chance in excess of 76 per cent of the animal ever starting in a race. If every foal born in the world started on a racecourse we would soon exhaust the supply of races available to them, or have a field of quite unmanageable proportions. So the fact that three-quarters of Nijinsky's stock do race is probably an unusually high proportion. This is bearing in mind that breeders/owners may react in two ways to structuring the career of their Nijinsky, especially if it is a filly. Some may not want to risk the horse to the rigours of a racing career. A filly of that pedigree is an asset valuable to any stud and just maybe an unraced mare is of more worth than one which ran and did not place. Alternatively, the odds are relatively high that the horse may gain black type should it race, in which case the owner may think it worth risking and send the Nijinsky on to a more arduous career. For, after all, what is the industry and sport of thoroughbred racing all about if it is not the thrill of racing itself?

Of Nijinsky's stock, then, 95 did not race. This number does include a high proportion of the juvenile crop of 1984 (28 in fact), so in actual fact there is probably greater than 76 per cent chance of the horse racing because many of these two-year-olds of 1984 will make their debuts in 1985. As we shall see, a far greater proportion of fillies than colts were unraced, mainly for the above reasons. Of course, there are other factors to be borne in mind that may restrict the colt or filly to other activities outside the racecourse due to numerous ailments and accidents that Nature may design to befall them.

Of those that ran (307) no less than 243 of them won flat races and two others won only over obstacles. This 79.41 per cent is phenomenal by any standards. In fact it is almost too phenomenal to be true but a glance at the lists of Nijinsky's foals will confirm it. So, although 23.63 per cent did not actually run, when they get on a racecourse the odds of having a winner are enormous. It is unlikely that any other of the world's leading sires can match this ratio of winners to runners. This is no temporary sensational first season stallion. These averages and percentages are taking into consideration Nijinsky's first *eleven* crops.

Obviously, to get winning brackets on a well-bred horse increases its value dramatically whether as a future broodmare or stallion. In addition to these winners, 38 were placed (including one National Hunt winner) and so showed some measure of ability. For one reason or another a few of them were obviously unlucky not to win. Three others were placed fourth, just out of the frame and on occasions only just. Six others ran just once, which is hardly enough to get them over any greeness and to accustom them to most unusual surroundings. This leaves us with just 15 horses out of the 307 that ran which made two or more trips to the racecourse. Of these 15, 6 ran just twice, 4 ran three times and 3 ran four times. Only four ran more than this: two running over hurdles and winning, the third has reportedly won several races in Israel though this is hard to confirm, while the last was a two-year-old of 1984 who may redress the situation in 1985.

Taking that information at its face value it is hard to point to many of Nijinsky's progeny who could be termed as definitely useless for some sphere of the sport. Though not wanting to illuminate the point too far, it is of interest that Nijinsky has a great success rate of progeny who have run over hurdles and fences (15 runners, 9 winners of 37 races) and has sired four stakes winners. Not only can they run but they can jump too and though it is unusual for his stock to race to the ages of seven or eight and above, some members of his first crops are still flying the flag in the "winter sport". Indeed Amen Wadeen, then a ten-year-old son of the Oaks winner Monade, was still counting them up in the United States in 1983 by winning his first flat races over 8½ furlongs showing there is still some speed there too.

But it is, of course, the earning of black type that is the all-important point in this day and age of commercialism and sales catalogues. It is here too that Nijinsky excels. Second only to his own sire in terms of stakes winners on the list of active sires today, Nijinsky has sired more stakes winners than even Northern Dancer at the same age. At the end of 1984 he was 24 adrift of his sire, six years his senior and, problems apart, must be odds on to surpass that. In one season's racing in 1983 Nijinsky had 18 stakes winners to represent him, more than any other stallion had ever achieved.

Of his 245 winners under both rules, 85 won stakes races, a percentage of just under 35 per cent, or just over one third. So, over one in three of Nijinsky's winners won a stakes race and 21 per cent of all foals, whether they be unraced or not. Of those that ran (307) 27.77 per cent won stakes races. So, over one quarter of Nijinsky's runners win a stakes race. It has been said that 11 per cent stakes winners is to be expected of a good stallion and it is Nijinsky's tremendous ratio that makes him one of the truly outstanding stallions in the world today, where such emphasis is placed on the production of good winners in the regimented and patterned systems in use all over the world.

Apart from these 85 stakes winners there are also 47 who gained black type by placing in graded or listed races, over half as many. One would possibly have expected there to be more stakes placed than winners, as there are automatically double as many stakes place opportunities than winning ones but Nijinsky has superseded all expectations in this department too.

Nijinsky's percentages of 21.14 per cent stakes winners to foals, 27.77 per cent stakes winners to runners and 34.69 per cent stakes winners to winners stand as irrefutable evidence as to the quality of the stock of this stallion.

At the end of the 1984 season, in terms of the Average Earnings Index, Seattle Slew, Northern Dancer and Nijinsky led the world by a large margin. Only two other stallions (Vaguely Noble and His Majesty) accomplished a figure of 4.00 or above. [AEI. The Average Earnings Index indicates how much money the progeny of one sire has earned (average) in relation to the average earnings of all runners in the same year. The average earning of these runners in any year is represented in an index of 1.00 (Stallions with 100 foals plus in 1984).] Even more striking was the Comparable Index. This is becoming even more of a widely used guideline by racing statisticians. The Comparable Index indicates the average earnings of progeny from mares bred to a particular sire and measured against the results when these mares are bred to other stallions. Only 30 per cent of all sires have an AEI higher than their mares' Comparable Index.

Nijinsky is not only one of the 30 per cent but he has a comparable margin over Northern Dancer (4.23 to 2.98) and shows just how he can "move up" his mares – how he fares with mares who have already been put to other stallions. Nijinsky has undoubtably been bred to some outstanding broodmares and he has done better with them than have the other stallions they have visited.

Of course the United States is far ahead of Europe in compiling and using these figures as a meaningful evaluation of stallions. The big drawback with their methods and usage of statistics is that there is little room for acknowledging the results from parts of the world other than North America. So many computer based stallion statistics are suspect on these terms when it comes to evaluating the stallions who stand in North America, but whose majority, or at least a good proportion, of runners end up in Europe. To give Nijinsky as an example: on the recognised American sires computer records, Nijinsky is recorded as only having 48 per cent starters to foals (instead of 76 per cent), 36 per cent winners to foals (instead of 60.94 per cent) and 76 per cent winners to starters (instead of 79.80 per cent). This is because the total number of foals registered in the United States (nearly all of them) are taken into account but not those that then performed abroad.

This is not only misleading but also wholly inaccurate and does do a stallion who is a success outside North America no credit at all. American breeders and owners would do best to treat with some scepticism any figures produced by American based institutes who do not keep a watchful eye on European racing as much as they should. Yet the number of stakes winners tends to be correct. This too will give the picture another side. The correct worldwide number of stakes winners are assumed but then compared only with horses that started in North America.

So, on a computer programme one gets 85 stakes winners giving a 42 per cent ratio stakes winners to runners because any horses that started in North America are included and not the 175 or so that came to race in Europe and elsewhere outside the United States and Canada. If any stallion computed 42 per cent stakes winners to starters, one could not hazard a guess at his value and one would probably assume he would be housed in a golden shrine for ever and have sacrifical offerings made to him.

However, sires tables do often give a more complete picture. The best known leading sires lists, as published for example in *The Blood Horse* magazine, do take into consideration European runners of American stallions in their figures both in money totals and Indices. There will necessarily be some disparity, because of the relatively poor financial rewards in Europe rather than the United States but it does give a much clearer picture. That point is noticeable in that the 1983 leading stallion, Halo, owed his success (and half of his total earnings) to one horse, Sunny's Halo, who earned US$1,011,062 alone. No European horse could really hope to earn the equivalent in sterling or francs in one season. Nijinsky, who finished runner-up (quite a feat in itself regarding his extra-high proportion of European runners) had 42 winners to represent him, the leading representative (in terms of money) being Nijinsky's Secret who accounted for a mere US$371,547 of the total of US$2,494,378 indicating Nijinsky's tremendous strength in depth.

This closeness of the 1983 leading sires tables brings to notice another point. Stallions such as Nijinsky, Blushing Groom and The Minstrel are often at a disadvantage because of their high proportion of European raced stock. It is unlikely that there will ever be another Bold Ruler, or any stallion, who can dominate the sires table in the United States in quite the same fashion purely because of the worldwide distribution of blood that now is the order of the day. For this reason, and the aforesaid disparity between financial rewards for racehorses on either side of the Atlantic, it is highly

	USA & CANADA	ENGLAND & IRELAND	FRANCE	ITALY	JAPAN	TOTAL CROP FOALS
1972	13	11	5	0	1	30
1973	18	6	3	0	1	28
1974	14	8	4	2	2	30
1975	18	10	3	0	1	32
1976	20	11	3	0	1	35
1977	22	11	5	0	1	39
1978	24	14	3	0	0	41
1979	25	9	4	0	2	40
1980	26	11	4	0	0	41
1981	21	12	7	0	1	41
1982	26	12	7	0	0	45
TOTALS	227	115	48	2	10	402

TOTAL CROP FOALS – refers to live foals who attained the age of two years, that is, of racing age.

World distribution of Nijinsky's progeny to foals of 1982

unlikely that Nijinsky will be champion sire on the American lists. It was all the more commendable that he should be only just pipped in 1983; while in those lists that included American racing alone he hardly ever gets a mention – like all the other stallions, Northern Dancer included, whose greatest successes are in Europe.

The world distribution of Nijinsky's progeny to foals of 1982 ably shows just how large is the proportion of horses raced outside the United States and which is so often overlooked by American racing statisticians.

Colts versus Fillies

So much for the general ability of Nijinsky to sire winners and stakes horses. But should a breeder be happier that his Nijinsky produce is a colt or a filly, or should the buyer be more interested in colts or the feminine representatives? Leaving aside the question of future potential value, that is, as a stallion or broodmare, let us look at the relative merits of colts and fillies and how likely it is for either one to be an exceptional racehorse.

Here too we shall be able to gauge Nijinsky's true consistency. Unlike Sir Ivor, and to some extent Lyphard and Nijinsky's own son Green Dancer who have shown a marked leaning towards producing a better class of filly than colt on the racecourse, Nijinsky is seen to spread ability through his stock right across the board.

To start, let us ascertain how many animal we are dealing with. Of Nijinsky's 402 foals, 214 are colts and 188 are fillies. Usually there are roughly half and half but the difference here is not enough to lead one to believe that Nijinsky has necessarily sired an appreciable amount fewer good fillies than colts.

Understandably fewer colts (39 or 18.2 per cent of total colts) than fillies (56 or 29.787 per cent) were unraced. As there are necessarily fewer stallions than mares there is a greater emphasis placed on a colt proving himself to be worthy to be put to stud by winning good races. It is the whole principle of thoroughbred selection. If all well-bred colts went straight to stud without racing none of them would even win The Derby. However, there is considerable paddock value for a well-bred filly without risking her on the racecourse.

Of the 131 fillies which ran, 102 won (a ratio of 77.86 per cent winners to starters). Of 176 colts which ran, 141 won flat races (80.11 per cent). So, percentage wise, one would expect colts to slightly outgun the fillies in terms of winning races, the first all-important goal in the life of any racehorse. However, there is not much to choose between them. This is not perhaps surprising in that one would expect owners to persevere more with colts than fillies because even a non-winning filly of good breeding has a high paddock value. Do not forget that these figures refer only to those that ran.

Of the fillies 17 (12·97 per cent) were placed but never won; while 21 colts (11.9 per cent) were placed but one of their number did win over hurdles. Twelve fillies (9·16 per cent) failed to make the first three whereas 14 (7·95 per cent) were unplaced amongst the colts although one of these also won "over the sticks". So much for individual performances. Now to the next question. Do fillies win more races? Nijinsky sired the winners of 737 races worldwide to the end of 1984. Of these 41.11 per cent were accounted for by fillies, which is a fair percentage all things considered.

However, though the colts and fillies appear to account for roughly equal an amount of foals and races there is a marked differentiation between stakes horses which is what it is all about when one talks about the higher echelons of the thoroughbred world. Of the 131 fillies which ran, 31 won stakes races (23·66 per cent), and 24 others (18·32 per cent) were placed in them without winning. Of the 176 colts, 54 were stakes winners (30.68 per cent) and 23 (13.06 per cent) were placed. So, colts come out slightly better in terms of their numbers accounting for a stakes race.

Yet it appears that a larger number of the best fillies appear in the United States and Canada rather than Europe whereas the best colts seem to race in England, Ireland and France. One only has to compare the performances:

Fillies

European Group and Stakes winners	*North American Stakes and Graded winners*
African Dancer, Cherry Hinton, Galletto, Leap Lively, Lighted Glory, Princesse Lida, Vidalia	Ballare, Balletomane, Bemissed, Dearly Too, De La Rose, Down Stage, Excitable, Folk Art, Javamine, Key Dancer, La Jalouse, Nijana, Number, Rose Crescent, Rosy Spectre, Shimmy, Sis C, Street Ballet, Summer Fling, Summertime Promise, Terpsichorist, Water Dance, Waving
TOTAL 7	TOTAL 23

A glance at the above table will show immediately that over three times the number of fillies won stakes and graded races in North America. Yet as the following list of the graded and stakes winning colts depicts, well over twice as many were triumphant in Europe as on the other side of the Atlantic.

Colts

European Group and Stakes winners

Beaudelaire, Bright Finish, Brogan, Caerleon, Caucasus, Empire Glory, Esperanto, Fabuleux Dancer, Golden Fleece, Gorytus, Greek Sky, Green Dancer, Ile de Bourbon, Kings Lake, Lucky Sovereign, Moscow Ballet, Muscovite, Nice Havrais, Night Alert, Niniski, Nizon, Nuclear Pulse, Pas de Deux, Peacetime, Piaffer, Quiet Fling, Russian Roubles, Shadeed, Shining Finish, Solford, Stradavinsky, Tanzor, Valinsky, Western Symphony, Yeats, National Hunt – Gleason, Half An Hour
TOTAL 37

North American Stakes and Grade winners

Baldski, Caucasus, Czaravich, Dancing Champ, His Honor, Hostage, Khatango, Nagurski, Nijinsky's Secret, Sportin' Life, Ultramate, Upper Nile, Val Danseur, Vision, Tights,
National Hunt – Popular Hero, Netherby
TOTAL 17 (Note that Caucasus appears in both lists)

Why has this marked difference occurred?

There may well be several reasons why this should be the case. Regarding the colts: in the latter years the largest buyers of Nijinsky stock, the Sangster/O'Brien combine, have been leaning towards buying higher priced colts of any sire than fillies – in 1983 O'Brien had only two fillies amongst his three-year-olds. No less than 15 of Nijinsky's European stakes winning colts were trained by Vincent O'Brien but only one of the fillies. There is still magic in the quest for the Derby goal and a general belief that Nijinsky colts are more suited to European turf conditions. They do certainly seem to prove it on these figures.

This also, of course, applies to the fillies. But there does not seem to be such a demand for them at public auction and buyers seem content to leave them in the United States with their futures at stud in mind. None of the European filly stakes winners went through the sales ring at public auction. There are also undoubtedly more opportunities in North America for fillies to gain black type especially as they get older; it is relatively limited in Europe especially for four-year-old fillies and older. There is also a trend towards fewer home-bred Nijinsky's in Europe. Apart from the fact that it is often cheaper to buy Nijinsky fillies at auction than colts a great many of the established owner breeders, who are depleting in number by the minute, are tending to use home based stallions. One notable example of this is Eric Moller who regularly used to have three or four Nijinskys in training at any one time (notably Cherry Hinton, Lucky Sovereign and Silky) out of home bred mares and whose numbers have dwindled to nothing because of this policy. Only Sheikh Mohammed at present is attempting to reverse this trend of bringing Nijinsky colts to come to Europe rather than fillies and he is possibly thinking of building up his broodmare band rather than sending his English based mares to visit Nijinsky.

While there are greater opportunities for fillies in the United States of course breeders and buyers are going to keep their filly representatives at home. The number of Nijinsky fillies in Europe from the first eleven crops has been almost half of those racing in North America (43/90 of fillies to run) though a slightly higher percentage of winners (39/74). However, taking into consideration Nijinsky's ratios of stakes winners to winners the seven filly stakes winners in Europe from 39 winners is rather below average. The 23 stakes winners from American raced fillies from 74 winners is almost 1 in 3, quite a different story altogether. The way the sales of Nijinsky fillies, as against colts, are going it does not seem likely to change much.

But in contemporary terms, whichever way one looks at it, Nijinsky is without doubt one of the truly great sires of this century. The criteria of the 1980s, of course, is rather difficult to apply to stallions, say, before the Second World War. But any stallion who gets over one third stakes winners from winners and 27.7 per cent stakes winners from runners with an AEI of 4.23 has to be respected as a very great sire indeed.

CHAPTER 5

Distance and Going Aptitudes

The true distance capacities of Nijinsky's stock in Europe, North America and Japan; the relative performances on dirt and turf; the aptitude shown on various types of ground

Until the close of 1984 Nijinsky had sired 243 winners of 737 races worldwide. In order to establish the average winning distance (AWD) of his progeny, to gain a general impression and to use as a sample of the relative aptitudes to grass and dirt tracks, it is these 243 horses we are concerned with here.

For the purposes of our investigation, it should be noted that many of Nijinsky's winners in North America won on both grass and dirt surfaces. In the figures used here then, they have been treated as separate animals. Those who, for example, won exclusively on good grass tracks may also have won on a fast dirt course.

Often in the following investigations it will be necessary to look separately at each area of the world involved because of the very different conditions that prevail. It is worth remembering throughout that Nijinsky himself raced exclusively on grass and in Europe and that his own winning distance was 6.6 furlongs as a juvenile, 10.83 as a three-year-old, averaging out at 8.7 furlongs and so was not himself a true stayer, in the European sense of the word.

Europe

For our purposes, Europe is here made up of the British Isles, Eire, France, Italy and also including (Brehon Law's) two wins in Holland. Very few excursions have been made into Germany and perhaps Krassata's third in the Consul Bayeff Rennen (Group 3) was the most successful. As none of the horses were trained in Italy the overseas raiders were not plentiful either though that trend is changing. For Nijinsky's progeny it resulted in a Group

1 victory for Nizon, the top race for juvenile fillies won by Vidalia and a second place finish for Brogan in the Italian Derby (Group 1).

To say that Nijinsky's progeny in Europe by all winners is a particular distance is too much of a generalisation but for the record the average distance of his winning progeny in Europe and North America is 8.58 furlongs. In Europe alone it is recorded as eleven furlongs. However many of these won at two years when the distance is necessarily limited. Of his 104 winners in Europe 41 were two-year-old winners, 15 over six furlongs, 17 over seven furlongs and 12 over eight furlongs and one over a distance in excess of eight furlongs. All in all this evolves a figure of 6.78 furlongs as Nijinsky's AWD of his European juveniles.

Nijinsky, though a brilliant two-year-old himself, was primarily a middle distance classic horse and thus not expected to sire precocious horses, though as we have seen in his success as a juvenile sire is not to be underrated in terms of quality. Because of this many horses were unraced at two years. We shall be taking a closer look at this later. Of his 104 European winners, 78 won at three years, from distances ranging from 6 to 16 furlongs. This results overall in an AWD of 10.78 furlongs, which compares favourably with the AWD of 10.83 of Nijinsky himself at the same age.

Because of the current trend of retiring horses to stud at the end of their three-year-old season Nijinsky had less horses to race at four years and up than he had at three. However, 15 of them won over an average distance of 10.95 furlongs.

These figures show how each crop of European raced progeny have uncannily matched almost exactly their sire's performances. Of course a calculation of the AWD of any sire's stock incorporates the two extremes of short and long distance performers but this method of divining the expected optimum distance at which the progeny would be expected to excel seems to be very popular these days. So, from these figures, any buyer of a Nijinsky foal or yearling to race in Europe can reasonably expect it to resemble its sire in the best distances over which it is likely to be successful.

United States and Canada

Grass—It is necessary to differentiate between performances achieved on turf and dirt in North America. It has been proved many times over that a horse's ideal distance on grass is not necessarily its best on the American "main" track. This will be seen to be proven using Nijinsky also as an example of the whole, as well as to see how his own progeny react on different surfaces. We will be seeing how the going affects performances but for the purpose of this survey we have to assume that the horses won over distances unaffected by the going in their particular case. Obviously there are many influencing factors in the win of any horse (for example, weight, human error, and so on), but if all these were taken into consideration then every stallion's AWD of progeny would never be any guideline at all. By establishing the average one assumes with this number of horses and wins that mitigating factors have sorted themselves out.

The majority of American horses race on dirt. This is to some extent reflected in the fact that 78 of Nijinsky's 149 American winners won on grass, only just over 50 per cent of the total. Of these 48 also won on dirt tracks, even though it is generally acknowledged that the Nijinsky's in North America adapt better to grass courses, which can actually be said about a number of European raced American bred stallions (for example, Blushing Groom, The Minstrel). Of these grass performers, twelve won at two years, two over seven furlongs, the remainder over eight furlongs plus. As there were plenty of two-year-old winners in North America by Nijinsky it shows how loathe the Americans are to race horses on turf as juveniles and the resulting lack of opportunities.

The Americans are, on the other hand, much more inclined to race their juveniles (on dirt of course) yet the differentiation as seen in Europe is almost reflected between two and three years on grass in North America. As three-year-olds 49 won and the AWD was 8.85 furlongs. Equally however, the Americans tend to keep their animals in training into their more mature years than is the trend in Europe. As a result 41 won at four years and up on turf courses (AWD 9.17 furlongs). This number is a little inflated as it includes most of the European exports who left British or French shores at the end of their three-year-old career.

It is particularly interesting to compare the performances on grass of the Nijinsky progeny on both sides of the Atlantic. It will be seen that at two years the American raced progeny are expected to win at distances greater than the European raced counterparts – in fact as much as 1½ furlongs. However, much of this must be attributed to opportunity. For the older horses the European raced horses are expected to succeed over distances averaging up to 2½ furlongs longer than those in North America. These may well be a reflection of the lack of long distance events (over ten furlongs) available in North America on grass. We shall see if that also applies to the majority, the dirt performers, below and how much they vary from their North American turf colleagues.

Dirt—As already noted 118 of Nijinsky's 149 American winners scored on the main surface. This appears to be especially true of the two-year-olds and, notably, also of Nijinsky's first crops before their grass affinity was even considered.

To take the juveniles first: five won over 5/5½ furlongs; 19 over 6/6½ furlongs; twelve over 7/7½ furlongs and eleven over distances in excess of 8 furlongs. This came from a total of 41 individual two-year-old winners in North America and their average distance of 6.73 furlongs, rather different from the eight furlongs plus of the turf scorers.

We have seen that there is a reverse trend in comparing American and European horses' winning distances between two and three years. Does this happen with the American dirt horses when compared to their grass counterparts? Nijinsky had 70 three-year-old winners on dirt to the end of 1984 accounting for 142 races. Their AWD was 7.41 furlongs, almost a furlong shorter than the grass three-year-olds and 3½ furlongs shorter than the European turf winners.

The differences in racing Nijinsky's progeny on turf and dirt are already becoming apparent in a rather dramatic way. In placing all the older horse winners in one group in actual fact hides the notable inclusions that many of the main track horses did race for several seasons beyond that of four years.

Nijinsky had 57 winners aged four and above which averaged 7.78 furlongs, not a considerable increase on the 7.41 furlongs accounted for by the three-year-olds.

At this point it might be as well to look at those 48 horses who won on both turf and dirt; to attempt to glean some idea of the relative merits of the grass and dirt performers' distances. Of the 48, nearly all won over longer distances on turf than on dirt. All either won over longer distances on grass or over similar distances over both but only His Honor won consistently over longer distances on dirt than on grass. It is usual for 6 furlong dirt specialists to score more than once over 8 or 8½ furlongs on turf.

Japan

Nijinsky has had 6 winners of 20 races in Japan including the champion Maruzensky. Like the Americans, the Japanese race on both types of surface and, as in North America, Nijinsky's progeny there have shown a greater liking for the turf courses. As there are so few representatives of Nijinsky they are worth dealing with separately.

Maruzensky, champion juvenile of 1976 and unbeaten in eight races, won four times as a two-year-old over 6 (twice) and 8 (twice) furlongs, all on turf. His four victories at three ranged from 6 to 9 furlongs but his lone victory over 6 furlongs was on dirt.

Yamanin Sukih won at four and five years in Japan. He scored from 7 to 10 furlongs at four years and over 9 and 10 furlongs at five. All his victories were on turf.

Meiwa Sukih was a two-year-old winner over 6 furlongs on dirt. Aino Saintsky won the first of his three starts as a three-year-old in 1984 over 9 furlongs on dirt.

Group winner Yamanin Penny won over 6 furlongs on dirt as a juvenile and twice over 8 furlongs on turf at three. Her contemporary Nishino Northern won twice on dirt at two years over 5 and 6 furlongs. Taking grass and dirt together the average winning distance of progeny at two years was 6.44 furlongs, but if divided to grass it was 7 furlongs and dirt 5.87 furlongs. The three-year-old's and up resulted in only two winners on dirt: over 6 furlongs – a distance not won over by the grass course runners (average 8.5 furlongs) – and 9 furlongs.

So, even in this small sample, we can see how horses can attain a greater winning distance over turf than on dirt, even as two-year-olds. If these are taken together with no differentiation a very false impression can be given as to the true average distance of a stallion's progeny. It is a point to bear in mind when comparing American stallions, whose progeny regularly race in the United States and Canada and those stallions whose progeny have proven themselves best suited by European conditions.

European Performers in North America

It is, obviously, extremely difficult to evaluate the relative merits of European and North American form. At the present time, the trend is very much one way – initially European raced horses are being sent in quest of the top races in North America rather than the other way around, especially now that All Along has become the first foreign trained Horse Of The Year and the birth of the Breeders' Cup series.

The American attitude to distances over which races are run is also very different from their European counterparts. While both may in some way share the prejudice against real staying blood, shown in North America by the lack of any real Pattern of events over distances in excess of twelve furlongs and in Britain by the lack of patronisation of staying horses at stud, there is also a tendency to regard the European raiders as able to win good races and be raced over far shorter distances than they have been in Europe. This may possibly be because of the sheer lack of financially rewarding longer distance races across the Atlantic.

However, this does not stop European raced horses trying and the success has been phenomenal. Many have been American breds actually returning to the land of their birth after a European campaign but also, with the successes of such as All Along, Royal Heroine, Trevita and Erin's Isle, there is an increasing number of European bred horses proving themselves capable of holding their own.

Perhaps the only way of examining the merits of either style of racing is to look at how these European raced horses have fared in North America.

Nijinsky has had 16 of his sons and daughters return to the land of their conception and win, having already won in Europe. It is these winning performances that we are therefore using to gauge the distance capacity of Nijinsky's stock, and they also show in some way how a horse's distance appears to alter when raced in North America. This, of course, also means it may be that Nijinsky's stock, racing over shorter distances in North America, may have shorter or longer AWD of stock in either country and the two may not be compatible. These 16 are then a possible way of proving or disproving this theory.

It does not necessarily follow that it is just the best horses that are sent to try their luck or add to their laurels on the rich North American circuit. The 16 do include Irish classic winner Caucasus, who went on to maintain that standard of performance; the Group placed Krassata, desperately unlucky not to annex a Pattern race in the United States; French stakes winner Nuclear Pulse, subsequently very disappointing in terms of class races in the United States; Group 2 placed two-year-old Borodine, similar to Nuclear Pulse; the Geoffrey Freer Stakes (Group 2) winner Valinsky, who had only a very limited career in America; Irish minor stakes filly Rissa; the enigmatic London Bells, who never fulfilled his undoubted promise on either continent; and the French stakes placed Val Danseur. Weighed against them however, are the decent handicapper King of Darby; Bundle of Kisses; and two just below stakes class, Russian Fox and Water Dance – an American stakes winner; and Nijinsky's Secret who was among the best turf horses in the United States and Canada plus minor Irish winners Lath and Gentleman Jinsky, and a good two-year-old winner Chivalry. So, although all these horses had some measure of ability they certainly did not have an equal amount of it. As regards distance, it is clearly misleading to consider European juvenile winners that won at later stages in North America for two-year-old races are naturally going to be run over far shorter distances than the horse is later capable of getting. This qualification necessarily excludes London Bells, Russian Fox, Krassata, Borodine and Chivalry.

Of the eleven that remain, no less than seven consistently won over shorter distances than they had in Europe, the other four were basically over similar stretches of ground. Significantly, the latter four were of Nijinsky's best representatives in this department: Caucasus, Nijinsky's Secret, Water Dance and Val Danseur. Perhaps this is due to a similarity in distance in the top turf events available in North America. Nijinsky's Secret and Caucasus won their Group races exclusively on grass as was Val Danseur's Blue Larkspur success. Maybe the difference is seen in that the majority of winners were three-year-old victors in Europe and at four or older in North America. The strength accumulated as the European raced horses matured gave them the ability to stay with the American horses over shorter distances. But, more likely, it was just a matter of opportunity and prejudice, human created conditions. Only three horses managed to win in Europe and North America in the same season: Water Dance won over 8 furlongs in England at three and over an 8½ furlong turf course in the United States, Gentleman Jinsky over 13 furlongs in Ireland and 9 furlongs (turf) in America, and Lath over 10 furlongs in Ireland and twice over 8 furlongs on dirt in Canada.

Classwise, broadly speaking, it can be said that Caucasus, Krassata, Lath, Rissa, Gentleman Jinsky, London Bells, Chivalry, Russian Fox, Val Danseur, and Bundle of Kisses maintained the level of ability shown in Europe in terms of the races in which they competed and performances attained; King of Darby, Valinsky, Borodine and Nuclear Pulse probably did not perform on equal merit as before (though Valinsky had hardly time to acclimatise after just three runs) and Nijinsky's Secret and Water Dance improved their form to a marked degree, but maybe in their case it was due to general maturity.

However, it is important to realise that these horses were bred on exactly the same lines as their exclusively American raced counterparts in Nijinsky's progeny; they were not bred with the European racing circuit exclusively in mind any more than were the others. It is therefore quite conceivable that had otherwise totally American raced horses spent their initial seasons in England, Ireland or France they would have been capable of gaining victories over longer distances than they are recorded to have attained, purely because of opportunity and the European attitude to longer distances being the true test of the classic racehorse (10–12 furlongs).

Female Influence on Winning Distances

Everything we have been concerned with until now had been based on the male influence upon the resultant progeny. It is foolish to suggest that the progeny of a stallion will necessarily receive the genes determining stamina from the sire alone. We therefore need to look at how the dams of the progeny may have had some influence. For the purpose of this study it is best to select only the progeny which won three or more races and which also had dams who won three or more races at whatever age. This is to enable us to have some sort of *average* winning distance.

DISTANCE AND GOING APTITUDES

It is essential to note that these average winning distances involve two-year-old performances and as we have already seen a notable difference between European and American aspects, that these dams and horses won in different countries. However, if we forget that Nijinsky won as a two-year-old and just take his three-year-old average winning distance of 10.83, the majority of foals from mares whose AWD is less than this have come up with something somewhere in between. But Nijinsky did win as a two-year-old like most of the dams and foals listed here and computed an AWD of 8.7. Occasionally horses have got longer AWD's but it is best to remember that these were usually European raced horses from American dams, for example, Caucasus (AWD 11.5) from Quill (7.6) who was exclusively American raced.

However this also leads us to the point that Nijinsky is able to sire horses of all distances, greater or smaller than he personally achieved. This is especially true of those with stamina. Though the furthest Nijinsky won was over an extended 14 furlongs (and it is generally agreed that was due to his sheer class rather than genuine stamina) he was able to sire two mile plus horses, like Bright Finish and Thahul, from mares whose AWD was nothing like this distance. Of course these are European raced horses as there is little or no scope for these kind of performances in the United States and Canada. This fact does not appear to be to everybodys liking. However he has also his fair share of five and six furlong performers and quite how much the female influence is felt here is not quite so clear. It will be noted that not many of Nijinsky's stock come from mares from sprint sires. It is best to remember also that Nijinsky won three times over distances around six furlongs as a two-year-old and there was nothing in his style of running to suggest that five furlongs would have been too sharp for him if tried. It is worth mentioning that Ile de Bourbon, who excelled at around twelve furlongs, was known to be able to defeat Champion Sprinter Double Form comfortably at that horse's best distance at home. A great many (62) of Nijinsky's progeny won at six furlongs, 38 as juveniles and 33 at three years and upwards. Those who won over 5–5½ furlongs are of course rarer and will demand closer inspection.

SIRE's AWD	FOAL	DAM
8.7 (2–3)	Caucasus 11.5 (3–5)	Quill 7.6 (2–5)
	Copernica 7.1 (2–3)	Copper Canyon 6.6 (2–4)
	Bakor 6.86 (2–6)	Copper Canyon
	Copper Kingdom 8.5 (3–4)	Peace Movement 7 (3–4)
	Nataraja 8.16 (2–5)	Peace Movement
	Dancing Champ 8.2 (3–4)	Mrs Peterkin 7.33 (2–3)
	Lord of The Dance 12 (3)	Monarchy 6.28 (2–3)
	State 8.16 (2–3)	Monarchy
	Krassata 8.25 (2–4)	Bonnie Google 6.25 (2–3)

SIRE's AWD	FOAL	DAM
8.7	Miss Mazepah 8.83 (3)	Monade 9.38 (2–5)
	Over Served 8.375 (2–5)	Nautical Miss 6.16 (2–3)
	Sportsky 7.125 (3–4)	Sports Event 7.4 (2–4)
	Bright Finish 13.08 (3–4)	Lacquer 6.4 (2–3)
	Shining Finish 12 (3)	Lacquer
	Javamine 9.07 (3–4)	Dusky Evening 7.83 (3)
	Sir Jinsky 9.07 (3–4)	Dusky Evening
	La Jalouse 6.875 (2–3)	Quadruple 7.83 (2–3)
	Miss Nijinsky 7.16 (2–4)	Kylin 8.125 (2–4)
	Nijana 8.1 (2–4)	Prodana Neviesta 7.4 (3–4)
	Nuclear Pulse 10.6 (3–5)	Solometeor 6.875 (2–3)
	Royal Jete 7.5 (3–5)	Bid High 6 (2–3)
	Baldski 7.28 (3–5)	Too Bald 7.5 (3–5)
	Edziu 6.3 (3–7)	Shahtash 6.6 (2–3)
	Lady Jinsky 6.5 (2–3)	Lady Victoria 7.875 (2–3)
	Milina 6.5 (2–3)	Tender Word 9 (2–3)
	Upper Nile 8 (2–4)	Rosetta Stone 6.83 (2–3)
	De La Rose 8.3 (2–3)	Rosetta Stone
	Fecund 8.4 (4–5)	Farm 10.2 (3–5)
	Ile de Bourbon 11.86 (3–4)	Roseliere 11.2 (2–4)
	Rose Crescent 8.75 (3–4)	Roseliere
	La Nijinska 8 (2–3)	Street Dancer 8.2 (2–5)
	Nijinska Street 8.33 (4)	Street Dancer
	Street Ballet 6.9 (2–3)	Street Dancer
	Makarova 10.4 (3)	Midou 7.5 (2–3)
	Piaffer 8 (4–5)	Strong Drink 5 (2–4)
	She Can Dance 7.6 (3)	Yanina II 7 (2–3)
	Terpsichorist 9.09 (3–4)	Glad Rags 6.33 (2–3)
	Classical Ballet 7.25 (2–4)	Fragile Witness 6 (3)
	Czaravich 7.85 (3–4)	Black Satin 7.25 (2–3)
	Gist 8.125 (4)	Deb's Darling 6.33 (3–4)
	Kyras Slipper 9.375 (4–5)	Drumtop 9.176 (2–5)
	Bedford 12 (3–4)	Drumtop
	Audley End 10.75 (3–4)	Favoletta 6.75 (2–3)
	Ballare 8.25 (2–3)	Morgaise 6 (2–4)
	Come Rain or Shine 10 (4–5)	Sign of the Times 7.875 (2–4)
	London Bells 7.125 (2–3)	Shake A Leg 5.66 (2–4)
	Nijit 6 (2–4)	Bitty Girl 5.5 (2–4)
	Beaudelaire 6.375 (2–3)	Bitty Girl
	Royal Nijinsky 9 (3–4)	Princessnesian 8.7 (3–5)
	Thahul 15 (4–5)	Queen City Miss 6.58 (3–4)
	Vatza 9 (2–4)	Shuvee 9.26 (2–5)
	Balletomane 7.875 (3–4)	Nanticious 6 (2)
	Gala Mood 8 (3–5)	Let's Be Gay 6.375 (2–4)
	Hapai 10.16 (3)	Hypavia 6.625 (2–3)
	Russian Fox 8.5 (2–4)	Flying Fur 8.03 (2–5)
	Shimmy 8.5 (3–4)	Amalesian 6.5 (3)
	Tournament Star 7.7 (3–4)	Chris Evert 8.1 (2–4)
	Dearly Too 7.19 (2–3)	Dearly Precious 6.08 (2–3)
	Khatango 10.9 (3–4)	Penny Flight 7.25 (3–4)
	Leap of The Heart 6.8 (3–4)	Ivory Wand 6.6 (3–4)

SIRE's AWD	FOAL	DAM
8.7	Waving 7.14 (3–4)	Top Round 8.1 (2–6)
	Bemissed 8.2 (2–3)	Bemis Heights 7.2 (2–3)
	Dancing Lesson 6.33 (2–4)	Trim The Sail 6 (2–4)
	Down Stage 8.2 (3)	Flying Above 6.33 (3–4)
	Rosy Spectre 7.83 (3)	Like A Charm 5.66 (2)
	Serheed 11.9 (3–4)	Native Partner 7.045 (2–4)
	Ultramate 6 (3)	Gala Party 6 (2–3)
	White Birch 7.83 (2–3)	Snow Peak 8 (2–5)
	Dancing Crown 8.33 (3)	Too Many Sweets 6.85 (2–3)
	Nagurski 8.5 (2–3)	Deceit 6.59 (2–4)
	Tights 8.5 (2–3)	Dancealot 7.5 (2)
	Caerleon 8.68 (2–3)	Foreseer 6.66 (2–3)
	Vision 9.3 (2–3)	Foreseer

Copernica 5½ (twice) at 2	Copper Canyon 5f at 2 AWD 6.6
Silky 5f at 2	Close Up 5f at 2
Bakor 5½f at 6	Copper Canyon 5f at 2 AWD 6.6
La Jalouse 5, 5½f at 2	Quadruple 6f at 2 (AWD 7.83)
Mixed Applause 5f at 2	My Advantage 5f at 2
Swan 5½f at 2	Her Demon 7f at 2 (AWD 8.0)
Bev Bev 5½f at 2	Native Partner 5½f at 2 (7.0)
Encino 5f at 2	Crimson Saint 4f at 2 (5.14)
Princesse Lida 5f at 2	Princess Lee 5f at 2
Street Ballet 5½f (twice) at 2	Street Dancer 6f at 2 (6.0)
Beaudelaire 5f at 2	Bitty Girl 5f (5 times) at 2
Western Symphony 5f at 2	Millicent Non winner

The list of Nijinsky's progeny who won over 5–5½ furlongs and at what age and their dams' AWD performances

As the above figures show Nijinsky gets a few five furlong flyers but the majority of cases involve a mare who also won over similar distances, mainly at two years. It seems to be more important to put fast mares to Nijinsky if it is intended to race the progeny over the shorter distances in North America where a greater accent is put on precocity.

To take this a step further: does Nijinsky inject speed into mares whose AWD's are greater than his own? Nijinsky's AWD is 8.7 furlongs. How do the resultant foals fare coming from mares whose AWD is greater than this? This survey will only apply to produce from mares who won three times or more.

Most of the mares concerned were European raced of course and therefore are more likely to have an AWD more relative to Nijinsky himself. The produce however did not necessarily race in Europe.

We will then take each foal in turn:

WINNER	SIRES AWD	DAMS AWD
Caught In The Act	8.7	Bamboozle 11.8
Kazatska	8.7	Comtesse de Loir 9.66
Kyra's Slipper	8.7	Drumtop 9.176
Brogan	8.7	Drumtop 9.176
Bedford	8.7	Drumtop 9.176
Pas de Deux	8.7	Example 12.33
Fabuleux Dancer	8.7	Fabuleux Jane 11.25
Fecund	8.7	Farm 10.2
Umabatha	8.7	Hardiesse 9.25
Miss Mazepah	8.7	Monade 9.38
Amen Wadeen	8.7	Monade 9.38
Ipi Tombi	8.7	Oraza 8.75
Cherry Hinton	8.7	Popkins 8.75 (UR at 2)
Royal Nijinsky	8.7	Princessnesian 8.7
Ile de Bourbon	8.7	Roseliere 11.2
Rose Crescent	8.7	Roseliere 11.2
Vatza	8.7	Shuvee 9.26
Milina	8.7	Tender Word 9
Vidalia	8.7	Waya 9.69

Caught In The Act — won over 8.5 furlongs in USA at 3 years. Bamboozle an European raced performer like Nijinsky himself.

Kazatska — out of Arc placed Comtesse de Loir; won over 12½ furlongs in France and stakes placed.

Kyra's Slipper — ex the exclusively American raced Drumtop. Kyra's Slipper won 4 races (AWD 9.375) in USA at 4 and 5 years.

Brogan — also out of Drumtop; won 2 races at 8f and 15f in Europe at 2 and 3 years.

Bedford — again out of Drumtop; won 5 races in England (AWD 12).

Pas de Deux — out of European Group winner Example; won over 10 furlongs at 3 years in England.

Fabuleux Dancer — ex European Group winner Fabuleux Jane; won stakes race over 12f in France at 3.

Fecund — American raced from champion Argentine mare; won 4 times in USA over 8–8½f.

Umabatha — ex European raced Hardiesse; won over 8f at 3 in England.

Miss Mazepah — ex French raced Epsom Oaks winner; won three times over 8½–9f in USA at 3.

Amen Wadeen — out of Monade (as above); won many times over jumps in USA but also won twice over 8½f at 10 years of age on the flat.

Ipi Tombi — ex German champion; Good hurdler in England and won over 12f on flat at 4.

Cherry Hinton — Nijinsky and European Group winner Popkins produced the champion juvenile filly of 1977; won over 6 and 8f at 2.

Royal Nijinsky — out of US Champion; won 3 races 8½–10f at 3 and 4 years in USA.

Ile de Bourbon	out of champion Roseliere. Champion Three Year old and Older Horse; won 5 races 10–13¼f at 3 and 4 years.
Rose Crescent	own sister to Ile de Bourbon; won 3 races in USA 6–11½f from 3 to 5 including a Gr 3 event.
Vatza	out of US Champion; won 3 times over 9f in USA at 2 and 4 years.
Milina	out of American and British raced mare; won 4 times over 8½f in the USA.
Vidalia	out of French and American champion; won over 8f at 2 (Gr 3); looked to need 12f at three in 1984.

As most of these foals were out of ex-European mares most have come back to Europe to race. Not many won at two years which is not surprising considering the AWD's of their parents. However those that won at three and conform nearer to Nijinsky's AWD of 10.83 than his general AWD of 8.7. In many cases the combination of a staying mare has added just a little bit more stamina. In North America most have won over shorter distances than their European raced parents which is not surprising bearing in mind American trends. It is to be concluded that Nijinsky does not sire true sprinters nor indeed true stayers unless helped by speed and stamina influence from the dam, but is a true catalyst for producing top-class classic distance runners, from 6–14 furlongs like himself. The dams AWD is affected greatly by whether she ran in Europe or North America. However, naturally, there are odd exceptions to every rule.

Going

Europe

FIRM/GOOD TO FIRM   Of Nijinsky's European winners 48.07 per cent won on firm or good to firm going but only 18 did not win on any other surface. Only Peacetime, Beaudelaire and Empire Glory were firm ground "specialists" and possibly Solford, who won four of his five races on this kind of going. The majority won on several different types of ground.

GOOD   It would only be expected that the majority of Nijinsky's European winners won on good going, which most racecourses do their utmost to achieve if possible. Firm ground will often be watered days in advance to bring it to "perfect" going. However, only 46.15 per cent of Nijinsky's European winners won on good going including the stakes winners Stradavinsky, Muscovite, Valinsky and Tanzor who showed an especial liking.

SOFT/GOOD TO SOFT   What will be a surprising number to many people of Nijinsky's progeny won on going very much on the soft side. No less than 23.07 per cent won on soft/good to soft going (which include those who showed aptitude on the infamous Irish good to yielding). Of these, four individuals only won on ground with severe indentation. The stakes winners who showed an especial aptitude include Lucky Sovereign, Shining Finish, Fabuleux Dancer, Western Symphony and Greek Sky.

HEAVY/YIELDING   A certain number of Nijinsky's progeny can win on this extreme of surface. Of those relatively few of Nijinsky's progeny (7.69 per cent) the most notable winners have been major stakes winners who did also win on other types of going including Green Dancer, Bright Finish, Ile de Bourbon, Nizon, Piaffer, Niniski and Kings Lake.

As reported, good horses win on any ground. Those who have especially reflected this truism include Green Dancer (French 2,000 Guineas, Prix Lupin, Observer Gold Cup), who won four races on yielding through all points to firm; Bright Finish (Yorkshire Cup, Jockey Club Cup) who won six races from heavy through to firm; Galletto (Galtres Stakes) who won three races in Ireland on good to yielding, good and firm ground; the champion Ile de Bourbon who won the Coronation Cup in very soft going, the Clive Graham on yielding and his three-year-old triumphs on good to firm surfaces; dual Leger victor Niniski who won six races on ground varying from heavy through all degrees to firm ground; Group 3 winner Shining Finish who won five races, three on soft, one on good and one on firm going; the Irish classic winner Kings Lake, winner of five races including three on good and two on soft and yielding going and the Derby winner Golden Fleece whose four successes were gained on soft, good and firm ground. Perhaps with Group races there is less of a tendency to take a horse out because of the ground; the prize and prestige is too valuable.

Nijinsky's European stock have, in the main, been able to win on various types of going and have proved themselves extremely adaptable. It seems virtually impossible to say that Nijinsky's stock win only on good ground as, when asked, they have proved themselves rather more versatile than that.

United States and Canada (Turf)—As has already been stated, the turf courses in North America are regarded rather more as the poorer relation to the dirt. However with the influx of more and more European performers into the United States "grass" is becoming much more popular which is greatly to the benefit of Nijinsky's better American representatives, many of whom have shown a liking for the more natural surface. Of Nijinsky's 149

American winners 79 won on a turf course, 31 exclusively so. As things are rather more definite in North America, degrees of ground such as good to firm and good to soft are not recorded: tracks are firm, good, soft or yielding.

FIRM   An exceptionally high proportion of Nijinsky's North American turf winners, 65 (82.27 per cent), won on firm going and an abnormal, 42 (53.16 per cent), won only on firm ground. Perhaps there is a propensity of firm ground in North America on the turf courses and also because many Nijinsky's are racing in the winter at courses in Florida and California which are predominately in dry areas giving fast going. Stakes winners who have especially excelled include European exile Caucasus, Excitable, His Honor, Shimmy, Dearly Too, Down Stage, Key Dancer and also champion De La Rose of whose ten grass victories, nine were registered on firm ground (she did achieve a success on yielding going).

GOOD   Only 16 of Nijinsky's American turf winners (20.25 per cent) won on good going and of these seven won on nothing else. However, none of the major Graded winners were "good ground specialists" though several did win on it: none showed an especial liking for it. This does lead one to wonder if those who make the decisions regarding the declaration of going tend to err towards the firm side consistently.

SOFT   Because of the number of United States courses who operate in relatively arid conditions not quite so many contests are held on soft and yielding tracks as in Europe. As a result only eight (10.12 per cent) of Nijinsky's turf winners won on soft going and only one exclusively so. Only Summertime Promise of the major winners showed any especial liking for soft going but she also won twice on the firm.

YIELDING   Perhaps surprisingly more horses, 11 (13.92 per cent), won on yielding going though only three won on it. This is perhaps because American racing is more geared to extremes and, in fact, Europeans often call American "yielding" equivalent to soft. The stakes winners to win on yielding turf tracks were Terpsichorist, Street Ballet, De La Rose, Bemissed and Tights, the latter being the only colt in the quintet.

The American horses appear not to be quite so flexible as the European. They tend to race more on one type of surface rather than over different variations. One can only reiterate that much of this may be due to the paucity of ground with any real give in it. Nijinsky's American turf stakes winners who have shown top-class form on ground both on the firm and soft side include Summertime Promise (6 turf wins: 4 soft, 2 firm); Javamine (7 turf wins: 5 firm, 2 soft); Nijana (7 wins: 5 firm, 2 soft); and Terpsichorist (7 turf wins: 4 firm, 2 good, 1 yielding).

United States and Canada (Dirt)—Of course the majority of Nijinsky's American winners were on dirt courses and this also includes the major stakes winners. Unlike the turf tracks not quite so many degrees of going are recorded, these "sub-divisions" being on the wetter side. For this survey I shall assume that sloppy and muddy mean basically the same thing.

FAST   As on turf in North America the greatest proportion of Nijinsky's winners achieved their success on fast going and presumably for basically the same reasons. Of Nijinsky's 118 dirt winners, 104 (88.13 per cent) won on fast going of which 68 won only on fast going. Stakes winners among these 68 include Dancing Champ, La Jalouse, Ballare, Water Dance, Balletomane, Shimmy, Hostage, Key Dancer and Folk Art.

GOOD   The figures for this division again follow the trend set by the turf runners: only 22 (18.64 per cent) succeeding on dirt courses of which five won exclusively on this surface. No stakes winner showed an especial aptitude to this type of ground but several scored on it.

SLOPPY/MUDDY   Probably easier to recognise and divide from other classifications unlike "good" and "fast". Of Nijinsky's winners 30 (25.42 per cent) won on this surface, eight exclusively so. Several stakes winners won at least once on this going, including Baldski, Upper Nile, His Honor, Terpsichorist, Street Ballet, Dearly Too, Rose Crescent, Rosy Spectre and Vision.

Not so many of Nijinsky's stakes winners have shown quite so much versatility over different surfaces as have the turf performers but quite a number have triumphed on both "fast" and "sloppy" going including major Graded winners Nijana, Baldski, Upper Nile, Terpsichorist and Rose Cresent.

All in all Nijinsky's winning progeny, of whatever class, show quite a remarkable adaptability to different types and degrees of going especially when bearing in mind the apparently general opinion that Nijinsky's leaning is especially towards producing solely top of the ground specialists. When it comes to the higher echelons of performers however, the old adage of "a good horse can win on any going" is a proven one and, where they have found it necessary, Nijinsky's major winners have been able to come up trumps over all racecourse surface adversity.

CHAPTER 6

Quality of Mare Books

The class of mare visiting Nijinsky and how this affects the performance of the resulting foals; does it matter what kind of mare Nijinsky has?; can Nijinsky "move up" his mares?; relative merits of full brothers and sisters

While it is necessary to take into consideration the part played in thoroughbred genetics by the female partner, it is equally necessary to realise that Nijinsky does have a higher quality book of mares than the average stallion. He always has had and always will have, but it does not follow that his mares are necessarily any finer than those of his rivals in the leading sires' lists. Indeed at this time the best book of mares in the world probably belongs to Northern Dancer. It does not make him any less of a sire.

It has been proved by statisticians in the United States that Nijinsky can upgrade the mares he receives. In other words the foals produced from these matings can, to a high percentage, achieve more than those the same mares have produced to other stallions. For this reason it will be most rewarding to look at various categories of mares and what they have produced when sent to Nijinsky.

Stakes Winners

The cream of any crop is its necessarily restricted number of stakes winners, be they fillies or colts. Such is the process of selection that victory in a stakes race automatically raises a filly to a different level of mate when she goes to stud. The old adage of breeding "the best to the best to get the best" still holds and without a common belief in this maxim the whole basis of thoroughbred selection would be undermined and founder.

Up until 1981 (the matings which produced the juveniles of 1984) Nijinsky had been put to 328 different mares resulting in 402 produce. (Only mares who produced live foals have been counted here as it is impossible to assess the ability of the resultant foal should it have died or the mare not conceive.)

Of these 328 mares 141 were Group or stakes winners, an above average percentage (over 42 per cent) by any standards. So what are the likelihoods of the produce of these two stakes winners being a stakes winner too?

Bemis Heights (SW)	Bemissed (Gr 1 W)
Be Suspicious (SW)	Half An Hour (SW)
Bitty Girl (Gr 1 W)	Beaudelaire (GW)
Black Satin (Gr 1 W)	Czaravich (Gr 1 W)
Dancealot (Gr 1 W)	Tights (SW)
Dearly Precious (Gr 1 W)	Dearly Too (SW)
Deceit (Gr 1 W)	Nagurski (GW)
Drumtop (Gr 1 W)	Brogan (GW)
Fabuleux Jane (GW)	Fabuleux Dancer (SW)
Fish Bar (SW)	Kings Lake (Gr 1 W)
Flying Above (SW)	Down Stage (SW)
Gaia (Gr 1 W)	Galletto (SW)
Glad Rags (Gr 1 W)	Gorytus (GW)
	Terpsichorist (GW)
Gleam (GW)	Gleason (SW)
Lacquer (Gr 1 W)	Bright Finish (GW)
	Shining Finish (GW)
Lady Victoria (Gr 1 W)	Tanzor (SW)
Like A Charm (Gr 1 W)	Rosy Spectre (SW)
Lisadell (GW)	Yeats (SW)
Miba (GW)	African Dancer (GW)
Morgaise (GW)	Ballare (SW)
Mrs Peterkin (GW)	Dancing Champ (GW)
Nanticious (SW)	Balletomane (GW)
Peace (SW)	Quiet Fling (Gr 1 W)
	Peacetime (GW)
Popkins (GW)	Cherry Hinton (GW)
Prodana Neviesta (GW)	Nijana (GW)
Quill (Gr 1 W)	Caucasus (Gr 1 W)
Roseliere (Gr 1 W)	Ile de Bourbon (Gr 1 W)
	Rose Crescent (GW)
Solometeor (Gr 1 W)	Nuclear Pulse (SW)
Sovereign (GW)	Lucky Sovereign (GW)
Spearfish (Gr 1 W)	Empire Glory (GW)
Squander (Gr 1 W)	Russian Roubles (SW)
Street Dancer (SW)	Street Ballet (SW)
Strong Drink (SW)	Piaffer (SW)
Too Bald (SW)	Baldski (SW)
Top Round (SW)	Waving (SW)
Valoris (Gr 1 W)	Valinsky (GW)
Waya (Gr 1 W)	Vidalia (GW)

The stakes winning mares who produced stakes winning foals to Nijinsky

Obviously, no stallion would be expected to sire 42 per cent stakes winners from all foals; most would be happy with 42 per cent winners. So the odds are not necessarily for the resultant foal being a stakes winner too.

So 37 (26.24 per cent) of the 141 stakes winning mares have produced 41 stakes winners by Nijinsky which represents about 50 per cent of his total stakes winners which supports the adage of breeding the best to the best to the hilt. But what of the other 104 stakes winning mares: what have they produced? 18 (12.7 per cent) have produced black type performers who did not actually win a stakes race. Some may have been unlucky not to do so. 44 (31.2 per cent) produced "ordinary" winners and 10 (7 per cent) produced placed horses. And 23 (16.3 per cent) had produce which never ran. The other 9 (6.3 per cent) had produce which ran but did not reach the first three. Bearing in mind Nijinsky's own outstanding ratio of winners to runners it must be accepted that a mare has probably a greater chance of breeding a winner than to most other stallions. Quite the likelihood of a stakes winner producing a stakes winner can really only be seen when other types of mares are considered. It must be borne in mind the number of foals born each year and that the odds are strongly against any of them being a stakes winner no matter how well bred. Is a stakes winner more likely to be bred by sending a stakes winner to Nijinsky rather than an ordinary winner or a proven dam of stakes winners? Mares have been taken here as being represented by their best produce by Nijinsky. The relative merits of full brothers and sisters where mares have returned to Nijinsky are discussed later.

Per cent	
22.14	stakes winners
11.69	stakes placed
28.85	ordinary winners (stakes winners and stakes placed winners not included)
7.9	placed (stakes placed non-winners not included)
7.8	not in first three
23.63	unraced

Nijinsky's percentages of runners

If these figures are taken into consideration it will be seen that the figures for the mares producing stakes and ordinary winners, is a little higher than Nijinsky's average while the placed and unplaced horses are almost identical but not the stakes placed horse. What is perhaps most surprising is the figure for the unraced horses. Only 16.3 per cent of foals produced by stakes winning mares to Nijinsky did not run, but 23.63 per cent of all his runners never saw a racecourse. The obvious conclusion is that horses out of stakes winners are most likely to see a racecourse which is strange as one would possibly have expected that the better bred animals, especially fillies, would have been most likely to have been kept for stud.

Stakes and Group placed Mares

Just below the absolute higher echelons of the racing world are those horses who did not quite make the top drawer in racecourse competition. These are the animals who proved themselves capable of competing in the best races but not quite able to win them. They must be regarded as superior to the ordinary race winners for the latter must constitute anything from moderate handicap winners to those successful in maidens.

Of Nijinsky's 328 mares, 41 (12.5 per cent) fall into this category. If we divide up their progeny as before one finds that 6 (14.6 per cent) produced stakes winners.

Bendara (GPW)	Esperanto (SW)
Brave Lady (SP)	Popular Hero (SW)
Foreseer (SPW)	Caerleon (Gr 1 W)
	Vision (Gr 1 W)
Homespun (SPW)	Sportin' Life (GW)
	Folk Art (Gr 1 W)
Penny Flight (GP)	Khatango (GW)
Princess Lee (GP)	Princesse Lida (Gr 1 W)

Taken a few steps further: 6 (14.6 per cent) produced stakes placed runners like themselves; 13 (31.6 per cent) produced ordinary winners; 5 (12.19 per cent) placed horses; 3 (7.3 per cent) unplaced horses; and 9 (21.9 per cent) whose progeny never saw a racecourse.

Compared with the stakes winning mares it seems that the stakes placed runners are as likely to produce ordinary winners, more likely to produce stakes placed and placed horses and have considerably more produce (21.9 per cent to 16.3 per cent) who never see a racecourse. They are less likely to produce stakes winners, but are also more likely to produce unplaced animals. When compared to Nijinsky's figures, these mares have produced rather more placed horses but less unplaced animals than perhaps might have been expected.

Ordinary Winners

It is only to be expected that there would be more ordinary winners than mares belonging in either of the above categories in Nijinsky's books of mares because of the sheer size of the thoroughbred population and relative scarcity of stakes races. However, due to the high quality mares Nijinsky is demanding, only 79 ordinary winners have gone to Nijinsky, virtually twice the number of those stakes placed but almost half that of the stakes winners.

It is in these categories that the upgrading by the stallion also comes into force. Of these 79, 17 (21.5 per cent) have produced stakes winners by Nijinsky:

Alyne Que	Muscovite (GW)
Amalesian	Shimmy (SW)
Continual	Shadeed (SW)
Dusky Evening	Javamine (GW)
Exit Smiling	Nizon (Gr 1 W)
Gala Party	Ultramate (SW)
Fond Hope	Sis C (SW)
Greek Victress	Greek Sky (SW)
Lady Graustark	Excitable (SW)
Key Partner	Key Dancer (GW)
Quadruple	La Jalouse (SW)
Quilloquick	Leap Lively (GW)
Rosetta Stone	De La Rose (Gr 1 W)
	Upper Nile (Gr 1 W)
Seximee	Stradavinsky (GW)
Shoubra	Nice Havrais (GW)
So Chic	Pas de Deux (GW)
Virginia Hills	Niniski (Gr 1 W)

Of the remainder of the 79, 10 (12.6 per cent) have produced stakes and Group placed horses; 23 (29.1 per cent) have produced winners; 7 (8.8 per cent) placed horses; 4 (5 per cent) unplaced; and 19 (24 per cent) that never ran.

These figures would seem to suggest that ordinary winners are less likely than stakes winners to produce stakes winners but much more likely than stakes placed horses; similarly so in producing stakes placed horses; are less likely to produce ordinary winners like themselves than either of the stakes type mares; are less likely to produce placed horses than the stakes placed mares but more so than stakes winners; are less likely to produce unplaced horses as stakes placed mares and also stakes winners and are likely to produce as many unraced horses in proportion to other types of mares as the stakes placed, but more than half again as many as those of the stakes winners.

Regarding Nijinsky's figures, the ordinary winners seem to account for a similar percentage of stakes winners and stakes placed performers than Nijinsky's overall performance, an equally similar number of ordinary winners, and placed non-winners, less unplaced horses and very slightly more unraced animals.

Placed and unplaced Mares

Needless to say not a large number of placed and unplaced mares have gone to Nijinsky: most mares selected as suitable mates for the stallion have shown some winning ability. However most are extremely well related and those unplaced actually ran only a few times.

These facts should not however be allowed to count against them, for they have come up with probably more than their fair share of stakes horses and more than anywhere else is demonstrated the stallion's power to upgrade. Of the 16 placed mares that have gone to Nijinsky (only 4.7 per cent of the total), 4 have produced stakes winners, 5 ordinary winners, 5 unraced and two unplaced.

Entente	Hostage (Gr 1 W)
Prides Promise	Summertime Promise (GW)
Secret Beauty	Nijinsky's Secret (Gr 1 W)
Lighted Lamp	Lighted Glory (GW)

The stakes winners produced by placed mares

These were four of Nijinsky's very top performers.

Of the 13 (3.8 per cent) unplaced mares 3 have produced stakes winners, one a stakes placed horse, 4 winners, 3 unraced and 2 placed horses.

Bold Honor	His Honor (SW)
Fast Approach	Summer Fling (GW)
Special	Number (GW)

The stakes winners produced from unplaced mares

So these mares must not be written off, though quite how much is contributed by the stallion and how much by the mare – in this case to produce these high quality horses – can only be guessed at.

Unraced Mares

Many fillies are kept for stud and not risked on a racecourse because of their outstanding bloodlines. Many of these often find their way to the court of the most expensive stallions.

In Nijinsky's case, 36 (10.9 per cent) of his 328 mares fall into this category. Though their potential to produce good winners is, of course, largely untapped beforehand as no one had a real idea as to their own ability, nine (25 per cent) have nevertheless produced eleven stakes winners to Nijinsky:

Exotic Treat	Golden Fleece (Gr 1 W)
Fairness	Solford (Gr 1 W)
Green Valley	Green Dancer (Gr 1 W)
	Val Danseur (SW)
Lower Lights	Yamanin Penny (GW)
Luiana	Water Dance (SW)
Millicent	Western Symphony (GW)
	Moscow Ballet (GW)
Moment of Truth	Night Alert (GW)
Shill	Maruzensky (Gr 1 W)
Sweet Satina	Netherby (SW)

The produce of these mares, of course, represents some of the very best of Nijinsky's progeny.

Only two (5 per cent) mares have produced a stakes placed horse but eleven (30.5 per cent) produced ordinary winners, five (13.8 per cent) placed horses, only two unplaced horses and seven (19.4 per cent) unraced stock like themselves. From these figures one would deduce that more unraced mares are likely to produce stakes winners than any other category except stakes winners themselves, in proportion to the number of each type of mare Nijinsky receives; that they are far less likely to produce a stakes placed horse – they produce a similar number of ordinary winners and unplaced horses but less unraced horses than stakes placed or ordinary winning mares but a good many more than stakes winners – but more placed horses than any other category.

Going by these figures then, stakes winners and unraced mares are more likely to produce stakes winning foals than other categories of mares sent to Nijinsky, but stakes placed mares seem to give the poorest return of stakes winners. The greatest proportion of unraced stock come from winning mares, those of average ability in themselves but below top-class. All categories of mares seem to produce a similar percentage of winners.

In the above calculations it is important to note that the mares who have had more than one foal by Nijinsky have been treated as having just one produce and the best representative has been taken for statistical purposes. The results of full brothers and sisters will be investigated later, in which we see what effect the mare's previous ability to breed stakes winners to other stallions has on Nijinsky foals. We have already seen how Nijinsky can upgrade racing stock with poorer records, now it is time to see what effect he can have on proven stakes producing mares.

Stakes producing Mares

In a number of surveys carried out in the past few years by American racing statisticians, the likes of Nijinsky and Northern Dancer have been proven to be truly outstanding sires because they upgrade even a high quality book of mares; or, in other words, do better with a certain mare than previous stallions have done. When considering stallions like Nijinsky who have a universally higher class book than the "average" stallion it must be realised that in terms of producing top-class animals the better stallions have an even harder task than perhaps a lower regarded sire. A great deal is expected of champion racehorses when they go to stud for, in many respects, they can have no excuses if they fail. Everything is going for them.

When discussing the upgrading achieved by Nijinsky the best produce are really the only ones to be considered. Nijinsky has his share, albeit a lower share, of "ordinary" animals; he certainly has more than his fair share of the higher echelons. Of the 328 individual mares who visited Nijinsky to produce live foals, 64 had a Nijinsky as her first foal. These can now be eliminated as a stallion can only really be said to upgrade a mare if she has had other produce before visiting him. These 64 (19 per cent), included such stars as South Ocean, Example, Street Dancer, Lisadell, Bitty Girl, Cloonlara, Dearly Precious, Swingtime, Waya and Fabuleux Jane. The progeny from these 64 included Green Dancer, Javamine, Maruzensky, Nizon, Niniski, Princesse Lida, Bemissed and many more stakes winners.

Obviously one would expect there to be a greater number of mares who had produced stakes winners before visiting Nijinsky than those who had not, as a breeder is more likely to splash out one of the highest fees in the world for a proven mare rather than an unproven one, whatever her pedigree credentials. In Nijinsky's case 109 of his mares had previously produced a stakes winner, 155 had not by the time the Nijinsky foal was a juvenile.

To begin to narrow this still further to the very cream of the produce of mares who had produced stakes winners before their Nijinsky foal, 29 had also produced stakes winners both to Nijinsky and to other stallions beforehand.

MARE	NIJINSKY SW	PREVIOUS SW
Quill	Caucasus	One for All (Northern Dancer)
Peace	Quiet Fling (Peacetime)	Peaceful (Crepello)
Lady Victoria	Tanzor	Northern Taste (Northern Dancer) Canadian Victory (Canadian Champ)
Prodana Neviesta	Nijana	Zingari (Northern Dancer)

MARE	NIJINSKY SW	PREVIOUS SW
Too Bald	Baldski	Exceller (Vaguely Noble)
So Chic	Pas de Deux	Beau Brummel (Round Table)
		Fashion Verdict (Court Martial)
Rosetta Stone	Upper Nile	Lie Low (Dr Fager)
	(De La Rose)	
Valoris	Valinsky	Val's Girl (Sir Ivor)
Roseliere	Ile de Bourbon	Rose Bowl (Habitat)
	(Rose Crescent)	Rose Bed (Habitat)
Moment of Truth	Night Alert	Convenience (Fleet Nasrullah)
		Indulto (Royal Coinage)
		Proliferation (Warfare)
		Puntilla (Never Bend)
Seximee	Stradavinsky	Nonoalco (Nearctic)
Glad Rags	Terpsichorist	Mirthful Flirt
	(Gorytus)	(Raise A Native)
Drumtop	Brogan	Topsider (Northern Dancer)
		War of Words (Arts and Letters)
Greek Victress	Greek Sky	Greek Answer (Northern Answer)
		Grecian Victory (Dr Fager)
		Lawmaker (Round Table)
Luiana	Water Dance	Little Current (Sea Bird)
Nanticious	Balletomane	Group Plan (Intentionally)
Fish Bar	Kings Lake	Cloonlara (Sir Ivor)
Sweet Satina	Netherby	Red Debonair (Lucky Debonair)
Top Round	Waving	Practitioner (Dr Fager)
		Bends Me Mind (Never Bend)
Amalesian	Shimmy	Chauffeur (Jacinto)
Exotic Treat	Golden Fleece	Office Wife (Secretariat)
Special	Number	Nureyev (Northern Dancer)
Foreseer	Caerleon	Palmistry (Forli)
	(Vision)	
Like A Charm	Rosy Spectre	Herecomesthebride
		(Al Hattab)
Fairness	Solford	No Bias (Jacinto)
Bendara	Esperanto	Ida Delia (Graustark)
Millicent	Western Symphony	Peterhof (The Minstrel)
	(Moscow Ballet)	
Deceit	Nagurski	Accomplice (Graustark)
Spearfish	Empire Glory	Kings Bishop (Round Table)
		Gaily (Sir Gaylord)
		Crown The Prince (Damascus)

One can probably judge for oneself whether the Nijinsky foal was a better racehorse than those preceding him. Certainly in the cases of Quill, Peace, Prodana Neviesta, Rosetta Stone, Valoris, Glad Rags, Exotic Treat, Foreseer, Fairness and, perhaps, Roseliere and Fish Bar, this is certainly true. So Nijinsky can be seen to be able to upgrade even proven stakes producers. In several cases the Nijinsky stakes winners are bred on the same lines: for example, Nijinsky's stakes winners Caucasus, Tanzor, Nijana, Brogan and

Number are half brothers and sisters to stakes winners by Nijinsky's sire Northern Dancer. Western Symphony is half brother to Peterhof (by Nijinsky's three parts brother The Minstrel). Stradavinsky is half brother to Nonoalco, by Northern Dancer's sire Nearctic. It is notable that of Roseliere's four stakes winners, two are by Nijinsky and two by Habitat, Nijinsky on Habitat is already a proven cross in Europe.

However the true test of any stallion is to produce stakes winners from mares who have had foals previously but have not been able to breed a black type winning horse. In Nijinsky's case 26 mares had bred stakes winners to Nijinsky whereas they had not before. This is only three fewer than the number of mares producing stakes winners to other stallions before the Nijinsky stakes winner.

The list of these 26 and their produce is printed below:

Mrs Peterkin	Dancing Champ
Lighted Lamp	Lighted Glory
Prides Promise	Summertime Promise
Miba	African Dancer
Lacquer	Bright Finish (Shining Finish)
Be Suspicious	Half An Hour
Solometeor	Nuclear Pulse
Gaia	Galletto
Sovereign	Lucky Sovereign
Popkins	Cherry Hinton
Lady Graustark	Excitable
Bold Honor	His Honor
Strong Drink	Piaffer
Black Satin	Czaravich
Gleam	Gleason
Morgaise	Ballare
Secret Beauty	Nijinsky's Secret
Quilloquick	Leap Lively
Homespun	Sportin' Life (Folk Art)
Entente	Hostage
Penny Flight	Khatango
Lower Lights	Yamanin Penny
Dancealot	Tights
Squander	Russian Roubles
Gala Party	Ultramate
Continual	Shadeed

Two of these mares have bred stakes winners since to other stallions: Mrs Peterkin (Sweet Alliance, by Sir Ivor) and Lady Graustark (Bel Bolide, by Bold Bidder). The fact that these are the only ones speaks volumes for Nijinsky's ability. As can be seen from the above list these stakes winners include some of the very best of his stock.

Significantly, a large proportion of mares whose first foal was by Nijinsky have bred nothing as good as that foal in subsequent years: these include Green Valley (Green Dancer), Dusky Evening (Javamine), Quadruple (La Jalouse), Shill (Maruzensky), Exit Smiling (Nizon), Virginia Hills (Niniski), Fond Hope (Sis C), Shoubra (Nice Havrais), Princess Lee (Princesse Lida) and Bemis Heights (Bemissed). A few of the mares from this group have so far only had foals of classic age by Nijinsky having not visited another stallion including Street Dancer (Street Ballet, La Nijinska, Nijinska Street and Prince Street), Dearly Precious (Dearly Too and Preciously Dear), Flying Above (Down Stage and Suspend), Fabuleux Jane (Fabuleux Dancer and Alezan Dancer) and Swingtime (Countertrade and Tunic).

Of course there are also a few who have bred stakes winners where Nijinsky has not since these first foals. They include Alluvial who was dam of Belmont Stakes victor Coastal but her Nijinsky filly, Dancing Detente, never saw a racecourse and it would be unfair to say that Nijinsky had failed where another stallion had succeeded. This also applies to South Ocean who was later the dam of Northernette and Storm Bird. Her first foal Sevastopol was also unraced. Several of the mares who had already produced stakes winners by other stallions had produced foals to Nijinsky who had gained black type but had just failed to win a stakes race. In several cases, however, the placings were probably better than some of the minor stakes successes gained by their maternal half brothers and sisters, also a large proportion of these stakes producing mares came up with a subsequently unraced foal by Nijinsky.

Added to all this is the fact that Nijinsky has a far greater percentage of winners to runners and stakes winners to winners than probably any other stallion in the world. Against any criterion Nijinsky has proved himself worthy of the accolades.

Repeated Matings

Bruce Lowe said that one successful mating should not be repeated as the resultant foal would have too much of the sires blood and overbalance the genetic make-up in the foal, some elements being left over inside the mare from the previous union and therefore the second foal would almost certainly not have the ability of the first.

With this in mind let us take the mating that produced Nijinsky himself. According to Lowe the foal which followed Nijinsky would not receive the same dosage from Northern Dancer and Flaming Page as did Nijinsky as there would be a surplus element of Northern Dancer left from the mating which produced Nijinsky. The resultant foal was Minsky. Chestnut, with a white blaze and white stockings resembling The Minstrel type of Northern Dancer rather than Nijinsky or Flaming Page, Minsky proved to be a champion two-year-old in Ireland and subsequently a "sire sensation" in Japan until his premature death. No Nijinsky, certainly. But has there ever been a case of full brothers both having the exceptional ability of a Nijinsky?

In investigating full brothers and sisters we will see that there will be cases of the foals being of comparable merit and those where one foal is definitely better than the other and a significant proportion where one foal never made the racecourse at all.

Of mares revisiting Nijinsky at least once more, 62 produced two *live* foals: 12 of these for three or even four seasons. These figures include the 1981 season which resulted in foals of 1982. Many of these foals of 1982, have of course, been unraced as juveniles but will no doubt be seen in their second season. This must be borne in mind as this will account for the disproportionately large number of unraced animals. Some mares have returned to Nijinsky and have not produced more than one live foal and are therefore not admissable in this discourse.

There are 12 mares which produced foals which were both stakes winners, that is, in the top percentage of racing stock. To these we may add Glad Rags and Bitty Girl, two of whose three foals were black type and the third unraced; and also the case of Rosetta Stone whose own sister to De La Rose and Upper Nile was a juvenile winner in France in 1983.

These mares are listed below with an indication of the abilities of their stock.

Bonnie Google, 1959 by Better Self, winner of 4 races. Dam of

Masqued Dancer (1972) won 2 races, second Queen Alexandria Stakes
Krassata (1973) 6 races in Ireland and USA and second Azalea Stakes, third Silken Glider Stakes (Gr 3), Consul Bayeff Rennen (Gr 3) Brownstown Stakes, Queen of The Stage Handicap, Parlo Handicap and La Prevoyante Handicap, fourth Irish 1,000 Guineas Gr I and Irish Oaks Gr I.
Bonnie Google had earlier produced Gr 1 winner Bonnie And Gay and Ohio Oaks winner La Noticia, both by Sir Gaylord

Drumtop, 1966 by Round Table, champion racemare, winner of 17 races. Dam of

Brogan (1980) won 2 races including Gr 3 Prix Berteux, second Italian Derby Gr I, third Prix de l'Esperance Gr 3
Bedford (1978) 3 races, second Houghton Stakes, third Irish St Leger Gr I
Kyra's Slipper (1976) 4 races, second Grassland Handicap
Had earlier produced stakes winners Topsider (1974 by Northern Dancer) and War of Words (1977 by Arts And Letters)

Foreseer, 1969 by Round Table, stakes placed winner of 3 races. Dam of

Caerleon (1980) won 4 races viz French Derby, Gr I, Benson & Hedges Gold Cup Gr I,

Ballsbridge/Tattersalls Anglesey Stakes Gr 3, Tyros Stakes
Vision (1981) won 5 races at 2 and 3 years including the Gr 1 Secretariat Stakes on turf and the dirt Gr 3 Pilgrim Stakes by 5¼ lengths
Earlier dam of stakes winner Palmistry (by Forli)

Lacquer, 1964 by Shantung, won Irish 1,000 Guineas Gr 1. Dam of

Bright Finish (1973) 6 races including Gr 2 Yorkshire Cup, Gr 3 Jockey Club Cup. English champion three year old stayer.
Shining Finish (1977) 5 races including Gr 3 St Simon Stakes, third John Porter Stakes Gr 2, Yorkshire Cup Gr 2
Only stakes winners produced by Lacquer to date

Lady Victoria, 1962 by Victoria Park, winner of Gr 1 Princess Elizabeth Stakes (Canada). Dam of

Tanzor (1972) won Acomb Stakes, Nijinsky's first stakes winner, third Chesham Stakes
Lady Jinsky (1974) 4 races in Canada, second Canadian Oaks Gr I, Mazarine Stakes
Lady Victoria had already produced Group winners Canadian Victory (1968 by Canadian Champ), Northern Taste (1971 Northern Dancer) and stakes winners Titled Hero and Canadian Taste

Peace, 1966 by Klairon, won Blue Seal Stakes, second 1,000 Guineas Trial. Dam of

Quiet Fling (1972) won 5 races including Gr 1 Coronation Cup, Gr 2 John Porter Stakes, second Irish St Leger Gr I
Peacetime (1979) won 3 races including Gr 3 Guardian Classic Trial, Schroder Life Predominate Stakes and Valdoe Stakes, third Houghton Stakes, Earl of Sefton Stakes Gr 3
Peace also dam of stakes winners Peaceful (1971 by Crepello), Intermission (1973 by Stage Door Johnny) and Group winner Armistice Day (1976 by Rheingold)

Roseliere, 1965 by Misti IV, French Oaks Gr I, Prix Vermeille, Gr I. Dam of

Ile de Bourbon (1975) champion 3 and 4 year old colt; 5 races including King George VI & Queen Elizabeth Stakes Gr I, Coronation Cup Gr I, etc
Rose Crescent (1979) 4½ races to date in USA including Athenia Handicap Gr 3
Roseliere also bred champion Rose Bowl (1972) and Group winner Rose Bed (1971), both by Habitat

Secret Beauty, 1967 by Raise A Native, placed. Dam of

Dancing Secret (1977) 6 races and third Martha Washington Handicap
Nijinsky's Secret (1978) 14 races including Gr I Hialeah Turf Cup, twice, Gr 2 Bougainvillea Handicap, W. L. McKnight Handicap and Tidal Handicap, and Gr 3 Jockey Club Stakes and King Edward Gold Cup
These are the only stakes performers produced to date by Secret Beauty

Dancealot, 1971 by Round Table, 4 races including Gr 1 Selima Stakes. Dam of

Dancing Again (1980) 2 races and second Ancient Title Stakes
Tights (1981) 7½ races including Graded events Silver Screen Handicap, La Jolla Mile and Volante Handicap
These are the only stakes performers out of Dancealot. She also has a 3YO of 1985 by Nijinsky.

Green Valley, 1967 by Val de Loir. Unraced. Dam of

Green Dancer (1972) 4 races including the Gr 1 events French 2,000 Guineas, Prix Lupin and Observer Gold Cup
   Val Danseur (1980) 3 races in France and USA including the Blue Larkspur Stakes on his first start in the latter country
   In between Green Valley produced French Group winner Ercolano (1974 by Sir Ivor)

Homespun, 1969 by Round Table, dual winner and twice stakes placed. Dam of
   Sportin' Life (1978) 8 races including 5 stakes events including the Allegheny by 7½ lengths
   Folk Art (1982) a leading juvenile filly in the USA in 1984; winner of the Oak Leaf Stakes (Gr 1)
   The only stakes winners produced by Homespun.

Millicent, 1969 by Cornish Prince, unraced. Dam of
   Western Symphony (1981) juvenile Group winner in Ireland
   Moscow Ballet (1982) won the P. J. Prendergast Railway Stakes (Gr 3) at 2 years in 1984.

Glad Rags, 1963 by High Hat, winner of 1,000 Guineas Gr I. Dam of
   Terpsichorist (1975) won 11 races including Gr 2 Sheepshead Bay Handicap, Gr 3 Rutgers Handicap, Long Island Handicap
   Vaslava (1977) unraced
   Gorytus (1980) won Laurent Perrier Champagne Stakes (Gr 2), Acomb Stakes
   Glad Rags also dam of Gr 3 winner Mirthful Flirt (1972 by Raise A Native)

Bitty Girl, 1971 by Habitat, champion juvenile in England. Dam of
   Nijit (1977) won 5 races, second Primonetta Handicap, Ocean City Stakes, third Cotillion Stakes
   Bivouac (1978) unraced
   Beaudelaire (1980) won 4 of his 7 races including Gr 2 Prix Maurice de Gheest, Beeswing Stakes and Coolmore Try My Best Stakes, second Kilfrush/What A Guest Stakes and Coolmore Hello Gorgeous Stakes
   Bitty Girl had produced stakes winner Memento (1979 by Roberto)

Rosetta Stone, 1964 by Round Table, won 3 races. Dam of
   Upper Nile (1974) 6 races including Suburban Handicap, Gr I, Gr 3 Nassau County Handicap
   De La Rose (1978) Champion Turf Filly, 11 races including Gr I Hollywood Derby
   Rose O'Riley (1981) winner in France at 2 years
   Rosetta Stone bred Group winner Lie Low (1971 by Dr Fager)

These are the select band of mares who have bred all top-class stock to Nijinsky. Obviously the majority of Nijinsky's mares are selected for their own exceptional racing merit, or the ability to breed his quality racing stock, so it is not surprising that these mares had often bred stakes horses to other stallions. In terms of potential, as in the case of Rosetta Stone, we can possibly add Dearly Precious, who has already produced a Nijinsky stakes horse and had a three-year-old of 1984 which had already shown winning form and was potentially of true black type calibre but was not seen out in her second season.

Dearly Precious, 1973 by Dr Fager, Champion Two Year Old Filly, 12 races including Spinaway Stakes Gr I, Sorority Stakes Gr I and Acorn Stakes Gr I. Dam of

> Dearly Too (1979) won 7 races including Starbright Stakes and Violet Handicap
> Preciously Dear (1981) winner at two in USA, three times fourth including Gr 2 Hollywood Futurity and It's In The Air Stakes
> Her only foals to date

Of the remainder of the 62, 27 also bred a black type performer including Dusky Evening who bred the Graded winner Javamine, stakes placed Sir Jinsky and the winner Debussy, and Street Dancer who went to Nijinsky five times up to the 1981 season, and produced Street Ballet (stakes winner), stakes placed La Nijinska, winner Nijinska Street and the unraced Prince Street and Words 'n Music, a two-year-old of 1984. Of these 27, in the case of ten mares the other foal was a winner (this is without Rosetta Stone and Dearly Precious). For a further 14 the second foal was unraced.

We have now accounted for 42 of the 62 mares. In three cases neither foal saw a racecourse so we can eliminate them. Of the 16 mares left, four have bred two winners from the two foals, and for Argentine champion La Sevillana two of her three foals won and the other was unraced. Of the eleven remaining six had one winner and one unraced foal.

The five we have left look something like this:
(a) Bold Liz, dam of an unraced filly and a placed filly
(b) Shinnecock, dam of a winning colt and one who ran twice
(c) Swift Lady, dam of a placed filly and an unraced filly
(d) Swift Symbol, dam of a winning colt and a colt who ran three times
(e) Rose Bowl, dam of an unraced filly and a filly who ran twice.

The conclusions to be drawn must be that for the majority of mares the return mating has been a worthwhile exercise. For those whose second produce never ran, it cannot be judged as to what might have happened had they done so. For the unraced fillies who have stakes horses for full brothers or sisters it cannot harm their paddock value in the least. It is to be seen that for Nijinsky the black type produce from successive matings is far above that to be expected from an ordinary stallion but so too is his stakes ratio to runners to that of an average sire.

In the seasons subsequent to 1981 more mares have gone back to Nijinsky than ever before and many of the above have two-year-old full relations to previous Nijinsky performers to represent them in 1985 with yearlings coming on behind.

CHAPTER 7

Searching for a "Nick"

Trying to ascertain whether the combination of Nijinsky with other sire lines has a particular success rate, the key to breeding good horses; notable characteristics of these crosses

One of the most fascinating aspects in the science of thoroughbred genetics is that of blood affinity or "nicks". Certain lines of blood appear to have an affinity when mated to other specific lines to produce exceptional results. For example, Isonomy on Hermit mares. This does not necessarily work the other way around, Hermit on Isonomy mares, assuming that both stallions are active at the same time. One of the most famous and effective was Phalaris on Chaucer mares, a union of blood which produced Fairway, Pharos, Colorado and Fair Isle, amongst others. Seen the other way around over 50 per cent of Chaucer's best winners as maternal grandsire were by Phalaris. The only notable exception in this case was Hyperion (by Gainsborough, by Bayardo). This process could not be reversed as Phalaris retired to stud after Chaucer had died.

Is it purely a result of opportunity? The problem with Nijinsky's stock arises with the large number of mares from one particular line, especially Bold Ruler and his sons. Being a Claiborne produced strain this relationship between the two lines has been given plenty of time to flourish, yet so far it has resulted in just two Group winners (Western Symphony and his own brother Moscow Ballet) and one stakes winner (His Honor) out of 20 foals.

Occurrence of "nicks" cannot be foretold but if they work . . . Inbreeding has also produced many good horses and it may be as well to start here by looking at Nijinsky's record when put to mares also from the Phalaris male line but, as yet, excluding Bold Ruler as he appears to be very much a special case.

Phalaris

VIA NEARCO To start with the closest aligned bloodline: Nearco himself was, along with Ribot, probably the best colt ever seen on a racecourse in Europe. According to his breeder Federico Tesio he was not a true stayer but won longer races (up to 15 furlongs) due to his "superb class and brilliant speed". This could also apply to his great grandson. He has however, founded a dynasty of top-class middle distance horses both through the male and female lines. The vast majority of the mares put to Nijinsky from his line are descended from Nearco's sons Nasrullah and Royal Charger. There are just five who do not come from either of these. Three of them were Group winners, one a decent winner, the fifth unraced. The Group 1 winning Solford was out of a daughter of the Belmont Stakes winning Cavan; African Dancer, Group 2 winner in England, was out of the Group winning Miba, by the Arc and Leger hero Ballymoss; while Lucky Sovereign, a middle distance Group winner, was out of the brilliantly fast Sovereign, who was by Pardao, a very similar performer to Lucky Sovereign, having won the Lingfield Derby Trial, Gordon Stakes and Jockey Club Cup, all twelve furlong races.

No less than 36 of Nijinsky's progeny come from mares descended from Nasrullah (other than through Bold Ruler), a tough and classy middle distance horse but whose temperament often got the better of him and which trait has often been seen in his descendants. However, there is nothing to show in the Nijinsky progeny with this blood that there is any more "hot blood" than through any other strain, though in one or two cases it may explain a certain amount of wilfulness. Silky, for example, is out of a Nearula (by Nasrullah) mare and therefore displays very close inbreeding to sons of Nearco (3 × 3). It is this tight relationship that has produced those performers who had greater temperament problems.

Of these 36, seven (19.4 per cent) were stakes or Group winners: La Jalouse and Empire Glory, out of mares by the Californian Stakes winner Fleet Nasrullah, Balletomane (mare by Nantallah), Baldski (out of a Bald Eagle mare), Esperanto (ex Never Bend mare), and Rosy Spectre, whose dam Like A Charm was by the Camden Handicap winner Pied d'Or, and Pas de Deux, out of the Nasrullah mare So Chic. Three (8.3 per cent) more were stakes placed: the aforementioned Silky (ex Nearula mare), Vatza (ex Shuvee, by Nashua) and Mixed Applause (out of a Princely Gift mare). Of the others eight (22.2 per cent) won a race of some description, two (5.5 per cent) were placed and five (13 per cent) did not reach the first three. A perhaps surprising 13 (36.1 per cent) did not make the racecourse, though this has included one unraced as a juvenile in 1984.

Many of these winners showed surprising speed and precocity as two-year-olds, notably La Jalouse, Mixed Applause and Silky and also Sportsky, all of whose wins at three and four were over seven furlongs. Indeed, many of Nijinsky's "shorter" runners such as Great Performance and Miss Nijinsky were also in this category; the only winners amongst these who were victorious over 8½ furlongs were Vatza (9 furlongs) Esperanto (10–11 f), Empire Glory (10–12 f) and Drumnadrochit (12 f); all the others recorded victories over less than 8½ furlongs.

The maternal sires of the Nijinsky produce in this case were Fleet Nasrullah (4), Grey Sovereign, Immortality, Jaipur (2), Kythnos (2), Lt Stevens, Nantallah (2), Nashua (3), Nearula, Never Bend (7), Pied d'Or, Bald Eagle, Princely Gift, Sovereign Path, Tillman, T. V. Lark (4) and Nasrullah himself. Many of these are great influences for speed. Perhaps it is to here that those seeking to inject speed into Nijinsky should be looking rather than to Raise A Native and his ilk, but bearing in mind that too close inbreeding may produce particularly wilful customers.

Apart from Nasrullah and Bold Ruler the other great progenitor of the Nearco line is Royal Charger. Of Nijinsky's produce 36 come from mares by sires descended from him, six (16.6 per cent) won stakes and Group races, a startling percentage; Grade 3 winner Summer Fling (ex Fast Approach, by First Landing), Lighted Glory (ex Sir Gaylord mare), Yamanin Penny, a Japanese Group 3 winner also out of a Sir Gaylord mare, Princesse Lida, Nijinsky's champion two-year-old daughter, out of a Habitat mare, Beaudelaire, also from a Habitat mare, and Sis C, a stakes winning daughter of the Sir Ivor mare Fond Hope. A further four (11.1 per cent) were stakes and Group placed: Beaudelaire's sister Nijit, Come Rain or Shine (out of a Francis S mare), Lightning Leap (ex First Landing mare), and Leap Of The Heart, out of a Sir Ivor mare. A further eleven (30.5 per cent) won, three (8.3 per cent) were placed but only one failed to make the first three. Ten (27.7 per cent) never ran but included six unraced two-year-olds of 1984 and Debutante Bob, who died in training at two years before she could race.

Winners to have come from this blood seem to cover a range of distance performers up to 12½ furlongs and the immediate influences seem to reflect this too. Royal Charger himself was a top sprinter but was placed in the 2,000 Guineas (8 furlongs). He was not a high-class two-year-old unlike some of his descendants. The maternal grandsires of Nijinsky's stock have a familiar ring: Hail To Reason (2), Sir Gaylord (8), Habitat (9), Sir Ivor (7), Mongo (3), First Landing (4), Turf Charger, Francis S and Riva Ridge.

VIA SICKLE   Sickle was a half brother to Hyperion and was the third best two-year-old of his year ultimately finishing third, like Royal Charger, in the 2,000 Guineas. His line is almost exclusively through the top-class sprinter Polynesian (by Unbreakable) and his champion son Native Dancer. Nijinsky's 22 produce from mares of his line all come down from Native Dancer. However these 22 only come from 15 different mares.

It is noticeable among these 22 that a remarkable number ran and an equally remarkable number won. Remember that stakes winners and stakes placed ordinary winners are counted separately.

Three (13.6 per cent) were stakes and Group winners: Street Ballet (ex the Native Dancer mare Street Dancer who had five foals by Nijinsky), Muscovite and Nijinsky's Secret, both out of daughters of Raise A Native. Six others (27 per cent) were stakes or Group placed: Nijinsky's Secret's sister Dancing Secret, Street Ballet's sister La Nijinska, London Bells, Father Matthew, and Bev Bev, all out of Raise A Native mares, and Rissa, a daughter of the Sea Bird II mare Kittiwake. Of the remainder five (22.7 per cent) won, two (9 per cent) failed to make the frame and five (22.7 per cent) were unraced including two-year-olds Dancing Brownie and Words 'n Music.

The maternal grandsires consist of six furlong winner Elevation, Native Dancer (6), Polynesian, Raise A Native (12) and Sea Bird II (2). As Raise A Native has the reputation of putting speed into staying blood it will be worth looking at him separately. Ten of the twelve produce of his daughters won; those that won at three years and up won from every distance from 7 to 12 furlongs and Bundle of Kisses even won over 15 furlongs. Most showed enough speed to win over 6 furlongs at two years and Bev Bev even over 5½ furlongs but these do not seem necessarily to show any more speed than other lines and certainly not as much as those from Nasrullah line mares. More than half did have best distances of around a mile however. Of the remainder the same is true; the majority had their best distance of 8½–9 furlongs, in fact more so than those derived solely from Raise A Native.

VIA FAIRWAY Eight of Nijinsky's progeny are from mares from the Fairway line. Pharos's St Leger winning brother had more ability on the racecourse than Nearco's sire but had more of the Phalaris nervousness. He was a very versatile horse, winning the Coventry Stakes as a two-year-old and the 10 furlong Eclipse by eight lengths, the 14 furlong St Leger and the 10 furlong Champion Stakes (twice). Only Fair Trial of his sons was a real success at stud and in the main this line does not have much stamina and so is fading from the classic scene being maintained by the success of milers such as Brigadier Gerard. The best middle distance racehorse Blue Peter was a relative disappointment at stud but does figure as a broodmare sire in

Nijinsky's progeny as the maternal grandsire of Running Ballerina, a successful broodmare.

The results from this particular branch have been poor compared with other descendants of Phalaris. None of the seven won a stakes race or was even placed in one; three did win, two out of daughters of Court Martial and one by Blue Peter, three were unplaced though ran little and two were unraced including a two-year-old of 1984 in Abeesh.

The broodmare sires here were Court Martial (3), Blue Peter, Palestine, Sensitivo, Tatan and Quibu. Although a thin bloodline one, it seems, to be avoided.

VIA MANNA   The horse to win the Derby by the furthest distance until Shergar in the twentieth century. There is only one representative of Manna amongst Nijinsky's progeny; the French stakes winner over hurdles Half An Hour, out of a Porterhouse mare.

VIA PHARAMOND   The last major representative of the Phalaris line, Pharamond was not a great racehorse though he did win the Middle Park at two. An own brother to Sickle his line is carried down by Menow, sire of Nijinsky's grandam Flaring Top. Of Nijinsky's progeny 28 come from mares of this line.

Four (14.2 per cent) of the 28 were Group or stakes winners: champion Maruzensky and Russian Roubles, both out of Buckpasser mares, Dancing Champ (out of a mare by Buckpasser's sire Tom Fool) and Javamine, a daughter of Dusky Evening, by Tim Tam. Two (6.1 per cent) were stakes placed: Javamine's brother Sir Jinsky, and Gallantsky (out of a Buckpasser mare).

Eight (28.5 per cent) were winners, three (10.7 per cent) placed, none were unplaced but eleven (37 per cent) never saw a racecourse.

Menow himself was best at distances of eight furlongs and under. His son Tom Fool got ten furlongs and was unbeaten at four years over distances such as these despite great imposts of weight. His son Buckpasser won 25 races and also got ten furlongs well.

The maternal grandsires of Nijinsky progeny are as follows: Buckpasser (16), Jester, Tim Tam (5), Tom Fool (5), and Tompion. All the progeny showed a tendency to distances above eight furlongs much like Nijinsky himself and which should only be expected from a union between him and mares from the Pharamond/Menow line. Even Goldye's Miss, a juvenile of 1983, scored her success over an extended mile.

For what it may be worth the majority of the Nijinsky stakes winners and placed animals descended from other lines from Nearco tend to be fillies (17 to 9) but with the Pharamond line colts have the upper hand (5 to 1).

Bold Ruler

Because of the large number of progeny from mares from the Bold Ruler line and because of the apparent relatively poor results, especially when compared to other representatives of the Phalaris male line, it is as well to treat Bold Ruler as a separate entity.

Of Nijinsky's progeny 20 come from mares from Bold Ruler and his sons. Of the 20 there are plenty of winners but there is a distinct scarcity of quality at the top, especially when one considers the quality of mares sent to Nijinsky.

Only three were Group or stakes winners: Western Symphony, from Mill Reef's Cornish Prince half sister, his own brother Moscow Ballet and His Honor, out of Bold Ruler's daughter Bold Honor. Of the rest only Ranking Beauty (ex Chieftain mare) was stakes placed (twice) and did not win in three starts.

However eight (40 per cent) did win, three (15 per cent) were placed (apart from Ranking Beauty), and five (25 per cent) were unraced (one two-year-old of 1984) but none were unplaced.

The maternal grandsires were Bold Ruler himself (7), and his sons Bold Bidder, Bold Lad (IRE), Bold Lad (USA) (3), Boldnesian, Chieftain, Cornish Prince (2), Jacinto (2) Dewan and Reviewer. Bold Ruler was the champion three-year-old and Horse Of The Year. Though he stayed ten furlongs himself, his lack of distance capacity has been the most serious limitation in his stud career. The majority of Nijinsky's runners from this line have been best at eight furlongs but as there are plenty of stakes opportunities in the United States it does not excuse the poor performance of stock. There are also opportunities in Europe for specialist milers, more and more a coming trend. Regarding the Group winners, Western Symphony, gained his Group 3 success over seven furlongs as a juvenile having been successful at five and six furlongs. In 1984 he was not successful when tried over longer distances and fell far short of expectations. His brother, Moscow Ballet, won two races as a juvenile in 1984, both over six furlongs, and including the P. J. Prendergast Railway Stakes (Group 3). Neither seemed to train on past their two-year-old days.

Hyperion

In total contrast to Bold Ruler, Nijinsky on mares from the Hyperion line has resulted in some of the best performers in recent years on both sides of the Atlantic. Of Nijinsky's progeny 40 are from mares descended from the Derby and St Leger winner's line. Hyperion could not have been much more unlike Nijinsky in appearance: chestnut, short legged, standing barely 15.1½ h.h. at three years and as calm in temperament as could be possible. He has become the greatest sire to stand in England in modern times, with the possible exception of Nearco, and his influence has come down the generations from many sons of many diverse natures.

Of the 40 foals, six (15 per cent) were stakes and Group winners, perhaps not a staggering percentage in itself, but in the six were some of Nijinsky's very best performers, headed by the unbeaten Derby winner Golden Fleece (ex Vaguely Noble mare); the brother and sister Gorytus and Terpsichorist (out of High Hat's classic winning daughter Glad Rags); Czaravich (out of Black Satin, by Linacre); Nureyev's three parts sister Number and Yeats, both out of Forli mares. Added to these are five (12.5 per cent) Group and stakes placed winners: Olamic (ex Forli mare); Borodine (ex Gun Bow mare); She Can Dance (ex Inca Yata mare); Stetchworth, out of a Right Royal V mare; and Makarova (ex Saint Crespin III mare). Hyperion's influence certainly has a varied and vast perimeter.

There were 13 (32.5 per cent) other winners, five (12.5 per cent) were placed and nine (22.5 per cent) unraced (three juveniles of 1984). Apart from the abnormally large number of unraced stock, only two were among Nijinsky's least able runners being unplaced, though Lucy Blue only ran once.

The influence coming from several Hyperion sons is reflected in the varied and large number of maternal grandsires: Creme dela Creme, Eighty Grand, Forli (4), Gin Tour, Gun Bow (2), Helioscope, High Hat (3), Hornbeam, Inca Yata (2), Flow Line, Linacre, Right Royal V, Dumpty Humpty, Rigoberto, Saint Crespin III (2), Salvo, Sky High, Swaps (7), Tudor Melody, Tudor Minstrel, Vaguely Noble (5), Warfare and Windy Sands.

One would probably expect the majority of stock of Nijinsky on Hyperion mares to be best over 10–12 furlongs and so about 30 per cent of them are. But more are better over shorter distances, another 30 per cent best at six and seven furlongs. Obviously the female line will have something to do with it, but it seems that the Hyperion line is also a surprising source of speed and representatives like Golden Fleece, Terpsichorist, Stetchworth, Russian Noble and Mansky, who got twelve furlongs, seem to be more of an exception than the rule. The vast majority were winners over 7–9 furlongs and the likes of Czaravich and Number are perhaps most typical.

St Simon

Via Persimmon

VIA PRINCEQUILLO If opportunity plays a great part in the creation or finding of nicks then Nijinsky on Princequillo certainly is an example. Of Nijinsky's progeny 44 come from Princequillo and his sons (especially Round Table) mares alone. It had been noted how well Nasrullah did on Princequillo. Both stood at Claiborne so there was great opportunity. It was here that Bull Hancock practised his theory of the practicality of selection – that the nick "gives an outcross in which some things in the stallion compensate for their absence in the mare". Here it was Nasrullah's fiery temper on such as Round Table's calm disposition. Round Table was also not very big, Nasrullah mares were big and rangy. The results included Bold Bidder, Bold Lad (USA), Mill Reef, Riverman, Secretariat and Seattle Slew.

We can see the same theories being practised in Nijinsky on Princequillo. Temperament, size and opportunity. As Nijinsky stands at Claiborne so there are a great many Princequillo line mares available. Most Nijinsky mares are big and rangy and there is more of a nervous streak in Nijinsky than in Round Table and Princequillo.

Of these 44, 14 (an outstanding 27.2 per cent) won stakes or Group races. This is really a quite staggering percentage, over a quarter of all the produce of Nijinsky on Princequillo line mares. These Group winners also include some of the very best Nijinsky has sired: Group 1 winners, the own brother and sister Upper Nile and De La Rose (ex Round Table mare); Caucasus (ex Princequillo mare); the French Derby winner Caerleon and his brother Vision (ex Round Table mare); Nizon (ex Stage Door Johnny mare); outstanding juvenile Folk Art (ex Round Table mare) and Kings Lake (ex Baldric II mare) plus Nagurski (ex Prince John mare), while Ballare, Sportin' Life, Waving, Brogan and Tights were all stakes and Group winning sons and daughters of Round Table mares. Added to these are seven (15.6 per cent) stakes placed winners: Avodire (Princequillo mare); Equinol (Round Table mare); Fortunate Dancer and Nishino Northern (both out of Prince John mares); Tights's brother Dancing Again and Brogan's brother and sister Bedford and Kyra's Slipper.

Eleven (25 per cent) also won other races, only two were just placed and three ran once without being in the frame. The remaining seven were unraced including three juveniles of 1984.

By any standards these are phenomenal figures and outstrip any other unions in terms of stakes and Group winners and performers.

Princequillo was a small horse and had indifferent sires in his own pedigree and though his dam had been a good class racemare there had been no good colt produced by the first three dams. More importantly there was no speed. His best performers had speed on the female line but most were on the small side. Most of his sons have sired stock with the full range of stamina.

The maternal grandsires in the Nijinsky's are: 2,000 Guineas victor Baldric II (2); American Derby and Preakness victor Hill Prince; the two-year-old Prince John (4), best known as a juvenile sire; Princequillo himself (10); the 43 race winner Round Table (23); and the Louisiana Derby winner Royal Union and Belmont Stakes winner Stage Door Johnny (2) and one representative for Longacres Derby victor Table Run.

A relative lack of speed might be expected in the union with a horse whose AWD is around 10–12 furlongs as a three-year-old. Yet nine, a third of the 27 horses who won at three years and up won over a distance less than 8½ furlongs and there are a number of "specialist milers" such as Ballare, Tights, Nagurski, Kings Lake and Waving, though a large number, such as Kings Lake proved themselves equally effective over longer distances. However, because a number in Europe won over more extreme trips, such as Thahul, Brogan and Nizon, it may be partly from here that Nijinsky gets much of his reputation for siring stayers.

VIA THOSE EXCEPT PRINCEQUILLO The maternal grandsires representing the Persimmon line through other bloodlines are Charlottesville, Court Harwell, Sicambre, Shantung, and Tiziano who were all specialists at twelve furlongs and up. They have been responsible for mares producing 13 Nijinsky progeny. Four (30.7 per cent) have won stakes races: Galletto (ex Charlottesville mare); Valinsky (ex Tiziano's Oaks winning daughter Valoris); and the brothers Bright Finish and Shining Finish, both sons of Lacquer, by Shantung. Susanna (out of Full Dress II, by Shantung) never managed to win but was stakes placed. Nijinsky's Melody was a Graded placed winning juvenile in 1984. Four (30.7 per cent) others won and two were unraced. Only one, Rare Splendor, ran once and did not reach the frame.

Though there are fewer representatives there is a very high proportion of top-class stock, certainly up to the other representative of the Persimmon line, Princequillo. All are 8–12 furlong performers, the better (stakes and Group runners) being twelve furlong plus specialists. Notably the stakes winning and placed horses from mares from the Persimmon line tend to be colts (17–6) rather than fillies.

Via Chaucer—This is represented by only two horses, both out of Gallant Man mares. The filly Entrancing, never ran and the colt Bolshoi, was a winner over twelve furlongs in the United States but died in training.

Via Rabelais—Rabelais is represented almost exclusively by Tenerani and Ribot and the sons of Ribot, the only exceptions being Bon Mot and Le Fabuleux. The only Nijinsky to have been produced by a Bon Mot mare was a Group winning one, Nice Havrais. Le Fabuleux has just two, both sons of his champion daughter Fabuleux Jane. The first colt was stakes winning Fabuleux Dancer, the second, Alezan Dancer, did not race. Tenerani himself has just one representative, Milina, who won four races over 8½ furlongs.

So the remaining 28 representatives of this line are due to Ribot and his line. There is not, of course, any necessity for much explanation of Ribot. Maybe the greatest racehorse seen in the twentieth century he was unbeaten in 16 races, including the King George VI & Queen Elizabeth Stakes and the Arc (twice). Being very small he was not nominated for the Italian classics. He has been a great sire and exceptional broodmare sire but there has been a question mark over the temperament of many of his progeny and their descendants, notably Alleged, especially once they have gone to stud.

A measure of excitability, but not necessarily exceptional, has been observed in a number of Nijinsky progeny from mares of this line. Ribot did not seem suitable to American racing wanting early maturity and sheer speed. Characteristic of Ribot's progeny was a lateness in maturity and as a result many of the best were seen in Europe. Occasionally he did get a horse of precocious brilliant speed, notably Graustark.

The 28 representatives have shown a great variety in ability. Seven (25 per cent) were stakes and Group winners: fillies Excitable, Key Dancer and Leap Lively (ex Graustark mares); Niniski (ex Tom Rolfe mare); Down Stage and Ultramate (ex Hoist The Flag mares); and juvenile champion Cherry Hinton (ex Romulus mare). Dancing Lesson and Loose Cannon (ex Graustark mares), plus Vestris (ex Hoist The Flag mare) were stakes placed winners.

Three others won and two were placed. Only two failed to reach the first three while ten (35.7 per cent) were unraced. This shows a very much higher percentage of unraced stock but less with lesser ability. Of those unraced five were two-year-olds of 1984.

The maternal sires consisted of: Graustark (10); Hoist The Flag (4); Key To The Mint (3); Romulus (2); Tom Rolfe (5); and Ribot himself (4). Perhaps it is a little too close up, with no other moderating influences, to have Ribot mares straight to Nijinsky for of the four produce none were stakes horses, two were winners and in at least one case temperament certainly got the better.

Distance wise one would certainly expect the produce of Nijinsky on Ribot line mares to be of a stouter breed than, say, that of the Polynesian line. This is certainly the case with Niniski (ex Tom Rolfe), King of Darby (Ribot),

Leap Lively (Graustark) and Loose Cannon (Graustark), but Excitable (Graustark) and Down Stage (Hoist The Flag) were certainly best at eight furlongs, and Dancing Lesson (Graustark), Miss Nut Cracker (Tom Rolfe), Vestris (Hoist The Flag) and 1984 multiple stakes winner Ultramate (Hoist The Flag) were all certainly excellers at six furlongs, and possibly seven, showing more speed than possibly could have been expected. Cherry Hinton (ex Romulus mare) was a champion filly at two years though admittedly won her Group race over eight furlongs having won at six beforehand and Leap Lively also at two years was an eight furlong Group winner.

Combined Nijinsky with Graustark has probably resulted in the injection of speed on top of Nijinsky's ability to sire seven and eight furlong runners in most cases. Others are not quite so easy to explain. Ultramate, three parts brother to Terpsichorist and Gorytus, can only be regarded as an out and out sprinter. His maternal grandsire Hoist The Flag was a brilliant juvenile and never had the chance to prove his stamina at three. It could be he is a factor for speed but more investigation would have to be done into all his winning stock for correct confirmation.

Swynford

The male line of the St Leger winner Swynford relies heavily on just three sons, two of which are extremely tenuous. Better known for his fillies than his colts, only two of these sons have any bearing on Nijinsky's progeny: St Germans and Blandford.

The Coronation Cup winner St Germans, a half brother to Buchan, is represented by his Gulfstream Park Handicap winning grandson Vertex whose daughter Overstreet produced Sabre Street, one of Nijinsky's less endowed performers whose best effort was to finish fourth in a Latonia maiden.

The Swynford male line rests therefore on the high-class Blandford, who was not entered for the classics because of his terrible forelegs. Though not over fertile he did very well, being champion sire three times and he died comparatively early. The Swynford line mares visiting Nijinsky all come from three of Blandford's sons, the unbeaten Triple Crown winner Bahram, the Derby winner Blenheim and Brantome, one of the most influential sires in French breeding.

Of Nijinsky's stock 16 come from these mares. Three (18.7 per cent) were Group winners: Nijinsky's first classic winner and probably most successful sire son to date, Green Dancer, his own brother Val Danseur, and Hostage, who was very unlucky in being injured a week before the Kentucky Derby, all out of Val de Loir mares. Kazatska, also out of a Val de Loir mare, was a stakes placed winner.

Four (25 per cent) were ordinary winners, two were placed and five were unraced, the latter all fillies. Indeed nine of the 15 are fillies, apart from the lone juvenile of 1984, Smartinsky. One ran twice unplaced.

All the black type animals were from Val de Loir mares which suggests that middle distances would be to their advantage. Hostage, though denied the opportunity to prove his stamina, won his best race over nine furlongs, Green Dancer seemed happiest at 8–10 furlongs as did Val Danseur but Kazatska was clearly at home at distances around twelve furlongs.

For what it is worth the other winners were out of mares by Exbury, Mount Marcy, Alcide and Idle Hour. Those placed, Le Haar and The Axe II while Meadow Dancer, who ran just twice without being placed, was out of a High Perch mare. Those with unraced stock were Vieux Manoir, Quadrangle, Restless Wind and Acropolis (2).

So, apart from noting that Nijinsky does exceptionally well on Val de Loir mares, there is not enough evidence to pass any judgement on the other representatives of the Swynford line.

Teddy

The Teddy line is also numerically very strongly represented amongst Nijinsky's stock, accounting for 24 of racing age to 1984. Teddy was unfortunate in that he raced in France during the Second World War years but ably demonstrated himself a top-class racehorse over middle distance (twelve furlongs). Both sides of his pedigree possessed staying blood yet his progeny became known for their stamina limitations when pitched against the best.

His blood comes down to Nijinsky's produce through three sons who made their mark in the United States, Bull Dog, Sir Gallahad III and Sun Teddy and all have been responsible for producing some of the best stock of Nijinsky. Of the 24, six (25 per cent) won Group or stakes races and another was a stakes winner over hurdles and stakes placed on the flat: Stradavinsky, a three parts brother to 2,000 Guineas winner Nonoalco, was out of the Hasty Road (by Sir Gallahad III) mare Seximee; Khatango and Shadeed, out of the Damascus (descendant of Sun Teddy) mares Penny Flight and Continual; Tanzor and his classic placed sister Lady Jinsky, out of the Victoria Park (Sir Gallahad III line) mare Lady Victoria and also Nuclear Pulse and Greek Sky (ex Victoria Park mares). Gleason, the stakes winner over hurdles and stakes placed on the flat was out of a Spy Well (Bull Dog line) mare.

Added to Gleason and Lady Jinsky, Tournament Star (ex Chris Evert, by Swoon's Son, a grandson of Bull Dog) and White Birch (out of a Sword Dancer mare. Sword Dancer being the sire of Damascus) were Group and stakes placed. Three others were winners while two placed. Eight (33 per cent) were unraced.

Bull Dog in particular did not have much maturity or speed himself and in that way it is perhaps a little surprising that he was so influential in the United States. None of the other sons, including his brother Sir Gallahad III, bred quite so many horses who had early maturity and who had severe distance limitations. As a result one would think that it would be best to look at the three Teddy sons differently to ascertain any distance heredity to be seen in the union with Nijinsky.

However, virtually all the descendants from this line in Nijinsky's progeny show a tendency to shorter distances, most being happy over shorter trips than nine furlongs. Only Oulanova and Gleason of the Bull Dog line, Khatango from the Sun Teddy and Nuclear Pulse and Greek Sky from Sir Gallahad III showed any liking for distances in excess of nine furlongs. Tanzor (Sir Gallahad III) is the joker in the pack as he did not win at any age above two years. His sister, Lady Jinsky, though second in the Canadian Oaks, proved her winning forte was 6–8 furlongs. It may be that this line has not been exploited enough with Nijinsky in the expectation of producing stout runners when in fact it has produced a number of class horses who had a certain amount of noticeable speed and precocity with them. Mares from Teddy's line have so far produced a notable emphasis on colts in the stakes winning and placed horses.

Tourbillon

The French Derby winner was not in fact a natural stayer which may explain why mares from this line are so popular amongst the band which have visited Nijinsky. If conserved, Tourbillon's decisive burst of speed was devastating but he also had the associated highly nervous disposition and developed quite a temper.

Of Nijinsky's progeny 21 come from mares descended from Tourbillon via his sons Ambiorix, Djebel, Meridien and Timor. The first two being by far the most numerical. Eight (giving an almost unreal percentage of 38 per cent) were stakes and Group winners and included the full brother and sister Ile de Bourbon and Rose Crescent, whose dam, the French Oaks victress Roseliere, was by Misti IV, grandson of Meridien and the only stallion from that line to play a part in Nijinsky's history. The others all came from the Ambiorix and Djebel lines: Quiet Fling and his brother Peacetime were from a Klairon (grandsire Djebel) mare; Little Current's half sister Water Dance, from a My Babu (son of Djebel) mare; Summertime Promise, a daughter of a Crozier (a son of My Babu) mare, Shimmy, out of the Ambiorix mare

Amalesian; and Vidalia from champion Waya, herself a daughter of Faraway Son, a grandson of Ambiorix.

Ten (47.6 per cent) more were winners including Testily, who was out of a Timor mare and the only representative of that particular Tourbillon line in Nijinsky's progeny. Kirov (ex My Babu mare) was also a good winner over hurdles. As a result, all the rest came from Ambiorix and Djebel and consisted of one placed horse and only one which had not made the racecourse and that a two-year-old of 1984. This shows a near 100 per cent success rate in the progeny reaching the racecourse and also a very high percentage of it at least winning there and often being in the top bracket.

Djebel was a Group 1 winning two-year-old and went on to capture the 2,000 Guineas and Arc de Triomphe. He was small and quick but not so fast as Ambiorix who had less distance capacity though he was second in the French Derby having been champion two-year-old and captured the Prix Lupin (10½ furlongs) at three. He did not really stay twelve furlongs. Standing at Claiborne he has become a great broodmare sire and sire of fillies.

From the distance point of view, the Nijinsky produce has shown a full range of distance capability, from those capable of winning at six furlongs, like Summertime Promise (who won at distances up to 8½ furlongs) and Rose Crescent, who won up to eleven furlongs, through to Rose Crescent's brother Ile de Bourbon (10–13 furlongs), Quiet Fling (12–14 furlongs), Mariinsky (14 furlongs), Kafouaine (11–15½ furlongs) and Peacetime (10–12 furlongs) with the others winning at all distances in between. Mares from this line have, however, produced some of Nijinsky's very best performers in Quiet Fling, Ile de Bourbon and Summertime Promise.

West Australian

One of the most poorly represented and perhaps surprisingly so as the great Man O'War is a member of this line. Just seven horses have been produced from mares from this line, six from that of Man O'War. The results have not been over encouraging as three (the brothers Nissr and Speedy Nijinsky out of the brilliant Mr Busher producer Fast Line and 1984 juvenile Grenada Pride, ex In Reality mare) have not run though Dancing Crown (ex Full Pocket mare) was a triple winner in 1984 and Solstein (ex Tentam mare) was a Group placed winning two-year-old in 1984. The sole representative of the line tracing through Solon was the Sheshoon mare Vela who produced the Group placed winner Nikitina to Nijinsky.

Clearly this line is too badly represented to allow any conclusions to be made from it.

Bay Ronald (excluding Hyperion)

After the resounding success of the Hyperion line when crossed with Nijinsky one might expect similar results from other aspects of the line tracing to Bay Ronald through Solario and Bosworth. In fact, just three maternal grandsires are involved and seven horses in total.

The sole representative of the Solario branch of the Bay Ronald line is Fly To Arms, out of a Dark Star mare, who won over 10½ furlongs in France at three years. The other six are from mares by Herbager (5) and his son Grey Dawn II. One, Bemissed, was a Grade 1 winning two-year-old filly and another, Popular Hero, was a good stakes winner over obstacles in the United States. Swan was a winner while Dawnballet (the only Grey Dawn II mare being his dam Dauntu) and Dance In Snow were just placed. Dancing Slippers (winner in 1985) ran three times as a three-year-old in 1984 not making the first three. So, the members of Nijinsky's progeny from this line are necessarily few in number and very diversified in ability, Bemissed standing head and shoulders above the rest and also coming from a female line which had not produced anything as good as herself in several generations though she did trace back eventually to Knight's Daughter.

Obviously also with a juvenile Group winner and a multiple stakes winner over jumps there has been no real continuity in producing a particular type of racehorse in uniting Nijinsky with mares from this side of the Bay Ronald line.

Himyar

A line indigenous to the United States in its significance, the most important branch being that of Domino through his son Commando to Colin and Peter Pan, the only one of significance for Nijinsky being the latter, through his son Black Toney to his sons Black Servant, Balladier and Brokers Tip. The other Himyar branch comes down through Plaudit ultimately to Dr Fager. For Nijinsky this means just two mares. Firstly, the champion Dearly Precious, who has had two daughters by Nijinsky: Dearly Too being a stakes winner and Preciously Dear a winning juvenile of 1983 and who was placed fourth in the Grade 2 Hollywood Futurity to Althea. Secondly, Charm School, whose daughter Perfect Point was placed at two years in 1984. Not a bad return.

The other 15 of Nijinsky's progeny come down through the sons of Black Toney, himself a long way behind the best of his age in ability but subsequently one of the best sires. Mares descended from his sons have accounted for one flat Group winner and one National Hunt stakes winner among Nijinsky's progeny: Nijana, whose dam Prodana Neviesta descends from Black Servant via Blue Larkspur and Revoked to Reneged; and Netherby, from a mare by Crimson Satan, a grandson of the Champagne winner Balladier.

The Domino sire line is renowed for its unsoundness and certainly there are some up and down performers in Nijinsky's sons and daughters out of these mares. Three others were Group and stakes placed however: the full brother and sister Masqued Dancer and Krassata, who were out of Better Self's daughter Bonnie Google, and Encino (ex Crimson Satan mare).

Of the remainder, five others won; out of mares by the grandson of Balladier, Bagdad (3), Better Self and Reneged, the last being Quick Dance, an own brother to Nijana. Two managed places while only one did not reach the frame. Only one, Masked Dancer, never raced and he seems to be making up for that in the paddocks.

Many of the Domino sires suffered by being at the same stud that had developed the line. The one who benefitted by being stood elsewhere was Double Jay, sire of Bagdad.

Many of Nijinsky's stock from mares of this line have shown good speed as juveniles and indeed two only won at two years. Only Masqued Dancer showed the ability to stay up to twelve furlongs though Nijana won from all distances in her second and third seasons from six to twelve furlongs. All the remaining winners were best at distances under nine furlongs.

St Albans

The nine representatives of this line are all out of mares by Sailor, bar two: Sugary Mist, an unraced daughter of a mare by the Preakness winner Candy Spots, and Jinsky, a winning daughter of a Nigromante mare.

Sailor, a brilliant handicapper, was a son of the unsound Suburban and Travers Stakes winner Eight Thirty. Of the seven Nijinsky sons and daughters out of his mares, none showed ability to gain a stakes win or place though three won, one more was placed and three never saw a racecourse. The winners gained their successes over distances between seven and twelve furlongs, the latter being achieved by the successful Australian sire Whiskey Road in Ireland and the other two being 7–8½ furlongs winners in the United States.

St Albans was a son of Stockwell as was Doncaster, ancestor of Phalaris. However the results are poles apart when seen reflected in Nijinsky's progeny.

Orby, Speculum and Athanasius

Though not from the same sire line these three are the most poorly represented among Nijinsky's stock, though Speculum was a son of Vedette, the sire of Galopin, in turn the sire of St Simon. Just one filly has been from a mare tracing to him, Misinskie, whose best performance was to place several times in England at two and three years. The German sire line of Athanasius has also just one member: Ipi Tombi, a winner from the Zank mare Oraza and who was stakes placed over hurdles in England.

Orby, through the speedy stallions Sound Track and Matador, is responsible for the mares who produced two of Nijinsky's better runners, the miler Piaffer and Night Alert, who won the Group 2 Prix Jean Prat and Group 3 Gladness Stakes before sadly dying in the United States at four. The third representative of this blood, his winning own brother Mr Justice, is starting to make a name for himself as a sire with his first crop of three-year-olds in the United States in 1984.

So, is there a nick between Nijinsky and any of the other bloodlines available? Quite evidently opportunity does have a say but it has been proved here that this is not the overriding factor in the poor performance of a cross of Nijinsky on Bold Ruler. However, the union with Princequillo mares and his line seems to have a very potent effect and inbreeding to other Nearco lines does tend to evolve a surprising amount of early speed. Raise A Native does not appear to be quite the element for speed that it was once believed though is responsible for a high number of successful racehorses while the Pharamond/Menow line seems to throw a tendency to stayers. Some of the very best performers among Nijinsky's progeny come from mares of the Hyperion line, while Tourbillon has provided a very high percentage of stakes winners when crossing Nijinsky with mares of this line.

A very great emphasis on speed seems to have been injected by the introduction of Ribot's line, especially through his son Graustark, perhaps a little surprising in view of Ribot's middle distance tendencies both of himself and a great many of his offspring. This is also the case with mares from the Teddy line. Individual stallions with whom Nijinsky has done especially well are Forli, Habitat, Hoist The Flag, Princequillo, Raise A Native, Round Table, Victoria Park and Val de Loir.

The Phalaris line mares (apart from Pharamond) have shown a tendency to produce more fillies among their best (stakes winning and placed) runners than colts but those from Teddy, Persimmon and Pharamond err towards colts. There is no appreciable favouring of the sexes amongst the other sire lines.

CHAPTER 8

Physiology of the Nijinsky Progeny

Physique; temperament; chestnut coat colour; grey coat colour; white markings (possible merits of)

One of the first things stud managers look for in a first crop of foals is whether the sire is recognisable in the progeny. Nijinsky does not fail in that respect: he is a great stamper of his stock. It is very easy to recognise a first time out Nijinsky colt in the packed pre-parade ring for a three-year-old maiden race, or a Nijinsky mare in a paddock full of broodmares. It does, of course, help if the animal concerned is bay in colour – one connects a son or daughter to its father much quicker if it shares the same coat colour.

The main factor in the Nijinsky heredity is size. The vast majority, if not all, of Nijinsky's best winners have shared their sire's size. Nijinsky stands not far off 17 h.h. though his presence makes him appear even taller. It is very difficult to find many of the equine population standing taller than that, but two notable Nijinsky Group 1 winners do: Solford, just inches out his sire to reach the 17 h.h. mark, and Quiet Fling stands a towering 17.2 h.h. and his tremendous physique makes him a formidable proposition. Most of Nijinsky's progeny are over 16 h.h. For example, Golden Fleece stood 16.3 h.h. No matter what colour they are they share the same picture of strength and power. Nijinsky does occasionally throw smaller versions of course and, in the main, these are often of lesser ability. For example, H.M. the Queen's Pas de Deux takes very much after her dam, Example, in colour and appearance. Compared to such as Quiet Fling she is absolutely minute and on the racecourse she managed one solitary win at Windsor, although by twelve lengths.

Niniski is perhaps one of the smaller of Nijinsky's Group 1 winners standing 16.1½ h.h. But he is almost an identical scaled down replica of Nijinsky and possibly appears even smaller to the observer having a noticeably shorter neck than his sire. Nijinsky fillies tend to be a little on the large rangy side and occasionally may lack a little in quality, especially those chestnut mares who do not take after their sire in all aspects. They can lack a little of the femininity that Green Dancer and Ile de Bourbon pass on to their daughters. But the emphasis is on the sheer power they possess and it is this strength that often makes them more difficult to handle than other strains.

All this makes it all the more remarkable that Nijinsky gets high-class juvenile winners, or that he gets two-year-old winners at all. Many of the larger specimens were given an easy introduction to the racecourse but that is often the trait for the particular stable to which they belong. But no one could say that Cherry Hinton, the champion juvenile filly of 1977, was small. Leap Lively and Gorytus are others that readily spring to mind.

Nijinsky's yearlings often give the impression that they still need time to grow, they are very much on the leg and have plenty of bone. Scope is the one word perhaps most apt to describe them. However many grow extremely rapidly towards filling their spacious frame and make imposing two-year-olds less than twelve short months later. Nijinsky, it has been said, is a little cow hocked and sickle hocked at the same time, the only physical fault that can be ascribed to him, and occasionally this is transmitted to his progeny.

One of the most noticeable aspects about Nijinsky's stock, especially the best of them, and which makes them so easily recognisable is the distinctive Nijinsky head and intelligent expression. Nijinsky has unusually bold eyes which carry that famed "look of eagles", which is often ascribed to the very best racehorses. He has been reported as being especially reminiscent of the flying machine The Tetrarch in this respect. He always appears to be looking at something else, somewhere else, staring out across the landscape to regions beyond the scope of the human eye. So many of Nijinsky's best progeny, especially the colts, are so reminiscent of him around the head and shoulders, the large eyes giving the shape of the face an almost Arabian dished appearance. Hostage, a Grade 1 winner who possibly would have won the Kentucky Derby but for accident, is probably the closest replica of Nijinsky; he has the colour, the size and the head. Just one turn of the head can give many a Nijinsky away ... Bright Finish, Kings Lake, Caerleon, Gorytus, Niniski. One of the most striking seen in 1984 was a colt foal out of Caucasus's half sister, Last Feather, in whom the resemblance is uncanny.

So much in evaluating and judging the conformation of a horse is instinct or a whim of personal preference. Buyers have evidently realised that the size of a Nijinsky yearling is no detrimental factor in that animal's potential racecourse ability and the Nijinskys which command the highest prices are often some of the largest Nijinsky has produced – Solford was a record priced yearling. But they are sought after for their *potential*. The scope is there for all to see. It is not what the yearling colt or filly is at the time of purchase but what he or she *will* be in twelve or 24 months time. The

ABOVE
The dual classic winner Niniski who has had such a superb start at stud

LEFT
Nijinsky's only Group 1 winner on both continents, Caucasus was the first to open American eyes to the durability of Nijinsky's stock

ABOVE *Nijinsky's most brilliant two-year-old Gorytus is now at stud in Ireland* OPPOSITE, ABOVE *Nijinsky's champion juvenile daughter Cherry Hinton in the summer of 1983* OPPOSITE, BELOW *The author's special favourite, the handsome Quiet Fling, a gentle giant of a horse*

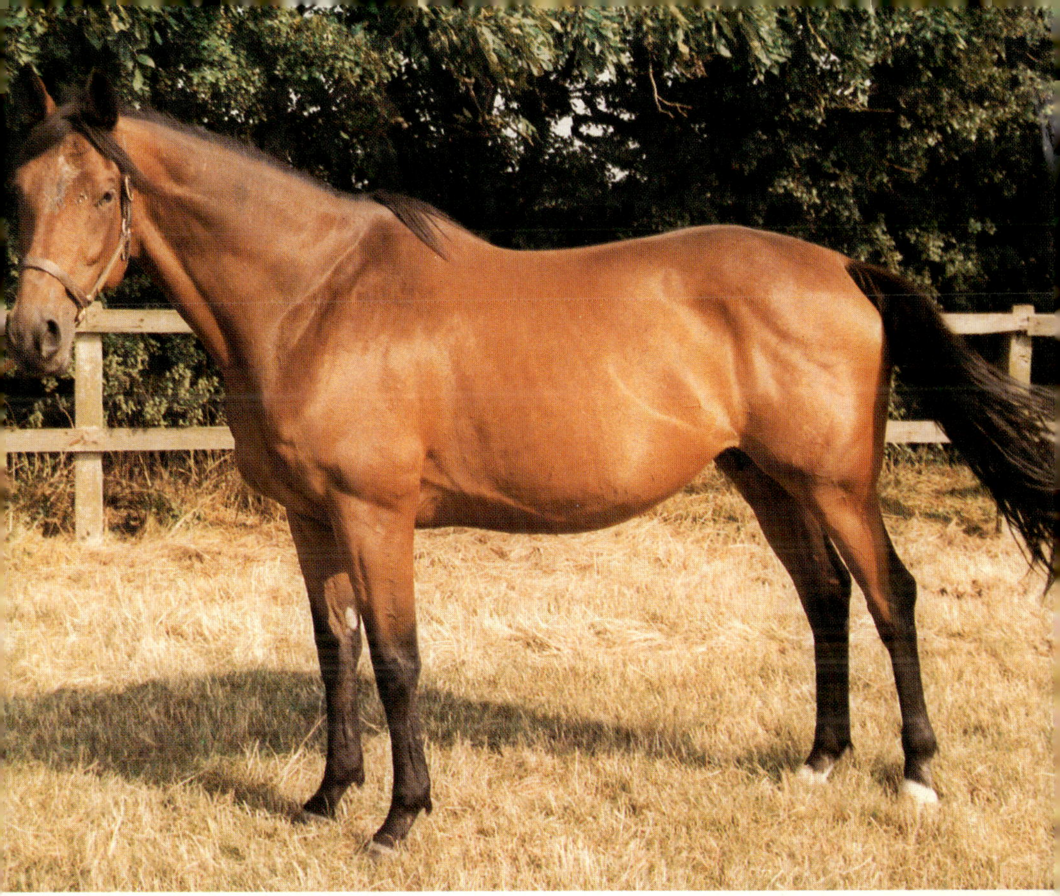

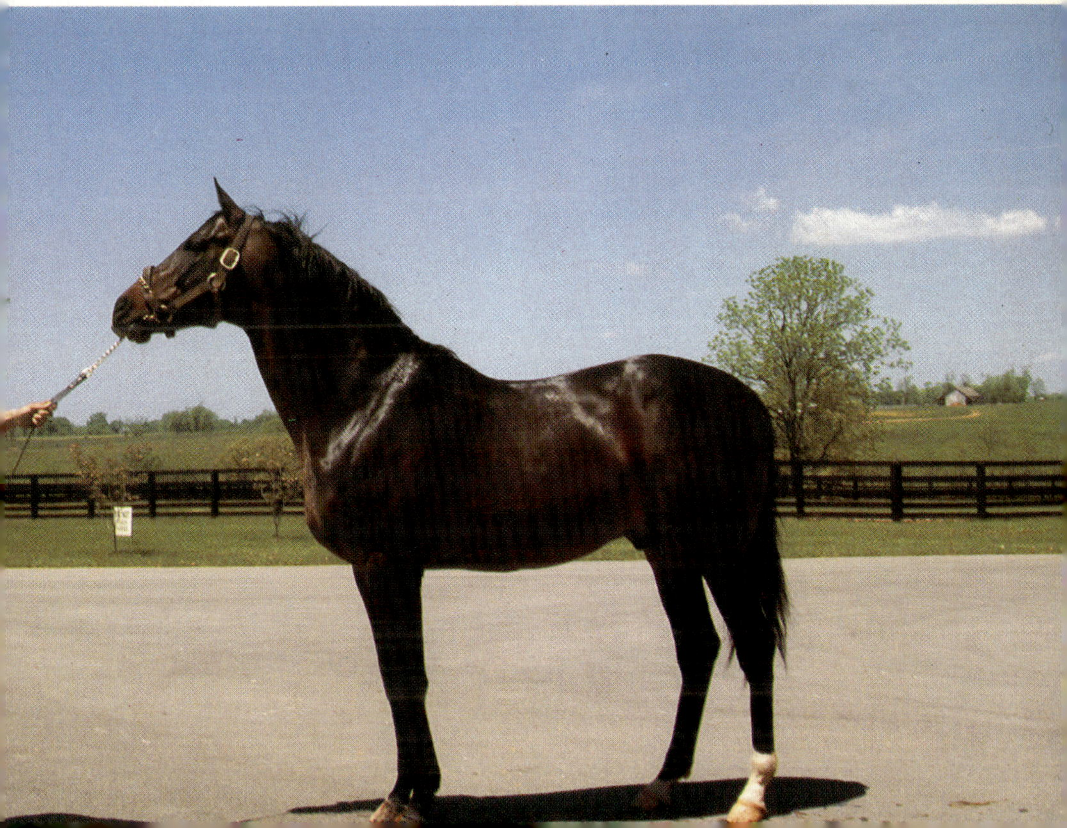

The star of 1985 . . . Shadeed

watchword is power. And Nijinsky is not reticent in endowing his sons and daughters with that. It is this power that makes champion two-year-olds of animals which appear to need time. Nijinsky was a champion two-year-old himself of course, even though as an atypical son of Northern Dancer there must have been doubts as to any precocious ability.

Small horses will often stay sounder than their larger counterparts and the fact that Nijinsky passes on his size to his progeny could well be the main factor in the inherent weakness some of his sons and daughters have to risk in their legs. Golden Fleece and Maruzensky both suffered lameness injuries which closed their careers. However there is always another side of the coin. Many of Nijinsky's fillies in particular raced for several seasons and remained totally sound throughout. They often ran on dirt courses, which ultimately puts a greater strain on tendons and ligaments than does a grass surface.

There are so many different theories as to perfect conformation and so many variations due totally to what pleases one eye from another. What is indisputable about Nijinsky is no matter that his sons and daughters are of a larger than average size . . . they can run.

Temperament

The more Nijinskys one studies the more convinced one becomes that the doubt about the Nijinsky temperament is a myth. High mettled yes, but not deliberately nasty. Doubtless there will be a few trainers who will point to certain individuals who have passed through their hands as defying this belief, but experience has shown that Nijinskys seem to be no more especially difficult to handle than are many other lines, and less than many such as those descending from Ribot and Nasrullah.

If a horse's temperament goes beyond the mere nervous, which in itself is not a bad sign and actually turns mean then it will usually be apparent after that stallion or mare has been at stud a few seasons. Visits to a good many Nijinsky stallions and mares in the paddock, conversations with many of their handlers, give convincing evidence that there is no Nijinsky who can be termed nasty or even savage.

Admittedly some of the fillies in particular can be difficult and this has come out more as stubbornness in later life. (The author well remembers attempting to stand Silky, whose 1983 Shergar colt had recently been weaned, in the paddock for a photograph. The difficulty was not in making her stand or pose, but in coaxing her to leave the shade of her running shed! Unfortunately, Silky is big and strong enough to make this quite a difficult manoeuvre.)

The problem with Nijinsky colts tends to be more of a question of over confidence and thinking too much which leads them to become a little "cheeky" and, therefore, a little difficult for a trainer to teach the horse to accept the routines of training. Becoming bored, frustration is a real enemy. Lucky Sovereign is probably a particular example of this.

Many Nijinskys do get hotted up on a racecourse. This sign of nervous temperament was apparent in Nijinsky himself but, over the years, it has become synonymous with top-class racing ability. As mentioned earlier, Ribot and Nasrullah have passed on a greater degree of their highly strung natures and it has certainly not made their illustrious descendants run with any less distinction.

Very occasionally it does badly affect that particular progeny's career. A few of Nijinsky's fillies have burned themselves up as two-year-olds and thereafter made no real mark at three. Silky is, of course, one example. London Bells may be an example of a colt. Quite often however, this has been blamed upon the relevant animals "temperament" when, in fact, there were other factors involved – as with Running Ballerina and Tanzor, and even to some degree Silky herself, whose careers were certainly compromised by contracting a severe virus towards the end of their two-year-old careers.

Nijinsky was a highly strung racehorse. In his case it was strongly allied to ability and certainly many of his major runners have been of a similar mould, notably Sportin' Life. However, no one could say there was anything wrong with Golden Fleece's temperament when he won the Derby.

Anyone who has visited Nijinsky's sons at stud will realise just how stable the majority are. Ile de Bourbon and Niniski in Europe, Solford, Green Dancer, and Hostage in the United States. (Ile de Bourbon would not even canter around his paddock to please the photographer let alone restrict anyone from entering it!)

Therefore, Nijinsky's stock are not possessors of a mean or dicey temperament; they are, at worst, merely highly strung thoroughbreds who want to get on with the job in hand. Nijinsky's fillies are often difficult and may take strong handling but fillies often are no matter who their sire may be. Being by Nijinsky they are often more noticeable as they have the eyes of the world on them – and nothing knows the better time to make a fool of a man than does a horse. Stallion men are not dealing with a Halo or an Alleged when they have a Nijinsky stallion in their care.

Many of Nijinsky's more wayward characters often come from families where there are other sources of "hot blood". I cite Silky again as she was really the only one of Nijinsky's progeny who obviously had a real mind of her own. Her dam was by Nearula, a son of Nasrullah, who was noted for passing on his own firebrand qualities. This also compounded the blood of Nearco in Silky – Nearco of course being the grandsire of Nijinsky's sire Northern Dancer. She is not the only one where the combination of Nijinsky with other influences may have affected the progeny.

Nijinsky has crossed quite well with mares from the Ribot line. The results have included stakes winners Excitable, Leap Lively, Niniski, Down Stage, Fabuleux Dancer, Nice Havrais and Cherry Hinton, very few of which could have been said to have a less than tractable nature. In this cross it is noticeable in some of the animals of lesser ability that they are often very much on their toes and happier when not being asked to stand still.

Nijinsky and his progeny must be treated with respect certainly but often their sheer size is daunting enough. They are often not what can be called friendly animals and Nijinsky himself seems to belong to another world. To be patient with a Nijinsky can reap untold rewards.

Coat Colour

Mendelism and the thoroughbred may seem rather remote bedfellows to the average racing man. Perhaps even the breeders themselves may not at first see the relevance. However, in relation to coat colour, Mendelism can have a real meaning in attempting to explain the distribution of colour.

Mendel experimented with two varieties of peas; the tall and the dwarf. In crossing these one might have expected the resultant plants to be medium sized, but not so, they were tall hybrids. So Mendel crossed them with each other and the resultant proportion evolved at three tall to one dwarf.

The horse is already a hybrid. There might be full brothers; one might be bay and useless, the other chestnut and a great racehorse. They are not pure, like animals who will never vary – brown bears will never be anything but brown.

So, in relation to coat colour, the horse follows closely Mendel's findings with the peas. Bay (including related colours brown and black) dominates the recessive chestnut gene so much that bay occurs in a proportion of three to every one chestnut. Nijinsky has 292 bay/brown foals and 99 chestnuts virtually following exactly this ratio. There are very, very few pure breeding bays – St Simon was a notable example and produced no chestnuts at all. The bays in Nijinsky's case are too numerous and probably well enough investigated already to need much more looking into here. Nijinsky is a bay and seems to be expected to produce bays and for the best produce to be that colour. This is not necessarily the case.

Chestnut Coat Colour in Nijinsky's Progeny—For some reason British racing people do not associate the best Nijinsky's with being chestnut. Whenever a chestnut Nijinsky wins a Group race, their enquiry is inevitably the same: "What other good chestnuts has Nijinsky had?"

Usually, to name Czaravich, Nijinsky's Secret, Bemissed and Nizon is enough reply for all these were Group 1 winners. To add the Group winners Leap Lively, Beaudelaire, Pas de Deux, Nice Havrais, Nijana and Terpsichorist is sufficient to convince. Of course, the answer to British unawareness is that only Leap Lively and Beaudelaire ran with success in England and Ireland, though Nice Havrais, Nizon and Pas de Deux were European. Nijinsky's Secret did not fulfil his potential until he travelled back from France to the United States for his four-year-old season and has not looked back. So the United States has certainly seen the best of the chestnut Nijinskys.

Of the 99 chestnuts registered to Nijinsky, 45 had chestnut dams including the Group and stakes winners Nijana, Excitable, Nizon, Terpsichorist (who had a bay full sister and brother), Water Dance, Leap Lively, Nijinsky's Secret and Fabuleux Dancer. There has been one case of a roan mare producing a chestnut foal to Nijinsky – Royal Jete who was definitely a chestnut as a yearling and it would be fascinating to discover if he stayed chestnut as he got older.

But two bays can produce a chestnut as they are carrying recessive genes in the Mendel ratio of 3 to 1. This is unless they are pure breeding bays, which is unlikely especially in the case of the stallion. Bay mares put to Nijinsky have produced the chestnut La Jalouse, Nuclear Pulse, Pas de Deux, Czaravich, Nice Havrais, Waving, Bemissed, Ultramate, and Rosy Spectre amongst his stakes winners.

Several mares have been sent back to Nijinsky's court for a second, or even more, mating. The resultant full brothers and sisters need not necessarily be as "peas from the same pod". As we have seen previously 62 mares (including the coverings which resulted in the foals of 1982) visited Nijinsky twice or more. Of these 62, twelve went back for a third, fourth or even fifth time. For this survey I shall concentrate just on these, as it gives a better evaluation of the Mendel ratio and the resultant racing quality of the foals. Nine of these mares were bay, three were chestnut. Starting with those of bay colour we look at these in detail below.

BITTY GIRL   The two-year-old champion visited Nijinsky three times. The first foal, Nijit, was a bay and thrice stakes placed winner of five races; Bivouac, also a bay, foaled a year later, never ran and two years later followed the Group 2 winner Beaudelaire who was a chestnut. Notably the chestnut produce of two bay champions was the best racehorse.

DRUMTOP   The champion handicap mare also went to Nijinsky three times, producing three bay foals. All had stakes ability but Brogan became the only one to win a black type race, the Group 3 Prix Berteux. His full brother Bedford won five races and was placed in the Group 1 Irish St Leger, his sister Kyra's Slipper won four races and was stakes placed in the United States.

DUSKY EVENING   Had three bay foals by Nijinsky: Javamine, the only filly, being the major winner with four Graded wins. Her full brothers, Sir Jinsky and Debussy, also won, the former being stakes placed.

LA SEVILLANA   Champion in Argentina, presented three bay fillies, two of which won, Foolish Redhead and The Temptress, plus the unraced Lucky Us.

MRS PETERKIN   Has also produced three bays: the unraced colt Top Rank and filly Nijistar and the Graded winner and successful sire Dancing Champ.

NATIVE PARTNER   Best foal of her three by Nijinsky was probably the bay filly Bev Bev. Her bay colt Serheed won five races at three and four years and her chestnut colt Northerly Native was a winner and twice stakes placed in France at three years.

ROSETTA STONE   Has produced two bay Grade 1 winners to Nijinsky in Upper Nile and the champion De La Rose. Their 1981 bay sister won in France as a juvenile.

STREET DANCER   The first mare to fetch two million dollars at public auction, she is the only mare to go to Nijinsky to produce five live foals, producing three bays and two chestnuts. Her one colt (a bay) did not race, nor has her 1982 bay filly, while the other three won including the stakes winner Street Ballet (bay) and stakes placed La Nijinska (chestnut).

DANCEALOT   The last of the bays, she has produced three consecutive foals to Nijinsky, all colts. The lone chestnut Dancing Again was the first, foaled in 1980 and winning two races and being stakes placed. Her second, the bay Tights was a major Graded winner in the United States in 1984 over distances around a mile. Their bay juvenile brother Starsalot ran three times in 1984 managing two fifth places but may come good in 1985.

The three chestnuts were:

COPPER CANYON   Produced three bay foals: Copernica, Bakor and Cherokee Phoenix. All won but Copernica was very much the best performer winning three races and being placed in Grade and stakes races eight times including the Grade 1 races the Matron and Frizette Stakes.

GLAD RAGS   The winner of the 1,000 Guineas is dam of the chestnut group winning filly Terpsichorist, the brilliant bay colt Gorytus and the unraced bay filly Vaslava.

SECRET BEAUTY   Has produced two chestnut foals and one bay to Nijinsky. The dual Grade 1 winner and only colt, the chestnut Nijinsky's Secret, was the best of them though his year older bay sister Dancing Secret won five races and was placed in a stake. Their chestnut sister Dancing Brownie was an unraced juvenile of 1984.

Grey Coat Colour in Nijinsky's Progeny—In a rough estimate there are three times as many bay (incorporating brown and black) thoroughbreds as chestnuts and three times as many chestnuts as grey/roans. The great Italian breeder Federico Tesio went as far as to call the grey coat colour a "disease", a discolouration of the bay and chestnut coat. Grey is a speckled combination of different colours, with two fundamental types: white on a bay background and white on a chestnut background.

It is generally agreed that grey colour does not genetically skip a generation. Every grey foal must have a grey parent. Though exceptions may be found in the Stud Books they probably occur through inaccurate registration, or registration of the dam before she was seen to change to her natural grey from a darker shade.

There are a mere eleven grey or roan Nijinskys and, as owners will be reassured to hear, all have registered grey or roan dams. This is far below the average for the thoroughbred racehorse but also their performances on the racecourse are slightly below that for other colours of Nijinsky.

We have already seen that the ratio of winners to runners of Nijinsky's stock is abnormally high. The eleven grey Nijinskys represent the range of racecourse performance except for one aspect. None of them won a Group or listed race. Two of them had no chance of proving the theory amiss, Blue Nijinsky and Edelene did not race and Niqua was a once raced juvenile of 1984 and may redress the balance in 1985. However this ratio is no different for any other colour. Only four of the eleven were winners, slightly below Nijinsky's average. They were White Birch, a highly regarded potential classic colt after winning successive races at two but who badly disappointed at three, despite winning his third start and being placed second in the

Grade 3 Hill Prince Handicap. He was probably the most accomplished of Nijinsky's grey stock and thought worthy of running in the Grade 1 classic Belmont Stakes, the first Nijinsky to start in one of America's Triple Crown races. Makarova was stakes placed in France where she won three races and Russian Fox was a shade below stakes class finishing a close fourth in the Appleton Handicap and running Nijinsky's Secret to 1½ lengths in his first start in France as a two-year-old. However, he was only twice (his last starts) out of the first four in twelve races in France and the United States, having accounted for four events. Nijinsky Sentiment won over seven furlongs in England as a three-year-old in 1984 while Super Gray was perhaps the unluckiest only to clock up a single start in which he finished fourth. Grey Ballet only ran twice. The remaining horse, Dronacharya, was the only one to consistently fail to show any form though he is reputed to have won several times in Israel but there has to be a question mark over the type of opposition he faced.

All this does not mean that those standing grey sons of Nijinsky need panic. The relative lack of stakes performance in themselves will not necessarily mean a transmission into the next generation. For example, Super Gray (who knows, he might have gone on to greater things had his career not be curtailed), though not setting the Antipodes alight in terms of stakes winners does turn out a remarkable number of winners – accounting for 131 races in his first five seasons including two Group winners.

White Markings—There are probably more superstitions surrounding white markings such as stars, blazes and socks than in any other aspect of the thoroughbred. This is probably because no one has ever really been able to explain the reasons behind their occurrence.

No doubt too, it is partially explained, as we have seen with coat colour, by the fact that the thoroughbred is a hybrid animal. In other animals and birds, white markings are usually symmetrical, where both sides of the animal are the same, as in pandas and various bird species. With the horse the white markings come in all shapes and sizes.

The most famous belief is that four white feet are unlucky and that white hind feet are better than white forefeet, while white marks on the off hind are to be avoided as it means disastrous performance. Quite how this places many of Nijinsky's best winners it is hard to ascertain! Tesio agreed in some measure with these superstitions in that he believed large white markings to be less "energetic". One can only wonder what the achievements of Czaravich might have been had he been whole coloured!

In the summer of 1982 David McCall, manager to Charles Engelhard and one of the co-owners of the totally brown Ile de Bourbon, was heard to make a somewhat rash assertion that the best of Nijinsky's progeny were "whole coloured". This was made just as the whole coloured Golden Fleece and Peacetime were establishing themselves at Derby contenders. This was probably the influencing factor and an erroneous one. A list of Nijinsky's *Group* (not listed) winners and their respective markings, are certainly enough to give a guide as to the evidence for McCall's opinion at that time and a sample of the overall picture.

YEAR OF FOAL-ING	HORSE	RACE(S)	MARKINGS
1972	CAUCASUS	Irish St Leger Gr 1 Sunset H Gr 1 Manhattan H Gr 2 San Luis Rey S Gr 1 Arcadia H Gr 3	large star, off hind sock
1972	DANCING CHAMP	Massachusetts H Gr 2 Woodlawn S Gr 3	white snip on nose
1972	GREEN DANCER	French 2,000 Gns Gr 1 Observer Gold Cup Gr 1 Prix Lupin Gr 1	large star & snip, near hind sock
1972	LIGHTED GLORY	Prix de Flore Gr 3	None
1972	QUIET FLING	Coronation Cup Gr 1 John Porter S Gr 2	white star & snip, both hind socks
1972	SUMMERTIME PROMISE	Apple Blossom H Gr 2 Gallorette S Gr 3	narrow blaze, off fore & near hind socks
1973	AFRICAN DANCER	Park Hill S Gr 2 Cheshire Oaks Gr 3	sock on near hind
1973	BRIGHT FINISH	Yorkshire Cup Gr 2 Jockey Club Cup Gr 3	socks on near hind and off fore
1973	JAVAMINE	Long Island H Gr 2 Diana H Gr 2 Knickerbocker H Gr 3 Arlington Matron Gr 2	large star
1973	NIJANA	Schuylerville S Gr 3	chestnut, near hind sock
1974	LUCKY SOVEREIGN	Mecca Dante S Gr 2	None
1974	MARUZENSKY	Asahi Hai Sansai S Gr 1	None
1974	PAS DE DEUX	Prix du Palais Royal Gr 3	chestnut, near hind sock
1974	UPPER NILE	Suburban H Gr 1 Nassau County H Gr 3	star, socks both hind feet and near fore

YEAR OF FOAL-ING	HORSE	RACE(S)	MARKINGS
1974	VALINSKY	Geoffrey Freer S Gr 2	large star
1975	CHERRY HINTON	Argos Star Fillies S Gr 3	small star, both hind socks
1975	ILE DE BOURBON	King George VI & Queen Elizabeth S Gr 1. Coronation Cup Gr 1 King Edward VII S Gr 2 Geoffrey Freer S Gr 2	None
1975	NIZON	Premio Roma Gr 1 Prix du Lys Gr 3 Prix de Lutece Gr 3	chestnut, white stripe on face
1975	STRADAVINSKY	Whitehall S Gr 3	blaze
1975	SUMMER FLING	Open Fire S Gr 3	star
1975	TERPSICHORIST	Rutgers H Gr 3 Sheepshead Bay H Gr 2 Long Island H Gr 3	chestnut, small star
1976	CZARAVICH	Metropolitan H Gr 1 Carter H Gr 2 Jerome H Gr 2 Withers H. Gr 2	chestnut, blaze, two large hind socks
1976	NINISKI	Irish St Leger Gr 1 French St Leger Gr 1 Geoffrey Freer S Gr 2 Ormonde S Gr 3 John Porter S Gr 2	star, front feet socks and near hind
1977	MUSCOVITE	Whitehall S Gr 3	hind feet socks
1977	NICE HAVRAIS	Prix de Fontainebleau Gr 3	chestnut, blaze, three large stockings
1977	NIGHT ALERT	Prix Jean Prat Gr 2 Gladness S Gr 3	None
1977	PRINCESSE LIDA	Prix Morny Gr 1 Prix de la Salamandre Gr 1	star, near hind sock
1977	SHINING FINISH	St Simon S Gr 3	small star, front coronets, off hind sock
1978	BALLETOMANE	Princess S Gr 3	narrow blaze, off fore & hind socks
1978	DE LA ROSE	Hollywood Derby Gr 1 Saranac S Gr 2 Diana H Gr 2 Long Branch S Gr 3	small star, near fore sock, off hind sock

YEAR OF FOALING	HORSE	RACE(S)	MARKINGS
1978	KINGS LAKE	Athenia H Gr 3 E. P. Taylor S Gr 3 Irish 2,000 Gns Gr 1 Sussex S, Gr 1 Joe McGrath Memorial Gr 1	small star
1978	LEAP LIVELY	Lingfield Oaks Trial Gr 3 Hoover Fillies Mile Gr 3	chestnut, white stripe, two hind socks
1978	NIJINSKY'S SECRET	Hialeah Turf Cup Gr 1 twice, W. L. McKnight H Gr 2, Tidal H Gr 2 Bougainvillea H Gr 2 King Edward Gold Cup Gr 3 Jockey Club Cup Gr 2	chestnut, star & snip, socks near fore and near and off hind
1978	SPORTIN' LIFE	Wm Dupont Jr H Gr 3	star, off fore coronet, near hind coronet, off hind sock
1979	GOLDEN FLEECE	Derby Gr 1 Ballymoss S Gr 2 Nijinsky S Gr 2	None
1979	HOSTAGE	Arkansas Derby Gr 1	small star, off fore coronet, near hind sock
1979	KHATANGO	Dixie H Gr 2 Seneca H Gr 3	None
1979	NUMBER	Hempstead H Gr 2 First Flight H Gr 3	large star
1979	PEACETIME	Guardian Classic Trial Gr 3	None
1979	ROSE CRESCENT	Athenia H Gr 3	star, snip, near fore coronet, off hind sock
1979	YAMANIN PENNY	Yonsai S Gr 3	star
1980	BEAUDELAIRE	Prix Maurice de Gheest Gr 2	chestnut, star, near hind sock
1980	BEMISSED	Selima Stakes Gr 1 Miss Grillo S Gr 3 Natalma S Gr 3	chestnut, large star, hind socks
1980	BROGAN	Prix Berteux Gr 3	near hind coronet
1980	CAERLEON	French Derby Gr 1 Benson & Hedges Gold Cup Gr 1	faint star

YEAR OF FOAL- ING	HORSE	RACE(S)	MARKINGS
1980	GORYTUS	Anglesey S Gr 3 Laurent Perrier Champagne S Gr 2	faint star
1980	SOLFORD	Coral Eclipse S Gr 1 Prix du Lys Gr 3	blaze, off hind sock
1981	EMPIRE GLORY	Royal Whip Gr 3	off hind sock
1981	KEY DANCER	Athenia S Gr 3	faint star
1981	NAGURSKI	Woodlawn S Gr 3	star, near hindsock
1981	TIGHTS	Silver Screen H Gr 2 La Jolla Mile Gr 3 Volante H Gr 3	small star and snip, hind socks
1981	VIDALIA	Criterium Femminile Gr 3	star, off hind sock, near hind coronet
1981	VISION	Secretariat S Gr 1 Pilgrim S Gr I	star, off hind sock
1981	WESTERN SYMPHONY	Larkspur S Gr 3	star, near fore sock, off hind sock
1982	FOLK ART	Oak Leaf S Gr 1	large star and snip, hind socks
1982	MOSCOW BALLET	P. J. Prendergast Railway S Gr 3	off hind sock

The conclusion to be drawn from this seems to be that, if anything, the majority of Nijinsky's progeny seem to inherit many of their sire's markings. Of the 56 Group winners across the world only Lighted Glory, Lucky Sovereign, Ile de Bourbon, Night Alert, Golden Fleece, Peacetime, Maruzensky and Khatango are whole coloured and it is noticeable that the last named five of these were all racing in the early 1980s, the time of McCall's remark.

Nijinsky himself has a large heart shaped star and white socks on both hind feet and a white coronet on the off fore. It is noticeable that many of his progeny carry one or more of these marks while, of the Group winners, Upper Nile, Niniski, Shining Finish, De La Rose, Hostage, Sportin' Life, Vidalia and Western Symphony approximate the closest to this distribution of markings and Sportin' Life as near as exactly. On their foreheads 31 Group winners carry their sire's star (though not necessarily the exact shape,

Number's is the closest imitation). In contrast, very few have large markings on their face. Only Czaravich, Stradavinsky, Solford, Balletomane and Nice Havrais have blazes while Nizon, Leap Lively and Summertime Promise bear narrow stripes. In addition to the star Quiet Fling, Green Dancer, Nijinsky's Secret, Rose Crescent, Folk Art and Tights also have snips on the nose.

As regards the myths about socks, Quiet Fling, Upper Nile, Niniski, Nice Havrais, Shining Finish, Sportin' Life, Balletomane and Nijinsky's Secret have the favoured white socks like their sire; Bright Finish, Cherry Hinton, Czaravich, Muscovite, De La Rose, Leap Lively, Hostage, Bemissed, Vidalia, Western Symphony, Summertime Promise, Tights, Folk Art, and Rose Crescent carry two and Nijana, Caucasus, Green Dancer, African Dancer, Pas de Deux, Princesse Lida, Beaudelaire, Brogan, Solford, Empire Glory, Nagurski, Moscow Ballet and Vision have just one – and all but Caucasus, Empire Glory, Moscow Ballet and Solford on the near hind. No Nijinsky Group winner carries one sock on a forefoot alone.

So with the majority of the socks on the hind feet, it is perhaps of note that only four of Nijinsky's Group winners carry the dreaded off hind sock alone. Of the four, Caucasus was one of the most consistent sons of Nijinsky over several seasons; Solford was unbeaten in the first five of his six races including the Group 1 Coral Eclipse Stakes; and Empire Glory and Moscow Ballet were among the best of their age in Ireland!

All the chestnut Group winners carry white markings of some sort. Pas de Deux is probably the nearest to being "whole coloured" with just that one near hind sock.

In a strange way, perhaps even Nijinsky's laminitis poses a doubt about the affirmation that white socks mean shelly or vulnerable feet, for the disease struck the front feet, one of which has no white colouring, the other is only around the coronet. Both Nijinsky's "socked" feet are untouched by the disease. Just an old wives' tale?

CHAPTER 9

A Commercial Success

Nijinsky's success at the world's sales and how the animals have fared compared with home bred stock; the likelihood of buying a champion

A good deal has been written and said in the last few commercialised years about the reasons for, and results of, the escalating price of the thoroughbred racehorse. Nijinsky's stock has consistently been of the most keenly sought after kind since first appearing on the market back in 1973. Perhaps by investigating the course of the sales records of Nijinsky's yearlings we may get an insight into the overall picture.

The overriding question is: has this money been well spent? The colts and fillies who were the highest priced yearlings of the years under review (that is, when Nijinsky's stock were also offered) may act as a control or yardstick:

YEAR	HIGHEST PRICED US YEARLINGS	SELLING PRICE IN US DOLLARS
1973	WAJIMA (c. Bold Ruler/Iskra) major sire	$600,000
	SUCH NOBILITY (f. Vaguely Noble/Sail Serenely) winner in France	$240,000
1974	KENTUCKY GOLD (c. Raise A Native/Gold Digger) winner in USA	$625,000
	DANCERS VIXEN (f. Northern Dancer/Ran Tan) won 3; placed in minor stakes	$250,000
1975	ELEGANT PRINCE (c. Raise A Native/Gay Hostess) Unraced; sire	$715,000
	SPRING ADIEU (f. Buckpasser/Natalma) won 3 races	$260,000
1976	CANADIAN BOUND (c. Secretariat/Charming Alibi) placed in France	$1.5m
	THIRTY NINE J.E. (f. Hoist The Flag/Hornpipe) ran twice	$310,000

YEAR	HIGHEST PRICED US YEARLINGS	SELLING PRICE IN US DOLLARS
1977	FOREIGN SECRETARY (c. Secretariat/Lady Victoria) placed fourth	$725,000
	HONOR TRICKS (f. Bold Bidder/Cosmah) Unraced; broodmare	$400,000
1978	NUREYEV (c. Northern Dancer/Special) Group winner; disqualified 2,000 Guineas Gr I	$1.3m
	PRICELESS COUNTESS (f. Vaguely Noble/Priceless Gem) placed in France	$500,000
1979	HOIST THE KING (c. Hoist The Flag/Royal Dowry) placed in France	$1.6m
	BARBS BOLD (f. Bold Forbes/Goofed) winner; fourth in Gr 3 in France	$1.45m
1980	LICHINE (c. Lyphard/Stylish Genie) stakes winner in France	$1.7m
	MINSTRELSY (f. The Minstrel/Mrs Peterkin) winner at 4	$900,000
1981	BALLYDOYLE (c. Northern Dancer/South Ocean) won a maiden at 3 in Ireland	$3.5m
	MUSICAL RIDE (f. The Minstrel/Directoire) won 2 races	$1.2m
1982	EMPIRE GLORY (c. Nijinsky/Spearfish) Group winner in Ireland at 3 years	$4.25
	KANZ (f. The Minstrel/Treasure Chest) Group winner in England at 3 years	$2.1m
1983	SNAAFI DANCER (c. Northern Dancer/My Bupers) Unraced	$8.25
	MA PETITE JOLIE (f. Northern Dancer/Ballade) ran once at 2 years in England	$2.5

Admittedly the pedigree alone of these animals will give a certain amount of paddock and stud value. But, of all these "creme de la creme" of the horse world, apart from the 1982 sales toppers, only Nureyev and Wajima have done what they were bought to do – win in races of the highest class. All the others who have run for two seasons or more are, frankly, disappointing. It will be interesting to see if the 1984 sales toppers Imperial Falcon (Northern Dancer/Ballade) at US $8.25m and Alchaasibiyeh (Seattle Slew–Fine Prospect) at US $3.75m can reverse the trend. Incidentally, both are in training in England/Ireland in 1985.

So, on the face of it, buyers who are willing to pay the very highest prices for potential top-class racehorses seem to be out of pocket. However, as paddock and stud values continue to soar so does the cost of sales yearlings. Quite a vicious circle. To turn to Nijinsky. Although Nijinsky's sales average is very much higher than the United States National Average, his stock do reflect a range in demand. How do the buyers fare in purchasing Nijinsky stock? A list by sales year of the Nijinsky yearlings sold at public auction in order of price and how they subsequently fared on a racecourse. The prices of the top priced colt (TPC) and top priced filly (TPF) are included for comparison. For a point of information the National Average for all American sales yearlings are printed below with that of Nijinsky beside it. The sudden soaring of bloodstock prices can be seen in these figures especially when noting the slump of 1974–6 and how the average has shot up again in leaps and bounds every year since then.

YEAR	US NATIONAL AVERAGE	NIJINSKY AVERAGE	% SOLD FOR $50,000+
1973	12,255	114,111	3.3
1974	10,689	74,342	4.7
1975	10,943	72,778	3.2
1976	13,021	75,777	9.0
1977	16,337	86,875	6.8
1978	19,846	235,833	8.0
1979	24,768	390,769	11.0
1980	29,683	261,563	13.0
1981	35,409	386,900	15.0
1982	32,991	738,462	13.0
1983	41,258	942,593	14.0

There is no doubt that in dealing with Nijinsky's stock at auction we are talking about the very highest echelon but this has also to be seen with such as Northern Dancer and Lyphard in mind.

YEARLING	SALES PRICE	SUBSEQUENT CAREER
1973, sales of		
WHISKEY ROAD (c)	$225,000	winner, successful sire in Australia
MASQUED DANCER (c)	200,000	won 2, Gr placed; successful sire in Argentina
LORD OF THE DANCE (c)	180,000	won 3; sire in Australia
SUPER GRAY (c)	100,000	placed 4th; sire in New Zealand
OVER SERVED (c)	90,000	won 4; successful sire in Japan; died early 1980's
BALLETIC (f)	70,000	Unraced; dam of winners
DANCING CHAMP (c)	60,000	GW; successful sire in USA
HELENOUCHKA (f)	52,000	winner; dam of Group and stakes winners
TANZOR (c)	50,000	SW; sire in Australia and Japan

YEARLING	SALES PRICE	SUBSEQUENT CAREER
TPC $600,000		
TPF $240,000		
1974		
CAUGHT IN THE ACT (f)	170,000	winner; dam of winners
KRASSATA (f)	130,000	6 races; Group placed; dam of winners
THE TEMPTRESS (f)	130,000	winner; dam of Group winner
GREY BALLET (f)	100,000	ran twice
RASIMOVA (f)	65,000	unraced; dam of stakes winner
NUCLEAR PULSE (c)	60,000	SW; sire in New Zealand and USA
DANCING DETENTE (f)	60,000	Unraced; dam of winners
ROYAL JETE (c)	56,000	won 6
AVODIRE (c)	45,000	winner; GP, sire in USA
LA JALOUSE (f)	40,000	SW; dam of stakes winner
JINSKY (f)	35,000	won 3; dam of stakes winner
TPC $625,000		
TPF $250,000		
1975		
MASKED DANCER (c)	120,000	unraced; sire of stakes winners
NIJINSKAIA (f)	115,000	won 2
LATH (c)	100,000	won 4
BALDSKI (c)	75,000	SW; a leading first season sire in USA in 1983
LADY JINSKY (f)	75,000	won 4, classic placed
MILOVA (f)	55,000	winner
DANCE IN SNOW (c)	40,000	placed
EDZIU (c)	40,000	won 8
RASKOLNIKI (c)	35,000	placed
VALETCHKA (c)	35,000 Gns	won 2; sire in USA
ex Requited (c)	27,000 Gns	
TPC $715,000		
TPF $260,000		
1976		
LA NIJINSKA (f)	232,000	won 3; stakes placed
SPACEFARER (c)	155,000	winner
SIR JINSKY (c)	50,000	won 3; stakes placed; sire in USA
JENNER (c)	48,000	winner
NORTHERN WALK (f)	45,000	won 2
HIS HONOR (c)	42,000	SW; sire in Argentina
NIZON (c)	40,000	GW; sire in USA & Japan
EXCITABLE (f)	35,000	SW
MEADOW DANCER (f)	35,000	ran twice
STRADAVINSKY (c)	64,000 Gns	GW; sire in Ireland
TPC $1.5m		
TPF $310,000		
1977		
SKIBINOFF (c)	300,000	placed
RISSA (f)	210,000	won 2; stakes placed
BO JINSKY (c)	115,000	winner

YEARLING	SALES PRICE	SUBSEQUENT CAREER
SWAN (f)	105,000	winner
GALLANTSKY (c)	100,000	winner; stakes placed
NINISKI (c)	90,000	dual classic winner; leading first season sire in UK
MIXED APPLAUSE (f)	75,000	won 2; Group placed
CHEROKEE PHOENIX (f)	70,000	won 2
DRONACHARYA (c)	55,000	unplaced; sire in Israel
CLASSICAL BALLET (c)	50,000	won 4; sire in USA
GIVE OR ELSE (c)	46,000	unraced
QUICK DANCE (c)	45,000	winner; sire in USA; died 1982
BREAKERS ROW (c)	43,000	fourth
CHARMING DANCE (f)	35,000	unraced
TUBAC DANCER (c)	31,000	unraced
PERSONATOR (c)	20,000	placed; sire in USA
BROOKDALE (c)	25,000 Gns	placed

TPC $725,000
TPF $400,000

1978

YEARLING	SALES PRICE	SUBSEQUENT CAREER
VATZA (c)	800,000 SAR REC	won 3; stakes placed; sire in USA; died 1982
ENCINO (c)	525,000	winner Group placed; sire in USA
NISSR (c)	335,000	unraced; sire in Zimbabwe
MUSCOVITE (c)	285,000	GW; sire in USA
GENTLE LINNA (f)	250,000	unraced
NIJIT (f)	220,000	won 5; stakes placed
PALACIOS (c)	220,000	ran 4
STREET BALLET (f)	200,000	SW
NIGHT ALERT (c)	190,000	GW; died at 4
LONDON BELLS (c)	185,000	won 4; Group placed; sire in Ireland & USA
UNREHEARSED (f)	185,000	unraced
GENTLEMAN JINSKY (c)	160,000	won 2
LADY HARDWICK (f)	155,000	won 2
FLY TO ARMS (c)	150,000	winner; sire in USA
ROYAL NIJINSKY (c)	150,000	won 3; sire in Japan
LUCY BLUE (f)	120,000	ran once
BONNIE HOPE (f)	65,000	winner
THAHUL (c)	50,000	won 5; sire in Australia
ENCHANTING DANCER (f)	18,000 Gns	unraced

TPC $1.3m
TPF $500,000

1979 Nijinsky leading sales sire

YEARLING	SALES PRICE	SUBSEQUENT CAREER
SAILOR KING (c)	1,400,000	placed; sire in USA
WORLDWATCH (c)	825,000	winner; sire in Chile
DE LA ROSE (f)	500,000 SAR REC	Champion Turf Filly
NIJISTAR (f)	410,000	unraced
GREAT PERFORMANCE (c)	385,000	winner
RANKING BEAUTY (f)	360,000	SP
BIVOUAC (c)	300,000	unraced

YEARLING	SALES PRICE	SUBSEQUENT CAREER
RUSSIAN FOX (c)	230,000	won 4; sire in S. Africa
LODGENSKI (c)	190,000	unraced; sire in Japan
EDMOND DANTES (c)	140,000	placed; sire in USA
CANOE (c)	130,000	winner
NETHERBY (c)	110,000	winner; SW over jumps
NATIVE BALLET (f)	100,000	winner

TPC $1.6m
TPF $1.45m

1980

GOLDEN FLEECE (c)	775,000	Derby winner; sire in Ireland; died 1984
VALSE NOBLE (f)	500,000	placed
SOPHISTICAL (f)	375,000	unraced
BALLET STYLE (f)	275,000	placed
CZARINSKY (c)	270,000	unraced; sire in India
NINOUSHKA (f)	260,000	placed
SUPER JAIME (f)	255,000	unraced
DRUMNADROCHIT (c)	250,000	winner
PRESTO LAD (c)	245,000	winner; sire in USA
ATMOSPHERE (c)	210,000	unraced
MISS NUT CRACKER (f)	180,000	winner
NISHINO NORTHERN (c)	150,000	won 2; GP
FIREBIRD (f)	125,000	unraced
EVASION (f)	105,000	unraced
ROMANOV (c)	105,000	ran 3; sire in USA
VASLOV (c)	105,000	won 2
DAWNBALLET (c)	58,000 Gns	placed

TPC $1.7m
TPF $900,000

1981

SOLFORD (c)	1,300,000 FTK REC	Gr 1 winner; sire in USA
COUNTERTRADE (c)	1,107,000	won 2
CAERLEON (c)	800,000	French Derby winner; sire in Ireland
SERHEED (c)	600,000	won 5
DANCININTHERAIN (f)	515,000	won 2
LA CONFIDENCE (f)	400,000	winner
SPEEDY NIJINSKY (c)	400,000	unraced
JILLINSKY (f)	385,000	won 2
TOP RANK (c)	350,000	unraced; sire in USA
MISINSKIE (f)	300,000	placed
ROSY SPECTRE (f)	250,000	SW
PAS DE CHEVAL (c)	210,000	winner
FABULEUX DANCER (c)	210,000	SW; sire in Canada
L'AVALANCHE (c)	190,000	unraced
DANCING HEIRESS (f)	180,000	unraced
EYE DAZZLER (F)	175,000	winner
KARENSKY (c)	150,000	placed (winner in 1985)
ULTRAMATE (c)	135,000	SW

YEARLING	SALES PRICE	SUBSEQUENT CAREER
WHITE BIRCH (c)	100,000	won 3; GP
BLUE NIJINSKY (c)	13,000	unraced; sire in USA
TPC $3.5m		
TPF $1.2m		

1982

EMPIRE GLORY (c)	4,250,000 WORLD REC	GW
ESPERANTO (c)	2,100,000	SW
RUSSIAN NOBLE (c)	800,000	winner (SP in 1985)
ALEZAN DANCER (c)	525,000	unraced; sire in USA
KAFOUAINE (c)	260,000	won 2
NAFKA (f)	255,000	unraced
INSTINCTIVE MOVE (f)	250,000	winner
KINSKI (c)	240,000	winner
GREEK SKY (c)	220,000	SW; sire in USA
GOLDYE'S MISS (f)	210,000	W2; stakes placed
NIJINSKY SENTIMENT (f)	200,000	winner
NAGURSKI (c)	170,000	GW
TRENDY GENT (c)	120,000	winner (SW in 1985)
TPC $4.25m		
TPF $2.1m		

1983

GALLANT ARCHER (c)	4,100,000	winner (GP in 1985)
FATHER MATTHEW (c)	1,900,000	winner; stakes placed
SAINTE CROIX (f)	1,700,000	unraced
SHADEED (c)	800,000	SW (Gr 1 classic winner in 1985)
WORDS 'N MUSIC (f)	800,000	unraced
ABEESH (f)	650,000	unraced
BALTIC DANCER (c)	575,000	unraced
TOLSTOY (c)	500,000	unraced
RUSSIAN RIBBON (f)	450,000	unraced
NIGHT MIRAGE (c)	300,000	unraced
MYJINSKI (c)	190,000	unraced
NIJINSKY'S SHOW (f)	175,000	unraced
NIJINSKY'S MELODY (f)	113,708	winner; Group placed
TPC $10.2m		
TPF $ 2.5m		

1984

NIJINSKY'S BEST (f)	2,100,000
SWEET MOVER (f)	1,100,000
HOPAK (c)	1,000,000
NADEED (c)	750,000
DANCING ON A CLOUD (f)	632,000
VERUSCHENKA (f)	625,000
NEVER EASY (f)	600,000
NEW DIRECTION (c)	500,000
RUSSIAN LOGIC (c)	500,000
GLORIOUS CALLING (f)	425,000
BUTTERFIELD STAGE (c)	410,000

YEARLING	SALES PRICE	SUBSEQUENT CAREER
PRODIGAL DANCER (c)	400,000	
LA CODORNIZ (f)	400,000	
REHEARSING (c)	400,000	
LIPIKA (f)	320,000	
MANZOTTI (c)	300,000	
ex Blackmail (c)	300,000	
NOBLE NIJINSKY (c)	300,000	
PRINCE OF TRICKS (c)	200,000	
STARJINSKY (c)	160,000	
ex Blackmail (c)	220,000 Gns	
FANAAN (c)	195,000 Gns	
TPC $8.25m		
TPF $3.75m		

A glance at the figures above leads one to correlate a connection between the high rise in prices with a better class of horse being put on the market. But though there is a probable chance of buying a winner the outlook on the Group front is distinctly unpromising. Looking at the Nijinskys in this light:

1973	9 sold	2 Group and stakes winner
1974	11 sold	2 stakes winners
1975	11 sold	1 stakes winner
1976	10 sold	4 Group and stakes winners
1977	17 sold	1 Group winner
1978	19 sold	3 Group and stakes winners
1979	13 sold	1 Group winner
1980	16 sold	1 Group winner
1981	20 sold	5 Group and stakes winners
1982	13 sold	4 Group and stakes winners

However in the years since 1979 the pattern has changed slightly in that four subsequent Group 1 winners were sold at auction: De La Rose, Solford, Caerleon and Golden Fleece. Only Niniski and Nizon had made it before that. Apart from De La Rose, all were European raced and it is no coincidence that the higher quality Nijinskys found their way onto the market from 1978, significantly the year that Vincent O'Brien and Robert Sangster began their onslaught for Nijinsky stock on the United States market. Their involvement began with the purchases of Muscovite, London Bells and Night Alert at that 1978 Keeneland July Sale and they have not looked back since. A minor setback with Sailor King was swiftly healed over with the purchases of Golden Fleece, Caerleon and Solford, until that heady moment in 1982 when they paid out US $4.25 million for the 1984 Group winner Empire Glory.

But has the subsequently better stock commanded the best prices? In

1973 the best racehorse was undoubtedly Dancing Champ but he was sold for the third to lowest price of Nijinskys. Those more expensive did win but all have increased their reputation as sires in various parts of the world. None of the Nijinskys sold at auction that year could be said to be a failure.

The products of the sales of 1974 produced two stakes winners from the middle to lower end of the Nijinsky market, Nuclear Pulse and La Jalouse, while Krassata (second highest price) was a consistent racemare of similar class. Apart from the unraced Dancing Detente only Grey Ballet (ran only twice) let the side down as all the others won.

The draft for 1975 were a really varied collection and the overall brevity of the price not only reflected the general slump in bloodstock prices but also perhaps the relative class of the animals. Only Baldski was a stakes winner though Lady Jinsky was runner-up to the brilliant Northernette in the Canadian Oaks. Dance In Snow and Raskolniki, neither of whom commanded a high price, were among the most moderate of Nijinsky's stock and while Edziu won eight races they were mainly claimers. The top priced lot, Masked Dancer, never saw a racecourse but has already sired a promising number of stakes winners.

In 1976 there was a small representation of ten. His Honor and Excitable made smallish prices but were good stakes winners, while of the two Group winners, Stradavinsky, was the fourth top priced yearling sold in England and Ireland in 1976. Again, apart from the low priced Meadow Dancer (ran twice) all won. The onset of the larger Nijinsky representation at the sales was seen in 1977: 17 lots this time. The buyer took a gamble and lost when laying out US $300,000 (top) for Skibinoff and certainly the lowest priced animals did nothing to make them seem cheap. Out of the 17, only Niniski (US $90,000) won a Group race though he was successful in Group 1 contests.

A change was seen to begin in 1978. Amongst the 19 lots there were 13 winners, including Group and stakes winners Muscovite, Street Ballet and Night Alert, the more than useful London Bells, Encino, Vatza and Nijit. All these black type animals were in the top half in terms of prices paid. Four were unraced and the other two ran a total of five times between them.

The floodgates being unlocked, Robert Sangster and partners paid a massive US $1.4m for Sailor King in 1979. Unfortunately this was a gamble which had no satisfactory ending. Sailor King was placed second in an Irish maiden and finished fifth and sixth in Group races when asked from a limited career. On the other side of the coin was the record priced Saratoga filly De La Rose who went on to fully redeem her purchase price by winning eleven races and being named Champion Turf Filly. Of the remainder, six won but only the non-winner Ranking Beauty attained a stakes placing.

Sangster and partners were not deterred. At the 1980 Keeneland July Sale they purchased the Derby winner Golden Fleece for US$775,000 and swiftly recouped it from the stallion's first (and only) season at stud. This single purchase, however, overshadowed the rest of the Nijinskys sold that year for only one of them attained a stakes position. This apparent lack of overall ability on the racecourse did not discourage the buyers in 1981. Some were more than rewarded with the high priced Group 1 winners Solford (Fasig Tipton record of US$1.3 million), Caerleon, and the lesser priced stakes winners Rosy Spectre, Ultramate and Fabuleux Dancer. This crop of sales youngsters produced a consistent collection: twelve winners, five unraced, two placed. The top five were all winners including Solford and Caerleon.

So to 1982 and the climax of the Nijinsky drafts to the international sales. Sangster and his partners splashed out US$4.25 million for Empire Glory, a world record, and followed it up with US$2.1 million for Esperanto. Both horses claimed stakes or Group winning status as three-year-olds and they were supported by others in this category: Greek Sky (US$220,000) and Nagurski (US$170,000), six other winners including the stakes placed Goldye's Miss (US$210,000) and two which have yet to run. It certainly seems that in latter years at least money has talked and the horses have run – if one was prepared to pay for it. It is too early to gain much from the sales which produced the two-year-olds of 1984 for nine of the 13 were unraced as juveniles. Of those that did race all won: two were stakes and Group placed and the other was Shadeed, the Houghton Stakes winner, and subsequent victor of the 1985 2,000 Guineas.

But what of the horses left at home? As one can see from the sales returns, relatively few of Nijinsky's 85 stakes winners have gone through the ring.

Despite the outnumbering of "home bred" (that is, not sold at public auction) to sales winners (do not forget that the larger numbers of a stallions progeny do not go through the ring) the popularity of Nijinsky has remained undimmed. He has broken records at every major American sale: Keeneland, Saratoga, Fasig Tipton. In accordance his stud fee has shot up to a massive US$450,000 no guarantee in 1984. While vast sums are still to be paid for the get of the leading stallions it is highly unlikely to fall!

Nijinsky has always been amongst the world's leading stallions in terms of sales demands apart from the results of his stock on the racecourse. That very first sales season of 1973, Nijinsky was second on the list of stallions by sales average to Bold Ruler. Raise A Native was third and Northern Dancer fourth. The esteem in which Northern Dancer is held says a great deal for this eclipse by his own son before any of his progeny had seen a racecourse.

From 1974 to 1977, however, saw a slump in the fortunes of the Nijinsky sales yearlings when Nijinsky was ninth, seventh, ninth and tenth behind

YEAR	GROUP WINNER SOLD	GROUP WINNER NOT SOLD
1973	Dancing Champ	Green Dancer
		Caucasus
		Lighted Glory
		Quiet Fling
		Summertime Promise
1974		African Dancer
		Javamine
		Nijana
		Bright Finish
1975		Valinsky
		Lucky Sovereign
		Maruzensky
		Pas de Deux
		Upper Nile
1976	His Honor	Cherry Hinton
	Nizon	Ile de Bourbon
	Stradavinsky	Summer Fling
		Terpsichorist
1977	Niniski	Czaravich
1978	Muscovite	Nice Havrais
	Night Alert	Princesse Lida
		Shining Finish
1979	De La Rose	Balletomane
		Kings Lake
		Sportin' Life
		Leap Lively
		Nijinsky's Secret
1980	Golden Fleece	Hostage
		Khatango
		Number
		Peacetime
		Rose Crescent
		Yamanin Penny
1981	Solford	Beaudelaire
	Caerleon	Bemissed
		Brogan
		Gorytus
1982	Empire Glory	Vision
	Nagurski	Key Dancer
		Vidalia
		Tights
		Western Symphony
1983		Folk Art
		Moscow Ballet

Round Table (1974 and 1975) and Secretariat (1976 and 1977). This did not deter someone paying US $240,000 for a share in 1976.

In 1978 there was a real turn however. Nijinsky was fourth on the sales list with an average of US $235,833, Northern Dancer was top for the first time since his son entered the fray with US $304,071. Thomas P. Whitney paid US $340,000 for a share which put a value on the then eleven-year-old stallion of US $10,880,000, precisely double his original syndication price in 1970.

In terms of sales, 1979 was the year for Nijinsky. He was the leading sales sire with an average of US $390,769, Hoist The Flag second on US $374,091 and Northern Dancer trailing in third with US $327,813. Two shares in Nijinsky both made US $500,000 in November that year to bids from the BBA and Ted Curtin, the highest price ever paid at public auction for a stallion share.

Northern Dancer was back on top in 1980 with Nijinsky in fifth place but, by 1981, Nijinsky was back to third place behind Northern Dancer and Hoist The Flag. Northern Dancer for the first time topped the one million mark with US $1,260,000. In 1982, with his stud fee recorded at US $175,000 and a share sold for US $750,000 in January, Nijinsky was third again on the list behind Northern Dancer and Alydar with an average of US $738,462.

In 1983 Nijinsky just missed the magic one million mark himself, finishing second to Northern Dancer again with a figure of US $942,593. His stud fee a reported US $250,000, Nijinsky actually outgunned his sire in the list of covering sires at the 1983 Keeneland November Sale, his four mares averaging US $2,612,000. At the same sale he established a new shares record of US $4 million; for 1984 his stud fee increased US $200,000 to US $450,000.

A lack of a really outstanding colt caused Nijinsky to slip back to fifth in 1984 behind the inevitable Northern Dancer and 1984 sire sensation Seattle Slew. However a season to the, then, ailing stallion was sold for US $475,000 on the open market and another at US $400,000 in November, while at that same sale a share was purchased for US $900,000 in the name of Josephine Abercrombie. Overstate was also sold for US $850,000 in foal to Nijinsky, while he was second on the list of broodmare sires, Spanish Riddle's position being entirely due to the US $4.1 million for Love Sign. Two of Nijinsky's daughters, Waving and Olamic, fetched in excess of US $2 million.

Despite the challenges of ever younger stallions Nijinsky seems more than capable of holding his own a little longer yet. Danzig and company will have to be patient. In 1985 Nijinsky's popularity is at its zenith, his US $13.1 million son testimony to the pulling power of the Nijinsky magnet.

CHAPTER 10

Sons as Sires

The probability of Nijinsky founding an enduring dynasty; the performance of his sire sons to date

When English journalists have nothing better to do than persecute Gorytus, they turn their attention to searching for a natural successor to Nijinsky at stud. This can cause panic to spread, that Nijinsky is not about to add to his dynasty in the near future and that an heir apparent must be found instantly to follow the sire's footsteps, perferably at Claiborne Farm. Quite whether the stud concerned is as obsessed with this search is not as yet readily apparent.

On the face of things there does not seem to be much backing for the statement in one advertisement for a new Nijinsky stallion in Florida that Nijinsky is the "greatest sire of sires in the world today". Not while Northern Dancer is still alive anyway. However, Nijinsky's sons are still young and their stud seasons as yet in their infancy. Also their number is growing so rapidly that we now have even 1982 foals carrying out their first stud seasons in 1985. The fact is that the oldest foals of Nijinsky's sons at stud were only the seven-year-olds of 1984 and only five stallions accounted for them. A closer examination reveals a little more than the apparently obvious.

Sire Sons with Oldest Foals 7-year-olds of 1984

As already mentioned only five stallions went to stud at four years, all coming from Nijinsky's first crop. Foremost of these is Nijinsky's most established sire son **Green Dancer**. Nijinsky's first classic winner, annexing the French 2,000 Guineas following success in the Observer Gold Cup (Group 1) and en route to the third Group 1 win in the Prix Lupin, Green Dancer initially stood in France at the Haras du Quesnay, in the hoofprints of other great modern day sires such as Riverman. As Green Dancer had been the flag bearer for Nijinsky in his first crop with a French Guineas success, so Aryenne signalled the explosive start at stud of Green Dancer.

Green Dancer, like his own sire, was leading first season sire in Europe in 1979, siring 6 winners of 7 races in France for 657,100 F; and 3 winners of 4 races in England/Ireland for £15,739 finishing fourth in the sires list of two-year-olds in France that year to his own sire. To set the pattern for Green Dancer's stud career to date his most accomplished performers were fillies; Aryenne, despite being a little in the shadow of Nijinsky's champion daughter Princesse Lida, won the Group 1 Criterium des Pouliches and, in England, The Dancer won the May Hill Stakes. In 1980 Aryenne came out of the shadow. Again Green Dancer's major earner, she defeated Princesse Lida first in the Prix de la Grotte (Group 3) and then in the French 1,000 Guineas (Group 1). Aryenne later finished a gallant short head second to English raider Mrs Penny in the French Oaks. Aryenne was ably supported by 17 other winners including Bold Green (Prix Coronation) and four other black type collectors. Together the 18 winners accounted for 23 races and 2,645,400 F, putting Green Dancer eighth on the French sires list (to Riverman) and sixth on the juvenile list (to Targowice). In England The Dancer won the listed Sir Charles Clore Memorial Stakes and finished third in both the Epsom and Lancashire Oaks, her only starts due to a worsening condition of moon-blindness. Green Dancer was reponsible for two other winners in England and Ireland and his superb looking stock were in such demand at the yearling sales that year that one, Dillingham, established a new European record of 530,000 guineas at the Tattersall's Houghton Sales in Newmarket.

The following year it was again fillies which led Green Dancer's assault on the major European prizes. Anitra's Dance won the Group 3 Prix de Minerve and finished second in the Prix de Pomone (Group 3) and Premiere Danseuse accounted for the Prix de la Calonne and was also Group 3 placed. Aryenne, racing for a limited third season, finished third in the Group 3 Prix Gontaut Biron. In France alone Green Dancer was responsible for 23 winners of 30 races and 2,868,200 F finishing eighth again on the general sires list to Riverman. He was spreading his wings a little further however. His five winners in England/Ireland included Dancing Rocks (Blue Seal Stakes) and in Italy he was sire of stakes winner Helenio and, in the United States, Verduret. And it was the United States, forever on the look out for top-class European stallions, that snapped up Green Dancer in the summer of 1981. Following the drain of Riverman, Lyphard, and Caro, Green Dancer was established at Gainesway Farm for the 1982 stud season, his fee set at US $80,000.

Of course, it will be a couple of years before Green Dancer's influence is felt in the United States. For 1982 it was still Europe which was at the mercy of the high-class products of Green Dancer's French seasons. Again it was a filly that led the way, a two-year-old filly of infinite promise, Maximova, a daughter of Stradavinsky's half sister Baracala. Dead heating for the Group 1 Prix de la Salamandre with the rather lucky Deep Roots, Maximova had already won the Prix du Calvados (Group 3) and Prix du Cabourg. She was supported in France by Group 2 winning colt Cadoudal (Prix Hocquart) and the multiple stakes winner No Attention. Green Dancer had established himself as the best of the living French stallions, finishing a close second to Luthier on the sires list and to the exported Riverman on the juvenile table. As ever a year after *his* export Green Dancer proved what a great loss he was likely to be to French breeding. Meanwhile in England, Dancing Rocks had trained on to win the Group 2 Nassau Stakes. Responsible for a dozen black type horses in 1982 Green Dancer had sired 23 winners of 34 races in France and 4,181,000 F; in England/Ireland 3 winners of 3 races and £50,225 and also sire of stakes horses in the United States and Germany.

In 1983, though no longer in France, Green Dancer strongly maintained his position as the leading French based sire (when his 1983 runners were foals) his best performers being Lovely Dancer (Prix du Prince d'Orange Group 3, second Prix Lupin, Group 1), Maximova (Prix de Meautry, Group 3, Prix de Seine-et-Oise Group 3) and placed in both French and Irish Guineas), Brilliante (Prix de la Seine, Group placed), Green Lucia (stakes winner in Ireland, second in Yorkshire Oaks, Group 1, third Irish Oaks Group 1), Oak Dancer (Prix de Reux) and juveniles Greinton (Prix du Cabourg) and Harifa (Prix Soya, third Prix Robert Papin, Group 1). The French products combined to place him fourth on both lists, to Luthier and Solicitor. His 40 winners netted 94 races for a tally of 4,608,897 F.

To rub in the salt, 1984 proved to be probably Green Dancer's best year yet in terms of strength in depth and overall consistency. There may not have been a star like Aryenne in France but his 25 winners accrued 36 races and 4,586,200 F and, up until the Prix de l'Arc de Triomphe at the beginning of October when Luthier and Northern Dancer were responsible for the first two, Green Dancer was leading the French sires table. Even as a result of this race he was still less than 400,000 F behind the leader Luthier, at the end of the season, in fourth place. He was represented by ten black type animals in France, the best of which was trained in England. Lovely Dancer, part of the Douieb stable that was transferred to Newmarket in 1984, returned to France to win the Prix d'Harcourt, Group 2, and the Group 3 Prix du Prince d'Orange.

In England and Ireland his runners won seven races and over £50,000 the leading horses being the fillies Corps de Ballet and the infinitely promising

Dance Machine. Even in Italy Green Dancer was well to the fore with three black type representatives, including the leading juvenile colt Will Dancer, winner of the Group 1 Gran Criterium. Solo Dancer finally won a stakes race in Germany while Green Dancer also had two stakes winners in the United States including Greinton, one of the leading lights in early 1985.

Green Dancer can only be seen as a sad loss to French breeding but, despite the success of Lyphard, Riverman, Caro et al since their export to the United States, there seems no hint of resistance to the mighty dollar for since Green Dancer, Nureyev and Arctic Tern have been spirited away. Somehow however, at least for the time being, French racing still maintains its position as one of the most competitive in the world, though quite how their home bred representatives will fare in years to come is another matter.

Establishing himself as a real sire sensation in quite another part of the world is **Whiskey Road**. A rather different specimen in terms of racing performance, Whiskey Road had given Australian racing, with its emphasis on staying power, quite another dimension. At US $225,000 as a yearling Whiskey Road was the highest priced of Nijinsky's first crop at auction. Out of the champion Bowl of Flowers and racing in Ireland with Vincent O'Brien, Whiskey Road chalked up just one win, albeit by eight lengths, over twelve furlongs at Leopardstown. A fellow member of that first crop, Masqued Dancer, had twice proved himself far superior to Whiskey Road in two earlier starts at Phoenix Park. Whiskey Road had just one subsequent start, finishing second at the Curragh and was promptly sent up to Tattersalls December Sales in Newmarket where he was bought for 10,500 guineas by the Newmarket Bloodstock Agency and sent to the Strathallan Stud in Australia.

Whiskey Road made a fairly modest start in his first season when he was responsible for 8 winners of 15 races worth Aus $56,770. Plenty of quality, yes. From his first crop of 26 foals, 22 were ultimately to win. The quality came from the 7 winners of 48 races (Aus $263,960) of the 1980–81 season. The name was Just A Dash. During the season he accounted for the Adelaide Cup (Group 1) and South Australian St Leger (Group 3). It was in the 1981–82 season however that Just A Dash really advanced his sire into the spotlight. In winning Australia's leading prize, the Group 1 Melbourne Cup by 2½ lengths, Just A Dash had proved himself for Whiskey Road, the equivalent of Aryenne for Green Dancer and Green Dancer for Nijinsky. Whiskey Road was not just a one horse wonder however. In that 1981–82 season he was responsible for 21 winners of 41 races and Aus $382,470 and in 1982–83 he finished fifth on the general sires list with 31 winners of 71 races and Aus $737,820. But in this year it was not only Just A Dash who was responsible for this lofty placing but also the triple Group 1 winner Strawberry Road, ultimately elected Horse of The Year.

It was Strawberry Road which made 1983–84 even more memorable for it was the globe trotting performances of this horse that lifted Whiskey Road to world recognition; a Group 1 winner in Germany, Strawberry Road ran creditably in similar contests in Europe and the United States as well as annexing a Group 1 race in his own country. Back home he was supported by 24 winners of 47 races and Aus $503,955 including stakes winner Whisky Lover.

As a measure of the esteem in which Whiskey Road is now held his initial stud fee of Aus $1000 has soared to Aus $12,000 (now reduced to Aus $10,000 to compensate for the recession which has hit Australia). Also, the three leading produce of Whiskey Road to date have been produced from mares who were not themselves good racehorses. Whiskey Road is a magnificent looking horse of 17 h.h. and he is certainly stamping his stock with his own distinctive physique and seems to be able to sire stock that can race in any conditions. The future seems assured for this particular son of Nijinsky.

Two of Nijinsky's three other contemporary sire sons also stood in the Antipodes: "stood" as Tanzor has recently left for Japan, another area where Nijinsky's sons have been doing exceptionally well. **Tanzor**, though not in the class of Whiskey Road, has proved himself an able sire, responsible to the end of the 1983–84 season in Australia for the winners of 129 races. He is remarkable in that he also has a representative in the United States, his lone stakes winner Admiration. Winner to date of 15 races, including the Sears Distaff Stakes, Distaff Stakes, Duchess Stakes, Manitoba Matron Stakes and the CHTS Matchmaker Stakes. A rather better racehorse than Whiskey Road, Tanzor was Nijinsky's first stakes winner, taking the Acomb Stakes at York as a two-year-old. A disappointing three-year-old, he nonetheless began his career in Australia at twice the fee of Whiskey Road.

Across the water in New Zealand stands the once raced **Super Gray**, a grey son of Loyal Land, half sister to Secretariat and Sir Gaylord. Sire of five foals from a test crop in the United States which accounted for 22 races there, Super Gray has so far established himself as a prolific winner-getter, his foals totalling 131 races in five seasons, including two Group winners in Martian's Son and Super Dude. After a tardy start in this calibre of field Super Gray is now showing signs of picking up with five stakes horses in 1983–84.

Nijinsky's fifth son is **Valodi**, an unraced half brother to Lonesome River and the dam of Barrera. Standing in Oklahoma at an initial fee of US $1,000 he is finding the opposition tough and has so far sired the winners of 32 races from limited opportunities.

Sire Sons with Oldest Foals 6-year-olds of 1984

The eight representatives are led by **Dancing Champ**, like the older stallion sons from Nijinsky's first crop. The most distinguished racehorse, Dancing Champ, comes from one of the foremost families of the last decade being a half brother to Sweet Alliance (Kentucky Oaks), dam of the 1983 European Champion Shareef Dancer (by Northern Dancer). Though not a Grade 1 winner Dancing Champ was nevertheless a top-class racehorse, being named co-champion older horse in Canada. His 7 victories included the Grade 2 Massachusetts Handicap and Group 3 Woodlawn Stakes. At the end of his career he was retired to the Canadian division of E. P. Taylor's Windfields Farm and sired a stakes winner from his first crop of 6 winners in Vimy's Champ. His second season total rose to 16 winners of 26 races in the United States and Canada and although sire of black type placers he did not quite manage to have a stakes winner to represent him. All that changed in 1982 however. His 29 winners included If Winter Comes who showed she could compete with the best with victories in the Grade 2 Diana Handicap and Grade 3 Knickerbocker Handicap. She was ably supported by Grade 3 victress Au Printemps and stakes winners Chic Dancer, Dance Pavilion and Gallant Risk.

In 1983 Dancing Champ was responsible for his first Grade 1 winner Archdeacon, winner of one of the Canadian Triple Crown races, the Prince of Wales's Stakes. Au Printemps and Ring Dancer won stakes races and If Winter Comes, though not managing a Graded victory herself, was placed in the Grade 1 Flower Bowl, Diana (Grade 2) New York (Grade 2) and Long Island (Grade 3) Handicaps and the Grade 3 E.P. Taylor Stakes. Dancing Champ also sired seven other black type animals. In 1984 his 37 winners included Grade 3 winner Island Champ. The total money won by his progeny stands at well over three million dollars.

However, just as Dancing Champ really seemed to be making his mark in the northern hemisphere it was announced in mid-1983 that he had been sold to stand at the Excelsior Stud in South Africa. It will be interesting to see what he makes of the change in climate.

A US $200,000 yearling from Nijinsky's first crop and winner of two races in Ireland, **Masqued Dancer** has come to the fore on stallion lists in Argentina with the victory of his daughter Miss Carlotita in the Group 1 Gran Premio Enrique Acebal at the beginning of the 1983–84 season. Earlier responsible for Group performers Martincha and Matera, Masqued

Dancer was the first son to stand in Argentina but he has now been joined by His Honor and Halpern Bay.

Nearby in Venezuela is **Umabatha**. An English winning representative of his sire's second crop, Umabatha's only other start was a fourth place finish in the Houghton Stakes (listed) at two. Though it is very difficult to get information from Venezuela, it appears that Umabatha is doing well, already being responsible for one Group 1 performer.

Now the only American representative left of this group, Storm Bird and Northernette's three parts brother **Sevastopol** seems to be able to hold the fort. Standing in Upperville, Virginia, having, like Dancing Champ, initially been at Windfields, Sevastopol has sired the winners of 116 races including the stakes winners Toporal, Grade 1 placed Futurette and The Cat Came Back. Given the opportunities Sevastopol could prove himself a sire to rank with the more established of Nijinsky's sire progeny.

Now the sole representative in Australia of this selection **Lord of The Dance** was never to fulfill the promise of an unbeaten three-year-old career (he was favourite for the Doncaster St Leger but was injured and retired). A son of champion Monarchy, he was sold to an Australian syndicate in 1976 for £110,000. Perhaps a trifle disappointing, he has nevertheless sired the winners of 65 races from his first three seasons including the Group 3 winners Money Game and Unique Dancer. Like Super Gray he seems at last to be coming good.

Another who has vacated the shores of Australia for Japan, **Sportsky** was a five times winner over seven furlongs in England. The first Nijinsky yearling to be offered at public auction in England (he failed to reach his reserve when the bidding stopped at 51,000 guineas), he has sired the winners of 72 races in his first few seasons including Sports Ruler (Kaiser Stuhl Quality Stakes). He has made an explosive start in Japan with a Group 1 winning juvenile in 1984 in Daigo Totsugeki.

Meiwa Iran, already in Japan having been foaled there but never raced and **Diaghilev**, sent to France after a three-year-old season in England in which he was placed, have both sired winners from a limited number of foals. However as neither has had any real opportunity to prove themselves at stud it is too early to gauge whether they will have any real influence on the breed.

Sire Sons with Oldest Foals 5-year-olds of 1984

This group includes some of the most familiar names in Nijinsky's first crops as many of them raced into their third and fourth seasons.

Quiet Fling, a Group 1 winner himself and one of the relatively few sons of Nijinsky to be taller than their sire, followed Nijinsky and Green Dancer with a Group 1 classic winner in his first crop when Old Country won the Italian Derby. He later followed this up in 1983 with a victory in the all-aged French St Leger (Group 1). Old Country has been supported by the stakes placed horses Quite Shy, Ma Gonzesse, Fling Tiger and Lamiel and has had representatives win for him all over Europe and already in the United States.

Initially standing in England at the King Edward's Place Stud, at £1,250 no foal, no fee, Quiet Fling, one of the handsomest of Nijinsky's sons was bought by the Green brothers of Mint Lane Farm in Kentucky to stand the 1981 season at a fee of US $10,000 and his first American crop raced in 1984, resulting in 9 winners of 21 races accruing US $214,132.

Hitting the headlines are the two Japanese stallions Maruzensky and Lucky Sovereign. **Maruzensky**, a bred and raced Japanese champion, has made a sensational start with Group 1 winners in each of his first two crops. In his first season his two-year-olds won seven races and included several black type performers. His representatives of 1982 accounted for 23 races and 285,330 yen including the Japanese St Leger (Group 1) winner Horisky and the two-year-old Nishinosky, who carried off the Group 1 championship the Asahi Hai Sansai Stakes, as did his sire. In 1983 Maruzensky was high on the general and juvenile sires lists, finishing fourth on the latter, his Group winners including Horisky, Suzuka Koban, Sakura Toko and the Group 1 placed Yamanosky. His runners in 1983 tallied races worth over 1¾ million yen. This high standard was maintained into 1984 with the winners of 2½ million yen, including Group winners Suzuka Koban and Promaydoh.

Not far behind him was **Lucky Sovereign,** the same age as Maruzensky (1974), both being representatives of their sires third crop. An English raced Group winner and second to The Minstrel in the Irish Sweeps Derby, Lucky Sovereign has so far been responsible for the winners of 78 races and finishing a place below Maruzensky in both the 1983 general and juvenile sires lists. From his first two crops (1981–82) his leading winners have included Shin Wolf, while in 1983 he was the sire of the champion juvenile colt Long Hayabusa, an absurdly easy winner of the Daily Sansai Stakes (Group 2) in a record time and the Group 1 Hanshi Sansai Stakes. Unfortunately he sustained a fracture of the cannon bone and was an absentee from the 1984 spring classics. Suzu Mahah however was second in the Japanese Derby.

Nijinsky also had a notable third son in Japan in **Over Served** who sadly is now dead. He may well prove to be a great loss for he is already the sire of the winners of 97 races and was chasing his two colleagues all the way up the sires table. An established sire of stakes horses his best performer to date has undoubtedly been Yamano Shiragiku (Kyoto Daishoten, Group 2 and second in the Group 1 Hanshin Sansai Stakes).

A stallion joining them for the 1984 season from Australia is **Bright Finish**, winner of six races off the reel at three and four years in England culminating in the Jockey Club Cup (Group 3) and Yorkshire Cup (Group 2). Bright Finish was leading sales sire in Australia with his first crop of yearlings. From his first two seasons of runners they only managed eight races between them and Bright Finish was sent to seek more lucrative pastures in an area where Nijinsky stallions are fought over. As so often happens, however, Bright Finish had the winners of 29 races and US $169,790 in 1983–84 including a top-class horse running for him now that he has departed in the filly Entrancing and a second stakes winner in High Polish.

He leaves behind **Copper Kingdom**, a three time American winning chestnut, who stands at the Panorama Stud in Queensland. From his first three seasons he has sired the winners of an almost phenomenal (by European standards) 126 races including the stakes winning classic placed Foreign Interest. Copper Kingdom has made an impressive, if not spectacular, start in terms of headline getters but seems assured of a bright future.

In the United States there are two sons of Nijinsky with four crops to race but of a very different nature. **Caucasus** will be a familiar name to racing people as he was a Group 1 winner on both sides of the Atlantic and raced until he was five-years-old. Initially standing at Windfields Farm alongside Northern Dancer for a fee of US $15,000 he moved in 1981 to Hurstland Farm in Kentucky and his fee now sits at US $12,500. His runners have, like him, taken time to mature but Casus Belli and Royal Anthem were stakes winning representatives to run in 1982 when Caucasus sired 16 winners of 29 races with his first crop of three-year-olds plus winners in England and Italy. At the back end of 1983 probably Caucasus's best son appeared when Pied à Terre won the Grade 3 Pilgrim Stakes by seven lengths as a juvenile though he was disappointing at three. In 1984 Caucasus had 32 winners of 61 races and US $792,458 in the United States including Dundrum Dancer and Trust Us.

Two years Caucasus's junior and unraced, **Masked Dancer** has done startlingly well in 1983 and 1984. In his first few seasons, over 35 individual winners have amassed 82 victories including the stakes winning Holiday Dancer (Bryn Mawr Stakes, Free State Stakes and Typecast Stakes), Given (Ruthless Stakes, Rare Perfume Stakes, Lassie Dear Stakes), Masked Barb (Toddler Stakes, Gala Lil Stakes), He's Vivacious (Grade 3 Knickerbocker Handicap), Hollywood Dancer (Silver Spoon Handicap), and Masked Romance, a stakes winner outside of the United States. Masked Dancer is based at Green Willow Farm in Maryland. As a yardstick to his merit the US $750 fee for his first season stood at US $7,500 in 1984.

Sire Sons with Oldest Foals 4-year-olds of 1984

With the younger sons at stud it is very much a case of being patient and wait and see. As with the older generations the stallions with oldest foals four-year-olds are distributed to similar areas of the world. Unfortunately the Antipodes, initially well endowed with Nijinsky stallions, have found themselves bereft in 1984 as all three from this group have been lost to them one way or another.

Two, Pas de Deux and Valinsky, both members of their sires third crop, have died. A Group 3 winner in France and from the famous La Troienne family, **Pas de Deux** died of a twisted bowel only months after his arrival at Woodlands Stud, having only partially completed his book. So he has very few progeny to make his mark for him but they do include a winner in 1983–84.

A son of the Oaks winner Valoris, and winner of the Group 2 Geoffrey Freer Stakes at Newbury for Vincent O'Brien and Sir Charles Clore, **Valinsky** was imported into Australia after a win and a fourth place in the Grade 2 Tidal Handicap in the United States. He died in the autumn of 1983 but has sired winners of 15 races to the end of the 1983–84 season including the stakes placed Kahana Bay.

The third Antipodean representative, touching wood, is alive and well . . . and in Texas. A French stakes winning chestnut son of Canadian Oaks victress Solometeor, **Nuclear Pulse**, after a four year racing career that took him from England to France and thence to the United States, was bought to stand at the Gracious Farm in New Zealand. After half his runners proved themselves able to win races Nuclear Pulse found himself standing the 1984 season in the northern hemisphere.

Already in the United States were four other stallions of similar stud status, reflecting all types of racehorse. The oldest of these is **Avodire** (1973). Half brother to High Echelon (Belmont Stakes) he won in the United States after a career in France and his best performance was probably a neck second to Copper Mel in the Grade 2 San Luis Obispo handicap.

One of Nijinsky's most accomplished sons, **Upper Nile** won six races including the Grade 1 Suburban Handicap. His own sister De La Rose was named Champion Turf Female in 1981. Upper Nile sired the winners of ten races from his first crop of two-year-olds including Nile Smile (Vancouver Island Futurity) but had a somewhat disappointing second season with no stakes horse to represent him though 13 individual winners of 18 races in the

United States did keep him ticking over. It is also notable that his initial fee of US $12,500 in 1981 rose to US $30,000 for the following season. In 1984 his 28 winners in the United States of 48 races included stakes winner Its A Done Deal and he and Nile Empress have wasted no time early in 1985.

Half brother to Barrydown, **Saunders** came from the same crop as Upper Nile but ran just once at two years. However his first crop to race in 1982 yielded Ro Ro's Coffee (four races including Master Fairmount Stakes and Bunker Hill Stakes) from only a limited book.

The fourth American horse and very closely related to Whiskey Road is **Choreographer**, a three time winner at three and four years. He stands at West Wind Farm, Alabama, at a fee of US $2,000 (1983) and seems to be stamping his stock extremely well and having a stakes winner in 1984 in Dancing Heifer.

The lone European is **Stradavinsky** a Group 3 winner and closely related to Nonoalco. Initially based in Ireland and thence leased to Italy, Stradavinsky has been domiciled in France but after his successes of 1984 he was swiftly repatriated to Ireland for 1985 but sailed for Japan soon after. From the same crop as Ile de Bourbon (to whom he was second in the King Edward VII Stakes), it seems a great tragedy that Stradavinsky was not raced as a four-year-old as he only seemed to be coming to his great size and strength towards the close of his racing career. However he has made a particularly bright start to his stud life, siring plenty of two-year-old winners, surprising in that he was not a two-year-old or even an early three-year-old himself and was represented by a Group placed horse in his first crop. In 1983 Anita's Prince won the Goffs Stakes and was runner up to Western Symphony (Nijinsky-Millicent) in the Birdcatcher, and Escart Bay was a stakes winner in Malaya. In addition, Heisenberg was Group placed in Ireland and Stradavari in Italy. Even more surprising seems to be Stradavinsky's tendency to sire sprinters, notably Anita's Prince and Alpine Strings, and it is beginning to look as if his stud future will lie along these lines. In 1984 Anita's Prince became champion three-year-old sprinting colt by winning the Group 3 King George Stakes and being beaten the shortest of short heads by Habibti in the Kings Stand (Group 1). Mirco Umbro and Apolvinsky kept Stradavinsky to the fore in Italy.

Sires with Oldest Foals 3-year-olds of 1984

The first season classic sires of 1984 have proved themselves a very promising collection. Baldski in America and Ile de Bourbon in England seem to be the leaders of their generation, at the present each having sired a champion.

The champion three- and four-year-old of Europe **Ile de Bourbon** had a very successful first year with his first two-year olds considering he was such a late developer himself. In England he was represented by 4 winners of 5 races and also Glowing With Pride, a very promising third in the Blue Seal Stakes at Ascot. Island Smile was a good winner in France but it was in Germany that perhaps Ile de Bourbon's best runner to date has appeared, the two-year-old champion Lagunas, who trained on to capture the German Derby. Among the very promising juveniles of 1984 Kashi Lagoon in particular gives a 1985 to look forward to. It is on Ile de Bourbon that the Nijinsky dynasty largely rests in England and it would be far too early to write him off in that respect.

A year senior to Ile de Bourbon, **Baldski** was a stakes winning half brother to Exceller and had a tremendous first season siring 18 individual winners including the leading Norwegian juvenile, the later classic placed Missy Baldski as well as Grade 3 winner Baldski's Holiday in Canada, and the American stakes horses Bald King and Bald Admiral. His fee for his first two seasons of US $10,000 seems certain to increase rapidly with Baldski's ever increasing successes which included 42 three-year-old winners of 92 races in the United States including four stakes winners, notably Baldski's Holidays.

The supporting cast is led by **Nizon**, Group 1 winner in Italy and Group 3 in France but who bowed a tendon in his first start in the United States. Retired to stud he sired a stakes winner in his first crop, Nozin Man (Kindergarten Stakes), but by then Nizon was heading for Japan.

Four other young sires of note are to be found in rather different thoroughbred areas of the world. **Red Steps**, the leading first season sire in Belgium, maintained that standard with his first classic runners in 1984. His daughter Mika Red was champion Three-Year-Old Filly, her victories including the Belgian 1,000 Guineas and Group I Grand Prix d'Ostende, while Cheriestep was an unbeaten Group 1 winning juvenile.

Across the Atlantic **Mr Justice**, a winning own brother to Night Alert, has sired the winners of 36 races in his first crops including the stakes winner Jessica Briar. **King of Darby**, in Japan was the sire of two decent animals including the Group 1 placed Bingo Chimuro. **Yeats** in Australia is also making his mark. He has an interesting representative in Deal. Yeats's first runners were two-year-olds of the 1983–84 season.

There are second season representatives as far afield as Peru, Australia, India and Japan whose potential is still to be unveiled due to the seasonal time difference.

Sires with Oldest Foals 2-year-olds of 1984

Heads and shoulders above a number of highly promising sons to have their first runners in 1984 was **Niniski**. A great deal has been written about Niniski so this is no time to dwell on the dual Leger winner's racing qualities but on the success of his juveniles in 1984. Niniski was the leading first season sire in England as Nijinsky had been before him, through two sons in the Champion Juvenile Colt, Kala Dancer, and the dual stakes winning Petoski. Kala Dancer will always be remembered for his thrilling victory over Law Society and Local Suitor in the Group 1 William Hill Dewhurst Stakes while but for unusually less than inspired assistance from the saddle, Petoski would in all likelihood have been a triple "Champagne" winner. Apart from this pair Niniski had a leading son in Italy called Gianchi and overall a remarkable strike rate.

Also to make his mark in this part of the world, **London Bells** got off to a great start. Perhaps more predictable than Niniski, for he was a talented juvenile himself, London Bells has only two crops to represent him in Europe having been moved to the Pegasus Stud in Kentucky after the 1983 season in Ireland. However, his first runners included the Sirenia Stakes winner Northern Chimes and other promising colts include Beginner's Luck.

A Group 1 placed juvenile himself, **Nice Havrais** is the only son of Nijinsky in France apart from the five years senior Diaghilev. He was well to the fore in the French first season sires table behind Nureyev, with whom he was rated on the juvenile Free Handicap in 1979.

Standing in the United States, **Czaravich** was one of Nijinsky's fastest sons in that country yet won the Grade 1 Metropolitan Handicap. Though having a quiet start in 1984 he is firing on all cylinders early in 1985 notably with Golden Horde.

The Irish Group winner **Muscovite** stands at Spendthrift Farm for a fee of US$15,000 for his first three covering seasons. From his first crop in 1984 he has had the winners of seven races including the stakes winner Must Guarantee. On a stud where there are so many stallions it will be interesting to chart Muscovite's progress as he comes from the same immediate family as Exclusive Native and General Assembly.

Nijinsky's sons are flung far and wide over the world's surface and many are in the southern hemisphere. Their first runners are being seen in 1984–85 where such as Nissr in Zimbabwe has already had three juvenile winners from three runners. Other representatives are to be found in Argentina (notably in the form of Halpern Bay) and South Africa, as well as a number of young sires standing at small studs in the United States.

The story does not end here of course. Every year more and more sons of Nijinsky are finding their way to the stud farms of the world. Sires whose first crop race in 1985 particularly include the immaculate Kings Lake in Europe, Sir Jinsky in the United States and, in the southern hemisphere, Shining Finish, His Honor and Audley End. In 1986 the first representatives of Sportin' Life and Hostage will see the racecourse as will the one and only crop of the champion Golden Fleece. Foals only now arriving by the likes of Caerleon, Solford, Gorytus and Beaudelaire will be racing in 1987. Sons standing their first season in 1985 include Grade 1 winners Nijinsky's Secret and Vision.

And what of the stallions still to come? Perhaps the heir apparent is not amongst those named but, after all, is yet to arrive. Perhaps he is one of those long-legged individuals now seeing grass for the first time. Perhaps. However those already at stud seem set to do their sire proud.

CHAPTER 11

Daughters as Broodmares

The probability of Nijinsky mares breeding good horses; the merits of purchasing Nijinsky fillies at auction and their successes to date; with which sires have they crossed.

The facts which restrict the general appreciation of the success of Nijinsky's sire sons are equally relevant and perhaps even compounded in the success of his daughters as broodmares. Whereas a few of the unraced members of his first crop did have foals as early as 1976, the fact remains that a mare can only have one foal to represent her each year. Therefore, there are not so many from which to breed a winner, usually the first milestone in deciding whether a mare is going to be a viable proposition at stud. Nijinsky's daughters have already proved themselves in that sphere – and have gone far further.

It is a well known fact that stallions going to stud are generally of greater racecourse ability than the mares to which they are bred. It is all part of the process of selection and therefore a stallion can have fifty mates or more in a single stud season, a mare only one. So it stands to reason that there will be far fewer stallions at stud than mares so naturally only the best of the male breed can be selected. However, the daughters of Nijinsky not only have better than average performance on their side but also pedigree far superior than the "average" mare.

Bearing this in mind we can rate the success of Nijinsky's daughters at stud and gauge the success of Nijinsky as a broodmare sire. Of his daughters 76 have been recorded as being at stud and having produced *at least one foal of racing age* in 1984. They are not quite so widely distributed worldwide as are the sires, but are to be found in the United States and Canada, England and Ireland and just a few in France. This makes it just a little easier to catalogue the performances of their stock.

As Nijinsky naturally receives superior mates, so the stallions to which the Nijinsky daughters are sent are generally "out of the top drawer" too. This of course gives them a better chance of producing good horses, as is the purpose of selective thoroughbred breeding. However it will be seen that put to a variety of stallions, in terms of distance progenitors and the sire lines they represent, the Nijinsky mares are still producing better than average stock. Working on the theory that the stallion and the mare supply an equal half of the resultant foal's genes, the Nijinsky mares are more than holding their own.

Of the 76, 18 have yet to have a runner; these 18 are those with first foals, two-year-olds, or a few three-year-olds of 1984. Of the remainder, 50 have produced a winner of one sort or another and, considering their youth, a staggering 19, or over a third, have produced two winners or even more. Of the mares concerned, 19 never ran, 50 won and 25 were stakes horses. Four others were placed and so had some measure of ability. Racing the fillies does not seem to have had any adverse effect on their ability at stud, especially bearing in mind that the unraced fillies had probably at least one extra year at stud. All have produced their share of winners. The investors in the Nijinsky mares, whether in sending their own mare to Nijinsky and keeping the produce or buying from the breeders, cannot have much cause to complain. For those buying Nijinsky fillies at public auction the overall outlay must by all accounts be well spent:

1973 Yearling Sales

Balletic (ex Tims Princess)	$ 70,000	Unraced but dam of 2 winners by Lord Durham & Snow Knight
Helenouchka (ex Hypavia)	$ 52,000	winner; dam of 4 winners from first foals including GW Hortensia (by Luthier) and SW Hot (by Tennyson) and GP Heil (by Grundy)

1974

Caught In The Act (ex Bamboozle)	$170,000	winner; dam of winners in England by Tentam and Kings Bishop
Dancing Detente (ex Alluvial)	$ 60,000	Unraced; dam of 2 winners by Ack Ack, and another by Judger
Grey Ballet (ex Pinny Gray)	$100,000	Ran twice; first foal an unraced juvenile of 1984
Jinsky (ex Sheila Jan)	$ 35,000	won 2; dam of Jinxed (by Recaptured) SW of 6 races
Krassata (ex Bonnie Google)	$130,000	6 times SP winner of 6 races; dam of Safe Process (by Bold Forbes) winner and 4th Irish Oaks
La Jalouse (ex Quadruple)	$ 40,000	SW of 4 races; dam of 2 winners by Exclusive Native including SW Exclusive One and one by Raise A Native
Rasimova (ex Restless Sis)	$ 65,000	Unraced; dam of Italian SW Delices (by Artaius)

The Temptress (ex La Sevillana)	$130,000	winner; dam of winners by Tentam and Val de l'Orne; the latter Gr 3 winner La Lorgnette
1975		
Lady Jinsky (ex Lady Victoria)	$75,000	classic placed winner of 4 races; dam of winner by Exclusive Native
Milova (ex Moss)	$55,000	winner; dam of placed horse; her only foal to race
Nijinskaia (ex Gay Meeting)	$115,000	2 races in France; no foals of racing age
1976		
Excitable (ex Lady Graustark)	$35,000	dual SW of 3 races; dam of a stakes placed triple winner in France by Youth
La Nijinska (ex Street Dancer)	$232,000	stakes placed winner of 3 races; dam of winner by Snow Knight
Meadow Dancer (ex Meadow Saffron)	$35,000	ran twice; dam of one foal to race
Northern Walk (ex Lovers Walk)	$45,000	won 2; no foals
1977		
Rissa (ex Kittiwake)	$210,000	won 2; stakes placed; no foals of racing age
Swan (ex Her Demon)	$105,000	winner; dam of placed horse
Mixed Applause (ex My Advantage)	$75,000	Group placed dual winner; first foal unraced juvenile
Cherokee Phoenix (ex Copper Canyon)	$70,000	won 2; dam of 2 unraced foals
Charming Dance (ex Tamalesian)	$35,000	unraced; sent to Japan

Few younger fillies have produced racing age foals but even now their value is clear and despite the demand for Nijinsky fillies many can still represent what is paramount to a bargain:

1978	7 fillies	av	US $170,714	incl Street Ballet, Nijit
1979	4 fillies	av	US $342,500	incl De La Rose, Ranking Beauty
1980	8 fillies	av	US $234,375	
1981	7 fillies	av	US $315,000	incl Rosy Spectre
1982	4 fillies	av	US $228,750	incl Goldye's Miss
1983	6 fillies	av	US $648,000	incl Nijinsky's Melody
1984	8 fillies	av	US $775,250	

So while there are relatively few Nijinsky fillies for sale on the open market the prices paid are not quite so prohibitive as, say, those of Northern Dancer. Even if subsequently unraced, on pedigree alone these fillies would be a priceless asset to any broodmare band. The results, as we have seen, can be well worth the investment.

Stakes Producing Daughters

Of course the pinnacle of any criterion by which to measure the value of a broodmare, is the production of stakes horses, the black type necessary to place her in the top bracket. Even in these early years a very high proportion (35 per cent) of Nijinsky's daughters have already been responsible for a number of top-class racehorses by a variety of stallions on both sides of the Atlantic. Of these 17 bred stakes winners of which four were stakes fillies themselves.

Lighted Glory—A first crop daughter of the Sir Gaylord mare Lighted Lamp, Lighted Glory was the product of a British female line tracing to the Guineas victress Picture Play via Queen of Light, maintained with such success by H. J. Joel at his Childwick Bury Stud in Hertfordshire. Trained by George Delloye Lighted Glory raced exclusively in France, foraying to England on a sole occasion to record a close fifth placed finish behind Nocturnal Spree in the 1,000 Guineas. Victorious in the Group 3 Prix de Flore, Lighted Glory had been unfortunate in being foaled in the same year as Ivanjica and Nobiliary because she was fated to take second place to either filly in the Prix St Alary (Group 1), Prix de la Cascade and Prix de la Grotte (Group 3) apart from being placed in the Prix de l'Opera (Group 2) and Prix de Malleret (Group 3). Two of her first three produce to run have also been in France, including the four-time winner Lykon (by Vaguely Noble). But it was in Ireland that her son Last Light (by Round Table) duplicated her Group 3 success in the Royal Whip. He won two other races and has now taken up stud duties in Brazil. Lighted Glory also had a three-year-old winner by Great Nephew in 1984 to be followed by a yearling by Artaius and a filly foal by Shirley Heights, so there is plenty to which to look forward.

Silky—The wayward daughter of Close Up, from the famous Horama family so prolific in producing Group winners in the late 1970s and early 1980s, Silky was Nijinsky's first winner. She won in such brilliant style that she was expected to be the Nijinsky flag waver from his first crop although, always having a mind of her own and troubled by a virus towards the end of her two-year-old days, Silky never quite lived up to her promise at three. She was however second to Miralla in the Irish 1,000 Guineas in which she turned the tables on the English Guineas victress Nocturnal Spree and was also second in the listed Strensall Stakes to H.M. the Queen's Joking Apart.

At stud her first mate was the sprinter Jukebox and the resultant colt, Abington, was a good winner at Ascot at two but found it difficult to find his true distance thereafter, being out of a stoutly bred filly whose distance was probably around a mile. Sent to the Derby winner Grundy in 1977, Silky came up with her Group 1 winning son Kirtling who annexed the Dee Stakes (Group 3) prior to his triumph in the Gran Premio d'Italia. He had been a stakes winner at Royal Ascot at two years and was later to run Beldale Flutter very close in the Benson & Hedges Gold Cup (Group 1) before setting sail to stand in Kentucky. Silky's third foal, by leading miler and sire Habitat, was another colt Crossways who became her second stakes winner when winning the XYZ handicap (Listed Race) at Newcastle after running classy Electric to a length in the Group 3 White Rose Stakes. Crossways, after being burdened by the handicapper at four, was bought to stand in New Zealand. Silky had a particularly nice Shergar colt, already named Cigar, in 1983, following a filly by General Assembly, a three-year-old of 1985 called Rustle of Silk. She foaled a colt by Grundy in 1984, a full brother to Kirtling.

La Jalouse—From Nijinsky's second crop La Jalouse accounted for four races in Canada including the Selene Stakes, also being runner up in the Boniface and Fury Stakes. Her first foal, by Exclusive Native, hit the headlines by breaking the Saratoga Sales record commanding US$1.6 million as a yearling. Named Exclusive One, he won four races including the Palisades Handicap and was placed second on the Grade 2 Paterson Handicap and third in the Pegasus Handicap. He now holds court at Spendthrift Farm. His year younger full brother Socratic was a good winner in England and La Jalouse had a three-year-old winner in Jealous One, a Raise A Native filly, in 1984 to whom there is a full brother called Carajas to race as three-year-old in 1985. Her juvenile is an Affirmed filly.

Galletto—Out of the Irish Oaks victress Gaia from a sturdy German classic family, Galletto won three races at two and three years, culminating in the listed Galtres Stakes at York, her only excursion out of Ireland. She also ran second in the Brownstown Stakes (to Nanticious) and the Fasig Tipton C.T.B.A. Stakes. These five outings were her only visits to the racecourse. Kept in Ireland, Galletto produced Aras An Uachtarain to a mating with Habitat, who won the Coolmore Godwalk Stakes (listed) and proved himself an able stakes horse in Ireland when raced against the best. Galletto herself made the headlines when she was sold in foal to Alydar for half a million Irish punts at the 1983 Goffs November Sales, following into the ring her colt foal by Shergar – the first of this ill-fated sire's stock to see a public auction.

And it is not just the very best of Nijinsky's female progeny that have proved themselves capable of producing black type animals.

Far Beyond—A winning daughter of Soaring who had also produced Miss Swapsco. Far Beyond's grandam, Skylarking, won the Group 2 Prix Maurice de Gheest and bred French 1,000 Guineas winner Yla. Far Beyond herself won at three years, her only season to race. Retired to stud she produced Battle Creek Girl to His Majesty as her first foal who won three races and was third in the Polly Drummond Stakes. Her second foal, Wings of Grace (by Key To The Mint), did even better winning six races including the Grade 3 Boiling Springs Handicap and being placed in the Lamb Chop and the Nellie Bly. Far Beyond's next two foals by Roberto and Honest Pleasure, also won.

Helenouchka—A winning daughter of French Group placed winner Hypavia, whose dam was a half sister to the Oaks winner Sicarelle, Helenouchka produced three winners from her first three foals. Of these Hortensia (by Luthier) proved herself a leading filly in France in 1980 winning the Prix Cleopatre (Group 3) and Prix de l'Opera (Group 2) and finishing third in the Prix de Malleret (Group 3). Helenouchka's second foal, Hart (by Filiberto), won in Italy as did her third, Hot (by Tennyson), who won the listed Premio Niccolo dell'Arca and was second in the Group 3 Premio Lazio. Helenouchka, not having perhaps the absolute top flight of stallions (the horizons being a little limited in France) was sold to the United States in foal to Arctic Tern for over half a million dollars early in 1984 just before her daughter Heil (by Star Appeal) gained black type and later Group 2 placed. In 1984 she also had a two-year-old colt by Tyrnavos and a yearling by Artaius.

Oulanova—Like Helenouchka, a French winning mare from Nijinsky's first crop, but from primarily an American female line. Oulanova has been at stud in England but her foals have already raced in various parts of the world, her first two foals, by Great Nephew and Brigadier Gerard, being placed in France and the United States respectively. Her third foal however, was trained just down the road from her Dalham Hall Stud home, in Newmarket. Celestial Dancer, a brown colt by Godswalk, despite not having the best start in his racing life, proved himself in the top flight of European sprinters capturing the Group 3 Prix de Meautry and Goldene Peitsche.

Vaslava—An unraced own sister to Terpsichorist and Gorytus, Vaslava has taken advantage of her longer spell in the paddocks to produce Big Monday (by Hagley) as her first foal. To the end of 1984 she had won seven races, including the Lodi Stakes, Half Moon Stakes, Drop Me A Note Stakes, and Platinum Belle Stakes. As Vaslava is only a 1977 mare it promises much for the future.

Jinsky—A dual winning representative of the English family of Yellow God, Jinsky, like so many of Nijinsky's daughters, hit the jackpot at the very first time of asking, producing Jinxed to a mating with the below top-class stallion Recaptured. Jinxed won six races, including the Colfax Maid Stakes and the Anita Peabody Stakes. Jinsky has since produced an unraced full brother to Jinxed and her three-year-old by Barrera ran just once in her juvenile season. Jinsky had a juvenile by Barrera in 1984.

Rasimova—Though she never saw a racecourse herself, Rasimova's third dam was Firetop, ancestress of The Minstrel, Columbiana and Nijinsky himself. She had a top-class daughter by Artaius to represent her in Italy in Delices, amongst the best of her sex and age in 1983. A 43,000 guineas yearling in 1980, Delices won five races in Italy from two to four years including the listed Premio Delleana and Premio Seregno and was placed second in the Premio Novella, Premio Mario Peretti and Premio Apertura and third in the Premio Royal Mares (Group 3). She was also fourth in the Italian 1,000 Guineas. Rasimova had a colt by Cure The Blues in 1983 and was then brought back to the United States where she expects to Super Concorde in 1984.

Veroushka—A half sister to Wajima, Veroushka was only placed on the racecourse and therefore must be regarded as one of Nijinsky's less endowed racehorses but has already produced five winners and three stakes horses as her first progeny. The first was a 1978 colt by Reviewer who won six races and was third in the Alumni Handicap. Her second, Lucence (by Majestic Light), has recently retired to stud after a career in which he captured seven races including the Grade 2 San Marcos Handicap, the Round Table Handicap, also Grade 2, and the Exceller Handicap. Veroushka's third foal Archiviste (by Secretariat) was a winner at three years in France while Lucence's full sister Sconce won in the United States. Her juvenile in 1984, Find, a Mr Prospector filly, was a winner and also stakes placed. Along with Euryanthe and Helenouchka, Veroushka must be regarded as one of Nijinsky's best broodmare daughters.

Euryanthe—Possibly the largest diamond amongst Nijinsky's unraced daughters, Euryanthe, an own sister to Caucasus and half sister to the dam of

Maruzensky, has lived up to the family tradition producing three winners from her first three foals, two of which are Group winners. All are fillies which must make them very valuable prospects indeed: her first, Steambath (by Honest Pleasure), won in the United States but her two subsequent foals Air Distingue (by Sir Ivor) and Eastern Dawn (by Damascus) made their mark in France. Both won successive Prix d'Aumales (Group 3). Air Distingue was then transferred to England and perhaps her second season was a disappointment, but she was placed in the French Oaks. Eastern Dawn also had a quiet three-year-old career but both fillies were stakes winners in the United States in the winter of 1984–85.

State—A daughter of the famed Monarchy, and thus a full sister to the Australian sire Lord of The Dance, State has produced two winners from her first two foals: Threat (by Ack Ack) and Narrate (by Honest Pleasure). Narrate took great strides during her three-year-old season, culminating in the Grade 3 Falls City Handicap following victory in the Princess Doreen. Narrate was also placed in the Arlington Oaks (Grade 3) and Pucker Up Stakes (Grade 3).

The Temptress—A winning daughter of Argentinian champion La Sevillana, The Temptress produced two winners in 1984, one a three-year-old colt by Tentam while the other was La Lorgnette (by Val de l'Orne) who proved herself one of the leading juvenile fillies in Canada by capturing the Grade 3 Natalma Stakes and being placed second in the Grade 1 Princess Elizabeth Stakes. La Lorgnette subsequently won the Canadian Oaks and Queen's Plate, the first filly to do so since Flaming Page.

Lucky Us—An unraced sister to both The Temptress and another Nijinsky winner in Foolish Redhead (dam of the Irish trained French stakes filly Blushing Redhead in 1985), Lucky Us is dam of a stakes winner in Bid Us (by Bold Bidder) whose five victories included the Bel Air Handicap. Bid Us was her first foal and he is followed by a three-year-old colt by J. O. Tobin and an unraced juvenile by Exceller.

Mariinsky—On paper, Mariinsky carries less black type in the first two removes of her pedigree than most of Nijinsky's progeny. However, her grandam Royal Justice won the St Hugh's Stakes and was a half sister to Royal Charger while her third dam was a half sister to Nasrullah. Mariinsky is the only one of the mares to have so far produced a classic winner when her daughter Silver Ikon (by Godswalk), already a juvenile winner in England, won the Austrian Oaks in 1984.

Running Ballerina—She was one of Nijinsky's most promising juveniles of 1977 winning her only start at Lingfield. Unfortunately she contracted a severe virus in the months between her two- and three-year-old seasons which wrecked any chance of a successful second season though she still ran with the best throughout. At stud, however, she has more than redeemed herself producing one of the fastest juvenile colts of 1983 in Defecting Dancer (by Habitat), winner of the Windsor Castle Stakes and Sirenia Stakes and finishing a game second to Superlative in the Group 2 Flying Childers Stakes. Running Ballerina had a filly by deceased Derby winner Troy in 1982, but unfortunately produced a dead foal by Mill Reef in 1983. She had a colt by Habitat in 1984 and expects to Mill Reef in 1985.

As one can see from the above, the majority of Nijinsky's best grand-progeny were not necessarily by the world's very best stallions, given the fact that this necessarily involves the deletion of the Northern Dancer line from the computations. In these early stages, Nijinsky mares in Europe appear to have combined particularly well with Habitat to produce the highest class of progeny; but in North America there does not seem to be an individual stallion that has had particular success. Only two stallions in the United States have produced three winners or more from *different* Nijinsky mares: Honest Pleasure and Secretariat. It is this variety of mates, many of which are complete outcrosses (for example, the British bred Snow Knight, by Firestreak ex a Chamossaire mare), that shows how Nijinsky mares can produce good-class winners, even to lesser stallions. Though the thoroughbred industry seems to be losing a great many of its best blooded stallions through early death at present, it does not seem that it will unduly worry the daughters of Nijinsky.

CHAPTER 12

What of the Future?

Writing as the close season of 1984–85 sheds its winter woollies and the optimism of a new season flows back with the colour and sunshine of summer meetings and which had seemed so far away, the future for Nijinsky and to some extent and growth of his male line through his own sons, looks considerably brighter than it did twelve months ago. In that short time Nijinsky has fought and apparently won his battle with laminitis, an often fatal illness, and several new sons have proved themselves which lessens a little the loss of Golden Fleece; the success of some was expected, others not quite so.

During the early Spring of 1984 the laminitis in Nijinsky's front legs was so acute that he could no longer walk to the stallion barn and covering was a procedure of hobbling a few difficult steps out of his own box to a makeshift covering mat in the aisle outside his own door. At $450,000 per mare, this was not a time to be squeamish.

Rumour had it that 1984 would be his last season come what may. However, 1985 has seen another high-class book visiting Claiborne and with foals arriving from such as Blue Wind, Gold Beauty, Blush With Pride and Trillion, Nijinsky's name is assured to live around the racecourses of the world a little longer.

But the fact remains that Nijinsky is now 18 years of age and though he is some years junior to his sire, the books soon will necessarily decrease and fewer foals appear on the racecourse. So what have we to look forward to in preserving his influence in succeeding generations? The loss of Golden Fleece, probably the best son seen on a racecourse, is a cruel blow following on the heels of Valinsky, Pas de Deux, Vatza, Quick Dance and Night Alert. After a bout of colic a cyst was removed from the stallion in January 1984 and this was found to be cancerous. The stallion was allowed to commence the stud season and his first mares included Soba, the flying filly from the previous racing season. Golden Fleece's first foals were arriving to French Guineas winner Ukraine Girl, to Santa Roseanna and Merlin's Charm and to Princess Tiara. However after a further operation for a strangulated intestine, the stallion died on 18 March, the third Derby winner of the previous five years to be lost to breeders in 13 months. It seemed that the Derby was not the race to want to win.

Left behind at Coolmore is perhaps potentially the second best of Nijinsky's sons at stud (after Golden Fleece). Kings Lake's foals and yearlings were so well received at the 1983 and 1984 sales and most are of top quality. Kings Lake himself was basically an 8–10 furlong horse though was not asked over the classic Derby distance at the height of his powers. This little bit more extra speed may make all the difference in becoming a great stallion or merely a good one. Kings Lake also comes from one of the best modern families to which Assert, Bikala and Salmon Leap belong, and was a champion in his own right.

Sure of Coolmore patronage at least is the French Derby winner Caerleon who had the misfortune to come up against Shareef Dancer on one of his better days, otherwise surely Caerleon would have been more than just the French three-year-old champion (10–12 furlongs). The third stallion now at Coolmore is of course the enigmatic Gorytus. An indisputably brilliant two-year-old and a horse as near to perfection in conformation as one could wish to see, but one on which judgement has to be reserved especially as he does not carry a pedigree renowned for producing top-class stallions. It is to be seen whether the effects of whatever caused him to lose the Dewhurst are still with him but he has at least proved himself an exceptionally fertile horse.

Compared with Ireland's wealth England has to rely totally on the Newmarket based Group 1 winning Ile de Bourbon and Niniski. Thanks to Kala Dancer and Petoski the latter, hopefully, will not be doomed to be regarded as a stayer because his classic victories were in the French and Irish St Legers, which is akin to leprosy in the racing world at present. It almost leads one to foresee a time where the Derby winners will be outlawed and racing will be returning to four furlong sprints.

Ile de Bourbon was unfortunately a late developer on the racecourse, and this may well prove the case in his early years at stud. A late foal, he only really came into his own as a four-year-old in appearance. That he could carry off the middle distance crown as a three-year-old with his stunning victory in the King George VI & Queen Elizabeth Diamond Stakes says a great deal for his class. However, after his first season, Ile de Bourbon proved that he can sire two-year-olds including the German Champion Lagunas who enabled Ile de Bourbon to imitate Nijinsky in producing a classic winner in his first classic crop. Were it not for the current sire sensation, Shirley Heights, maybe Ile de Bourbon would get even better patronage. If English breeders think as much of the Nijinsky influence as the Coolmore syndicate then this paucity of Nijinsky blood in England narrows the field from which they have to choose.

France is in a similar situation. Due to her current trend of succumbing to the mighty dollar whenever one of her own stallions becomes successful, France is finding herself bereft of much of the best current international blood. The quality Nijinsky stallion in the country is Nice Havrais, whose first crop were two-year-olds of 1984 and which performed well enough to give their sire a healthy position on the French first season sires list.

France's losses are of course America's gain; they have benefited beyond price from the arrivals of Lyphard, Riverman, Caro, Arctic Tern and the classic son of Nijinsky, the leading European First Season Sire of 1979, Green Dancer. Like Nijinsky, Green Dancer had an explosive start at stud with Aryenne winning the French 1,000 Guineas. However his best produce to date, like Sir Ivor (who seems to have so few sire sons to carry on his line), seem to be fillies, though it was a colt, Lovely Dancer, who helped Green Dancer to such a lofty position on the French sires table. Of the established American based sire sons of Nijinsky, Caucasus maybe has not been given the best chances or type of mare and the line seems at present to rely on the very young stallions Czaravich, Sportin' Life and Hostage. Maybe it will be Hostage who will make the most noticeable mark. Tragically injured in his preparation just before the Kentucky Derby for which he must have had an outstanding chance, the Arkansas Derby winner is a fine example of the "Nijinsky type" and carries a great many of his sire's qualities. Almost certainly a better racehorse than his career allowed him to show, he and Golden Fleece were the only two Nijinskys bred by the Hexters in 1979 and hopefully Hostage will have a longer and more rewarding time at stud.

On current showing the rest of the world does not have to worry. Japan seems to be particularly well endowed with Maruzensky and Lucky Sovereign already having sired Group 1 winners in their first crops. Only the demise of the promising Over Served is the one black spot in an otherwise rosy future in the land of the rising sun. The Antipodes too can be satisfied in the performance of Whiskey Road and must be looking forward to the careers of the young stallions such as Shining Finish. While Super Gray, though not as yet an outstanding sire of pattern race winners, does produce a seemingly endless string of lesser winners in New Zealand, Nijinsky stallions in the Antipodes certainly seem to need time as both Lord of The Dance and Super Gray are only now turing out black type winners. It is now becoming all to clear that maybe Bright Finish was sent to Japan far too early.

Now that Dancing Champ has arrived in South Africa backed by Peacetime, that up and coming breeding area can only look forward. There is also a fair sprinkling of promising sires in lesser thoroughbred areas: Umabatha in

Venezuela, the highly successful young sire Red Steps in Belgium, Masqued Dancer and Halpern Bay in Argentina. In 1985 the first runners appear by Kings Lake while even more for the future are the sires with their first foals of 1985 ... Caerleon, Solford, Beaudelaire and Gorytus and the Group 1 winners standing their initial seasons ... Nijinsky's Secret and Vision.

As we have seen Nijinsky's daughters are declaring themselves a sound investment, proving a steady source of pattern and listed race winners in both North America and Europe and most, more often than not, have produced plenty of winners to credit their sire in the first years of their stud careers. At Keeneland November 1983, four of the five Nijinsky mares sold made over one million dollars. At the same sale in 1984 two made over two million.

So, despite the apparently ominous grey clouds that loomed in the Spring of 1984, the outlook for Nijinsky and his worldwide influence there seems to be plenty of star material to carry through into succeeding generations. Is the thoroughbred breeding community panicking unnecessarily about the lack of a natural successor to Nijinsky? Maybe we need look no further than the 1985 classic winner Shadeed. Or perhaps he is already here, in the shape of one of the young as yet unproven sons and let us not forget what starlets there might be in the as yet unraced or unseen foals of 1983–86. Perhaps one of those four-legged pipedreams may yet become a reality.

Appendix A

Nijinsky's Progeny 1972–82 and Foals of 1983

Abbreviations used:

b	= bay	GP	= Group (or Graded) placed
br	= brown	SW	= stakes winner
ch	= chestnut	SP	= stakes placed
b/br	= bay/brown	p	= placed
gr	= grey	UP	= unplaced
ro	= roan	R	= ran number of times
W	= winner and number of races	UR	= unraced
GW	= Group (or Graded) winner	NH	= National Hunt

Name	Col	Sex	Yr	Dam	Dams sire	Perf
Abeesh	b	f	82	Lady Bugler	Court Martial	UR
African Dancer	b	f	73	Miba	Ballymoss	W2 GW2
Aino Saintsky	b	c	81	Aino Crespin	Saint Crespin III	W
Alezan Dancer	ch	c	81	Fabuleux Jane	Le Fabuleux	UR
Amen Wadeen	b	c	73	Monade	Klairon	W2 W2 NH
Arctic Faun	b	c	80	Mira Femme	Dumpty Humpty	p
Atmosphere	b	c	79	Sphere	Round Table	UR
Audley End	b	c	77	Favoletta	Baldric II	W4
Avodire	b	c	73	Luquillo	Princequillo	W GP
Bakor	b	c	73	Copper Canyon	Bryan G	W5
Baldski	b/br	c	74	Too Bald	Bald Eagle	W7 SW
Ballare	b	f	77	Morgaise	Round Table	W4 SW
Balletic	ch	f	72	Tims Princess	Tim Tam	UR
Balletomane	b	f	78	Nanticious	Nantallah	W4 GW
Ballet Style	ch	f	79	Embroidery	Double Jay	p
Baltic Dancer	b	c	82	Flail	Bagdad	UR
Banana Split	b	c	75	Vanilla	Amerigo	W4 NH
Baronova	b	f	75	Tsessbe	Buckpasser	W
Beaudelaire	ch	c	80	Bitty Girl	Habitat	W4 GW SW2
Bedford	b	c	78	Drumtop	Round Table	W5 GP
Bell Rammer	ch	c	78	Shellshock	Salvo	W
Bemissed	ch	f	80	Bemis Heights	Herbager	W5 GW3 SW
Benefit Performer	b	c	79	So Social	Tim Tam	W SP
Bev Bev	b	f	77	Native Partner	Raise A Native	W2 GP
Bivouac	b	c	78	Bitty Girl	Habitat	UR
Blint	ch	f	82	Table Hands	Table Run	UR

APPENDIX

Name	Col	Sex	Yr	Dam	Dams sire	Perf
Blue Nijinsky	gr	c	80	Divine Grace	Wise Exchange	UR
Bo Jinsky	b	c	76	Swoons Symbol	Swoon's Son	W
Bolshoi	b	c	76	Gallant Demand	Gallant Man	W
Bolshoi Star	b	f	72	Luquillo	Princequillo	UR
Bonnie Hope	ch	f	77	Bonnie And Gay	Sir Gaylord	W
Borodine	b	c	74	Directoire	Gun Bow	W2 GP
Breakers Row	b/br	c	76	Minorstone	Ribot	4th
Brehon Law	b	c	74	Cambrienne	Sicambre	W2
Bright Finish	b	c	73	Lacquer	Shantung	W6 GW2
Bright Forecast	b/br	c	81	Optimistic Gal	Sir Ivor	W
Brogan	b	c	80	Drumtop	Round Table	W2 GW
Brookdale	b	c	76	Areola	Kythnos	p
Browser	b	f	80	Rose Bowl	Habitat	UR
Bundle of Kisses	b	c	79	Bundler	Raise A Native	W2
Caerleon	b	c	80	Foreseer	Round Table	W4 GW3 SW
Cancaniere	b	f	78	Play On Words	Never Bend	UR
Canoe	b	c	78	Shinnecock	Tom Fool	W
Caucasus	b	c	72	Quill	Princequillo	W9 GW4 SW
Caught In The Act	ch	f	73	Bamboozle	Alcide	W
Charming Dance	b	f	76	Tamalesian	Tatan	UR
Cherokee Phoenix	b	f	76	Copper Canyon	Bryan G	W2
Cherry Hinton	b	f	75	Popkins	Romulus	W2 GW
Chiffon	b/br	f	75	Trumpery	Tudor Minstrel	W
Chivalry	b	c	79	Cloonlara	Sir Ivor	W2
Choreographer	b/br	c	74	Green Finger	Better Self	W3
Circus Performer	ch	c	81	Dumfries	Reviewer	UR
Classical Ballet	b	c	76	Fragile Witness	Court Martial	W4
Come Rain or Shine	ch	c	77	Sign of The Times	Francis S	W4 GP
Considerable Risk	b	c	81	Raise Your Skirts	Elevation	UR
Copernica	b	f	72	Copper Canyon	Bryan G	W5 GP3 SP5
Copper Kingdom	ch	c	72	Peace Movement	Admirals Voyage	W2½
Cor Anglais	b	f	81	Royal Dilemma	Buckpasser	p
Countertrade	b	c	80	Swingtime	Buckpasser	W2
Count Nijinsky	b	c	72	Scaremenot	Bagdad	p
Crown of Crowns	b	f	76	English Silver	Mongo	W
Crystal Cup	ch	f	81	Rose Bowl	Habitat	R2
Czaravich	ch	c	76	Black Satin	Linacre	W8 GW4
Czarinsky	b	c	79	Straight Street	Never Bend	UR
Dance Call	b	f	78	Royal Warrant	Hill Prince	W
Dance Furlough	ch	c	82	Blitey	Riva Ridge	UR
Dance God	b	c	77	Parlor Game	Stage Door Johnny	p
Dance In Snow	b	c	74	Snow Sparkle	Herbager	p
Dance Light	b	f	78	Flood Light	Bold Lad (USA)	W2
Dancing Again	ch	c	80	Dancealot	Round Table	W2 SP
Dancing Brownie	ch	f	82	Secret Beauty	Raise A Native	UR

Name	Col	Sex	Yr	Dam	Dams sire	Perf
Dancing Champ	b	c	72	Mrs Peterkin	Tom Fool	W7 GW2 SW
Dancing Crown	b	c	81	Too Many Sweets	Full Pocket	W3
Dancing Czar	b	c	82	Mrs Warren	Hail To Reason	UR
Dancing Detente	b	f	73	Alluvial	Buckpasser	UR
Dancing Heiress	b	f	80	After Me	Mongo	UR
Dancing Lesson	ch	f	80	Trim The Sail	Graustark	W4 SP
Dancing Peach	b/br	f	77	Fleet Peach	Fleet Nasrullah	UR
Dancing Secret	b	f	77	Secret Beauty	Raise A Native	W6 SP
Dancing Slippers	ch	f	81	Chain	Herbager	R3
Dancinintherain	b	f	80	Show Lady	Sir Ivor	W2
Dawnballet	ch	c	79	Dauntu	Grey Dawn	p
Dearly Too	b	f	79	Dearly Precious	Dr Fager	W7 SW2
Debussy	b	c	77	Dusky Evening	Tim Tam	W
Debutante Bob	ch	f	79	Coiffure	Sir Gaylord	UR
De La Rose	b	f	78	Rosetta Stone	Round Table	W11 GW6 SW2
Diaghilev	b	c	72	Ya Ya	Primera	p
Didwana	b	f	82	Diamond Spring	Vaguely Noble	UR
Divine Etoile	ch	f	72	Directoire	Gun Bow	W
Down Stage	b	f	80	Flying Above	Hoist The Flag	W5 SW
Dronacharya	gr	c	76	Belle de Nuit	Warfare	up
Drumnadrochit	ch	c	79	Quadruple	Fleet Nasrullah	W
Duty Dance	b	f	82	Discipline	Princequillo	UR
Edelene	ro	f	77	Mama Ocollo	Sovereign Path	UR
Edmond Dantes	b	c	78	Gusher	Flow Line	p
Edziu	ch	c	74	Shahtash	Jaipur	W8
Empire Glory	b	c	81	Spearfish	Fleet Nasrullah	W2 GW
Enchanting Dancer	b	f	77	Exempt	Immortality	UR
Encino	ch	c	77	Crimson Saint	Crimson Satan	W GP SP
Entrancing	b	f	75	Gallant Bloom	Gallant Man	UR
Equinol	b	c	81	Equal Honor	Round Table	W2 SP
Esperanto	b	c	81	Bendara	Never Bend	W4 SW2
Ethics	b	f	82	Fairness	Cavan	UR
Euryanthe	ch	f	75	Quill	Princequillo	UR
Evasion	ch	f	79	White Lie	Bald Eagle	UR
Excitable	ch	f	75	Lady Graustark	Graustark	W3 SW2
Exquisite Miss	b	f	76	The Bride	Bold Ruler	UR
Eye Dazzler	ch	f	80	First Squaw	First Landing	W
Fabuleux Dancer	ch	c	80	Fabuleux Jane	Le Fabuleux	W SW
Fancy's Child	b	f	75	Rare Exchange	Swaps	UR
Far Beyond	b	f	72	Soaring	Swaps	W
Father Matthew	ch	c	82	Our Lady Queen	Raise A Native	W SP
Fecund	b	c	75	Farm	Idle Hour	W5
Firebird	b	f	79	Georgie	Damascus	UR
Fire of Life	b	c	82	Spark of Life	Key To The Mint	p
First Fling	ch	f	77	Fast Approach	First Landing	W
Fly To Arms	b	c	77	Fly By Venus	Dark Star	W

APPENDIX

Name	Col	Sex	Yr	Dam	Dams sire	Perf
Folk Art	b	f	82	Homespun	Round Table	W$_3$ GW
Foolish Redhead	b	f	75	La Sevillana	Court Harwell	W
Fortunate Dancer	b	c	82	Isle of Fortune	Prince John	p GP
Full Parade	b	c	73	Full Dress II	Shantung	UR
Gala Mood	ch	c	78	Let's Be Gay	Bagdad	W$_5$
Gallant Archer	b	c	82	Belle of Dodge Me	Creme dela Creme	W
Gallantsky	b	c	76	Queen Pot	Buckpasser	W SP
Galletto	b	f	74	Gaia	Charlottesville	W$_3$ SW
Gentle Linna	ch	f	77	Bold Liz	Jacinto	UR
Gentleman Jinsky	b	c	77	Blackfly	Mount Marcy	W$_2$
Gist	b	c	76	Deb's Darling	Sailor	W$_4$
Gleason	b	c	76	Gleam II	Spy Well	W$_2$ SP W$_5$NH SW
Give or Else	b	c	76	Give or Take	Swaps	UR
Golden Fleece	b	c	79	Exotic Treat	Vaguely Noble	W$_4$ GW$_3$
Goldye's Miss	b	f	81	Miss Suzaki	Tompion	W$_2$ SP
Gorytus	b	c	80	Glad Rags	High Hat	W$_2$ GW SW
Great Performance	ch	c	78	Chou Croute	Lt Stevens	W
Greek Sky	b	c	81	Greek Victress	Victoria Park	W SW
Green Dancer	b	c	72	Green Valley	Val de Loir	W$_4$ GW$_3$
Grenada Pride	b/br	f	82	Lacework	In Reality	UR
Grey Ballet	gr	f	73	Pinny Gray	Palestine	R$_2$
Haitien	b	f	73	Swift Lady	Sailor	UR
Half An Hour	b	c	73	Be Suspicious	Porterhouse	p W$_2$NH SW
Halpern Bay	b	c	77	Beja	Bagdad	W
Hapai	b	f	78	Hamada	Habitat	W$_3$
Hasty Nijinsky	ch	f	79	Hasty Cutie	Hasty Road	p
Helenouchka	b	f	72	Hypavia	Sicambre	W
Heza Fancy Dancer	b	c	80	Fascinating Rhythm	Never Bend	UR
Hico	b	f	79	Funny Funny Ache	Jester	UR
Hint	b	f	81	Glisk	Buckpasser	W
His Honor	b	c	75	Bold Honor	Bold Ruler	W$_9$ SW$_4$
Hostage	b	c	79	Entente II	Val de Loir	W$_4$ GW
Ile de Bourbon	br	c	75	Roseliere	Misti IV	W$_5$ GW$_4$ SW
Instinctive Move	b	f	81	Bold Bikini	Boldnesian	W
Ipi Tombi	ch	c	75	Oraza	Zank	W WNH SP
Jabbering	b/br	f	82	Poppycock	Dewan	UR
Javamine	b	f	73	Dusky Evening	Tim Tam	W$_7$ GW$_4$
Jenner	ch	c	75	Dihela	Hitting Away	W
Jillinsky	b	f	80	Pashamin	My Babu	W$_2$
Jinsky	b	f	73	Sheila Jan	Nigromante	W$_2$
Jump Ship	b	f	73	Port of Call	Sailor	UR
Kafouaine	ch	c	81	Stylish Pattern	My Babu	W$_2$
Kandinsky	b	c	75	Alanesian	Polynesian	W$_2$
Karajinska	b	f	78	Karelina	Sea Bird II	R$_1$
Karensky	b	c	80	Tuerta	Forli	p
Karsavina	ch	f	74	Glimpse	Eighty Grand	W

APPENDIX

Name	Col	Sex	Yr	Dam	Dams sire	Perf
Kazatska	b/br	f	79	Comtesse de Loir	Val de Loir	W SP
Key Dancer	b/br	f	81	Key Partner	Key To The Mint	W4 GW
Khatango	b	c	79	Penny Flight	Damascus	W6 GW2
Kicking Up	b	c	72	Rash Statement	Ambiorix	W2
King of Darby	b	c	75	Gibellina	Ribot	W5
Kings Lake	b	c	78	Fish Bar	Baldric II	W5 GW3
Kinski	b	c	81	Royal Kin	Sir Gaylord	W
Kirov	b	c	74	How I Wonder	My Babu	W2NH
Krassata	ch	f	73	Bonnie Google	Better Self	W6 SP4 GP3
Kremlin	b	c	82	Monolith	Ribot	UR
Kshesinskaya	b/br	f	80	Royal Kin	Sir Gaylord	UR
Kyra's Slipper	b	f	76	Drumtop	Round Table	W4 SP
La Confidence	b	f	80	La Dame du Lac	Round Table	W
Lady Hardwick	b	f	77	Zeal	Round Table	W2
Lady Jinsky	b	f	74	Lady Victoria	Victoria Park	W4 GP SP
La Jalouse	ch	f	73	Quadruple	Fleet Nasrullah	W4 SW
La Nijinska	ch	f	75	Street Dancer	Native Dancer	W3 SP
Lath	b	c	74	Moll Flanders	Swaps	W4
L'Avalanche	b	c	80	Soft Snow	T. V. Lark	UR
Lead The Dance	b	c	81	Ten Cents A Dance	Buckpasser	W
Leap High	b	c	82	Aces Full	Round Table	UR
Leap Lively	ch	f	78	Quilloquick	Graustark	W3 GW2
Leap of The Heart	b	f	79	Ivory Wand	Sir Ivor	W5 SP
Leap To Fame	ch	f	77	Quonset	Graustark	R4
Le Gosse	b	c	80	Quilly	Bagdad	W2
Leotard	b	f	81	Flapper	Graustark	p
Lighted Glory	b	f	72	Lighted Lamp	Sir Gaylord	W2 GW
Lightning Leap	ch	c	82	First Feather	First Landing	W SP
Lodgenski	b	c	78	Lodge	Bold Lad (USA)	UR
London Bells	b	c	77	Shake A Leg	Raise A Native	W4 GP SP
Loose Cannon	ch	c	80	Java Moon	Graustark	W2 SP
Lord of The Dance	b	c	72	Monarchy	Princequillo	W3
Lucky Sovereign	b	c	74	Sovereign	Pardao	W GW
Lucky Us	b	f	76	La Sevillana	Court Harwell	UR
Lucy Blue	b	f	77	Sandy Blue	Windy Sands	R1
Makarova	ro	f	75	Midou	Saint Crespin III	W3 SP
Mansky	b	c	77	Mandera	Vaguely Noble	W W2NH
Mariinsky	b	f	74	Iron Maiden	Klairon	W
Martha Norelius	ch	f	74	Nooky	Neptunus	UR
Maruzensky	br	c	74	Shill	Buckpasser	W8 GW2
Masked Dancer	b	c	74	Masked Lady	Spy Song	UR
Masqued Dancer	b	c	72	Bonnie Google	Better Self	W2 GP2 SP2
Meadow Dancer	b	f	75	Meadow Saffron	High Perch	R2

APPENDIX

Name	Col	Sex	Yr	Dam	Dams sire	Perf
Meiwa Iran	b	c	73	Princess of Iran	Prince Royal	UR
Meiwa Rikiya	b	f	74	Marching Matelda	Hasty Road	W$_4$
Meiwa Sukih	b	f	77	North Broadway	Bold Ruler	W
Milina	b	f	74	Tender Word	Tenerani	W$_4$
Milova	b	f	74	Moss	Round Table	W
Mischievous Lady	b	f	79	Fascinating Rhythm	Never Bend	UR
Misinskie	b	f	80	Kankakee Miss	Better Self	p
Miss Mazepah	b	f	72	Monade	Klairon	W$_3$
Miss Nijinsky	b	f	73	Kylin	Kythnos	W$_3$
Miss Nut Cracker	b	f	79	Shufleur	Tom Rolfe	W
Mixed Applause	b	f	76	My Advantage	Princely Gift	W$_2$ GP
Moscow Ballet	b	c	82	Millicent	Cornish Prince	W$_2$ GW
Mr Justice	b	c	75	Moment of Truth	Matador	W
Murmansk	b	f	78	Mohmond	Jaipur	p
Muscovite	b	c	77	Alyne Que	Raise A Native	W$_3$ GW SW
Myjinski	b	c	82	English Silver	Mongo	UR
Nafka	b	f	81	Easy Virtue	Native Dancer	UR
Nagurski	b	c	81	Deceit	Prince John	W$_4$ GW
Nataraja	b	c	76	Peace Movement	Admirals Voyage	W$_3$
Native Ballet	b/br	f	78	Miss Francesca	Raise A Native	W
Netherby	b	c	78	Sweet Satina	Crimson Satan	W, W$_4$NH SW
Nice Havrais	ch	c	77	Shoubra	Bon Mot II	W$_2$ GW
Night Alert	b	c	77	Moment of Truth	Matador	W$_3$ GW$_2$ SW
Night Mirage	b	c	82	Miracolo	Sir Gaylord	UR
Nijana	ch	f	73	Prodana Neviesta	Reneged	W$_{10}$ GW SW$_4$
Nijinskaia	b	f	74	Gay Meeting	Sir Gaylord	W$_2$
Nijinska Street	ch	f	76	Street Dancer	Native Dancer	W$_3$
Nijinsky Model	b	c	79	Model	Ribot	p
Nijinsky Sea	b	f	78	Nautical Miss	Sailor	UR
Nijinsky Sentiment	gr	f	81	Harrapan Seal	Habitat	W
Nijinsky's Melody	b	f	82	Shanghai Melody	Shantung	W GP
Nijinsky's Ruler	ch	c	82	Tourulla	Gin Tour	UR
Nijinsky's Secret	ch	c	78	Secret Beauty	Raise A Native	W$_{14}$ GW$_7$ SW$_2$
Nijinsky's Show	ch	f	82	Show Lady	Sir Ivor	UR
Nijinsky Star	b	f	80	Chris Evert	Swoons Son	UR
Nijinsky's Way	b	c	82	Waya	Faraway Son	UR
Nijinsukih Sutah	ch	c	72	Lunik	Rigoberto	p
Nijistar	b	f	78	Mrs Peterkin	Tom Fool	UR
Nijisty	b	c	74	Misty Bride	Hethersett	W$_2$
Nijit	b	f	77	Bitty Girl	Habitat	W$_5$ SP$_3$
Nikitina	b	f	77	Vela	Sheshoon	W GP
Niniski	b	c	76	Virginia Hills	Tom Rolfe	W$_6$ GW$_5$

Name	Col	Sex	Yr	Dam	Dams sire	Perf
Ninoushka	b	f	79	Periwig	Buckpasser	p
Niqua	gr	f	82	Bequa	Never Bend	R1
Nishino Northern	ch	c	79	Sun Valley Linda	Prince John	W2 GP
Nissr	b	c	77	Fast Line	Mr Busher	UR
Nizon	ch	c	75	Exit Smiling	Stage Door Johnny	W5 GW3
Northerly Native	ch	c	81	Native Partner	Raise A Native	W SP2
Northern Partner	ch	f	76	Dance Partner	Graustark	UR
Northern Walk	ch	f	75	Lover's Walk	Never Bend	W2
Nuage d'Or	ch	c	82	Exotic Treat	Vaguely Noble	UR
Nuclear Pulse	ch	c	73	Solometeor	Victoria Park	W3 SW
Number	b	f	79	Special	Forli	W8 GW2 SW
Olamic	b	f	79	Continuation	Forli	W5 SP4
Olympic Victory	b	c	78	Shama	Bold Ruler	W
Orlov	b	c	81	Something Super	Promised Land	UR
Oulanova	b	f	72	Our Model	Johns Joy	W
Our Tina Marie	b	f	78	Java Moon	Graustark	UR
Overall Image	ch	f	80	Bold Liz	Jacinto	p
Over Served	b	c	72	Nautical Miss	Sailor	W4
Page Nijinsky	ch	c	82	Sixteen Letters	Graustark	UR
Palacios	b	c	77	Fun Palace	Nashua	R4
Pas de Cheval	b	c	80	Bold Honor	Bold Ruler	W
Pas de Deux	ch	f	74	Example	Exbury	W
Pas de Deux	ch	c	74	So Chic	Nasrullah	W4 GW
Pavlova	b	f	72	Jan Jessie	Turf Charger	p
Peacetime	b	c	79	Peace	Klairon	W3 GW SW2
Perfect Point	b	f	82	Charm School	Dr Fager	p
Personator	b	c	76	Act of Faith	Promised Land	W3
Piaffer	b	c	75	Strong Drink	Sound Track	W4 SW
Pitriza	b	f	82	Hopesprings-eternal	Buckpasser	UR
Popular Hero	b	c	73	Brave Lady	Herbager	W, W14NH SW2
Preciously Dear	ch	f	81	Dearly Precious	Dr Fager	W
Preferred Steppe	b	c	78	Top Round	Round Table	p
Presto Lad	ch	c	79	Lassie Dear	Buckpasser	W
Princesse Lida	b	f	77	Princess Lee	Habitat	W4 GW2 SW2
Prince Street	b	c	78	Street Dancer	Native Street	UR
Professional Dance	b	f	79	Perfecta	Swaps	UR
Pueblo	b	c	81	Shinnecock	Tom Fool	R2
Pustinya	b	f	78	Desert Law	Court Martial	W4
Quick Dance	ch	c	76	Prodana Neviesta	Reneged	W
Quiet Fling	b	c	72	Peace	Klairon	W5 GW2
Radost	ch	f	82	Magnificence	Graustark	UR
Raininsky	b	f	78	Singing Rain	Sensitivo	R2
Ranking Beauty	b	f	78	Imsodear	Chieftain	p SP2
Rare Splendor	b	f	73	Rafale	Court Harwell	R1
Rasimova	b	f	73	Restless Sis	Restless Wind	UR

APPENDIX

Name	Col	Sex	Yr	Dam	Dams sire	Perf
Raskolniki	b	c	74	Yanina II	Inca Yata	p
Reckless Dancer	b	c	81	Squander	Buckpasser	UR
Red Steps	b	c	76	Croda Rossa	Grey Sovereign	R3
Rissa	b	f	76	Kittiwake	Sea Bird II	W2 SP
Roman Empire	b	c	82	Ivanjica	Sir Ivor	UR
Romanov	b	c	79	Swoons Symbol	Swoons Son	R3
Rose Crescent	b	f	79	Roseliere	Misti IV	W4½GW
Rose O'Riley	b	f	81	Rosetta Stone	Round Table	W
Rosy Spectre	ch	f	80	Like A Charm	Pied d'Or	W6 SW
Royal Jete	ch	c	73	Bid High	Bold Bidder	W6
Royal Nijinsky	b	c	77	Princessnesian	Princequillo	W3
Ruby Slippers	ro	f	82	Moon Glitter	In Reality	R2
Rue Lauriston	ch	c	79	Liberation Girl	Hail To Reason	p
Running Ballerina	b	f	75	Running Blue	Blue Peter	W
Russian Fox	ro	c	78	Flying Fur	Sky High II	W4
Russian Noble	b	c	81	Noble Fancy	Vaguely Noble	W
Russian Ribbon	b	f	82	Banderole	Hoist The Flag	UR
Russian Roubles	b	c	80	Squander	Buckpasser	W2 SW
Sabre Street	b	c	79	Overstreet	Vertex	4th
Sailor King	ch	c	78	Syrian Sea	Bold Ruler	p
Sainte Croix	b	f	82	Spearfish	Fleet Nasrullah	UR
Saunders	b	c	74	Foxy Quilla	Princequillo	R1
Scroll	ch	c	82	Quillesian	Princequillo	R5
Scrumptious	b	f	79	Queen Pot	Buckpasser	p
Serheed	b	c	80	Native Partner	Raise A Native	W5
Sevastopol	b	c	73	South Ocean	New Providence	UR
Shadeed	b	c	82	Continual	Damascus	W SW
Shalomar	b	f	78	Kerala	My Babu	W
She Can Dance	ch	f	75	Yanina II	Inca Yata	W3 GP
Shimmy	b	f	78	Amalesian	Ambiorix	W4 SW
Shining Finish	b	c	77	Lacquer	Shantung	W5 GW
Shujinsky	ch	f	80	Shufleur	Tom Rolfe	UR
Silky	b	f	72	Close Up	Nearula	W GP SP
Sir Jinsky	b	c	75	Dusky Evening	Tim Tam	W3 SP
Sis C	b	f	76	Fond Hope	Sir Ivor	W2½ SW
Skibinoff	b	c	76	Susceptible	Prince John	p
Skyjinni	ch	f	72	Swift Lady	Sailor	p
Smartinsky	ch	c	82	Smart Angle	Quadrangle	UR
Smart Steppin	b	f	81	Smartaire	Quibu	W
Solford	b	c	80	Fairness	Cavan	W5 GW2
Solstein	b	c	82	Solana	Tentam	W GP
Sophistical	b	f	79	Sophist	Acropolis	UR
Spacefarer	b	c	75	Plane	Round Table	W
Speedy Nijinsky	ch	c	80	Fast Line	Mr Busher	UR
Sportin' Life	b	c	78	Homespun	Round Table	W8 GW SW4
Sportsky	b	c	72	Sports Event	T. V. Lark	W5
Stack	ch	c	82	File	Tom Rolfe	W2
Starsalot	b	c	82	Dancealot	Round Table	R3
Start A Rumor	ch	f	80	Nosey Nan	Nantallah	W2
Star Topper	b	c	81	Top Banana	T. V. Lark	W
State	b	f	74	Monarchy	Princequillo	W3

APPENDIX

Name	Col	Sex	Yr	Dam	Dams sire	Perf
Stetchworth	ch	c	76	Grenadiere	Right Royal V	W5 GP
Stradavinsky	b	c	75	Seximee	Hasty Road	W GW
Stravinsky	b	c	78	Come To Market	To Market	R4
Street Ballet	b	f	77	Street Dancer	Native Dancer	W6 SW
Sugary Mist	ch	f	80	Sweet Mist	Candy Spots	UR
Summer Fling	b	f	75	Fast Approach	First Landing	W4 GW
Summertime Promise	b	f	72	Prides Promise	Crozier	W10 GW2 SW4
Super Gray	gr	c	72	Loyal Land	Tillman	4th
Super Jaime	b	f	79	Something Super	Promised Land	UR
Susanna	b	f	78	Full Dress II	Shantung	p SP
Suspend	b	f	81	Flying Above	Hoist The Flag	UR
Swan	b	f	76	Her Demon	Herbager	W
Tanzor	b	c	72	Lady Victoria	Victoria Park	W SW
Terpsichorist	ch	f	75	Glad Rags	High Hat	W11 GW4 SW
Testily	ch	f	78	Sofisticada	Timor	W
Thahul	b	c	77	Queen City Miss	Royal Union	W5
The Temptress	b	f	73	La Sevillana	Court Harwell	W
Tights	b	c	81	Dancealot	Round Table	W7½ GW3 SW3
Tolstoy	ch	c	82	Key To The Saga	Key To The Mint	UR
Topin	b	f	80	Top Banana	T. V. Lark	W
Top Rank	b	c	80	Mrs Peterkin	Tom Fool	UR
Torriglia	ch	f	76	Tour Nobel	Habitat	p
Tournament Star	b	f	78	Chris Evert	Swoons Son	W3 SP3
Tovarich	ch	c	76	Musical Chairs	Swaps	UR
Trendy Gent	ch	c	81	Pucheca	Tom Rolfe	W
Tubac Dancer	b	c	76	Romagna	Romulus	UR
Tunic	b	c	81	Swingtime	Buckpasser	UR
Ultramate	ch	c	80	Gala Party	Hoist The Flag	W7 SW2
Umabatha	b	c	73	Hardiesse	Hornbeam	W
Unrehearsed	ch	f	77	Impetuous Lady	Hasty Road	UR
Upper Nile	b	c	74	Rosetta Stone	Round Table	W6 GW2
Vacances	b	f	76	Vincennes	Vieux Manoir	UR
Val Danseur	b	c	80	Green Valley	Val de Loir	W3 SW
Valetchka	b	c	74	Sales Ring	Bold Ruler	W2
Valinsky	b	c	74	Valoris	Tiziano	W2 GW
Valodi	b/br	c	72	Heliolight	Helioscope	UR
Valse Noble	ch	f	79	Merry Jingle	Bold Lad (USA)	p
Vaslav	ch	c	78	Waterloo	Bold Lad (IRE)	W
Vaslava	b	f	77	Glad Rags	High Hat	UR
Vaslov	b	c	75	Flirting Lady	Swaps	W2
Vatza	ch	c	77	Shuvee	Nashua	W3 SP
Veroushka	ch	f	73	Iskra	Le Haar	p
Vestris	b	f	79	Respect The Flag	Hoist The Flag	W5 GP2 SP

Name	Col	Sex	Yr	Dam	Dams sire	Perf
Vidalia	b	f	81	Waya	Faraway Son	W GW
Virginia Princess	ch	f	82	Shuvee	Nashua	R1
Vision	b	c	81	Foreseer	Round Table	W5 GW2
Voglia Matta	ch	f	74	Velatura	Acropolis	UR
Water Dance	ch	f	77	Luiana	My Babu	W6 SW
Waving	ch	f	79	Top Round	Round Table	W7 SW2
Western Symphony	b	c	81	Millicent	Cornish Prince	W3 GW SW
Whiskey Road	b	c	72	Bowl of Flowers	Sailor	W
White Birch	gr	c	80	Snow Peak	Sword Dancer	W3 GP
Words 'N Music	b	f	82	Street Dancer	Native Dancer	UR
Worldwatch	b	c	78	Georgica	Raise A Native	W
Wunderkind	ch	c	81	Wonderful Gal	The Axe II	p
Yamanin Penny	b	f	79	Lower Lights	Sir Gaylord	W3 GW
Yamanin Sukih	ch	c	75	Unmentionable	Buckpasser	W5
Yeats	b	c	76	Lisadell	Forli	W3SW

Foals of 1983

Aquarina	ch.c.	Riverqueen	Luthier
Bad Connection	b.c.	Caronatta	Raise A Native
Bogus	ch.f.	Chappaquiddick	Relic
Breather	ch.c.	Relaxing	Buckpasser
Butterfield Stage	ch.c.	Impetuous Gal	Briartic
Colophon	ch.f.	Idmon	Dr Fager
Curl And Set	ch.f.	Coiffure	Sir Gaylord
Dance Of Life	b.c.	Spring Is Here	In Reality
Dancing Key	b.f.	Key Partner	Key To The Mint
Dancing On A Cloud	b.f.	Square Angel	Quadrangle
Dancing Show	b.f.	Show Lady	Sir Ivor
Dervish	b.c.	Crazy Music	Hail To Reason
De Stael	ch.f.	Peace	Klairon
Equator	ch.c.	Sound of Success	Successor
Fanaan	b.c.	Sensitive Lady	Sensitivo
Ferdinand	ch.c.	Banja Luka	Double Jay
Festival Town	b.c.	Quick Cure	Dr Fager
Foxy Prince	b.c.	Equanimity	Sir Ivor
Fred Astaire	b.c.	Late Bloomer	Stage Door Johnny
Glorious Calling	b.f.	Blue Blood	Round Table
Herald's Voice	b.c.	Spanked	Cornish Prince
Hopak	b.c.	Royal Suite	Herbager or Majestic Prince
Ightham	b.c.	Golden Alibi	Empery
In Excelsis	b.c.	Millicent	Cornish Prince
Jardiniere	b.f.	Fish Bar	Baldric II
La Codorniz	b.f.	Petit Rond Point	Round Table
Lipika	b.f.	Faultless Tudor	Tudor Grey
Manzotti	b.c.	Shufleur	Tom Rolfe
Martha Queen	b.f.	Rosetta Stone	Round Table
Missile Man	ch.c.	Entente II	Val de Loir
Nadeed	b.c.	Palmistry	Forli

Nepalais	ch.c.	Halietta	Habitat
Never Easy	b.f.	Easy Virtue	Native Dancer
New Direction	b.c.	Pretty Angela	Son Ange
Nijinsky's Best	ch.f.	Best In Show	Traffic Judge
Noble Nijinsky	b.c.	Vainly Noble	Vaguely Noble
Plaxtol	b.c.	Fruhlingstag	Orsini
Prince Of Tricks	ch.c.	Trick Chick	Prince John
Prodigal Dancer	b.c.	Miracolo	Sir Gaylord
Quadripartite	b.c.	Quadruple	Fleet Nasrullah
Rehearsing	ro.c.	Zerelda	In Reality
Russian Logic	b.c.	Feminine Logic	Bold Reasoning
Shahrastani	ch.c.	Shademah	Thatch
Sort	ch.c.	Special	Forli
Starjinsky	b.c.	Hillsham	Sham
Sweet Mover	ch.f.	Compassionately	Hail To Reason
Thundering Force	b.c.	Java Moon	Graustark
Veruschenka	b/br.f.	Veruschka	Venture
Video	b.f.	Foreseer	Round Table
Wunderwerk	ch.c.	Wonderful Gal	The Axe II
Yacht	b.f.	Furling	Hoist The Flag
	b.c.	Blackmail	Ack Ack
	b.f.	Sleek Belle	Vaguely Noble

Appendix B
Nijinsky's Stakes Horses 1974–84

AFRICAN DANCER   Cheshire Oaks Gr 3, Park Hill Stakes Gr 2, second Yorkshire Oaks Gr 1, third Epsom Oaks Gr 1, Lancashire Oaks Gr 3

AVODIRE   second San Luis Obispo Handicap Gr 2, third South Bay Handicap

BALDSKI   Gold Coast Handicap, second Ak-Sar-Ben Omaha Gold Cup Gr 3, third Ak-Sar-Ben Presidents Cup Gr 3

BALLARE   Senorita Stakes

BALLETOMANE   Princess Stakes Gr 3, second Hollywood Oaks Gr 1

BEAUDELAIRE   Prix Maurice de Gheest Gr 2, Beeswing Stakes, Coolmore Try My Best Stakes, second Kilfrush/What A Guest Stakes, Coolmore Hello Gorgeous Stakes

BEDFORD   second Houghton Stakes, third Irish St Leger Gr 1

BEMISSED   Selima Stakes Gr 1, Miss Grillo Stakes Gr 3, Natalma Stakes Gr 3, Japan Racing Association Handicap, second Anne Arundel Handicap, third Evening Out Stakes, Gallorette Handicap Gr 3, Kentucky Oaks Gr 1

BENEFIT PERFORMER   second Santa Gertrudes Handicap

BEV BEV   second Prix d'Aumale

BORODINE   third Prix des Chenes Gr 3

BRIGHT FINISH   Yorkshire Cup Gr 2, Jockey Club Cup Gr 3

BROGAN   Prix Berteux Gr 3, second Italian Derby Gr 1, third Prix de l'Esperance Gr 3

CAERLEON   French Derby, Gr 1, Benson & Hedges Gold Cup Gr 1, Ballsbridge/Tattersalls Anglesey Stakes Gr 3, Tyros Stakes, second Irish Sweeps Derby Gr 1

CAUCASUS   Irish St Leger, Gr 1, Ulster Harp Derby, Sunset Handicap Gr 1, Manhattan Handicap Gr 2, San Luis Rey Stakes Gr 1 Arcadia Handicap Gr 3, South Bay Handicap, second Hollywood Invitational Handicap Gr 1 (twice), third American Handicap Gr 2, Hollywood Gold Cup Gr 1, San Luis Capistrano Handicap, Gr 1

CHERRY HINTON	Argos Star Fillies Mile, Gr 3 second Fred Darling Stakes, Gr 3, Convivial Stakes, third Ribblesdale Stakes, Gr 3 fourth 1,000 Guineas Gr 1
COME RAIN OR SHINE	second Pan American Handicap Gr 2
COPERNICA	second Fashion Stakes, Colleen Stakes, Astarita Stakes Gr 3, Matron Stakes Gr 1, Frizette Stakes Gr 1, Sunshine Nell Stakes, Grey Flight Handicap, third Dark Mirage Handicap
CZARAVICH	Metropolitan Handicap, Gr 1, Withers Stakes, Gr 2, Jerome Handicap Gr 2, Carter Handicap Gr 2, third Wood Memorial Stakes, Gr 1, Woodward Stakes Gr 1, Man O'War Stakes Gr 1, Suburban Handicap Gr 1, Whitney Handicap Gr 1
DANCING AGAIN	second Ancient Title Stakes
DANCING CHAMP	Massachusetts Handicap Gr 2, Woodlawn Stakes Gr 3, City of Baltimore Handicap, second Gettysburg Handicap
DANCING LESSON	third Interborough Handicap
DANCING SECRET	third Martha Washington Handicap
DEARLY TOO	Starbright Stakes, Violet Handicap, third Prioress Stakes, Garden City Stakes
DE LA ROSE	Hollywood Derby, Gr 1, Diana Handicap Gr 2, Long Branch Stakes Gr 2, Saranac Stakes Gr 2, E. P. Taylor Stakes, Gr 3, Athenia Handicap Gr 3, Lamb Chop Handicap, Evening Out Stakes, second Miss Grillo Handicap, Demoiselle Stakes, Gr 2, Kentucky Oaks Gr 1, Flower Bowl Handicap Gr 2, Lexington Handicap Gr 2, Columbiana Handicap
DOWN STAGE	Wistful Stakes, second Busher Handicap
EMPIRE GLORY	Royal Whip Gr 3, second Jefferson Smurfit Memorial Irish St Leger Gr 1, Blandford Stakes Gr 2
ENCINO	second Haggin Stakes, third Hollywood Juvenile Championship Gr 2
EQUINOL	second Prix de Seine-et-Marne
ESPERANTO	Shanbally House Stud Stakes, Craddock Advertising Stakes
EXCITABLE	Miss Florida Handicap, Miss Tropical Handicap, second La Prevoyante Handicap, third Poinciana Handicap, Black Helen Handicap Gr 2, Columbiana Handicap
FABULEUX DANCER	Prix de l'Avre, second Prix Juigne
FATHER MATTHEW	second Tyros Stakes
FOLK ART	Oak Leaf Stakes Gr 1
FORTUNATE DANCER	third Sanford Stakes Gr 2
GALLANTSKY	third Prix de Menneval

GALLETTO	Galtres Stakes, second Brownstown Stakes, Fasig Tipton CTBA Stakes
GLEASON	third Prix de Saint Firmin; WON Aurelius Hurdle
GOLDEN FLEECE	Epsom Derby Gr 1, Nijinsky Stakes Gr 2, Ballymoss Stakes Gr 3
GOLDYE'S MISS	second Ballylinch & Norelands Stud Stakes
GORYTUS	Laurent Perrier Champagne Stakes Gr 2, Acomb Stakes
GREEK SKY	Prix Juigne, second Prix La Force Gr 3
GREEN DANCER	French 2,000 Guineas Gr 1, Prix Lupin Gr 1, Observer Gold Cup Gr 1, second Prix des Chenes Gr 3, Prix Niel Gr 3
HALF AN HOUR	Prix Gerald de Rochefort Hurdle
HIS HONOR	Governors Handicap, Seabiscuit Invitational Handicap, Happy New Years Invitational Handicap, Tellys Pop Invitational Handicap, second Berkeley Handicap, Silky Sullivan Invitational, third San Francisco Mile, Golden Gate Handicap Gr 3
HOSTAGE	Arkansas Derby Gr 1, third Nashua Stakes
ILE DE BOURBON	King George VI & Queen Elizabeth Diamond Stakes, Gr 1, Coronation Cup Gr 1, King Edward VII Stakes Gr 2, Geoffrey Freer Stakes Gr 2, Clive Graham Stakes, second Heathorn Stakes, Predominate Stakes
IPI TOMBI	second Tote Place-Pot Hurdle
JAVAMINE	Long Island Handicap Gr 2, Diana Handicap Gr 2, Arlington Matron Handicap Gr 2, Knickerbocker Handicap Gr 3, second Monmouth Oaks Gr 2, Alabama Stakes Gr 1, Queen Charlotte Handicap Gr 3 Long Island Handicap Gr 3
KAZATSKA	second Prix des Belles Filles
KEY DANCER	Athenia Handicap Gr 3, second Long Island Handicap Gr 2, third Ladies Handicap Gr 1, Desert Vixen Stakes
KHATANGO	Dixie Handicap Gr 2, Seneca Handicap Gr 3, third Lawrence Realization Gr 2
KINGS LAKE	Airlie/Coolmore Irish 2,000 Guineas Gr 1, Sussex Stakes Gr 1, Joe McGrath Memorial Stakes Gr 1, second St James's Palace Stakes Gr 2, third Ballymoss Stakes Gr 3, Prix Jacques le Marois Gr 1
KRASSATA	second Azalea Stakes, third Silken Glider Stakes Gr 3, Brownstown Stakes, Consul Bayeff Rennen Gr 3, Queen of The Stage Handicap, Parlo Handicap, La Prevoyante Handicap, fourth Irish 1,000 Guineas Gr 1, Irish Oaks Gr 1
KYRA'S SLIPPER	second Grassland Handicap
LADY JINSKY	second Canadian Oaks Gr 1, Mazarine Stakes

LA JALOUSE	Selene Stakes, second Boniface Stakes, Fury Stakes
LA NIJINSKA	third Constitution Stakes
LEAP LIVELY	Hoover Fillies Mile Gr 3, Johnnie Walker Oaks Trial Gr 3, second Yorkshire Oaks Gr 1 third Epsom Oaks Gr 1
LEAP OF THE HEART	second Garden City Handicap
LIGHTED GLORY	Prix de Flore Gr 3, second Prix de la Grotte Gr 3, Prix St Alary Gr 1, Prix de l'Opera Gr 2, third Prix de Malleret Gr 3
LIGHTNING LEAP	second To Market Stakes
LONDON BELLS	second Coventry Stakes Gr 2, Rochester Cup
LOOSE CANNON	second Nashua Stakes
LUCKY SOVEREIGN	Mecca Dante Stakes Gr 2, second Acomb Stakes, Irish Sweeps Derby Gr 1, third Great Voltigeur Stakes Gr 2, Ladbroke Craven Stakes Gr 3
MAKAROVA	second Prix des Tuileries
MARUZENSKY	Asahi Hai Sansai Stakes Gr 1, Nihontapa Shou
MASQUED DANCER	second Brownstown Stakes, Autumn Handicap, Queen Alexandria Stakes, third Player Wills Stakes Gr 2
MIXED APPLAUSE	second Cherry Hinton Stakes Gr 3
MOSCOW BALLET	P. J. Prendergast Railway Stakes Gr 3
MUSCOVITE	Whitehall Stakes Gr 3, Ballycorus Stakes, second Desmond Stakes Gr 3, third BMW Nijinsky Stakes Gr 2, Beeswing Stakes
NAGURSKI	Woodlawn Stakes Gr 3, second Hoist The Flag Stakes
NETHERBY	Delta Airlines Handicap Chase
NICE HAVRAIS	Prix de Fontainebleau Gr 3, second Grand Criterium Gr 1
NIGHT ALERT	Prix Jean Prat Gr 2, Gladness Stakes Gr 3, Houghton Stakes, third Larkspur Stakes Gr 3, 2,000 Guineas Gr 1, Waterford Crystal Mile Gr 2, Joe McGrath Memorial Stakes Gr 1
NIJANA	Schuylerville Stakes Gr 3, Parlo Handicap (twice), Shrewsbury Handicap, La Prevoyante Handicap, second Long Island Handicap Gr 3, Green Glade Handicap, Gallant Bloom Handicap, third Diana Handicap Gr 2
NIJINSKY'S MELODY	second Natalma Stakes Gr 3
NIJINSKY'S SECRET	Hialeah Turf Cup Gr 1 (twice), Tidal Handicap Gr 2, Bougainvillea Handicap Gr 2, W. L. McKnight Handicap Gr 2, King Edward Gold Cup Gr 3, Jockey Club Cup Gr 2, Miami Lakes Stakes, Americana Handicap, second Jockey Club Cup Gr 2, Arlington Handicap Gr 1, third Budweister Million Gr 1

NIJIT	second Primonetta Handicap, Ocean City Stakes, third Cotillion Stakes
NIKITINA	second Silken Glider Stakes Gr 3
NINISKI	Irish St Leger Gr 1, French St Leger Gr 1, Geoffrey Freer Stakes Gr 2, Ormonde Stakes, Gr 3, John Porter Stakes Gr 2, second Coronation Cup Gr 1, Gordon Stakes Gr 3, third Doncaster St Leger Gr 1
NISHINO NORTHERN	second Junior Cup, Okurayamo Tokubetsu, third Kytoto Sansai Stakes
NIZON	Premio Roma Gr 1, Prix du Lys Gr 3, Prix du Lutece Gr 3
NORTHERLY NATIVE	second Prix de Sassy, third Handicap de le Seine
NUCLEAR PULSE	Grand Prix de Clairefontaine
NUMBER	Hempstead Handicap Gr 2, First Flight Handicap Gr 3, Firenze Handicap, second Gazelle Handicap Gr 2, Shuvee Handicap Gr 2, Ballerina Stakes Gr 3, third Test Stakes Gr 3, Bewitch Stakes Gr 3
OLAMIC	second Politely Stakes, Eatontown Handicap, Pukka Princess Stakes, third Lamb Chop Handicap
PAS DE DEUX	Prix du Palais Royal Gr 3, second Prix de Pontarme, third Prix Daphnis Gr 3
PEACETIME	Guardian Classic Trial Gr 3, Schroder Life Predominate Stakes, Valdoe Stakes, third Earl of Sefton Stakes Gr 3, Houghton Stakes
PIAFFER	Rose of York Handicap, second Ultramar Jubilee Handicap
POPULAR HERO	International Gold Cup Chase, Blockhouse Hurdle
PRINCESSE LIDA	Prix Morny Gr 1, Prix de la Salamandre Gr 1, Prix du Pin, Prix Yacowlef, second Prix de la Grotte Gr 3, third Grand Criterium Gr 1, French 1,000 Guineas Gr 1
QUIET FLING	Coronation Cup Gr 1, John Porter Stakes Gr 2, second Irish St Leger Gr 1, Coronation Cup Gr 1, Houghton Stakes, third Hardwicke Stakes Gr 2
RANKING BEAUTY	second Kilruddery Stakes, Cornelscourt Stakes
RISSA	third Hennessy Handicap
ROSE CRESCENT	Athenia Handicap Gr 3, second Lamb Chop Handicap
ROSY SPECTRE	Regret Stakes, second Smart Deb Handicap
RUSSIAN ROUBLES	Houghton Stakes, second King Edward VII Stakes Gr 2, third Gordon Stakes Gr 2
SHADEED	Houghton Stakes
SHE CAN DANCE	third Suwannee River Handicap Gr 3, Miss Florida Handicap
SHIMMY	Senorita Stakes, third Del Mar Oaks Gr 2

APPENDIX

SHINING FINISH	St Simon Stakes Gr 3, third Yorkshire Cup Gr 2, John Porter Stakes Gr 2
SILKY	second Irish 1,000 Guineas Gr 1, Strensall Stakes
SIR JINSKY	third Thomas A Edison Handicap
SIS C	Camellia Stakes
SOLFORD	Coral Eclipse Stakes Gr 1, Prix du Lys Gr 3
SPORTIN' LIFE	William Dupont Jr Handicap Gr 3, Allegheny Stakes, Philmont Stakes, Leonard Richards Stakes, Cochise Handicap, second Pennsylvania Derby, third Hill Prince Handicap Gr 3
STETCHWORTH	second Chester Vase Gr 3, fourth Doncaster St Leger Gr 1
STRADAVINSKY	Whitehall Stakes Gr 3, second King Edward VII Stakes Gr 2, Queen Elizabeth II Stakes Gr 2
STREET BALLET	La Centinela Stakes, second Santa Ynez Stakes Gr 3, Santa Susana Stakes Gr 1, Blue Hen Stakes, Tempted Stakes, La Habra Stakes, third Selima Stakes Gr 1, Honeymoon Handicap Gr 3, Nettie Stakes Gr 3
SUMMER FLING	Open Fire Stakes Gr 3, second Alabama Stakes Gr 1, third Test Stakes Gr 3, Tuscarora Handicap
SUMMERTIME PROMISE	Apple Blossom Handicap Gr 2, Gallorette Handicap Gr 3, Yo Tambien Handicap (twice), Indian Maid Handicap (twice), second Columbiana Handicap, Black Helen Handicap Gr 2, Santa Margarita Invitational Gr 1, Indian Maid Handicap, Gallorette Handicap Gr 3, third Selima Stakes Gr 1, Sheepshead Bay Handicap Gr 2, Hawthorne Handicap, Columbiana Handicap, Apple Blossom Handicap Gr 2, Las Palmas Handicap Gr 3, Queens Handicap
SUSANNA	second Fern Hill Stakes
TANZOR	Acomb Stakes, third Chesham Stakes
TERPSICHORIST	Sheepshead Bay Handicap Gr 2, Rutgers Handicap Gr 3, Long Island Handicap Gr 3, Violet Handicap, second Boiling Springs Handicap Gr 3, Suwannee River Handicap Gr 3, Orchid Handicap Gr 3, Long Island Handicap Gr 3, third Gazelle Handicap Gr 2, Diana Handicap Gr 2, Flower Bowl Handicap, Lamb Chop Handicap
TIGHTS	Silver Screen Handicap Gr 2, Volante Handicap Gr 3 La Jolla Mile Gr 3, Cougar II Stakes, Santa Catalina Stakes, Spotlight Handicap, third Hoist The Flag Stakes, San Vicente Stakes Gr 3, Will Rogers Stakes Gr 3
TOURNAMENT STAR	second Busher Handicap, third Beaugay Handicap, My Fair Lady Handicap
ULTRAMATE	Forum Stakes, Terrapin Handicap, second E. Taylor Chewning Handicap

UPPER NILE	Suburban Handicap Gr 1, Nassau County Handicap Gr 3, second United Nations Handicap Gr 1, third Nashua Stakes, Bernard Baruch Handicap Gr 3
VAL DANSEUR	Blue Larkspur Stakes, second Prix de la Butte Mortemart
VALINSKY	Geoffrey Freer Stakes Gr 2, second Royal Whip Gr 3, Grand Prix de Paris Gr 1
VATZA	second Hill Prince Handicap
VESTRIS	second Matchmaker Stakes Gr 2, third Acorn Stakes Gr 1, Rampart Handicap
VIDALIA	Criterium Femminile Gr 3
VISION	Secretariat Stakes Gr 1, Pilgrim Stakes Gr 3, second Brooklyn Handicap Gr 1, Lawrence Realization Gr 2, third Lexington Handicap Gr 2, Rutgers Handicap Gr 2
WATER DANCE	Twilight Tear Stakes, second Beaugay Handicap, third Miss Liberty Handicap, Long Look Handicap Gr 2, Hannah Dustin Handicap
WAVING	Lamb Chop Handicap, Manta Handicap, third Las Cienagas Handicap
WESTERN SYMPHONY	Larkspur Stakes Gr 3, Birdcatcher Nursery, second Tap On Wood Stakes, Tara Sires Desmond Stakes Gr 3, third Windfields The Minstrel Stakes
WHITE BIRCH	second Hill Prince Stakes Gr 3
YAMANIN PENNY	Yonsai Stakes Gr 3, Junior Cup, second Kobai Shou, third Shirayuri Stakes, October Handicap
YEATS	Herbertstown Handicap

Appendix C
The Pedigree and Family details of Nijinsky

NIJINSKY Bay Horse, 1967	Northern Dancer (B. 1961)	Nearctic (Br. 1954)	Nearco (Br. 1935)	Pharos	Phalaris
					Scapa Flow
				Nogara	Havresac II
					Catnip
			Lady Angela (Ch. 1944)	Hyperion	Gainsborough
					Selene
				Sister Sarah	Abbot's Trace
					Sarita
		Natalma (B. 1957)	Native Dancer (Gr. 1950)	Polynesian	Unbreakable
					Black Polly
				Geisha	Discovery
					Miyako
			Almahmoud (Ch. 1947)	Mahmoud	Blenheim
					Mah Mahal
				Arbitrator	Peace Chance
					Mother Goose
	Flaming Page (B. 1959)	Bull Page (B. 1947)	Bull Lea (Br. 1935)	Bull Dog	Teddy
					Plucky Liege
				Rose Leaves	Ballot
					Colonial
			Our Page (B. 1940)	Blue Larkspur	Black Servant
					Blossom Time
				Occult	Dis Donc
					Bonnie Witch
		Flaring Top (Ch. 1947)	Menow (B. 1935)	Pharamond II	Phalaris
					Selene
				Alcibiades	Supremus
					Regal Roman
			Flaming Top (Ch. 1941)	Omaha	Gallant Fox
					Flambino
				Firetop	Man O'War
					Summit

NIJINSKY

Bay Horse 1967

TURF RECORD
2 Years: 1969

Ran five times.
WON Erne Maiden Stakes, Curragh, 6 furlongs by ½ length from Everyday; 5 ran.	£ 843
WON Railway Stakes, Curragh, Gr III, 6 furlongs 63 yards by 5 lengths from Decies; 7 ran.	2,140
WON Anglesey Stakes, Curragh, Gr III, 6 furlongs 63 yards by 3 lengths from Everyday; 6 ran.	2,185
WON Beresford Stakes, Curragh, Gr II, 8 furlongs by ¾ length and 6 lengths from Decies and Greenloaning; 7 ran.	4,272
WON Dewhurst Stakes, Newmarket, Gr I, 7 furlongs by 3 lengths from Recalled; 6 ran.	10,576

3 Years: 1970

Ran eight times.
WON Gladness Stakes, Curragh, Gr III, 7 furlongs by 4 lengths from Deep Run and Prince Tenderfoot; 12 ran.	2,025
WON 2,000 Guineas, Newmarket, Gr I, 8 furlongs by 2½ lengths from Yellow God and Roi Soleil; 14 ran.	28,195
WON Derby Stakes, Epsom, Gr I, 12 furlongs by 2½ lengths from Gyr and Stintino; 11 ran.	62,311
WON Irish Sweeps Derby, Curragh, Gr I, 12 furlongs by 3 lengths from Meadowville and Master Guy; 13 ran.	56,993
WON King George VI & Queen Elizabeth Stakes, Ascot, Gr I, 12 furlongs by 2 lengths from Blakeney, Crepellana and Karabas; 6 ran.	31,993
WON St Leger Stakes, Doncaster, Gr I, 14 furlongs 127 yards by a length from Meadowville and Politico; 9 ran.	37,082
Second Prix de l'Arc de Triomphe, Longchamp, Gr I, 12 furlongs, beaten a head by Sassafras, beating Miss Dan, Gyr, Blakeney, etc; 16 ran.	480,000
Second Champion Stakes, Newmarket, Gr I, 10 furlongs to Lorenzaccio, with Hotfoot third; 8 ran.	7,416
TOTALS	£246,031 F480,000

1st Dam
   FLAMING PAGE (1959 by Bull Page), won 4 races and $108,836, including Shady Well Stakes, Queen's Plate, Gr I and Canadian Oaks, Gr I, placed second 4 times, including Princess Elizabeth Stakes, Gr I and Kentucky Oaks, Gr II, third twice, including Coronation Futurity Stakes, Gr I.
   Dam of 3 winners:
      Fleur b.f.1964, by Victoria Park, won 3 races and third Summer Stakes, Gr II; dam of winners, including:
         FAR NORTH won 3 races and 201,480 francs at 2 and 3 years in France, including Prix Saint Roman, Gr III and Prix Omnium II*, successful sire.
         THE MINSTREL won 7 races and £570,605, at 2 and 3 years, including Derby, Epsom, Gr I, Irish Sweeps Derby, Curragh, Gr I, King George VI & Queen Elizabeth Stakes, Ascot, Gr I, Dewhurst Stakes, Newmarket, Gr I, Larkspur Stakes, Leopardstown, Gr III and Ascot 2,000 Guineas Trial, Gr III.

THE MINSTREL ...
  also second in Irish 2,000 Guineas, Curragh, Gr I and third 2,000 Guineas, Newmarket, Gr I; all his starts. Horse of the Year in England and Ireland; successful sire.

FLOWER PRINCESS won 3 races including Duchess Stakes, Fort Erie, dam of **DANCE FLOWER** won Vogue Stakes.

PILGRIM won Midsummer Scurry Handicap* and Youghal Stakes*, second The Minstrel Stakes*.

NIJINSKY b.c.1967, by Northern Dancer, as overleaf.

MINSKY ch.c.1968, by Northern Dancer, won 4 races and £17,051, viz. Beresford Stakes, Gr II, Railway Stakes, Gr III, Tetrarch Stakes, Gr III and Gladness Stakes, Gr III, second in Erne Stakes and Observer Gold Cup, Gr I; fourth in 2,000 Guineas, Gr I, also won 4 races and $52,550 in USA, including Durban Cup (twice); second in Discovery Handicap, Gr III; third in Niagara Handicap, Gr III; a leading sire in Japan.

Her only living foals.

2nd Dam

FLARING TOP (1947 by Menow), won 3 races and placed second twice at 2 and 3 years.

Dam of 11 winners:

Gleam, ch.f.1952, by Tournoi, won 2 races and placed second at 3 years; dam of winners, including:
  EVENING BAG won 11 races and $111,592, including Orchid Handicap, Gr III, second in Pageant Handicap, Gr III, third in Suwanee River Handicap, Gr III.
  Flaming Triumph won 6 races, second in Seagram Cup Stakes, Gr III.
  grandam of **ROYAL SKI** (won 8 races and $324,895, including Pimlico Laurel Futurity, Gr I, Heritage Stakes, Gr III, Remson Stakes, Gr II, Mayflower Stakes), third dam of **UTMOST CELERITY** (Susquehanna Handicap, Mill Race Handicap, Doylestown Handicap, Bristol Handicap, Falsington Handicap), **THUNDER RUNNER** (Warminster Stakes).

TOP TOURN ch.c.1953, by Tournoi, won 23 races from 3 to 9 years, and $61,460, including Inferno Handicap, Fort Erie Handicap (twice), Ultimus Handicap and Jacques Cartier Stakes, placed second 12 times, including Connaught Cup, Gr III, third 17 times, including Ultimus Handicap, Fairplay Stakes, Jacques Cartier Stakes, Vigil Handicap and Bold Venture Handicap; sire.

Flaming Wind, b.f.1955, by Windfields, won 3 races; placed second twice and third twice, at 2 and 3 years, dam of winners, including:
  FRENCH WIND won 4 races, including Display Stakes, second Tattling Handicap, dam of **Notra Joie** second in Natalma Stakes, Gr III, **La Giroulette** third in Criterium de Saint-Cloud, Gr II and **Flaming Reason** second Lady Fingers Stakes.
  Bahamas Wind won 27 races, second in Queenstown Stakes.
  grandam of **DOBBINTON** won Birdcatcher Stakes and Debutante Handicap, **FLAMME D'OR** won Mazarine Stakes and **BLONDY** won Gran Premio Joaquin Crespo, Gr I, Premio Prensa Nacional, Gr I, etc, in Venezuela; third dam of **SANDY ISLE** won Yearling Sales Stakes, **NEW REGENT** won Yearling Sales Stakes and William P Kyne Handicap, and **JORDY'S BABA** won San Francisco Invitational Handicap, Spectacular Invitational Handicap, Star Ball Invitational Handicap, and Alameda County Fillies and Mares Handicap.

Merry and Bright, ch.f.1956, by Menetrier, winner at 2 years; dam of winners, including:
  FANFARON won 4 races including Plate Trial, second in Queen's Plate, Gr I, Vandal Stakes and Victoria Stakes, Gr III.

third dam of **CHALDEA** (Iroquois Stakes, Ticonderoga Handicap).

QUINTAIN b.c.1957, by Tournoi, won 11 races from 2 to 6 years and $41,096, including Continental Handicap, placed second 13 times, including Queen's Plate, Gr I and Plate Trial Stakes, third 11 times, including Edmonton Special Handicap and Journal Handicap.

FLASHING TOP ch.f.1958, by Menetrier, won 7 races at 2 and 4 years and $30,457, including Shady Well Stakes, placed second 8 times, including Belle Mahone Stakes (twice), Gr II, Plate Trial and Star Shoot Stakes; third 4 times, including International Handicap and Quebec Derby; dam of winners, including:

> **Northern Flash** won 6 races; second in Highland Handicap, Gr III, sire in England and USA.
>
> **Arctic Flash** 17 races, third in Canadian Handicap; sire in Japan.
>
> **Vast Opportunity** 14 races, second in Saskatchewan Derby.
>
> **Police Car** 6 races, second in Eclipse Handicap, Achievement Handicap; sire.

FLAMING PAGE b.f.1959, by Bull Page, as overleaf.

Top Victory b.g.1962, by Victoria Park, won 9 races from 2 to 5 years and $33,455, placed second 9 times, including Canadian Handicap, third twice.

Flaming Victress, b.f.1963, by Victoria Park, won 3 races and placed three times at 2 and 3 years; dam of winners, including:

> **ALL FOR VICTORY** won 6 races and $118,851, including Canadian Derby, Gr II, Woodbine Invitational, second Fairbank Handicap and Thanksgiving Handicap.
>
> grandam of **RUMPOLE** (Prospect Stakes, British Columbia Stallion Stakes, New Westminster Stakes, British Columbia Nursery Stakes); third dam of **ROCKCLIFFE** (Stampede Park Sprint Championship, Norway House Handicap, Inaugural Handicap, Lieutenant Governors Handicap, Gr III, Polo Park Handicap).

Flamatory b.f.1964, by Victoria Park, won 3 races at 2 and 3 years; placed second once and third twice, including Bison City Stakes.

Friendly Relations, ch.f.1966, by Nearctic, winner at 2 years; placed second once and third 3 times; dam of winners, including:

> **VIENDRA** won Convenience Stakes, Hollywood and second in Sir Charles Clore Memorial* and Virginia Stakes* and Matinee Handicap.
>
> grandam of **MORNING FROLIC** won Canadian Turf Handicap, Gr III, Appleton Handicap, and **ICY TIME** won Twilight Tear Stakes.

All her living foals.

3rd Dam

FLAMING TOP (1941 by Omaha), ran three times.

Dam of 8 winners:

ILLUMINABLE ch.c.1946, by Sun Again, won five races at 2 years and $31,920, including Spalding Lowe Jenkins Stakes, placed second twice, including East View Stakes, third twice.

Flaring Top, ch.f.1947, by Menow, as above.

Quick Pick-Up, ch.c.1950, by Princequillo, won two races at 2 and 3 years and placed once.

DOUBLEDOGDARE b.f.1953, by Double Jay, won 13 races at 2 and 3 years and $258,206, including Matron Stakes, Gr I, Colleen Stakes, Alcibiades Stakes, Gr II, National Stallion Stakes, Spinster Stakes, Gr I, Falls City Handicap, Gr III, Ashland Stakes, Gr III, Coronet Stakes and Oaks Prep. placed second six times, including Spinaway Stakes, Gr I, Fashion Stakes, Kentucky Oaks, Gr II Cleopatra Handicap and Misty Isle Handicap, third in Arlington Classic; dam of a winner and grandam of **FOUR SPADES** won Prix des Yearlings*, and **FULL OF STARS** won Prix Maurice de Nieuil, Gr II.

Double Top, b.c.1955, by Double Jay, placed.

TOP DOUBLE b.c. 1956, by Double Jay, won eight races from 3 to 5 years and $72,715, including Yearling Sales Stakes, Escondido Handicap and Pomona Handicap, third 13 times.

Way To Go, b.f.1957, by Olympia, winner at 2 years, placed second four times and third five times; dam of winners, including:

    TOWARD won 9 races including Duchess Stakes, second in Fury Stakes, Selene Stakes, Gr III, Golden Poppy Handicap and Whimsical Stakes, Gr III, dam of **Split Opinion** 2 races and third Westwood Stakes.

    TRANSPORTATION won 4 races including Caliente Derby Handicap, third in Longacres Derby Handicap, Gr III.

    Camel Train won 13 races and second Journal Handicap, third Speed to Spare Championship Stakes, Inaugural Handicap and Province Handicap.

Nacelle, b.c. 1960, by Turn-to, won two races at 3 and 4 years, placed second three times and third six times.

Nike Site, b.c.1961, by Double Jay, won 15 races from 3 to 8 years and $89,905 placed second 26 times and third 13 times.

All her foals.

4th Dam

FIRETOP (by Man O'War), dam of winners, including **COLUMBIANA** (Widener Handicap, Gr I), and **RED VULCAN** (Raceland Handicap); grandam of **OCEAN WAVE** (Blue Grass Stakes, Gr I), **FREE AMERICA** (Churchill Downs Handicap), **KENTARIO** (Canada Cup), **EARLY ENGLAND** (Great American Stakes); third dam of **DECIMATOR** (Great American Stakes) and **ZINOV** (Lawrence Realization, Gr II), fourth dam of **CHORAL GROUP** (Princess Elizabeth Stakes, Gr I, Can).

5th Dam

SUMMIT by (Ultimus), bred **APOGEE** (Arlington Lassie Stakes, Gr II); third dam of **ACE OF ACES** (Sussex Stakes, Goodwood, Gr I).

6th Dam

TORPENHOW (by Torpoint), dam of **DARE SAY** (Phoenix Hotel Stakes) and **NOW HIGH** (Seneca Stakes); ancestress of **EL GRAN SENOR, TRY MY BEST, BLUSH WITH PRIDE, AVIANCE, MALINOWSKI** etc.

No. 8 Family

Index of Horses

Abeesh 53, 216, 249
Abington 273
Acamas 27, 28, 68, 69, 70
Acaroid 38, 100
Accomplice 205
Achieved 40, 61
Ack Ack 270, 276
Acropolis 223
Adios 139
Admiration 259
Affirmed 32, 47, 94, 273
Afifa 52
African Dancer 20, 21, 22, 70, 152, 159, 179, 198, 206, 213, 238, 242, 253
African Pearl 104
A Happy Butterfly 159
Aino Saintsky 51, 186
Air Distingue 154, 276
Akarad 121, 122
Alanesian 18
Alchaasibiyeh 244
Alcide 223
Alezan Dancer 129, 207, 221, 249
Al Hattab 205
All Along 127, 186, 187
Alleged 23, 24, 25, 54, 68, 70, 105, 221, 232
Allegretta 151
Allez France 66, 77
All For Victory 4
All Systems Go 146
Alluvial 16, 207, 270
Alpine Strings 265
Al Riyadh 150
Althea 50, 226
Alydar 54, 159, 254, 273
Alyne Que 201
Amalesian 191, 201, 205, 225
Amaranda 65
Amber Rama 9, 73

Ambiorix 224–5
Amen Wadeen 170, 175, 192
Amuigh Faoin Spier 6
Ancient Title 116
Andover Way 100, 101
Anifa 110
Anita's Prince 265
Anitra's Dance 256
Anne's Pretender 74, 76, 118, 119
Apolvinsky 265
Apollonia 135
Approval 7, 8, 9, 10, 11
April Run 83, 91, 102
April Slipper 91
April View 91
Aras An Uachtarain 273
Archdeacon 260
Archiviste 275
Arctic Tern 258, 274
Arctique Royale 64, 82, 83
Ardross 65, 83, 111
Areola 18
Argument 83, 111
Arkadina 65
Armistice Day 209
Artaius 154, 270, 272, 274, 275
Artfully 162
Arts And Letters 103, 205, 208
Aryenne 32, 34, 78, 135, 136, 148, 256, 257, 258
Assault 103
Assert 39, 42, 45, 46, 60, 61, 62, 79, 83, 88
Athanasius 228
Atmosphere 248
Audley End 190, 268
Aunt Jin 156
Au Printemps 260
Autumn Sunset 104, 105, 152
Avatar 115, 116
Avodire 22, 25, 170, 219, 246, 264

Bagdad 227
Bahram 13, 146, 222
Bakor 190, 191, 236
Bald Admiral 266
Bald Eagle 213, 214
Bald King 266
Baldric II 219, 220
Baldski 22, 24, 25, 170, 180, 190, 196, 198, 205, 213, 246, 251, 265, 266
Baldski's Holiday 266
Ballade 244
Balladier 226, 227
Ballare 23, 32, 33, 34, 36, 84, 172, 179, 190, 196, 198, 206, 219, 220
Balletic 17, 245, 270
Balletomane 23, 38, 40, 179, 191, 196, 198, 205, 213, 239, 242, 253
Ballet Style 248
Ballydoyle 85, 244
Ballymoss 213
Balmerino 68, 118
Baltic Dancer 249
Bamboozle 16, 18, 192, 270
Bandarilla 113
Baptism 31
Baracala 257
Barbs Bold 244
Baronova 26
Barrera 259, 275
Barrydown 265
Bastonera 158
Battle Creek Girl 274
Bayardo 147, 212
Baygo 157
Bay Ronald 226
Beau Brummel 205
Beaudelaire 30, 44, 45, 48, 49, 50, 104, 152, 180, 190, 191,

INDEX

Beaudelaire – *cont.*
   193, 198, 210, 214, 234, 240, 242, 253, 268
Beau Reef 110
Beautiful Contest 91
Bedford 36, 39, 40, 190, 192, 208, 219, 235
Beginners Luck 267
Beja 20
Bel Bolide 81, 169, 206
Beldale Flutter 40, 83, 273
Bella Paola 135, 136
Belle de Nuit 18
Belle Of Dodge Me 48
Belmont Bay 81, 82
Bemis Heights 30, 140, 191, 198, 207
Bemissed 30, 43, 44, 45, 46, 47, 49, 140–2, 149, 150, 170, 179, 191, 195, 198, 204, 207, 226, 234, 240, 242, 253
Be My Guest 5, 45, 52, 60
Be My Native 126
Bendara 43, 200, 205
Bends Me Mind 205
Bessabarian 55
Best In Show 47, 53
Be Suspicious 198, 206
Be Sweet 138, 140
Better Self 208, 227
Bev Bev 30, 31, 32, 120, 133, 191, 215, 235
Bid High 190
Bid Us 276
Big Monday 274–5
Bikala 79, 83, 121
Bingo Chimura 266
Bireme 32, 149, 150
Bishop's Choice 92
Bitty Girl 20, 23, 30, 32, 44, 104, 152, 169, 190, 191, 198, 204, 208, 210, 234
Bivouac 210, 234, 247
Blackmail 250
Black Satin 18, 29, 90, 190, 198, 206, 218
Black Servant 226–7
Black Toney 226
Blade 113
Blakeney 12
Blandford 222
Blenheim 222
Blondy 4
Blue Larkspur 227
Blue Nijinsky 236, 249
Blue Peter 215, 216
Blue Wind 38, 39, 52, 82, 83, 151
Blushing Groom 45, 159, 161, 177, 184

Blushing Redhead 276
Blush With Pride 52
Bohemian Grove 110
Boitron 137
Bo Jinsky 246
Bolak 138
Bold Bidder 206, 217, 219, 244, 276
Bold Forbes 165, 244, 270
Bold Frond 129
Bold Green 134, 256
Bold Honor 202, 206, 217
Bold Hour 120
Bold Lad (IRE) 217
Bold Lad (USA) 217, 219
Bold Liz 20, 30, 211
Bold 'N Determined 34
Boldnesian 217
Bold Ruler 212, 213, 214, 217, 228, 243, 253
Bold Run 126
Bold Venture 103
Bolkonski 75
Bolsa 110
Bolshoi 220
Bon Mot 221
Bonne Ile 72
Bonnie and Gay 15, 20, 113, 164, 208
Bonnie Google 17, 113, 164, 190, 208, 227, 270
Bonnie Hope 247
Borodine 21, 187, 188, 218
Bosworth 226
Bottled Water 123
Bourbonel 72
Bowl Game 32, 94, 97
Bowl of Flowers 15, 17, 113, 258
Brantome 222
Brave Lady 200
Bravo Native 97
Breaker's Row 247
Brehon Law 182
Brenn 75, 76
Brigadier Gerard 215, 274
Bright Crocus 142
Bright Finish 20, 21, 22, 25, 171, 180, 189, 190, 194, 198, 206, 209, 220, 230, 238, 242, 253, 263
Brilliante 257
Brilliantine 18, 151
Brogan 30, 44, 46, 47, 48, 50, 84, 145, 180, 183, 192, 198, 205, 208, 219, 220, 235, 240, 242, 253
Brokers Tip 226
Brookdale 247
Broom Dance 44
Browser 66

Bruni 77, 114, 117
Buchan 222
Buckpasser 13, 130, 216, 243
Buckskin 72
Bull Dandy 120
Bull Dog 223, 224
Bundle of Kisses 187, 188, 215
Bundler 26
Burslem 85
Bushti Music 104
Busted 33
Bustino 77, 110
Butterfield Stage 249

Cadoudal 257
Caerleon 30, 38, 42, 43–4, 45, 46, 47, 48, 49, 50, 52, 53, 54, 84–90, 103, 104, 105, 107, 112, 147, 152, 153, 171, 172, 180, 191, 200, 205, 208, 219, 230, 240, 248, 250, 252, 253, 268
Caesar's Wish 166
Calderina 167, 168, 169
Caliban 12
Call Me Prince 120
Cambrienne 16
Canadian Bound 243
Canadian Champ 204, 209
Canadian Taste 209
Canadian Victory 204, 209
Candy Spots 227
Canoe 248
Cantelo 139
Capture The Heart 143
Carajas 273
Caraquenga 139
Carlingford Castle 88, 105
Carmarthen 66
Caro 25, 256, 258
Carolina Moon 165
Cascapedia 118–9
Castle Keep 79, 122
Casus Belli 119, 263
Catherine Wheel 83
Caucasus 19, 20, 21, 22, 23, 24, 25, 49, 54, 75, 112–9, 130, 153, 162, 170, 180, 187, 188, 189, 190, 195, 198, 204, 205, 219, 230, 238, 242, 253, 263, 275
Caught In The Act 18, 20, 192, 246, 270
Cavan 38, 103, 213
Caveat 48
Celestial Dancer 274
Century Banker 99
Chamossaire 277
Chandelier 15
Charlottesville 220

INDEX

Charlton 13
Charming Alibi 243
Charming Dance 247, 271
Charm School 226
Chaucer 212, 220
Chauffeur 205
Cheriestep 266
Cherokee Phoenix 236, 247, 271
Cherry Hinton 24, 25, 26, 35, 67, 96, 132, 137–40, 143, 149, 151, 166, 179, 180, 192, 198, 206, 221, 222, 230, 233, 239, 242, 253
Chic Dancer 260
Chieftain 25, 217
Chivalry 39, 187, 188
Choreographer 265
Choucri 134, 135
Chou Croute 23
Chris Evert 23, 30, 39, 191, 223
Christmas Past 43
Chronicle 62
Cigar 273
Cistus 138
Citoyen 77
Clair Matin 152
Classical Ballet 33, 190, 247
Clever Trick 93
Cloonlara 26, 39, 78, 204, 205
Close Up 17, 191, 272
Clover Princess 164
Coastal 16, 32, 93, 94, 207
Cock Robin 87
Colin 226
Colombo 146
Colorado 212
Columbiana 4, 275
Come Rain or Shine 41, 170, 190, 214
Commando 226
Compassionately 53
Comtesse de Loir 26, 77, 134, 192
Concert Hall 54
Condessa 83, 101, 151
Condorcet 74, 75
Conquistador Cielo 15, 96, 103
Continual 201, 206, 223
Convenience 205
Copano 25
Copernica 17, 18, 19, 155, 156, 190, 191, 236
Copper Canyon 15, 190, 191, 236, 271
Copper Kingdom 20, 190, 263
Copper Mel 115, 264
Cornish Prince 210, 217
Corps de Ballet 257
Cosmah 244
Costly Dream 157

Countertrade 38, 46, 84, 207, 248
Countess Eileen 164
Count Nijinsky 16
Court Harwell 220
Court Martial 205, 216
Cracaval 31, 71, 109
Cremation 105
Creme dela Creme 218
Crepellana 12
Crepello 8, 204, 209
Cresta Rider 82
Crimson Beau 70
Crimson Saint 20, 191
Crimson Satan 227
Critique 80
Croda Rossa 18
Crossways 273
Crowned Prince 47
Crown The Prince 205
Crown Thy Good 91
Crown Treasure 153, 162
Crozier 224
Cry Baby 9, 10
Cryptic 140, 141
Crystal Cup 66
Crystal Water 118
Cumbernauld 8
Cupecoy's Joy 42
Cure The Blues 275
Cute Kiss 156
Cyane 108
Cynara 10
Czaravich 29, 30, 32, 33, 34, 35, 36, 90–6, 180, 190, 198, 206, 218, 234, 237, 239, 242, 253, 267
Czarinsky 248

Dactylographer 66, 67
Dahlia 20, 47, 77, 115, 116, 118
Daigo Totsugeki 261
Dalsaan 81
Damascus 124, 154, 161, 205, 223, 276
Dame Mysterieuse 98
Dancealot 30, 34, 37, 141, 153, 191, 198, 206, 209, 235
Dance Bid 80
Dance Call 39
Dance In Snow 226, 246, 251
Dance Machine 258
Dance Pavilion 260
Dancer's Countess 158
Dancer's Vixen 243
Dancing Again 50, 153, 209, 219, 235
Dancing Brownie 120, 215, 236
Dancing Champ 19, 20, 22, 100, 113, 180, 190, 196, 198, 206,

216, 235, 238, 245, 251, 253, 260, 261
Dancing Crown 51, 170, 191, 225
Dancing Detente 207, 246, 251, 270
Dancing Femme 161
Dancing Heifer 265
Dancing Heiress 248
Dancing Lesson 50, 51, 140, 191, 221, 222
Dancing On A Cloud 249
Dancing Rocks 256, 257
Dancing Secret 43, 99, 120, 123, 209, 215, 236
Dancing Slippers 226
Dancinintherain 46, 248
Dandy Blitzen 120
Dandy Lute 74, 75
Danzatore 45, 86, 104, 105, 152
Danzig 254
Darby Creek Road 167
Dark Star 226
Data Swap 125
Dauntu 35, 226
Dawnballet 226, 248
Day Is Done 125
Deal 266
Dearly Precious 19, 26, 34, 42, 162, 191, 198, 204, 207, 211, 226
Dearly Too 26, 39, 41, 43, 44, 45, 50, 179, 191, 195, 196, 198, 207, 211, 226
Deb's Darling 190
Debussy 211, 235
Debutante Bob 214
Deceit 34, 191, 198, 205
Decies 6, 7, 8, 132, 133
Deep Roots 257
Deep Run 7, 8, 9
Deesse du Val 20, 157
Defecting Dancer 154, 277
De La Rose 23, 31, 35, 36, 37, 38, 39, 40, 47, 50, 84, 96–103, 140, 141, 143, 152–3, 155, 165, 169, 179, 190, 195, 201, 205, 208, 210, 219, 235, 239, 241, 242, 247, 250, 251, 253, 264, 271
Delgado 86, 105
Delices 154, 270, 275
Derring Do 29
Desert Law 23
Determinant 126
Detroit 64, 83, 111
Dewan 217
Diaghilev 261, 267
Diamond Shoal 162
Diesis 45, 147

INDEX

Dillingham 256
Directoire 21, 244
Discovered 126, 128
Distant Land 103
Divine Grace 30
Djaura 162
Djebel 224, 225
Dogger Bank 79
Domino 226–7
Dom Pasquini 87
Dona Maya 160
Doncaster 227
Don Menzotti 128
Dottie's Doll 162
Doubledogdare 4
Double Form 71, 189
Double Jay 227
Dowdall 114
Down Stage 30, 48, 49, 50, 169, 179, 191, 195, 198, 207, 221, 222, 233
Dragon 32, 33, 133, 135
Dr Fager 205, 210, 211, 226
Dronacharya 237, 247
Dr Patches 96
Drumnadrochit 214, 248
Drumtop 18, 23, 30, 44, 145, 190, 192, 198, 205, 208, 235
Dr White 52
Duke of Marmalade 77
Dumpty Humpty 218
Dundrum Dancer 119, 263
Dunette 64, 65
Dunfermline 68, 69, 138
Durandal 134
Dusky Evening 159, 190, 201, 207, 211, 216, 235

Easter King 70
Eastern Dawn 154, 276
Edelene 236
Edmond Dantes 248
Edziu 25, 190, 246, 251
Effervescing 117, 118
Eight Thirty 227
Eighty Grand 218
Ela Mana Mou 111
Electric 89, 273
Elegant Air 156
Elegant Prince 19, 243
Elegant Tern 156
Elevation 215
El Gran Senor 50, 53
El Palomar 72
Embroidery 26
Empire Glory 43, 53, 54, 55, 56, 180, 193, 198, 205, 213, 214, 241, 242, 244, 249, 250, 252, 253
Enchanting Dancer 247

Encino 27, 30, 191, 227, 247, 251
End of War 123
English Harbour 67
Enstone Spark 26, 64, 67, 138, 140
Entente 59, 202, 206
Entente Cordiale 79
Entrancing (USA), 220
Entrancing (AUS), 263
Equal Change 103
Equal Venture 103
Equinol 48, 53, 54, 219
Ercolano 210
Erin's Isle 39, 65, 80, 82, 126, 187
Erwin Boy 116
Escaline 105
Escart Bay 265
Esperanto 43, 52, 54, 56, 180, 200, 205, 213, 214, 249, 252
Esprit du Nord 87
Euryanthe 54, 154, 275–6
Evasion 248
Evening Bag 4
Evening Boo Boo 166
Everyday 6, 7
Example 16, 192, 204, 229
Exbury 22, 223
Exceller 23, 119, 170, 205, 266, 276
Excitable 28, 29, 155, 166, 169, 179, 195, 201, 206, 221, 222, 233, 234, 246, 271
Exclusively Raised 151
Exclusive Native 267, 270, 271, 273
Exclusive One 270, 273
Exdirectory 27, 68
Exit Smiling 201, 207
Exotic Treat 60, 203, 205
Explodent 120
Explorer King 121
Explosive Bid 99, 129
Eye Dazzler 248

Fabiano 125
Fabled Monarch 113
Fabuleux Dancer 30, 38, 46, 87, 180, 192, 194, 198, 207, 221, 233, 234, 248, 252
Fabuleux Jane 30, 34, 46, 87, 192, 198, 204, 207, 221
Fabulous Fraud 167
Fair Davina 101
Fair Isle 212
Fairness 38, 103, 203, 205
Fair Salinia 139, 140
Fair Trial 215
Fairway 212, 215–6

Fairy Bridge 47
Fairy Footsteps 36, 151
Fairy Tern 156
Fanaan 250
Fanfaron 4
Faraway Son 225
Far Beyond 100, 274
Farm 190, 192
Far North 4
Fascinating Girl 157
Fashion Verdict 205
Fast Approach 202, 214
Fast Line 225
Father Matthew 48, 54, 55, 56, 215, 249
Favoletta 20, 190
Fecund 190, 192
Festive Mood 22
Field Cat 125, 126
Filiberto 274
Find 275
Fine Prospect 244
Fiordiligi 139
Firebird 248
Firestreak 277
Firetop 275
First Feather 37, 113
First Landing 214
Firyal 134, 135
Fish Bar 23, 78, 198, 205
Fit To Fight 53
Flama Ardiente 162
Flaming Page 3, 4, 5, 207–8, 276
Flaming Top 4
Flaring Top 4, 216
Flashing Top 4
Fleet Nasrullah 205, 213, 214
Fleet Peach 20
Fleet Victress 157, 159, 160, 163
Fleur 4
Fling Tiger 262
Flitalong 169
Florida Son 63
Flower Princess 4
Flow Line 218
Fluorescent Light 94
Flying Above 30, 34, 191, 198, 207
Flying Fur 23, 120, 191
Fly To Arms 226, 247
Folge 123
Folk Art 55, 56, 84, 140, 142–4, 153, 179, 196, 200, 206, 210, 219, 241, 242, 253
Fond Hope 201, 207, 214
Foolish Pleasure 36
Foolish Redhead 235, 276
Foolish Tanner 123
Forego 27

INDEX

Foreign Interest 263
Foreign Secretary 244
Foreseer 47, 84, 191, 200, 205, 208–9
Forli 84, 205, 209, 218, 228
Formidable 120, 138
Fortunate Dancer 54, 219
Four Bases 128, 129
Four Kids Only 92
Fragile Witness 190
Francis S 214
Fran's Valentine 55, 143, 144
Fray Star 126
Free Round 74
French Legionnaire 153
French Wind 4
Frere Basile 70, 71
Front Row 90
Frost King 124
Full Dress II 16, 23, 220
Full Pocket 225
Funalon 156
Funny Peculiar 162
Future Spa 61
Future Tense 153, 162
Futurette 261

Gaia 16, 21, 198, 206, 273
Gaily 205
Gainsborough 212
Gala Mood 191
Gala Party 145, 191, 201, 206
Gallant Archer 48, 53, 55, 249
Gallant Bloom 18
Gallant Man 220
Gallant Risk 260
Gallantsky 30, 216, 247
Galletto 21, 24, 179, 194, 198, 206, 220, 273
Gallina 113
Galopin 228
Gap of Dunloe 121, 122
Gate Dancer 52
Gato del Sol 42, 129
Gay Fandango 113
Gay Hostess 243
Gay Mecene 33, 70, 71, 72
Gay Meeting 16, 19, 271
General Assembly 65, 91, 92, 93, 267, 273
General Partner 158
Gentle Linna 247
Gentleman Jinsky 187, 188, 247
Genuine Risk 32, 36
Gianchi 267
Gin Tour 218
Gist 190
Given 263
Give or Else 247
Give Thanks 105

Gladiolus 158
Glad Rags 18, 20, 26, 30, 44, 47, 145, 166, 190, 198, 205, 208, 210, 218, 236
Gleam II 18, 198, 206
Gleason 29, 30, 180, 198, 206, 223
Glenoe 164
Glint of Gold 122, 162
Glorious Calling 249
Glorious Song 47
Glowing Tribute 160, 162, 163, 165
Glowing With Pride 72, 266
Godswalk 274, 276
Gold Beauty 43, 52
Gold Digger 243
Golden Act 91
Golden Bowl 66, 67
Golden Fleece 10, 26, 35, 39, 40, 41, 42, 43, 44, 45, 46, 49, 52, 59–65, 82, 85, 86, 104, 107, 130, 147, 180, 194, 203, 205, 218, 229, 231, 232, 238, 240, 241, 248, 250, 252, 253, 268
Golden Horde 267
Gold River 83, 111
Gold Source 142
Gold Standard 117
Goldye's Miss 43, 49, 52, 216, 249, 252, 271
Good Thyne 84
Goofed 244
Gormanstown Prince 152
Gorse Bush 164
Gorytus 30, 44, 45, 46, 52, 89, 132, 140, 144–7, 149, 150, 151, 166, 180, 198, 205, 210, 218, 222, 230, 236, 241, 253, 255, 268, 274
Graustark 205, 221, 222, 228
Great Career 120
Great Heron 6, 7, 8, 9
Great Nephew 272, 274
Great Performance 214, 247
Great Substance 81, 120
Great Wall 10
Grecian Victory 205
Greek Answer 205
Greek Sky 43, 52, 180, 194, 201, 205, 223, 224, 249, 252
Greek Victress 201, 205
Green Dancer 17, 18, 19, 27, 32, 34, 48, 49, 53, 56, 72–8, 87, 112, 113, 114, 122, 131, 133, 134, 135, 136, 148, 151, 152, 178, 180, 194, 203, 204, 207, 210, 222, 223, 230, 232, 238, 242, 253, 255–8, 262

Greenland Park 65
Greenloaning 7
Green Lucia 257
Green Valley 15, 72, 73, 203, 207, 209–10
Greinton 257, 258
Grenada Pride 225
Grey Ballet 237, 246, 251, 270
Grey Dawn II 73, 91, 226
Grey Sovereign 214
Group Plan 205
Grundy 18, 62, 64, 73, 74, 75, 76, 77, 113, 148, 151, 154, 270, 273
Guadinini 68
Guillaume Tell 76–7
Gun Bow 218
Gun Carriage 129
Gunner B 68
Guns of Navarone 106
Gyr 10, 11, 12, 15

Habibti 265
Habitat 66, 133, 154, 205, 206, 209, 210, 214, 228, 273, 277
Hagley 275
Hail Hilarious 158
Hail The Pirates 116
Hail To Reason 84, 214
Half An Hour 180, 198, 206, 216
Half Iced 127
Halo 50–1, 98, 177, 232
Halpern Bay 261, 267
Hapai 191
Harbour 65
Hardiesse 16, 192
Hard To Tell 83
Harifa 257
Hart 274
Hasty Road 223
Haul Knight 109
Hawaiian Sound 27, 47, 66, 68, 69
Heartland 103
Heavenly Cause 37, 97, 98, 141
Heil 270, 274
Heisenberg 265
Helenio 256
Helenouchka 245, 270, 274, 275
Helioscope 218
Henbit 41
Henri le Balafre 77
Herbager 84, 140, 226
Her Demon 191, 271
Herecomesthebride 205
Hermit 212
Heron Bay 86, 105
Herringbone 79
He's Vivacious 263

High Counsel 101
High Echelon 15, 113, 264
High Hat 210, 218
High Line 112
High Perch 223
High Polish 263
Hilal 136
Hill Prince 220
Himyar 226–7
Hinshi Suphido 130, 131
Hinterland 163
His Honor 26, 28, 35–6, 37, 170, 180, 185, 195, 196, 202, 206, 212, 217, 246, 251, 253, 261, 268
His Majesty 175, 274
Hogarth 12
Hoist The Flag 31, 163, 221, 222, 228, 243, 244, 254
Hoist The King 244
Hold Me Closer 141
Holiday Dancer 263
Hollywood Dancer 263
Home Love 143
Home Run 66, 67
Homespun 142, 143, 200, 206, 210
Honest Pleasure 274, 276, 277
Honey Fox 41, 102
Honor Tricks 244
Hopak 54, 249
Horage 85
Horama 272
Horisky 131, 149, 262
Hornbeam 218
Hornpipe 243
Hortensia 270, 274
Hostage 26, 39, 41, 42, 45, 46, 47, 59–60, 172, 180, 196, 202, 206, 222, 223, 230, 232, 240, 241, 242, 253, 268
Hot 270, 274
Hot Touch 89
Hula Dancer 135, 136
Huntercombe 8, 9
Hunza Dancer 119
Hush Dear 126
Hypavia 191, 270, 274
Hyperion 212, 214, 217–8, 226, 228
Hypermetric 110

Icy Time 142
Ida Delia 205
Idle Hour 223
I Enclose 45
If Winter Comes 100, 260
Ile de Bourbon 24, 26, 27, 28, 29, 30, 31, 33, 35, 49, 56, 65–72, 90, 109, 112, 166, 180,

189, 190, 192, 193, 194, 198, 205, 209, 224, 225, 232, 237, 239, 241, 253, 265, 266
Illa Laudo 7
Illuminable 4
Immortality 214
Imperial Falcon 244
Imperial Fling 109
Imsodear 23
Inca Yata 218
Indulto 205
In Fijar 81, 135
In Reality 225
Instinctive Move 249
Instrument Landing 91, 92, 93
Intentionally 205
Intermission 209
Intrepid Hero 77, 117, 158
Invision 167
Ipi Tombi 30, 192, 228
Irish Ball 79
Irish River 70
Iron Leader 104
Iskra 243
Island Champ 260
Island Smile 266
Isonomy 212
Its A Done Deal 265
Ivanjica 37, 52, 77, 83, 272
Ivatan 108
Ivory Wand 26, 191
Ivory Wings 47

Jabal Tarik 105
Jacinth 83
Jacinto 103, 205, 217
Jaipur 60, 156, 214
Jalmood 63
Jan Jessie 15
Jasper 87
Javamine 20, 21, 22, 24, 25, 28, 112, 155, 159–61, 163, 164, 165, 169, 170, 179, 190, 196, 201, 204, 207, 211, 216, 235, 238, 253
Java Moon 23, 30
Jealous One 273
Jellaby 70
Jenner 246
Jessica Briar 266
Jester 216
Jeu de Paille 87
Jillinsky 52, 248
Jinsky 227, 246, 270, 275
Jinxed 270, 275
Jiyou Kuitsukirih 131
John de Coombe 138
John French 89
John Henry 40, 49, 54, 107, 125, 126, 127, 129

Johnny D 119
Joking Apart 272
Joshua 9
J. O. Tobin 149, 276
Judger 270
Jukebox 273
Julio Mariner 66, 67, 69
Just A Dash 258, 259
Just A Game 47, 102

Kafouaine 225, 249
Kahana Bay 264
Kala Dancer 55, 56, 112, 150, 267
Kalaglow 45, 62, 83
Kalamoun 45
Kamaraan 77, 116
Kamicia 167
Kanz 244
Karabas 12
Karelina 113
Karensky 248
Karol 61
Kashi Lagoon 72, 266
Kasteel 77
Katonka 157
Kazatska 192, 222, 223
Kenmare 138
Kentucky Gold 243
Key Dancer 47, 53, 55, 56, 166, 179, 195, 196, 201, 221, 241, 253
Key Partner 201
Key To The Mint 221, 274
Key To The Saga 166–7
Khatango 26, 43, 44, 45, 47, 124, 170, 180, 191, 200, 206, 223, 224, 240, 241, 253
Kilijaro 102, 137
Kind of Hush 82
King of Darby 26, 27, 187, 188, 221, 266
King of The Castle 13
King Pellinore 113, 114, 115–6, 117, 119
Kings Bishop 94, 205, 270
Kings Lake 23, 35, 36, 37, 38, 39, 40, 47, 49, 78–84, 86, 90, 99, 104, 112, 147, 171, 172, 180, 194, 198, 205, 219, 220, 230, 240, 253, 268
Kingsview 90
Kinski 249
Kirov 225
Kirtling 154, 273
Kissapotamus 157
Kittiwake 18, 24, 215, 271
Klairon 209, 224
Knight's Daughter 226
Known Fact 34

INDEX

Koboko 135
Krassata 19, 20, 23, 24, 25, 155, 159, 160, 163, 164–5, 169, 182, 187, 188, 190, 208, 227, 246, 251, 270
Kylin 190
Kyra's Slipper 39, 155, 190, 192, 208, 219, 235
Kythnos 214

La Codorniz 250
La Confidence 248
Lacquer 16, 20, 190, 198, 206, 209, 220
La Dorga 113
Lady Abernant 138, 139
Lady Graustark 201, 206, 271
Lady Hardwick 247
Lady Jinsky 21, 23, 169, 190, 209, 223, 224, 246, 251, 271
Lady Randolph 158
Lady Roberta 36
Lady Singer 160, 164
Lady's Secret 143–4
Lady Subpet 165
Lady Victoria 15, 16, 113, 190, 198, 204, 209, 223, 244, 271
Lafontaine 106
Lagunas 56, 72, 266
Lagunette 83, 165
La Jalouse 20, 47, 159, 162, 169, 179, 190, 191, 196, 201, 207, 213, 214, 234, 246, 251, 270, 273
Lakeville Miss 166
La Lagune 65
La Lorgnette 154, 271, 276
Lamiel 262
Landaluce 142
Landscaper 115
La Nijinska 21, 25, 166, 190, 207, 211, 215, 235, 246, 271
La Noticia 208
Lark Rise 6
La Sevillana 16, 211, 235, 271, 276
Lassie Dear 26
Last Fandango 82
Last Feather 47, 230
Last Light 54, 272
Late Bloomer 31, 47, 168, 169
Lath 187, 188, 246
La Troienne 85, 264
L'Avalanche 248
Lawmaker 205
Law Society 112, 267
Lead The Dance 53
Leap Lively 23, 35, 36, 37, 38, 39, 40, 151–2, 179, 201, 206,

221, 222, 230, 233, 234, 240, 242, 253
Leap of The Heart 46, 49, 191, 214
Le Fabuleux 221
Le Haar 223
Lemhi Gold 45
Legendaire 119
Le Mamamouchi 122
L'Emigrant 86, 87, 107
Le Moss 72
L'Enjoleur 126
Lepanto 164
Leros 76
Let's Be Gay 191
Libra's Rib 20
Lichine 244
Lie Low 205, 210
Lighted Glory 18–9, 54, 113, 155, 179, 202, 206, 214, 238, 241, 253, 272
Lighted Lamp 15, 202, 206, 272
Lightning Leap 54, 55, 214
Like A Charm 30, 47, 191, 198, 205, 213
Linacre 90, 218
Lioubov 76
Lipika 250
Lisadell 18, 31, 65, 198, 204
Little Current 97, 205, 224
Lobkowiez 106
Local Suitor 112, 143, 267
Lodgenski 248
Lomond 47, 86, 107
London Bells 23, 27, 30, 33, 35, 53, 55, 120, 134, 187, 188, 190, 215, 232, 247, 250, 251, 267
Lonesome River 259
Long Hayabusa 262
Long Till 10
Loose Cannon 45, 48, 221, 222
Lord Durham 270
Lord Elgin 123
Lord of The Dance 17, 19, 113, 190, 245, 261, 276
Lords 61, 62, 104
Lorenzaccio 14
Lovely Dancer 87, 257
Lover's Walk 271
Love Sign 254
Lower Lights 203, 206
Loyal Land 15, 259
Lt Stevens 214
Lucence 275
Luck of the Draw 136
Lucky Debonair 205
Lucky For Me 113
Lucky Sovereign 21, 23, 24, 25, 180, 194, 198, 206, 213, 232, 238, 241, 253, 262

Lucky Us 235, 276
Lucy Blue 218, 247
Luiana 203, 205
Lunik 15, 113
Luth Enchantee 107
Luthier 257, 270, 274
Lykon 272
Lyphard 54, 87, 178, 244, 245, 256, 258
Lyphard's Wish 95

Madam Gay 151
Magesterial 80
Magnificent 167
Magnum 121
Ma Gonzesse 262
Mahmoud 11
Mairzy Doates 102
Majestic Light 25, 119, 275
Majesty's Prince 124, 126, 129
Makarova 26, 190, 218, 237
Malaak 152
Mandera 20
Manna 216
Man O'War 225
Mansky 218
Manzotti 250
Ma Petite Jolie 244
Marasali 121
Margouzed 87
Mariacci 73, 74, 75, 76, 77, 148
Mariacho 121, 122
Mariinsky 225, 276
Martian's Son 259
Martincha 260
Maruzensky 21, 22, 23, 54, 113, 130–1, 148–9, 185, 203, 204, 207, 216, 231, 238, 241, 253, 262, 276
Marwell 36
Masked Barb 263
Masked Dancer 19, 227, 246, 251, 263–4
Masked Lady 19
Masked Marvel 108
Masked Romance 263
Masqued Dancer 17, 19, 113, 164, 208, 227, 245, 258, 260–1
Master Guy 11
Master Thatch 79
Matador 228
Matahawk 75
Matera 260
Mattaboy 80, 81
Maximova 49, 148, 152, 257
Mbaiki 121, 122
Meadow Dancer 223, 246, 251, 271
Meadow Saffron 271

INDEX

Meadowville 10, 11, 13
Megalomania 113
Meiwa Iran 261
Meiwa Rikiya 22, 24
Meiwa Sukih 186
Memento 210
Memory Best 100
Meneval 23, 165
Menow 4, 216, 228
Meridien 224
Merry Lady III 160
Methane 75, 76
Miba 16, 198, 206, 213
Mickey's Echo 51
Midou 190
Mika Red 266
Milford 109
Milina 23, 166, 190, 192, 193, 221
Millicent 150, 191, 203, 205, 210, 265
Mill Reef 29, 44, 47, 67, 146, 150, 217, 219, 277
Milova 25, 246, 271
Minsky 5, 13, 65, 133, 207–8
Minstrelsy 244
Mira Femme 30
Miralla 19, 272
Mirco Umbro 265
Mirthful Flirt 145, 205, 210
Misgivings 167
Misinskie 228, 248
Miss Carlotita 260
Miss Francesca 23
Miss Mazepah 190, 192
Miss Nijinsky 190, 214
Miss Nut Cracker 222, 248
Miss Prism 159
Miss Suzaki 34
Miss Swapsco 15, 274
Missy Baldski 266
Mister Jacket 73
Misti IV 209, 224
Mixed Applause 26, 27, 132, 191, 213, 214, 247, 271
M-Lolshan 66, 69, 70, 109
Molly Ballantine 156
Moment of Truth 32, 203, 205
Monade 15, 16, 113, 170, 175, 190, 192
Monarchy 15, 16, 113, 190, 261, 276
Money Game 261
Mongo 214
Mon Plaisir 10
Monsanto 74, 75
Montcontour 68
Monteverdi 31, 33, 65, 83
Moorestyle 137
Moral Leader 104

More Light 109
Morgaise 20, 190, 198, 206
Morning Frolic 4
Morse Code 111
Moscow Ballet 47, 53, 56, 151, 180, 203, 205, 210, 212, 217, 241
Moss 271
Moulton 15
Mount Marcy 223
Mr Brea 94
Mr Busher 225
Mr Justice 228, 266
Mr Prospector 275
Mrs Penny 136, 256
Mrs Peterkin 15, 23, 30, 113, 190, 198, 206, 235, 244
Mrs Warren 37
Muscatite 106, 126
Muscovite 23, 27, 31, 33, 35, 120, 193, 201, 215, 239, 242, 247, 250, 251, 253, 267
Musical Ride 244
Must Guarantee 267
My Advantage 191, 271
My Babu 224, 225
My Bupers 244
My Charmer 47
Myjinski 249
Mystic Era 91

Nadeed 84, 249
Nafka 249
Nagurski 43, 50, 51, 52, 53, 180, 191, 198, 219, 220, 241, 242, 249, 252, 253
Nantallah 213, 214
Nanticious (USA) 23, 191, 198, 205
Nanticious (IRE) 273
Narrate 276
Nashua 213, 214
Nasrullah 213, 214, 215, 219, 231, 232, 276
Natalma 3–4, 5, 243
Nataraja 190
National Banner 141, 142
Native Ballet 36, 40, 248
Native Courier 167
Native Dancer 3, 113, 215
Native Heritage 15, 113
Native Nurse 47
Native Partner 20, 30, 34, 191, 235
Nautical Miss 190
Navajo Princess 168, 169
Nearco 3, 213–4, 215, 216, 218, 228, 233
Nearctic 3–4, 15, 205, 206
Nearula 213, 214, 232

Nebbiolo 50
Netherby 180, 203, 205, 227, 248
Never Bend 205, 213, 214
Never Easy 249
New Berry 108
New Direction 249
Nice Havrais 23, 32, 33, 133, 135, 180, 201, 207, 221, 233, 234, 239, 242, 253, 267
Nicholas Bill 67, 122
Night Alert 23, 27, 32, 33, 34, 35, 36, 55, 120, 149–50, 180, 203, 205, 228, 239, 241, 247, 250, 251, 253, 266
Night Mirage 249
Nigromante 227
Nijana 19, 20, 21, 22, 23, 24, 25, 28, 112, 153, 155, 159, 160, 161–4, 165, 169, 179, 190, 196, 198, 204, 205, 227, 234, 238, 242, 253
Nijinskaia 19, 23, 26, 246, 271
Nijinska Street 33, 190, 207, 211
Nijinsky's Best 53, 249
Nijinsky Sentiment 237, 249
Nijinsky's Melody 48, 55, 220, 249, 271
Nijinsky's Secret 23, 36, 37, 42, 43, 45, 46, 48, 49, 50, 51, 53, 54, 56, 99, 107, 119–29, 170, 177, 180, 187, 188, 202, 206, 209, 215, 234, 236, 237, 240, 242, 253, 268
Nijinsky's Show 249
Nijistar 235, 247
Nijisty 23
Nijit 27, 32, 33, 36, 38, 169, 190, 210, 214, 234, 247, 251, 271
Nikitina 225
Nile Empress 265
Nile Smile 264
Niniski 24, 27, 29, 30, 31–2, 33, 34, 35, 36, 47, 55, 56, 108–12, 171, 180, 194, 201, 204, 207, 221, 229, 230, 232, 233, 239, 241, 242, 247, 250, 251, 253, 267
Ninoushka 248
Niqua 236
Nishino Northern 41, 186, 219, 248
Nishinosky 131, 149, 262
Nissr 225, 247, 267
Nizon 24, 26, 28, 180, 183, 194, 201, 204, 207, 219, 220, 234, 239, 242, 246, 250, 251, 253, 266

No Alimony 74
Noalto 81, 82
No Attention 257
No Bias 103, 205
Nobiliary 18, 19, 76, 77, 272
Noble Damsel 100, 101
Noble Dancer 123, 167
Noble Mark 79
Noble Nijinsky 250
Noblesse 139
Nocturnal Spree 18, 19, 272
Nodouble 50
No Duplicate 103, 160
Noelino 109
No Lute 121, 122
Nonoalco 21, 67, 134, 205, 206, 223, 265
Nooky 16
North Broadway 20
Northerly Native 54, 235
Northern Answer 205
Northern Baby 109
Northern Chimes 267
Northern Dancer 3, 4, 5, 15, 48, 50, 88, 103, 172, 175, 177, 178, 204, 205, 206, 207–8, 209, 231, 233, 243, 244, 245, 253–4, 255, 257, 260, 263, 271, 277
Northernette 16, 23, 207, 251, 261
Northern Gem 16
Northern Monarch 6
Northern Taste 113, 204, 209
Northern Trick 47
Northern View 91
Northern Walk 246, 271
Northjet 39, 82
Northleach 34
Norwick 63, 64
Notably 165
Nozin Man 266
Nuclear Pulse 21, 170, 180, 187, 188, 190, 198, 206, 223, 224, 234, 246, 251, 264
Number 26, 40, 43, 44, 45, 46, 47, 48, 49, 169, 179, 202, 205, 206, 218, 240, 242, 253
Nureyev 33, 40, 47, 133, 136, 169, 205, 218, 244, 258, 267
Nuthatch 114

Oak Dancer 257
Obratzsovy 70
Office Wife 60, 205
Olamic 43, 48, 49, 169, 218, 254
Old Country 262
Old Testament 84
Ole Bob Bowers 40
Omaha 4

One For All 113, 204
One On The Aisle 116
Only Queens 142
On My Way 77
On Stage 146
Open Call 127
Optimistic Gal 19, 34, 160, 162
Oraza 18, 192, 228
Orby 228
Orchestra 68
Ore 61, 80
Oulanova 19, 224, 274
Our Lady Queen 48
Outstandingly 56, 144
Over Served 19, 22, 190, 245, 262–3
Overstate 254
Overstreet 222

Pacific Princess 163
Padroug 21
Paico 69
Pair of Deuces 124
Paisana 143
Palacios 247
Palestine 216
Palmistry 84, 205, 209
Panamint 90
Panaslipper 90
Panaview 90
Panorama 91
Pardao 213
Pareo 72
Partez 101
Parva Stella 110
Pas de Cheval 248
Pas de Deux (GB) 192, 229
Pas de Deux (USA) 23, 24, 26, 28, 180, 201, 205, 213, 234, 238, 242, 253, 264
Pass A Glance 163
Pass The Glass 115
Past Forgetting 38
Patch 77
Patriach 55
Pawneese 20
Peace 15, 26, 47, 204, 205, 209
Peaceful 204, 209
Peace Movement 15, 190
Peacetime 26, 39, 41, 42, 44, 46, 47, 63, 64, 123, 171, 172, 180, 193, 198, 204, 209, 224, 225, 238, 240, 241, 253
Pearl Necklace 32, 160, 161, 163, 165, 166, 168
Pearl Strand 138
Pebbles 107
Pelerin 126, 128
Penny Flight 124, 191, 200, 206, 223

Perfect Point 226
Perrault 83, 122, 125
Persepolis 63, 64
Persimmon 219–20, 228
Personator 30, 247
Pet Bird 143
Peterhof 61, 150, 205, 206
Peter Pan 226
Petingo 29, 112
Petipa 164
Petoski 112, 267
Phaeton 135
Phalaris 4, 212, 213–6, 227, 228
Pharamond 216, 228
Pharos 212, 215
Philyra 152
Phydilla 65
Piaffer 30, 31, 34, 35, 36, 180, 190, 194, 198, 206, 228
Pianist 91
Picture Play 272
Picture Pretty 97
Picturesque 92
Pied à Terre 119, 153, 262
Pied d'Or 213, 214
Pietru 87
Pilgrim 5
Piney Ridge 83
Pinny Gray 270
Pirate's Glow 144
Pisgale 36
Pisistrato 115
Pitcairn 36
Plaudit 226
Pola Bella 65
Polamia 72
Politico 13
Pollerton 109
Polynesian 215, 221
Pompoes 136
Popkins 18, 137, 192, 198, 206
Popular Hero 29, 180, 200, 226
Porterhouse 216
Posse 32, 149
Practitioner 205
Prayers 'N' Promises 97, 98, 99
Preciously Dear 50, 207, 211, 226
Premiere Danseuse 256
Presto Lad 248
Priceless Countess 244
Priceless Gem 244
Pride's Profile 156
Pride's Promise 155–6, 202, 206
Prima Voce 106
Prime Prospect 97
Primo Rico 73
Prince Dias 134
Prince Echo 80, 81
Prince John 16, 219, 220

INDEX

Princely Gift 213, 214
Prince of Tricks 250
Princequillo 219–20, 228
Princess Cabrini 143
Princesse Lida 23, 29, 31, 32, 33, 34, 36, 96, 133–7, 149, 179, 191, 200, 204, 207, 214, 239, 242, 253, 256
Princess Lee 133, 137, 191, 200, 207
Princessnesian 20, 190, 192
Princess Rooney 47, 142
Prince Street 207, 211
Prince Tenderfoot 7, 8, 9
Proclaim 146
Prod 161
Prodana Nevíesta 18, 161, 190, 198, 204, 205, 227
Prodigal Dancer 250
Prodigo 92
Producer 52
Proliferation 205
Promaydoh 262
Properantes 118
Proper Princess 158
Prove It Baby 110
Prowess 162
Prove Out 103
Provideo 112
Psidium 64
Punctilio 104
Puntilla 205
Pustinya 38

Quadrangle 223
Quadruple 190, 191, 201, 207, 270
Queen City Miss 190
Queen of Light 272
Queens Gambit 159
Queen To Conquer 102
Quibu 216
Quick Dance 162, 227, 247
Quick Tempo 156
Quiet Fling 18, 19, 20, 22, 23, 25, 37, 39, 47, 113, 114, 123, 171, 180, 198, 204, 209, 224, 225, 229, 238, 242, 253, 261-2
Quill 15, 18, 113, 130, 189, 190, 204, 205
Quilloquick 201, 206
Quintain 4
Quite Shy 262

Rabelais 221–2
Raconteur 61
Rafale 16
Ragapan 90
Ragstone 79
Rahotep 121, 122
Rainbow Connection 98
Raise A Native 120, 128, 205, 209, 210, 214–5, 228, 243, 253, 270, 273
Raise Your Skirts 34
Ranking Beauty 37, 217, 247, 252, 271
Ran Tan 243
Rapide Pied 55
Rare Splendor 220
Rare Treat 60
Rarity 7
Rash Statement 15, 113
Rasimova 154, 246, 270, 275
Raskolniki 246, 251
Recalled 8, 133
Recaptured 270, 275
Recitation 121, 122
Record Token 75
Recupere 116, 160
Red Debonair 205
Red Steps 266
Redundancy 157, 159
Regal Gal 158
Regal Gleam 84
Rehearsing 250
Reindeer 7
Relaxing 47
Relfo 26, 140
Reneged 227
Reprocolor 109
Requited 246
Restless Sis 270
Restless Wind 223
Revidere 159
Reviewer 84, 217, 275
Revoked 227
Rheingold 209
Riboccarre 108
Ribofilio 8
Ribot 5–6, 11, 94, 108, 213, 221, 228, 231, 232, 233
Right Away 73
Right Royal V 218
Rigoberto 218
Ring Dancer 260
Ring of Light 95, 96
Riot In Paris 116, 117
Rissa 24, 30, 187, 188, 215, 246, 271
Riva Ridge 214
River Lady 65
Riverman 54, 219, 255, 256, 257, 258
Riverqueen 47, 136
Robbie Burns 113
Robellino 81
Roberto 167, 210, 274
Rock 'N' Roller 85

Rock Roi 13
Rocky Trip 158
Roi Dagobert 79
Roi Soleil 9
Rokeby Rose 100
Romanov 248
Romildo 105
Romulus 137, 221, 222
Ronbra 129
Ro Ro's Coffee 265
Rosalba 97
Rose Bed 66, 205, 209
Rose Bowl 30, 34, 66, 67, 205, 209, 211
Rose Crescent 26, 49, 55, 67, 166, 169, 179, 190, 192, 193, 196, 198, 205, 209, 224, 225, 240, 242, 253
Roseliere 18, 26, 27, 65–6, 67, 190, 192, 193, 198, 205, 206, 209, 224
Rose O'Riley 50, 210
Roses For The Star 21
Rosetta Stone 34, 97, 190, 201, 205, 208, 210, 211, 235
Rosy Spectre 30, 38, 46–7, 169, 179, 191, 196, 198, 205, 213, 234, 248, 252, 271
Round Table 15, 84, 97, 142, 205, 208, 209, 210, 219–20, 228, 254, 272
Royal Anthem 119, 263
Royal Bowl 113
Royal Charger 213, 214, 276
Royal Coinage 205
Royal Dowry 244
Royal Glint 84
Royal Heroine 54, 129, 143, 187
Royal Hive 69
Royal Jete 20, 190, 234, 246
Royal Justice 276
Royal Nijinsky 190, 192, 247
Royal Ski 4
Royal Union 220
Rubescent Rumor 97
Ruffian 156
Running Ballerina 24, 154, 216, 232, 277
Run The Gantlet 113
Russian Fox 36, 40, 120, 187, 188, 191, 237, 248
Russian Logic 249
Russian Noble 53, 218, 249
Russian Ribbon 249
Russian Roubles 30, 44, 46, 47, 48, 50, 55, 150, 171, 180, 198, 206, 216
Rustle of Silk 273
Rye Tops 72

INDEX

Sabre Street 222
Sackford 107
Sacramento 7
Sadler's Wells 50
Safe Process 165, 270
Safita 136, 137
Saidan 103
Sailor 227
Sailor King 247, 250, 251
Sail Serenely 243
Saint Crespin III 218
Sainte Croix 48, 249
Saintly Song 9
Sajama 101
Sakura Toko 262
Salieri 44, 145–6
Sallust 33
Salmon Leap 86
Salutely 61
Salvo 218
Sandal 8
Sandy Blue 20
Sangue 101
Sans Arc 163, 167, 168
Sans Critique 168
Sarah Siddons 21, 64, 152, 164–5
Sassabunda 83
Sassafras 10, 14, 15, 79
Saunders 265
Sayes 8
Scaremenot 16
Schiaparelli 79
Sconce 275
Scorpio 109
Screen King 91, 92
Sea Bird II 6, 10, 11, 73, 76, 205, 215
Sea Boat 68, 69
Sea Break 74, 75
Sea Chimes 35, 111
Sea Hawk II 113
Sea Pigeon 97
Seattle Slew 28, 47, 149, 175, 219, 244, 254
Secretariat 15, 31, 91, 164, 205, 219, 243, 244, 254, 259, 275, 277
Secret Beauty 47, 120, 202, 206, 209, 236
Secret Script 164
Secret Sharer 164
Senior Citizen 62
Sensational 163
Sensitivo 216
Seraphima 140
Screncia 165
Serheed 52, 191, 235, 248
Sevastopol 207, 261
Seximee 201, 205, 223

Seymour Hicks 107
Shadeed 48, 55, 56, 150, 180, 201, 206, 223, 249, 252
Shafaraz 110
Shahtash 190
Shake A Leg 20, 190
Shamstar 121
Shanizadeh 47
Shantallah 114
Shantung 79, 209, 220
Shapina 139
Shareef Dancer 15, 47, 88, 89, 90, 150, 171, 260
Shark Song 102
Shearwalk 86
She Can Dance 27, 166, 167, 190, 218
Sheila Jan 270
Shergar 10, 41, 54, 65, 83, 146, 216, 231, 273
Sheshoon 225
Shill 113, 130, 131, 203
Shimmy 23, 37, 38, 40, 45, 179, 191, 195, 196, 201, 205, 224
Shining Finish 23, 36, 37, 40, 180, 190, 194, 198, 206, 209, 220, 239, 241, 242, 253, 268
Shinnecock 211
Shin Wolf 262
Shiny Tenth 9
Shirley Heights 26, 28, 29, 65, 67, 68, 69, 70, 83, 272
Shiyada Etsuse 130
Shoubra 201, 207
Shuvee 20, 27, 32, 37, 190, 192, 213
Sicambre 220
Sicarelle 274
Sickle 214–5, 216
Sign of The Times 20, 190
Sigy 70
Silky 17, 19, 132, 154, 155, 180, 191, 213, 214, 231, 232, 233, 272–3
Silver Cloud 135
Silver Hawk 62, 64
Silver Ikon 276
Silver Lad 68
Silveyville 102
Simply Great 63, 64
Singapore Girl 110
Singing Rain 23
Singing Susan 141, 142
Sir Gallahad III 223–4
Sir Gaylord 15, 205, 208, 214, 259, 272
Sir Ivor 9, 11, 15, 22, 42, 66, 154, 164, 178, 205, 206, 210, 214, 276

Sir Jinsky 28, 30, 159, 170, 190, 211, 216, 235, 246, 268
Sirlad 94
Sis C 28, 31, 179, 201, 207, 214
Sixty Sails 157
Skibinoff 24, 246, 251
Sky High 218
Skylarking 274
Slap Up 165
Slew O'Gold 16
Slip Screen 156
Sly Moon 152
Sly Pola 15, 72
Small Raja 163
Smartaire 34, 51
Smart Angle 37, 141
Smarten 91, 92
Smarten Up 139
Smartinsky 223
Smart Steppin 51
Smilin' Sera 98
Snaafi Dancer 48, 244
Snow Knight 62, 270, 271, 277
Snow Peak 30, 191
Soaring 274
So Chic 16, 201, 205, 213
Socratic 273
Soft Angels 139
Solario 226
Soleil Noir 32, 35, 109, 111
Solford 30, 37, 38, 44, 45, 46, 47, 48, 49, 50, 52, 84, 85, 86, 87, 103–8, 180, 193, 203, 205, 213, 229, 230, 232, 241, 242, 248, 250, 252, 253, 268
Solford (Champion Hurdler) 104
Solicitor 257
Solo Dancer 258
Solometeor 16, 21, 190, 198, 206, 264
Solon 225
Solstein 55, 56, 225
Something Super 26, 34
Son of Love 32, 109, 110
Sookera 139
Sophistical 248
Sound Track 228
South Atlantic 86, 105
South Ocean 16, 204, 207, 244
Sovereign 16, 198, 206, 213
Sovereign Path 214
Spacefarer 246
Spanish Riddle 254
Spark of Life 37, 168
Spearfish 34, 37, 43, 47, 198, 205, 244
Special 202, 205, 244
Spectacular Bid 15, 54, 92, 93, 94

316 INDEX

Speculum 228
Speedy Nijinsky 225, 248
Sphere 26
Spicy Story 161
Sportin' Life 23, 36, 37, 38, 42, 43, 55, 84, 142, 143, 153, 180, 200, 206, 210, 219, 232, 240, 241, 242, 253, 268
Sports Event 17, 190
Sports Ruler 261
Sportsky 17, 20, 21, 190, 214, 261
Spring Adieu 243
Spy Well 223
Squander 30, 34, 198, 206
Square Angel 47
Stage Door Johnny 209, 219, 220
Stage Door Key 99
St Albans 227
Stalwart 157
Stanerra 61, 62, 77, 103, 106, 107
Stanhoe 151
Star Appeal 77, 274
Star Ball 158, 160, 161
Starjinsky 250
Star Pastures 65
Starsalot 235
Start A Rumor 48
Star Way 135
State 23, 169, 190, 276
State Dinner 95, 96
Steambath 276
Steeple Bell 108
Stetchworth 29, 30, 32, 33, 109, 218
St Germans 103, 222
Stintino 10, 11
Stockwell 227
Storm Bird 16, 63, 79, 80, 85, 207, 261
Stout Fellow 110
Stradavari 265
Stradavinsky 21, 26, 28, 67, 180, 193, 201, 205, 206, 223, 239, 242, 246, 251, 253, 257, 265
Strawberry Road 259
Street Ballet 23, 27, 30, 31, 32, 33, 34, 35, 36, 179, 190, 191, 195, 196, 198, 207, 211, 215, 235, 247, 251, 271
Street Dancer 18, 20, 21, 23, 30, 37, 190, 191, 198, 204, 207, 211, 215, 235, 271
Stroller 5
Strong Drink 190, 198, 206
St Simon 219–22, 228, 233
Stylish Genie 244
Stylish Pattern 34

Such Nobility 243
Sugar Plum Time 162
Sugary Mist 227
Summer Fling 26, 27, 28, 33, 166, 179, 202, 214, 239, 253
Summertime Promise 18, 19, 20, 21, 22, 23, 25, 113, 155–9, 179, 195, 196, 202, 206, 224, 225, 238, 242, 253
Summing 37, 153
Sun And Snow 163
Sunny's Halo 51, 177
Sun Princess 87, 88, 89, 90
Sun Teddy 223, 224
Super Concorde 138, 275
Super Dude 259
Super Gray 237, 245, 259, 261
Super Jaime 248
Superlative 277
Super Sunrise 125
Susanna 37, 220
Sushila 112
Suspend 207
Suvero 136
Suzuka Koban 262
Suzu Mahah 262
Swale 84
Swallow Tail 79
Swan 191, 226, 247, 271
Swaps 218
Sweet Alliance 15, 88, 113, 206, 260
Sweet Bernice 163
Sweet Caprice 143
Sweet Mimosa 64
Sweet Mist 30
Sweet Mover 53, 249
Sweet Revenge 97, 98
Sweet Satina 203, 205
Swift Lady 15, 113, 211
Swift Symbol 211
Swingtime 30, 34, 38, 84, 113, 158, 161, 204, 207
Swoon's Son 223
Sword Dancer 223
Swynford 222–3
Syria 47
Syrian Sea 31

Table Hands 33, 37
Table Run 220
Takawalk II 72
Tamalesian 271
Tamil 9
Tanthem 95
Tanzor 18, 21, 151, 180, 193, 198, 204, 205, 209, 223, 224, 232, 245, 259
Tap On Wood 109
Targowice 256

Tartan Pimpernel 138, 139
Tatan 216
Teacher's Pet 102, 134, 135, 136, 137
Teddy 223–4, 228
Teenoso 47, 50, 87, 88, 89, 107
Tellurano 79
Tempest Queen 166
Tender Word 16, 190, 192
Tenerani 221
Tennyson 270, 274
Tenpointo 131
Tentam 225, 270, 271, 276
Terlingua 30
Terpsichorist 27, 28, 29, 30, 31, 32, 33, 44, 52, 96, 145, 162, 165–9, 179, 190, 195, 196, 198, 205, 210, 218, 222, 234, 236, 239, 253, 274
Testily 225
Thahul 41, 53, 171, 189, 190, 220, 247
Thatching 65, 72, 83
That's A Nice 68, 69
The Axe II 223
The Bart 126
The Cat Came Back 261
The Dancer 256
Theia 158
The Minstrel 4, 5, 23, 25, 30, 62, 87, 177, 184, 208, 244, 262, 275
The Neurologist 61
The Noble Player 86, 126
The Temptress 154, 235, 246, 271, 276
The Tetrarch 230
The Very One 47, 102, 168
The Wonder 82, 121, 122, 126
Thirty Eight Paces 36, 153
Thirty Nine J. E. 243
Thirty Years 163
Threat 276
Three Troikas 72, 111
Thundergay 8
Thunder Puddles 124, 125, 126, 127
Tights 50, 51, 52, 53, 54, 55, 56, 84, 153, 170, 180, 191, 195, 198, 206, 209, 219, 220, 235, 241, 242, 253
Ti King 52
Tillman 214
Time Charter 48, 88, 103, 106, 107
Time For Pleasure 163, 167
Timely Writer 45
Timor 224, 225
Tim's Princess 270
Tim Tam 216

INDEX

Tina Tina Too 98
Tipperary Fixer 122
Title 113
Titled Hero 113, 209
Tiziano 220
To Agori Mou 37, 38, 39, 40, 80, 81, 82, 83
Today 'N Tomorrow 119
Tolomeo 49, 103, 106, 107, 126, 127
Tolstoy 249
Tom Fool 216
Tompion 216
Tom Rolfe 108, 221, 222
Tonzarun 128
Too Bald 16, 190, 198, 205
Too Many Sweets 34, 191
Top Command 115
Top Crowd 117, 118
Top Dancer 122
Top Double 4
Topin 43
Toporal 261
Top O' The North 146
Top Rank 235, 248
Top Round 23, 26, 191, 198, 205
Topsider 205, 208
Torus 110
Touching Wood 64
Tourbillon 224–5, 228
Tournament Star 39, 191, 223
Tow 122
Town And Country 70
Transworld 24
Treacherous 120
Treasure Chest 244
Treasure Trove 85
Treizieme 83
Trendy Gent 249
Trepan 75
Trevita 126, 187
Trillion 52, 68, 69
Trim The Sail 191
Tromos 70
Troy 10, 30, 33, 41, 65, 70, 71, 108, 109, 111, 277
Truculent 52
True Rocket 8, 9
Trumpeter Swan 116
Trust Us 119, 263
Try My Best 53, 139
Try To Smile 134
Tsunami Slew 53, 54, 55
Tubac Dancer 247
Tudor Melody 218
Tudor Minstrel 218
Tuerta 30
Tunic 207
Turf Charger 214

Tuscarora 113
T. V. Lark 214
Two of Diamonds 111
Two Rings 47
Typecast 64, 83
Tyrnavos 274

Ukraine Girl 64, 82
Ultramate 38, 50, 52, 53, 55, 145, 170, 180, 191, 201, 206, 221, 222, 234, 248, 252
Umabatha 20, 192, 261
Unbreakable 215
Unique Dancer 261
Un Kopeck 77
Unreality 169
Unrehearsed 247
Upper Nile 21, 26–7, 28, 47, 84, 96, 97, 180, 190, 196, 201, 205, 208, 210, 219, 235, 238, 241, 242, 253, 264–5

Vaguely Noble 13, 45, 60, 66, 67, 115, 143, 175, 205, 218, 243, 244, 272
Vaisseau 150
Val Danseur 48, 52, 53, 180, 187, 188, 203, 210, 222, 223
Val de Fier 75
Val de Loir 15, 59, 72, 75, 209, 222–3, 228
Val de l'Orne 73, 75, 77, 154, 271, 276
Valdez 93
Valetchka 246
Valinsky 21, 23, 24, 25, 27, 54, 60, 180, 187, 188, 193, 198, 205, 220, 239, 253, 264
Valodi 259–60
Valoris 16, 21, 198, 205, 220, 264
Valse Noble 248
Val's Girl 83, 205
Valuation 69
Vanann 121
Varingo 134
Vaslava 145, 210, 236, 274–5
Vaslov 33, 248
Vatza 27, 32, 33, 37, 190, 192, 193, 213, 214, 247, 251
Vayrann 40, 83, 122
Vedette 228
Vela 20, 225
Venomous 120
Verduret 256
Veroushka 162, 275
Vers La Caisse 52
Vertex 222
Veruschenka 249

Vestris 39, 42, 43, 47, 49, 50, 51, 170, 221, 222
Victorian Queen 157
Victoria Park 4, 209, 223, 228
Vidalia 50, 132, 152, 179, 183, 192, 193, 198, 225, 241, 242, 253
Viendra 4, 101
Vieux Manoir 223
Vigors 118
Vimy's Champ 260
Virginia Deer 85
Virginia Hills 201, 207
Vision 47, 49, 52, 53, 54, 55, 56, 84, 112, 153, 180, 191, 196, 200, 205, 209, 219, 241, 242, 253, 268
Vital Season 109
Vitiges 135

Wajima 162, 243, 244, 275
Walky Talky 7, 8, 9
Warfare 205, 218
Warfever 168
War of Words 205, 208
Wassl 88, 107
Watch Out 139
Water Dance 23, 37, 39, 97, 99, 169, 179, 187, 188, 196, 203, 205, 224, 234
Waterloo 23
Water Malone 168
Waving 26, 43, 46, 49, 84, 179, 191, 198, 205, 219, 220, 234, 254
Waya 34, 37, 50, 166, 168, 192, 198, 204, 225
Wayward Lass 97, 98, 99
Wayward Pirate 143, 144
Welsh Garden 164
West Australian 225
West Coast Scout 120
Western Symphony 37, 47, 49, 50, 52, 53, 54, 56, 132, 150, 151, 180, 191, 194, 203, 205, 206, 210, 212, 217, 241, 242, 253, 265
What A Summer 161
What A Treat 60
Whip It Quick 74, 114
Whiskey Road 17, 113, 227, 245, 258–9, 265
Whisky Lover 259
White Birch 44, 46, 47, 48, 191, 223, 236–7, 249
Whites Creek 141
White Star Line 166
Whitstead 66
Who's For Dinner 54, 129
Wicked Will 100

317

Will Dancer 258
Winds of Thought 156
Windy Sands 218
Wings of Grace 100, 274
Winning Feature 104
Winter's Love 143
Winter's Tale 35, 95, 96
Without Fear 9
Without Reserve 150
Words 'N Music 211, 215, 249
Worldwatch 39, 247

Yamanin Penny 41, 186, 203, 206, 214, 240, 253
Yamanin Sukih 30, 185–6
Yamano Shiragiku 263
Yamanosky 262
Yanina II 16, 190
Yankee Lady 83
Yawa 113
Ya Zaman 136
Yeats 30, 31, 180, 198, 218, 266

Yelapa 108
Yellow God 7, 9, 275
Yes Dear Maggy 157
Yla 274
Youth 50, 115, 117, 271
Yumi 120

Zank 228
Zanthe 116
Zingari 161, 204